APRIL 10

Challenge and Response in England in 1848

Henry Weisser

UNIVERSITY
PRESS OF
AMERICA

LANHAM • NEW YORK • LONDON

Soc
HD
8396
W439
1983

Copyright © 1983 by

University Press of America,™ Inc.

4720 Boston Way
Lanham, MD 20706

3 Henrietta Street
. London, WC2E 8LU England

Library of Congress Cataloging in Publication Data

Weisser, Henry.
April 10 : challenge and responses in England in 1848.

Bibliography: p.
Includes index.
1. Chartism. I. Title. II. Title: April tenth.
HD8396.W439 1983   322'.2'0942   83–1259
ISBN 0–8191–3079–6
ISBN 0–8191–3080–X (pbk.)

To Betty, Tim, Jeanette and Steven

ACKNOWLEDGEMENTS

In dealing with 1848 in England, an American background has its advantages. The recent American civil rights movement, with its divisions, factions, debates over the use of physical force and great moral force demonstrations was not unlike Chartism, although this movement was for the rights of a minority rather than a majority. Mass moral force demonstrations against the war in Vietnam conditioned my appreciation of April 10 and the role of Feargus O'Connor. I saw the police lines, the angry counter-demonstrations, and people being roughly handled. One of the buildings on my campus, Colorado State University, was mysteriously burned to the ground at the height of the anti-war demonstrations, and it was revealing to see the flood of volunteers that came forth to protect the rest of the university. They had much of the spirit of the special constables of 1848. Many of them, as well as townspeople who were frightened by the wildest of rumors, made the hasty and erroneous identification of anti-war demonstrator and incendiary. It was a tense but informative time. I feel that all of these experiences enhanced my sensitivity as an historian of the last great surge of the Chartist movement.

Much of this study was written in the agreeable environment of the Centre for the Study of Social History at the University of Warwick. I am indebted to Professor Royden Harrison for inviting me to be a Visiting Fellow, which meant that I could use all of the facilities of the Centre, receive the criticisms and advice of staff and graduate students, and call upon Professor Harrison for his own insights.

A research fellowship from the National Endowment for the Humanities made it possible for me to spend the 1980-81 academic year at the Centre and work on this book. I am very appreciative of this support.

Many colleagues and friends helped me to persevere in this study. At Colorado State University, Professor Harry Rosenberg has continued in his cheerful, enthusiastic, and perceptive encouragement of scholarship within the history department. Professor Kenneth Rock, a Habsburg specialist, has offered many helpful observations on 1848 and on some of what I have written about it. I must also thank my colleague, Professor Arthur Worrall, for helping me to resist a penchant for the passive voice. Dr. Frank Vattano, Dean of the College of Arts, Humanities and Social Sciences, and Mark Gilderhus, Chairman of the Department of History, have supported this research in various ways.

Professor R. K. Webb of the University of Maryland, Baltimore County, has encouraged and lent support to my research projects ever since I was a graduate student of his at Columbia University in the late 1950's. I was able to rely upon Dr. Howard and Suzanne Leichman and Rev. Robert Schmidt, of the University of Washington, at a particularly critical stage in the evolution of this study. Professor C. Robert Cole, of Utah State University, has offered helpful support in recent years. I am thankful for the many helpful suggestions to come from various members of the Rocky Mountain Conference on British Studies as a result of papers that I have given at its gatherings for the past several years.

Numerous librarians in England and in the United States have offered courteous assistance, and I wish to thank Mrs. Pat Pugh of the University of Warwick's library in particular. Among scholars in the United Kingdom who have offered helpful advice, I wish to mention Dr. Raymond Challinor of Newcastle Polytechnic, Professor Norman McCord of the University of Newcastle upon Tyne, and Dr. David Jones of the University College of Wales at Swansea.

I offer the standard disclaimer that none of these good people are in any way responsible for the errors, omissions and misjudgements that critical readers may find in these pages.

Fort Collins, Colorado

Henry Weisser

CONTENTS

INTRODUCTION

The unifying theme of this book is given in the subtitle, "Challenge and Response in England in 1848". Both the government and the Chartists put forth challenges and developed responses to them in the year of revolutions, and the essential focus of the book rests upon this interaction. Deliberate limitations have been rigorously imposed on the material included so that the main theme can stand forth sharply. Therefore, this is not a history of everything in England in 1848. Developments in Europe, Scotland, Wales and Ireland are usually peripheral to the main theme, which is acted out on an English stage. This book does not retell the story of revolution and reaction on the Continent in 1848, nor does it retell the history of the Chartist movement. Readers wishing a deeper background on these subjects may consult the suggestions for further reading in the notes accompanying the very brief introductory remarks in the first chapter.

There are those historians whose quest is discovery and those who write history in order to make a demonstration on behalf of one or another ideology. I believe that this study has been carried out in the realm of discovery alone, although I must confess having empathy for the struggling Chartists as well as a desire to rehabilitate their much maligned leader in early 1848, Feargus O'Connor. In general, the book seeks to open up the sources, relive some of the events and analyse the nature of the confrontations and their participants.

Oral history is much in vogue these days, as historians clamber about laden with equipment. Since the last leading Chartist, George Julian Harney, died four years before Queen Victoria, the tape recorder will never capture the sounds of the Chartist movement. But through using some imagination, Chartist voices can still be heard. They have been tucked away in thousands of closely printed columns of newsprint. The Chartist years coincided with the great era of the newspaper press, when nothing rivaled the pages of dailies and weeklies for news, information and instruction. On those pages for 1848, the drama of Chartist resurgence and governmental repression comes to life in meetings, speeches, editorials and reports of arrests and trials. So do the individual voices of

the major and minor figures in the agitation for democracy. Whenever possible, I have used newspapers to
enable the Chartists to speak for themselves, so that
the reader might pick up the slogans, arguments,
sounds and flavour of the movement that year, and
thereby appreciate the rich textures and complexities
of the interaction of challenge and response.

The study breaks down into two roughly equal
parts. Chapters one through four have April 10 as the
focal point, before, during and after the events of
that historic day. Chapters five through seven take
up the various challenges and responses until the end
of the year. Chapter eight reconsiders the leadership
of O'Connor and Jones and goes on to examine what historians have said about April 10 and 1848 in England.

Within these chapters, the study seeks answers to
a set of questions: What was the impact of the French
Revolution of 1848 on Chartism? What role did the
Irish Confederates play in England? What was the
nature of public hysteria about revolution in England?
To what extent did those in charge share these fears?
Why did the government prepare itself for massive
"overkill" on April 10? How did the Chartists
approach April 10? Where did the myths of April 10
originate? How did the Chartists view the significance of that date? Why did euphoria overtake the
propertied classes after April 10? What was the
nature of the counter-revolution in England in 1848?
Did it have parallels to the pattern on the Continent?
How serious was the Chartist revolutionary threat?
Was this threat mostly rhetoric? What was the real
nature of the leadership of the two key national figures in 1848, Ernest Jones and Feargus O'Connor?
After April 10, what options did Chartists have besides revolutionary plotting? Into what stages can
the Chartist challenge of 1848 be organized? What was
the nature of Chartist strengths, weaknesses and attitudes in each of these chronological stages? How
loyal were the forces of authority? What was the true
nature of the celebrated force for law and order, the
special constables? Can a class conflict be seen on
April 10? Finally, what have historians said about
April 10 and 1848 in England heretofore?

Answers to these questions lie in an atmosphere
charged with many myths, fears, rumours, and overreactions. The events of April 10 were given two
widely differing interpretations from the outset, and

several myths have clung to that famous date in
English history. The most notorious is that of Feargus O'Connor as the cowardly Irish buffoon presiding
over a 'fiasco'. The portrayal of Ernest Jones as a
revolutionary leader after April 10 is another myth of
1848. Chartists suffered from their own myth that the
government was out to massacre them. During 1848,
people with property feared foreigners, Irish conspirators, Chartist conspirators, riot, arson, assassination, communism and democracy, and liberally plied
their fears with fantastic rumours. More realistic-
ally, Chartists feared arrest, imprisonment, the
destruction of constitutional freedoms and misinter-
pretation of their intentions.

    Men, women and children live by myths, fears,
rumours, overreactions and misjudgements in any age.
One of the most important tasks of any historian seeking a saner, more rational world, is to penetrate the
distortions of the past and come as close to perceiv-
ing reality as is humanly possible. Such an attempt
has been made in this study of 1848 in England, and it
is up to the reader to decide how successful the quest
has been.

CHAPTER ONE

TRICOLOR ALOFT

Men of England, ye are slaves,
Hark the stormy tempest raves --
Tis the nation's voice I hear,
Shouting: Liberty is near.

(Sung by Chartists in March, 1848)

Curtain Raiser

One evening late in February of 1848, the Fraternal Democrats, a group of Chartist internationalists and democratic Continental exiles, was holding one of their regular meetings. As usual, they were listening to speeches about the growing brotherhood of workers in all countries and the march of the rational mind. Suddenly someone burst in with news of a new revolution in Paris, the overthrow of Louis Philippe, and the creation of a new republic. It came like a shock of electricity. The members sprang to their feet, shouted, gesticulated, snatched decorative flags from the walls and waved them about in a crescendo of exaltation. The cry of "Vive la République" pierced the night air as the Fraternal Democrats poured into the street. With flags flying and arms linked, they strode to the meeting place of the Westminster Chartists where a similar scene ensued. By the end of the night, voices were hoarse with singing and shouting, heads were muddled from round after round of clinking toasts. Heads were clearer at a coffee house in Croyden where Chartists drank coffee or sipped lemonade, but feelings were just as joyous. One artisan summed up the significance of the news succinctly, as he thought back on how the Reform Bill of 1832 had been passed with the help of the impact from the July Revolution of 1830 in France. "Now we will get our rights," he said.[1]

That meant the People's Charter. It embodied the democratic program which British workers had sought for a decade. Universal manhood suffrage, vote by ballot, payment of members, no property qualifications for members, equal electoral districts and annual parliaments were its famous six points. The years 1839 and 1842 marked the crests of the movement, the first

1

accompanied with a minor uprising in Wales and the second by an attempted general strike. In 1847 the movement had built up again, with another petition for the Charter in the making and hard times stalking the land. 1847 had been shrouded in gloom: famine stalked in Ireland again; an acute financial crisis brought down many businesses; and unemployment was high.[2] Many wondered what would accompany the third crest of Chartism now that the stimulus of foreign revolution was at play.

The Charter meant many things to many people, but all its proponents could agree that it was a democratic solution for the ills of society. Whether aggrieved by the old wealth of the aristocratic "drones" or by the new wealth of the middle class "profit mongers," or both, British workers and many radicals felt that a democratically elected legislature would set things right, and enable those who toiled to have due recompense. Economic justice would be the fruit of political justice, and the Charter was the means to that end.

Viewed across its history, Chartism was a restless, seething hodge-podge, with individuals and groups moving in and out of it all through its years. It was really a movement of movements, gathering up various streams of radical concern and directing it all towards the one great goal of democracy. The bitter anti-Poor Law movement, the movement for workers' education, the trade union movement, early socialism, the movement for factory reform and the movement for a free, unstamped press all contributed hosts and leaders to Chartism. This movement of movements became the heir of the long tradition of British radicalism, stretching back through the times of Cobbett, Hunt, and Cartwright to the times of John Wilkes and Thomas Paine. The great impulse of the French Revolution of 1789 towards human equality lived in the organization.

The diversity that became unity returned to diversity again after Chartism's first crests. Decline and division set in after 1842, bringing specialized Chartist groups: Chartist internationalists, Temperance Chartists, Didactic Chartists, Chartist churches and the celebrated Land Plan to settle workers on agricultural small holdings. Yet something like unity came back for the last time in 1848, centering on the presentation of the third great petition for the Charter on April 10.

2

Temporarily regained unity sealed over the most
fundamental division in Chartism for a time. Chartists
used the terms 'physical force Chartism' and 'moral
force Chartism' to describe the deepest fissure. These
designations becloud the issues considerably in 1848.
Moral force Chartism usually referred to the London
Working Men's Association kind of Chartism, stressing
the need for gradual improvement through upgrading the
education, morals and rational abilities of the working
classes. The names of William Lovett, Henry Hetherington, and James Watson come readily to mind as leaders
of this wing of Chartism. In 1848 James Bronterre
O'Brien and Thomas Cooper were with them as well, the
former a Chartist theorist and the latter a poet and
lecturer of note. All of these men were now the
middle-aged veterans.

Mainstream Chartism or centerist Chartism, awkward
as these terms may seem, are better designations than
'physical force Chartism' for the great majority of the
movement who were members of the National Charter Association behind their maligned, colorful, and compassionate Irish leader, Feargus O'Connor. The foremost
internationalists were in this wing, led by George
Julian Harney and Ernest Jones.

Some of the younger and lesser known Chartists
veered off to the left after April 10 and actually became physical force Chartists, often in conjunction
with Irish Confederates.

Chartism had its geography. Unlike ancient Gaul,
modern England can be divided into two parts, London
and the rest of it. London was and is a unique
environment. In 1848 it was of paramount importance
for the Chartist challenge. Political force on the
Continent was most intense in the great capitals:
Paris, Vienna and Berlin, so it is appropriate that the
drama of 1848 in England was largely staged in London.
Many of the old centers of Chartism in the north and
Midlands, such as Manchester and Birmingham, were
quieter in 1848 than at the earlier crests. Vigorous
manifestations of Chartism in the north in 1848 in
such places as Bradford cannot be denied, but nothing
can detract from the central significance of London to
the challenge and response of 1848.

London Chartism had declined since its peak of
1842, sharing decline with the whole movement. Only
ten Chartist societies existed in 1848, down from a

total of 35 in 1842. But the sprawling, varied metropolis remained the most important Chartist center.
O'Connor's Northern Star, the only national Chartist
newspaper, moved there from Leeds in 1844. O'Connor's
Land Company had its offices in London, and Londoners
served as the secretaries of the project. Furthermore,
the Executive of the National Charter Association had
a majority of Londoners sitting on it. A Metropolitan
Delegate Council still sat regularly, organizing meetings, arranging for speakers and gaining publicity for
themselves in the Northern Star. Decline notwithstanding, London Chartism was fairly vigorous prior to the
electrifying news from Paris.[3]

    One divisive issue for Chartists everywhere was
the question of collaboration with the middle classes.
Moral force Chartists were apt to seek middle class
alliances; mainstream Chartists were sometimes
attracted and sometimes repelled at the possibility;
physical force Chartists ignored the prospect. These
Victorian middle classes were unique in their growing
numbers, self-confidence, wealth, political influence,
social power and aspirations to transform the world in
their image. Their England was unique as well, the
scene of the world's first industrial revolution, and
the place where the world's first urbanized society
was being created. It was the rich, colorful England
of Charles Dickens and the England of the grim Blue
Books at one and the same time. Everything seemed
faster, more efficient, and more powerful in England
than anywhere else. For a brief moment, the British
Isles were at the center of the stage in world history,
the most important, dynamic, influential and exciting
place in the whole universe. Should there be any
wonder that great interest and nostalgia for the Victorian era live on in Britain?

    The political system of Victorian Britain was
confidently described as the "envy and admiration of
the world." The propertied classes saw limited, constitutional monarchy and limited representative government as the most stable and progressive form known to
history. It was obviously superior to the despotisms
in varying stages of decay in Europe, the Near East
and Asia, as well as to the tribal anarchy perceived
in Africa and the democratic anarchy perceived in
America. The British system allowed a steady stream
of legislative improvements embody the undeniable
forces of progress and at the same time cope with the
needs of the new industrial environment. People of

property felt that a property qualification for voting was as sensible as they were. The poor but able could enrich themselves in such a free society and join the enfranchised if they had the will to do so. Ancient freedoms embodied in precious laws protected everyone, rich and poor alike, and enhanced the opportunities of all. Victorian society, politics, science, technology and arts steadily advanced, all as part of God's great ongoing Revelation.

The Chartist challenge did not fit into this scheme, except from the Chartist point of view. For most of the upper and middle classes, democracy meant the rule of the poor over the rich, the uneducated over the educated and the mob over all. Such fears of democracy might seem strange in the 20th century, since it has become the norm in Western industrialized states. It might be helpful to consider the Afrikaaners' fears of what one person one vote would do in South Africa to appreciate many middle and upper class attitudes towards Chartism in 1848.[4]

In the minds of the propertied classes, the very worst associations of democracy were tied up with the French Revolution of 1789, when democracy, the mob, a republic, the Terror, Robbespierre and the guillotine were all inextricably linked together. By contrast, Chartists blamed the excesses of the French Revolution of 1789 on the selfish resistance of its enemies. The French Revolution in the eyes of British democrats was essentially the destruction of irrational, hereditary oppression by the force of enlightened rationalism, a force which drove for human equality. Chartists felt that they were the British heirs of this tradition. In 1848, a new French Revolution, bringing a new republic and a new democracy, proved to them that the drive for equality was very much alive and on the surface again. It also made it certain that there would be a challenge and a response in England in 1848. The nature of both remained to be seen.

The French Breeze In Chartist Sails

The twenty-one odd miles of the English Channel at its narrowest has long served as a moat, guaranteeing insularity and protecting Britain from the full impact of sweeping changes on the Continent. The Renaissance, the Reformation, the era of absolutism, the age of the French Revolution, 19th century

nationalism and 20th century tyranny have all produced
distinctly different reflections, adaptations, or forms
of resistance in British history. Just as the first
and greatest French revolution produced a unique impact
on Britain, so, too, did the French revolution of 1848.

Its impact on Chartists deserves careful analysis.
It is well known that the outbreak of another revolution in France put a great wind into the hitherto
rather listless Chartist sails, but just how that blast
was used in the movement to navigate towards the at-
tainment of the Charter needs explanation.

France held the rapt attention of Englishmen in
1848 almost to the exclusion of all the other places
undergoing revolution, and for good reasons. France
was the home of modern revolution, and the insurrec-
tions of Italians, Germans and Slavs were regarded as
ramifications of the initial explosion in Paris.[5]
Moreover, France was what we would call today a super-
power, with size, resources, population, cultural
achievement and historic traditions all underlining
French greatness. So the shock of another revolution
in France in 1848 was deeply significant for contemporary Englishmen.

There is another reason for English preoccupation
with the French Revolution almost to the exclusion of
all the other revolutions of 1848. Daily bulletins
arrived from Paris, so news was fresh and immediate.
France was exciting in 1848.

The new French Revolution was different from the
great upheaval that began in 1789, a point its proponents stressed. A corrupt and narrow constitutional
monarchy came to an end when Louis Philippe, the
"Citizen King", was overthrown by a mixed force of
Parisians and the dissident National Guard. It happened in the midst of an economic crisis and after
repressive acts clamped down on freedom of assembly
and the press. It was all accomplished rather quickly
and many of the revolutionaries from the rising classes
of educated and professional men were surprised at how
far their agitation had carried in so short a time. A
democratic franchise, the abolition of slavery and at
least an attempt to do something about the unemployed
followed close on the heels of the proclamation of a
republic. Unlike French republicans in 1793, the ministers of the new provisional government were quick to
assure the world that a republic in France in 1848 did

not mean the danger of French expansionism abroad. The speed of the revolution, combined with the relatively short period of chaos, reassured many observers in other countries. The most optimistic amongst them felt sure that this revolution would avoid the tragedies of the 1789 to 1815 era. The pessimistic waited for new chaos to erupt and a new man on horseback to end it by imposing order on France as Napoleon had done.

The Chartists were the greatest of optimists. News of the glorious events in France filled the sails of Chartism quickly. But there was some momentum already at work. In the winter of 1847 and 1848, the third great petition had been circulating, with the familiar round of meetings, speeches and missionaries accompanying it. O'Connor's Land Plan, a scheme to resettle British workers on small, intensively cultivated farms through means of a national lottery, was in full swing, with several Chartists acting as Land Company circuit lecturers.[6]

Then came the French gale, and Chartism raced ahead, sails billowing, green flags flying, on to the last great surge for working class democracy in the early nineteenth century. Meeting followed meeting, in the halls, on the hillsides and on the wastelands. They were reported to be so crowded that people could not enter, and when held outdoors, multitudes filled the landscape. Cheers, shouts, laughter and roars of approval greeted the uniformly enthusiastic speakers. Chartism had a new lease on life; the spirit of 1839 and 1842 lived again. The Chartist Executive went on a nationwide campaign, rousing the north, the west, the Midlands, Scotland and Wales, and the closely printed pages of the Northern Star were jammed with information and extracts from speeches. Even the established press gave some of their space to Chartist news once again. Simultaneously, in the same heady atmosphere, delegates were chosen for a new Chartist National Convention. For Chartism, 1848 began with the same intoxicating enthusiasm that young revolutionaries on the Continent experienced.

Everywhere Chartists drew up resolutions and addresses to send to the French people congratulating them, although the content was usually more for home consumption than for French consumption. Addresses went forth to France from Chartist groups everywhere: from Salford, Manchester, Burnley, Halifax,

Macclesfield, and on and on.[7] The addresses more or
less repeated each other. The French were congratu-
lated, their good conduct was praised, and their victory was described as transcendent, something not just
for France but for all men everywhere. With such a
victory won in France, despotism abroad and oppression
at home were bound to give way. Because of what they
had done in Paris, Chartists were more determined than
ever to gain liberty, equality and fraternity in Britain. Such content was obviously aimed more at exciting
British workers' enthusiasm for the Charter than for
any impact on the French revolutionaries.

     Chartists were convinced that the French republi-
cans had raced ahead of them to gain the Charter. When
the Chartists of Salford addressed the French provisional government, they made it clear that the "basis"
of the French Republic consisted of "those principles
which the Chartists of England have long sought to
establish."[8] English Chartists were proud of the provisional government's desire for universal manhood
suffrage, the ballot, payment of members, and equal
electoral districts.[9] They also hailed the abolition
of capital punishment, freedom of the press, and the
promises to set up an arrangement for the benefit of
the unemployed.[10] Chartists felt they were hailing a
"model republic" which would put the interests of "the
operative workman" first, as well as uniquely apply
"the true principle of Christianity."[11] The new regime
in France was destined to have its influence felt all
over the world, since people were demanding their
rights everywhere. Chartists were sure that something
beneficial would come from it for England, but they
were not sure of where or when.[12] To an extent, they
identified with the victorious revolutionaries, because
they felt they faced some of the same wrongs that
Frenchmen had banished.[13] One Chartist orator graphic-
ally demonstrated this identity of interests by asking
thousands to "uncover their heads as a mark of respect
for the French people." When they had done so, the
speaker announced that the hatless were "prepared to
tell the government that the battle of France was the
battle of the world" and that "the sons of labor all
over the world were with the French."[14]

     Economic situations were emphasized, what Char-
tists called the 'knife and fork' issue. To put it
simply, too few had too much and too many had too
little. Under the new French constitution, one Chartist proclaimed, "every man" would be given "plenty of

the necessaries, the comforts, even the luxuries of life...."[15] Another saw both the revolutions of 1789 and 1848 as having had one object: "Food for the people."[16] Charles Keen, a Fraternal Democrat, saw "the men of capital" keeping people hard at work until the warehouses were "overflowing." Then they dismissed their workers or reduced their wages. The French Revolution that they celebrated "must put an end to such a state of things."[17] Feargus O'Connor saw the revolutionaries animated by the drive for "a fair day's wages for a fair day's work."[18]

One source of enthusiasm for the Chartists in the early months of 1848 was over the way the French revolutionists had been well behaved. The people of Salford thanked the people of France for "respecting property, preserving the public peace...[and]...maintaining order where all your enemies predicted nothing but anarchy and the wildest confusion." This showed, as one of the supporting speakers pointed out, that "the people were not, as alleged, ignorant and savage."[19] The National Charter Association and the Fraternal Democrats complimented the people of Paris on this particular point:

> As magnanimous in victory as heroic in
> combat, you have exhibited in the moment
> of triumph a spirit of clemency altogether
> unmerited by the miscreants who conspired
> to drown your liberties in a sea of blood;
> but mercy . . . reflects the more honour on
> the victor.[20]

A Macclesfield Chartist noted that "no damage had been done to property" except "destruction of the throne." If the French people behaved like this, could Chartists be called "levellers, anarchists and revolutionists?"[21]

Chartists of all kinds were sure, early in 1848, that the French Revolution would help in gaining the Charter for themselves. Chartists "rejoiced" at the French Revolution because "they could not enjoy perfect liberty in France without it being speedily extended to this country."[22] G. W. M. Reynolds, who was cited in the established press as an ardent revolutionary, said that when the French Revolution was given "fair play," its example would let no one deny Englishmen the same advantages.[23] Moral force Chartists looked to no "vain attempts at imitation" of the revolution, but to the example set of universal manhood suffrage and the ballot in action in that country. If democracy worked in France, "who shall dare refuse them to steady, prudent, calculating England?"[24] Time and again, the celebrated quotation of Lafayette was brought to bear: "That for a nation to be free, it is sufficient that she will it."[25]

Chartists bent their efforts towards revitalizing the will of Britain's workers to have the Charter, using the example of the French Revolution as a spur. "Organize! Organize!! Organize!!!," thundered the Northern Star. "France has a Republic, England must have the Charter!"[26] In their address to France, Macclesfield Chartists asked, rhetorically: "Should we remain quiescent, with arms folded, mere spectators of the glorious struggle for freedom...?"[27] Liverpool Chartists saw "the whole continent of Europe...struggling to obtain liberty..." and asked: "Was England to remain quiet?"[28] The Fraternal Democrats also wondered whether England would "remain an exception to the generous and glorious progress of nations."[29] Would they, asked Philip McDouall, "consent to remain in slavery?"[30]

Sometimes Chartists used the French Revolution to shame British workers into political activity. "Let not the world say that the French are free while Englishmen are slaves."[31] That was the usual message, repeated time and again in the Northern Star and at Chartist meetings all over the land. "How long, men of Great Britain and Ireland," the editor of the Northern Star asked, "will you carry the damning stigma of being the only people in Europe who dare not will their freedom?"[32] If they did not set about to work "at once" they were merely "the most despicable of slaves."[33] Another Chartist declared that the nation must be "lost indeed" if workers could not "profit by the mighty lessons" of the French Revolution. How could they go on, a once great people, "grovelling in misery and debt at the feet of the feeblest government...?"[34] Yet another "hoped Heaven's curse" would "fall heavily upon them" if they did not stir.[35] England, the former "pioneer of liberty," was now "demurely bringing up the rear-guard, instead of leading in the van."[36] The National Convention warned that if they did not stir "the liberty seeking German, the emancipated Italian, the struggling Pole and the proud French Republican" would all shame them.[37] The heroic French who rose against tyranny in the face of "100,000 soldiers" and "a deadly cordon of fortifications" were owed a debt. The only way for Englishmen to redeem themselves from their shame was by asserting their rights "as boldly and nobly."[38] The unemployed of Manchester were taunted that "if they had the courage of men in them" they would rise against tyranny also, but "they were not men; the spirit of men was not with them."[39]

There was a deliberately threatening tone in all of this rhetoric. Many older workers in 1848 remembered participating along with the middle classes in the struggle for the Reform Bill during the years 1830 to 1832, a time when violent oratory flowed freely. The French Revolution of 1830, which had instituted the July Monarchy of Louis Philippe, was an inspiration for the agitation, which did not hesitate to threaten the landed classes with the spectre of a similar revolution occurring in England if the Reform Bill were not passed. With this lesson of history so close chronologically, actually in the living experience of many Chartists, is it any wonder that they sought to use the French Revolution of 1848 to frighten the government into conceding the Charter?

Many of the threats were direct and clear: A multitude in Glasgow was exhorted to "do a deed worthy of the name in France."[40] Chartists in Macclesfield were instructed that the French had demonstrated again that "Kings could not do without people, but the people could do without kings." Therefore, should England "be so far behind in following the example which France had set?"[41] A speaker at a London meeting pointed to a huge placard reading: "The Republic for France -- The Charter for England," and declared: "Ay; and if they refused us the Charter, we should then begin to think about a republic."[42] Ernest Jones predicted that if the Charter were refused by Parliament, "the people" would "ask for a republic," and "the men of London were as good as the men of Paris, the men of Milan or the men of Berlin."[43] During his rousing speeches in Manchester, John Nutall urged imitation of the French. Young men were called upon to "imitate the conduct of the gamins and the students of France," and, just as English people had "hitherto imitated the fashions of France in their apparel," they should now "imitate her politically."[44] Nottingham Chartists moved to advise the government to adopt the Charter before the people of England "follow the example of the bold, noble and heroic people of France" and hurl their oppressors from power.[45] Halifax Chartists warned that the

11

"forebearance" of the people could not be relied upon
"beyond a certain point," and the government should
respond to them in order to prevent a "similar fate
befalling them" as happened to their counterparts in
France.[46] The message of the Blackburn Chartists,
similar to that of Chartists in many other localities,
was that only concessions could prevent violence and
bloodshed.[47]

Threats could be incorporated in comparisons.
The Northern Star's editor conspicuously juxtaposed a
column describing Lord John Russell's opposition to
democracy with a column describing the tide of revolution in various European capitals.[48] Russell was regularly called the "Guizot of England", a reference to
the French minister overthrown with Louis Philippe.[49]
G. W. M. Reynolds found the decree against the upcoming
meeting on April 10 "like that of M. Guizot," so it
might become necessary to meet in the same way that
Guizot's decrees were met.[50] The incident of Guizot
initially laughing at the French revolutionaries was
compared to the laughter that greeted Feargus O'Connor
when he gave notice in the House of Commons for his
motion for the People's Charter.[51] Many comparisons
with the new France were invidious for old England:
The "cold front" of Buckingham Palace was contrasted
with the "open doors" of the Hotel de Ville receiving
worker's deputations "at any hour of the day."[52] The
low pay of the ambassador from the provisional government was compared to the vast sums lavished on aristocratic ambassadors from England.[53]

Whether in making threats against the government
or in enthusing British workers for the Charter, so
much of the Chartist response to the French Revolution,
given in speeches, toasts, addresses and editorials,
consisted of repetitive clichés. There was nothing
new about the slogans and phrases; most had been used
to celebrate the first French Revolution and all revolutions ever since. Thomas Paine and the late 18th
century "march of the mind" radicals were the true
sources of inspiration for these sentiments. By 1848,
it was a litany of praise long sung.

The commonest expressions involved trumpets blown,
seeds sown and thistles thrashed. A promethian motif
was popular, with liberty, or oppressed nations, or
freedom, or peoples breaking free. In doing so, they
would "throw off the degrading bonds", or "burst their
chains", or break the "manacles of corruption", or the

12

"fetters of force."[54] Of course, the throwing off, breaking and bursting was done for "all people", and not just Frenchmen. Addresses to France almost uniformly stated that Chartists "rejoice in the overthrow of tyranny" and "hail" the coming of justice, or reason, or universal suffrage, or the fraternity of nations, or "virtuous" government. It was still a time when the struggle was between the kings and their peoples, a time when "knowledge, like an electric shock, played round the world."[53] France was once again "the temple of liberty," radiating "those holy principles of human emancipation." Therefore, the "bright era of the world's progress" was clearly at hand, at least in the early months of 1848,[56] for everywhere "thrones were crumbling" and "despots" were being "flung away."[57]

Some clichés were more pointed: The French had "kindled the torch" by whose light the British people could read the "Charter of their liberties."[58] There was a "terrible grandeur" in an armed, "omnipotent" people seeking their liberties.[59] The French had "consecrated the sacred right of insurrection," which was the last resort "of the oppressed."[60] Who would know, ran another common refrain, "what glorious revolution a single hour may bring forth?"[61] But patriots could not rest for "a single hour" until the "brave example" of the French was followed by "the universal race of man."[62] A favorite cliché of Ernest Jones found "the weather cocks on Lord John Russell's mansion" creaking "with the French breeze" and pointing to the Charter.[63]

Clichés linked up the French Revolution with English and Irish struggles: "A Republic for France, the Charter for England and Repeal for Ireland!"[64] Or a banner might proclaim: "Success to the Republic of France, Repeal for Ireland; the People's Charter for England and No Surrender."[65]

So many of these clichés testified to the full sweep of romanticism at play in 1848. For example, a Chartist placard appearing in Lancashire and Cheshire announced that Continental revolutionists were "struggling with manly vigour to rescue the fair but weeping form of liberty from the foul embrace of usurping faction."[66] Salford Chartist urged the French to become a "polar star for the guidance of surrounding nations."[67] An address of the National Convention struck the romantic chord of overpowering nature in describing revolution as a tornado, which, "in its awful but grand career", tore up the roots of despotism and swept along, "sublime in its fury...."[68]

Many clichés were enveloped in vagueness. An obscure Chartist at a Macclesfield meeting assured the audience that "in France they had done it, and what was sauce for the goose was sauce for the gander."[69] Vagueness and romanticism was also rife in the gush of poetry that came forth, which ranged from the merely bad to the awful.

Along with the clichés about the French Revolution went quite a bit of symbolism and trappings, which had been used to celebrate every revolution since the late 18th century. These included caps of liberty, sometimes on heads and sometimes on poles; fasces of the republic; the slogan, 'Liberty, Equality and Fraternity,' which appeared everywhere; cheers for the French revolution and the French Republic, especially 'Vive la République'; cries of 'Bread or Revolution!'; tricolor rosettes worn in buttonholes; red, white and blue outfits for women; and, above all, the French tricolor flag, seen flying on regular staffs or from pikes or spears. The great anthem of revolution, the Marseillaise, was regularly sung by Chartists, sometimes as they paraded arm in arm and sometimes in conjunction with 'Rule Britannia'.[70]

These trappings and clichés were just part of the diffuse enthusiasm for the French Revolution of 1848 that pervaded Chartism in March and early April. Certain groups and individuals need to be singled out for a closer focus, beginning with the moral force Chartists. This wing of Chartism, so marked by its hostility to O'Connor and his organizations, could share in welcoming the French revolution without compromising their unequivocally non-violent principles. William Lovett and his friends asked British workers to follow the example of France "in spirit", but not with arms and barricades, which were unnecessary because England had the right of public meeting.[71] Their rather small National Association, composed largely of skilled workers, sent an address to the French people offering "fraternal sympathies" and rejoicing at the victory in Paris. Yet they also deplored the "fate of the slain" and the sufferings of the wounded, and hoped that there would be no "further effusion of human blood." The address lectured the French on the impermanence of improvements for humanity through the use of force. Building up the "power and the stability" of the minds

of the people was the answer. Frenchmen should
"respect the opinions of those who differ", and make
friends out of their enemies by being "peaceful, kind
and courteous...." British workers would achieve their
own liberties "ere long" by their "moral energies", but
the success of the French republic would undoubtedly
help them. Still, success meant following a "prudent"
and "peaceful" onward course in France.[72]

Nothing is known of what French Republicans
thought of the National Association's moral instruction. It was translated and forwarded to the ambassador of the French Republic in London, and a copy was
sent to Lamartine, but no receipt of it was ever
acknowledged.[73] The French were very busy.

Feargus O'Connor was very busy also, preoccupied
with his great hope, the Land Plan. Yet O'Connor could
not keep from being swept along in the tide of excitement over the fresh French Revolution. But his
responses were usually careful, cautious and not unfree
from either a xenophobic tinge or from egotistical
idiosyncrasies. At first he was hesitant, explaining
in mid-March that he was "slow to comment upon the good
results to be anticipated" from the French Revolution
because "past history" had made him "skeptical". By
then it seemed that France had the Charter, but
O'Connor pointed out that they had been able to achieve
it because English Chartists had taught them the way,
through their assemblies, speeches and sufferings.
Since British workers were so well instructed on
account of his efforts, democracy would come to Britain
without the strife and carnage that had been necessary
in France.[74] After all, "there was not a principle" in
this "glorious reformation of France" which he himself
had not "thoroughly taught to the people of England."
Therefore, when the Charter came to England there would
not be "a single day's inter-regnum".[75] If the Charter
were proclaimed on Monday, April 10, on Tuesday, April
11, everything would be ready for "carrying out a new
system...".[76]

O'Connor could go along with the standard joyful
Chartist enthusiasm over the revolutions on the Continent, up to a point. For instance, he acknowledged
that France "had doubtlessly given an impetus to the
movement", for Englishmen could not be expected to
"remain in slavery" while thrones collapsed on the
Continent.[77] Still, in the House of Commons he boasted
of his restraint in refusing to go to France with a

fraternal deputation.[78] Above all, Feargus O'Connor
would not let the waving of tricolors distract him from
his current obsession: the Land Plan. "I tell you
that as long as I live," he editorialized in the
Northern Star, "the Charter and the Land Plan shall
never be lost sight of, nor placed in abeyance by any
foreign excitement or movement, however, we may use
events for the furtherance" of the Charter.[79]

        At the same time that O'Connor was so absorbed
with the Land Plan, several of his closest lieutenants
were regularly involved in Chartist internationalism.
Of all the Chartist groups, the Fraternal Democrats
might be expected to show the greatest excitement at
the news from the Continent in early 1848, and indeed
they did.

        The multi-national Fraternal Democrats had flour-
ished in London for almost three years when news of the
new French Revolution arrived. The organization was
led by a component of O'Connorite Chartists, including
Ernest Jones, Charles Keen, Thomas Clark and Philip
McGrath. George Julian Harney was the heart and soul
of the organization, the foremost Chartist internationalist who furnished the Fraternal Democrats and himself
with extensive publicity as editor of the Northern
Star. Harney endlessly devoted his energies to stirring Chartist enthusiasm for foreign movements.
Germans provided the main foreign component, and while
the organization gained lasting notoriety for their
association with Marx and Engels and the Communist
League, more obscure Germans, such as Karl Schapper,
were the regular speakers and members. Dr. Charles
Marx, as they called him, only showed up on rare occasions. A small number of French, Poles, Swiss and
Scandinavians composed the rest of the foreign membership.[80]

        At first glance these internationalists might be
suspected of being ardent supporters of a British
revolution, but this was decidedly not the case. The
Fraternal Democrats were never revolutionary in their
history, if 'revolutionary' is taken in the same clear
and simple sense with which Chartists ordinarily used
the term: revolution was thought of as an important
political change brought about by violence.[81] In fact,
Engels was instructed by Harney in 1846 that "a revolution in this country would be a vain and foolish project."[82] The Fraternal Democrats were devoted instead
to education and propaganda, functioning openly and

publicly, eschewing conspiracies, and, except for a degree of Gemütlichkeit, they can be said to have carried on with very English operations. They produced dozens of addresses, made hundreds of speeches, drank thousands of toasts, sang the Marseillaise endlessly and filled columns in the Northern Star newspaper with accounts of their meetings. Faith in democracy and the march of the rationalistic mind lay behind their internationalism. Despite the class conscious pronouncements of some of their leaders, Paine, not Marx, provided basic inspiration for them as well.

The powerful stimulus of Continental revolution in 1848 catapulted ecstatic Fraternal Democrats to the centre of the Chartist stage in March, where they organized meetings, drew up addresses and arranged to send a delegation to congratulate the victorious republicans in Paris.[83] Harney kept busy filling more columns than usual in the Northern Star with exciting accounts of Continental developments, thereby earning Engels' sobriquet, "Citizen Hip-Hip Hurrah!"[84]

None of this hectic internationalist activity had anything to do with fomenting a British revolution. Instead, the Fraternal Democrats' goal was the same old goal of Chartism, to have the six points of the Charter become law. Karl Schapper, a militant German revolutionary declared that the Charter would be passed "legally, peacefully and constitutionally."[85] In March, Harney's editorials promised the Charter in one month, "without breaking one law or committing one outrage.[86] In all of the addresses of the Fraternal Democrats in 1848, the only specific advice to British workers was: have large meetings; proclaim the Charter; sign the petition.[87]

In 1848 as before, their teachings on revolution were the same: violence might be the only means for, say, Poles or Italians to free themselves, because on the Continent both the oppressors and the oppressed would resort to physical force. By contrast, British workers had recourse to superior means of achieving reform, namely public meetings, petitions, free speech, a free press and at least some electoral influence.[88] In other words, the Fraternal Democrats did not draw analogies between Continental conditions and their own when it came to contemplating revolution. Nevertheless, they welcomed the revolutions of 1848 very enthusiastically, remembering also how the July Revolution of 1830 had helped the Reform Bill of 1832. As

17

we shall see, the year of revolutions that began so propitiously for the Fraternal Democrats turned out to be disastrous for the organization. Their first loss was the departure of some foreign members to seek glory on the Continent.[89]

Some of the Chartist Fraternal Democrats departed for the Continent to seek glory as well, but only for a brief visit to present an address. Their venture to Paris marked the high point of the Chartist celebration of a new republic in France. It was supposed to be a joint operation: The National Chartist Association Executive sent Philip McGrath; the Chartists of London sent Ernest Jones; the Fraternal Democrats sent George Julian Harney. But all three of them were Fraternal Democrats, showing that Chartists often wore several hats. They bore the congratulatory address which had been whipped up by the Fraternal Democrats on February 28, and agreed to by the Metropolitan Delegate Committee on the next day. A great public meeting ratified it on March 2. The address contained the usual congratulatory remarks and the hope that the French would preserve, among other things, a republican form of government, universal suffrage, the right to bear arms in a National Guard, the right of public meeting and complete freedom of the press. It assured the French government that British workers were determined never to aid any intervention against the new republic.[90]

When the delegation arrived in Paris they proceeded directly to the Hotel de Ville, the seat of government. The ministers received them promptly and Ernest Jones spoke to them in French -- how well no one knows. He said more or less the same things contained in the address, but did add the important point that they were there "not to ask for...aid." Jones then read a French translation of the address and the original, "adorned with the tricolor," was placed in the hands of Ledru-Rollin by Harney.

The reply of one of the ministers, Garnier-Pages, on behalf of the provisional government, was carefully constructed so as to dispel fears that Britons might have from familiarity with the course of the first French Revolution. The French minister pointed out that the republic would accomplish its mission "peaceably," through "the movement of ideas." There was no impending republican aggrandizement. "We desire to conquer the good opinion of all nations; we desire to invade them with our principles and ideas...." But

nothing would come from France "on the point of the
sword." Garnier-Pages stressed the "generous calm"
pervading republican France, free form cries of "vengeance or hate," and how order was immediately reestab-
lished after the upheaval. These sentiments were, of
course, the standard fare served by the French government to whatever delegations arrived from abroad. A
few remarks were for Chartists in particular: The
delegation was charged to tell their organizations at
home that they had the "liveliest sympathy" of the
republican government, which admired their principles
and respected their movement for its ability to regen-
erate British society.

After hearing this, the delegation withdrew,
crying Vive la République. The Chartist address was
taken and hung over the president's chair in the "Hall
of Audience."91

One historical event not celebrated at all at the
time has been given lasting fame by historians of
Marxism. While in Paris, Jones and Harney participated
in reconstituting the central committee of the Communist League.92 Marx, Engels and several German Fraternal Democrats were already in Paris, with their eyes
fixed on events across the Rhine. The Communist League
probably did not seem so significant to the Chartist
delegates, considering all of the excitement of the
times.

There was much for them to be excited about in the
Paris of the young republic, and they recorded their
favorable impressions: The guards at the gates of the
government were armed working men in blouses. No
"puerile ceremony" accompanied their audience, which
was straightforward. The French ministers had counte-
nances which displayed "the conscious power of mind".
When in the streets, dense crowds, so recently excited
by conflict, made no hostile remarks towards the Chartists, although they were easily identified by their
language as British. Everywhere they found friendly
people urging them to take note of their good feelings
towards England. The delegates saw a paradise under
the tricolor, with "peace, order and contentment" prevailing throughout. "Theft and outrage" were "unknown".
Dramatic improvements startled them: money from the
king's lavish civil list was now buying bread for the
starving; revolutionary slogans were scrawled on
palaces and churches; the wine from cellars that had
sloshed at "the orgies of the vicious" was now giving

19

"strength to the sick in the hospitals of Paris."
Meanwhile the shops were all open, trade flourished,
grain speculators were banished.[93]

When Jones and McGrath returned they told their
tale of French glory to throngs in London.[94] Harney
was detained in Paris for a short time with a gastro-
nomic disorder which he claimed was due to overexertion
in the democratic cause rather than rich French food.
This delayed his report for a few days, but soon he was
able to regale the Fraternal Democrats and readers of
the Northern Star with second hand descriptions of the
moving funeral of the revolution's martyrs. Upon re-
covery, the Civil Governor of the Tuileries, who Harney
called "a very civil governor", had him over for a
breakfast served on Louis Philippe's "crockery".
Harney's greatest moment came when he was brought to
Louis Philippe's old throne room, where he uttered a
prayer, "not loud, but deep", that all the thrones of
Europe would share the same fate. He also found time
to pay his "devotions" at the tombs of Voltaire and
Rousseau at the Pantheon. Harney breathed deeply in
the sweet French breeze of the springtime of Europe.

Tacking in the French Breeze

Republican France was hardly paradise regained in
the eyes of the British upper and middle classes.
Their initial response was of a "mixed character", to
quote Lord John Russell's early appraisal. He was
glad, nevertheless, that the French would now be able
to enjoy benefits long cherished by Englishmen, namely
political liberty and a free press. Perhaps the remarks of Lord George Bentinck, nominal leader of the
Conservatives, typifies the reaction of most Members of
Parliament: Bentinck hoped that a republic might prove
as "lastingly advantageous" to the French as it had to
the Americans, but he was somewhat worried about the
republic's potential for "territorial aggrandisement".
In general, the Members of Parliament approved of the
overthrow of Louis Philippe and his highhanded regime,
but were not obsessed with the event, as most Chartists
were. The increase in the income tax, Irish problems,
repeal of the Navigation Acts and the question of re-
moving Jewish disabilities absorbed them more.[95]

The Foreign Secretary could not avoid having deep
concern over the new republic. Palmerston was privately aggrieved over the prospect that it might lead to

war in Europe, although Lamartine, the leader of the
provisional government, gave all indications that he
wanted an Anglo-French entente. Palmerston was dis-
pleased by Chartist and Irish deputations to France,
and angered by allusions to British internal affairs
contained in the French government's replies to them.
He thought Garnier-Pagès insinuated to the Chartist
deputation that the English government did not possess
the entire confidence of the population. Palmerston
sent a protest via the British ambassador. Lamartine
disclaimed any such insinuation, saying that Garnier-
Pagès had been "misinterpreted." Lamartine had even
more difficulty maintaining correct diplomatic neutral-
ity when Irish groups arrived, and finally, taking
Palmerston's advice, the French leader was deliberately
cold to them.[96]

The government took no chances over the prospect
of fraternization between French republican agents and
Chartists in England. Frenchmen were watched everywhere. Officials at the Channel ports had to inform
the Home Office about the numbers of French visitors.[97]
Railway officials were on the lookout as well. Two
Frenchmen on the platform for the London train in
Manchester excited their suspicion one day, particularly when an Irishman came to meet them.[98] Various
other incidents involving seemingly mysterious Frenchmen and French connections were dutifully reported to
the Home Office by authorities and citizens. Perhaps
the most bizarre example of Francophobe fears involved
G. W. M. Reynolds, noted for his oratory at Chartist
meetings in March. An informant, W. W. Weston, a
Greenwich manufacturer of noise suppressants, described
Reynolds as "a naturalized Frenchman." Reynolds,
according to this report, had been in the Paris
National Guard. If the French invaded, he would be the
first to "hoist their republican flag". Until they
did, the Weekly Dispatch paid him to write republican
articles, but he was probably getting funds from "some
of the lowest republican clubs in Paris."[99] Hostility
never lurks far from suspicion. A French journal soon
complained that no Frenchman could walk the streets of
London without being insulted.[100]

Even the Chartist National Convention was temporarily seized by fear of foreign entanglements. When
a group of democratic Frenchmen presented them with an
address, the Convention at first declined it. After
some confusion, Thomas Clark, a leading member of the
Fraternal Democrats, explained that it was just a

21

friendly exchange, and ought to be reciprocated. Clark acknowledged that he could understand the reluctance of the Convention to accept the address, for fear that they might "appear desirous of seeking French aid." After his explanation, the Convention went along unanimously for an exchange of sentiments with the French democrats.[101]

Fraternization with Frenchmen was just part of a larger concern over the impact of the new French Revolution on Chartism. The Earl of Shaftesbury foresaw a social revolution against the rights of property, and feared most "the calm of Republican [sic] success" rather than the storm of revolution continuing. Such success would "inevitably breed a spirit of imitation" in England.[102] Palmerston was worried that "the example of universal suffrage might set our non-voting population agog." It might make them demand "an inconvenient extention of the suffrage, the ballot and other mischievous things."[103]

The established press shared no responsibility for anyone becoming 'agog' at the French Revolution of 1848. Its initial reaction was as mixed as that of Parliament, but in time it became increasingly hostile, particularly after the French seized railway property owned in part by British shareholders, without paying compensation. The Morning Chronicle complained that "the most mischievous and mistaken...superficial notions" about the French Revolution had been spread about, and thereafter set about to counteract them.[104] Dialogues supposed to take place between British workmen were contrived by The Staffordshire Mercury to show the revolution in the worst light. "It's the lazy vagabonds and not the steady workmen who have gained -- it's mob rule," proclaimed one of these ficticious workers.[105] The Leeds Mercury saw the Continental revolutions as a "rough storm" and expected the English "bark" to "ride uneasily, however well she may be moored."[106] The Times sought to pour oil on these rough waters by pointing out that the "mobs" in control in Europe had gotten their power because the army and the police forces of Continental states had been beaten "for want of a timely and energetic resistance." The Times urged such resistance in England.[107] The radical Weekly Dispatch joined the established press in pouring oil. An editorial stressed that Britain was much closer to "disturbance" during the first French Revolution than in 1848. The London Corresponding Society had been much more "formidable" than O'Connor and the

22

Convention in 1848. Moreover, people were less ignorant in 1848 than in the late 18th century, and the new
French republic was less "propagandist."[108]

All of this editorial comment fed into an ongoing
debate about the merits of France in 1848, a debate
destined to become a minor version of the classic Burke
versus Paine debate over the 1789 revolution. Lord
Brougham and John Stuart Mill became the antagonists in
the latter debate, which was far less interesting than
the original.

Increasing hostility in the established press towards France convinced Chartists that they alone
shouldered the responsibility for reporting the progress of the revolution truthfully. They thought the
established press deliberately distorted news of French
progress by always placing revolutionary developments
in the very worst light: The purpose of the press was
to discourage the revolution's English enthusiasts.
Feargus O'Connor cited the "ribald nonsense" which
sought to frighten readers about the "unsettled" state
of France, thus creating the "hobgoblin" of the
"horrors of change".[109] The Fraternal Democrats called
upon British workers to protect the "brave French working classes against the vile aspersions and foul calumnies" coming from the "prostituted press of England."
Workers should do this "everywhere...in your meetings
...your workshops...your homes...."[110] The Fraternal
Democrats accused "capitalists and profitmongers" of
setting up "a howl" against the provisional government's labor policies for fear that the English "proletarians...should get it into their heads that they have
similar rights...."[111] O'Connor thought the press was
destroying the influence of the French Revolution of
1848 just as Pitt had destroyed the influence of the
first French revolution.[112] Since this revolution of
1848 had "torn the mask from tyranny" and revealed its
"hideous features", the event had to be "run down" by
the established press in order to discourage the
British people from advancing against their own oppressors.[113]

Chartists noted how the press restricted coverage
of Chartist meetings celebrating the French Revolution.
O'Connor complained that "scores of enthusiastic, bold
and splendid meetings" had been held in the metropolitan area, "yet not a line had been reported...."[114]
As far as possible, the Northern Star tried to make up
for it.

British hostility to the point of bringing intervention against France was feared by the Chartists.
They sought to make it clear that British workers were
unwilling to participate in such an action. They
assured the provisional government that if "oppressive
governments" forget the "lessons of the past" and
"league against France," this time the people would not
march against the French.[115] Ernest Jones moved a
resolution at a metropolitan demonstration protesting
any "hostile interference" against the French Republic.[116] A meeting at the National Hall put the question of which side the audience would support if
England took up arms against the provisional government. Bronterre O'Brien recorded that a unanimous
answer was given in favor of the provisional government.[117]

     Unfortunately for the Chartist crusade to protect
the provisional government and the vision of paradise
regained in France, ugly French xenophobia flared
against British workers in that country. It struck
out at British workers in French factories and British
domestics in French households. In Normandy alone,
2,500 British workmen were employed, many of them from
Ireland. Riots and other forms of pressure drove them
out, and a sad exodus to Britain began. The Earl of
Shaftesbury organized a relief scheme for them, and
Lord Palmerston at the Foreign Office did what he could
to implement it. Shaftesbury felt considerable indignation at how British workers had been driven out "by
the bayonet." Without their labor, "not a railway
could have been constructed in France," nor "hardly a
factory carried on."[118] The expulsion became an issue
in Parliament, with descriptions of British workers
fleeing Rouen in haste by steamboat, without the wages
due to them and in possession of little more than the
clothing they wore.[119]

     For some, these acts of the French workers were
indicative of how illiberal British workers would be
should the Chartists gain power.[120] There was even
concern that British workers would make reprisals in
the Manchester area on French workmen, but so few of
them were in the vicinity that the authorities were at
ease about the prospect.[121]

     The established press made much of the affair,
repeating the indignant comments of those dismissed:
"I've been hunted like a wild beast out of France,"
reported one worker in the Staffordshire Mercury, "by

men as call themselves free and brothers of all the
world."[122] The _Morning Chronicle_ dwelt on the manner
in which "English artisans and laborers" were expelled
without their pay. This clearly showed that "equality
and fraternity" were nothing more than "unmeaning ab-
stractions."[123] The saga became material for a pamphlet, supposedly written by one of the expelled workers,
a man "thrust out almost naked...by the ferocious cries
of the disciples of 'Fraternity'." The same French
doctrine of that sort of fraternity, the author maintained, was "parading the streets of London in the disguise of Chartism."[124]

Chartists took up this difficult challenge as best
they could. They declared the news to be "a perfect
god send for our daily press," because their aim was to
"foment an enmity against the French Republic." Rather
weakly, the _Northern Star_ explained that many of those
dismissed were servants, out of work because the French
aristocracy had to trim their expenses in the republic.[125] French aristocrats, now in a state of "wholesome terror" could no longer "parade fat horses before
a hungry people," and so they were breaking up their
establishments and discharging their "useless idlers in
livery, French as well as English."[126] As for the dismissed British working men, it had to be remembered
that French capitalists had long and "cunningly" employed them in order to "bring down the prices of
French labor." Since French workers saw them as inter-
lopers, a reaction against them was natural.[127] Moreover, as Joseph Sturge pointed out in a Birmingham
meeting, French workers were doing the same thing to
English workers as they themselves had often done to
the Irish.[128] French democrats who were in London
declared that they "deplored" the expulsions and found
French workers mistaken in their xenophobic zeal.[129]

The whole subject was an embarrassing hot potato
for Chartists. There would be other, more serious,
more difficult issues confronting them as the drama of
revolution unfolded in France during the year. Eventually even the Chartists most enthusiastic about the
French Republic in March found it a struggle to continue to sail in the French breeze.

A Green, White and Orange Tricolor

Irish patriots had sailed far on a French breeze
before 1848, and they sought to do so again in the year

25

of revolutions. The Irish were always more important to Chartism than Chartism was to Ireland. The Irish in England provided many leaders for the Chartist movement and, in 1848, conspirators as well. Yet in Ireland, Chartism never seemed to flourish. O'Connor, O'Brien, Thomas Clark and Christopher Doyle were but a few of the Chartist leaders originally from Ireland. Many little known Irishmen were among those arrested in 1848, some of whom were transported to Australia.

In 1848 Irish nationalists and Chartists began to fraternize on both sides of the Irish Sea, on a scale that had never occurred before. The main reason for this was the death of Daniel O'Connell in 1847. The great leader of the Irish Repeal Movement had been antagonistic to Chartism and Feargus O'Connor. Up until the time of his death, fewer than 1,000 Dublin Chartists existed. Thereafter, Dublin saw enthusiastic joint meetings of Irish Confederates and Chartists, a scene repeated even more enthusiastically in English cities.[130]

Ireland in 1848 was in a grave state, after having endured several years of frightful famine that led to mass emigration. Nationalists formed the Irish Confederation, which was founded by a group called Young Ireland. Its leaders were socially, intellectually and physically out of touch with the hungry, suffering masses. Young Ireland was basically composed of romantic, non-sectarian journalists. Ireland's hero of the year, John Mitchell, was an icconoclastic young Protestant solicitor, the son of a Unitarian minister.[131] William Smith O'Brien, the man at the center of whatever violence there was in Ireland that year, was a Protestant landlord.[132]

How serious a revolutionary threat did the Irish Confederacy pose? This is a significant question in light of the English government's preoccupation with the threat of an Irish rising all through 1848. Robert Kee claims that there were only 70 Confederate clubs, half of them in Dublin, with 200 to 500 members in each.[133] Yet the Russell papers reveal that the Prime Minister was so gravely concerned with the possibility of rebellion in Ireland that before, during and after the English crisis of April 10, his attention was riveted on Ireland. When disturbance did eventually arise, in July, it was only an émeute, another Irish tragicomedy called the "battle of cabbage patch," because it all happened around the house of a widow

McCormack. The "escapade", as Smith O'Brien himself termed it, provided Punch cartoonists with yet another tableau of their brand of Irish history. Robert Kee says that it was not a rising at all, but "a confrontation of sorts".[134]

None of these events touched the masses, who were seeking to survive, often by fleeing over the Irish Sea or across the Atlantic. Severely insufficient caloric intake does not make vigorous revolutionaries.[135] Actual peasant resistance was so far from the anticipations of the British government that it raises suspicions about guilty consciences. They knew that while hungry Irish died in fields and ditches, shiploads of food exports left the country, testimonials to the strength of political economy's doctrines.

At any rate, the projected Irish insurrection fell far short of the image presented by Irish Confederates collaborating with Chartists in England. There were many old obstacles in the path of this collaboration in 1848. Irish workers faced discrimination, segregation and humiliating humor in England, prejudice stemming from their cheap competition for jobs, a situation exacerbated by the flood of refugees arriving since the great famine of 1846. Stereotypes of filthy, drunken, silly, devious and boorish Irish workers and servants were well entrenched in the 19th century, as any reader of Punch knows. Sadly, some of this still persists.

Chartist and Irish leaders worked against these prejudices and had a special reason for doing so in 1848: A disturbance in Ireland might add to the pressure for the Charter and would certainly shift government forces there; agitation or disturbances in England would take pressure off of Ireland.[136]

Irish oratory on this point, as on all others, made scant use of understatement. An Irishman at a Liverpool meeting warned that if the Irish were massacred, "the spark of ignition" might reach Liverpool and "the martyrs dying on the scaffold or on the plain will have the consolation in looking up to Heaven, to see the skies reddened with the blaze of the Babylon of England."[137] At Salford, another Irishman declared that "the first man shot in Ireland" would signal 50,000 Irishmen in London "to take...revenge" for "centuries of oppression and tyranny". These London Irish would not "stand quietly by and see their countrymen butchered."[138]

Collaboration in 1848 depended upon an identity of
interests, a realization that workers the world over
had common goals. Therefore, national differences had
to be submerged. Actually, there is little evidence of
anti-Irish feeling from the era of warm fraternization
in 1848. Both English and Irish democrats felt they
needed the Charter. Patrick O'Higgins, a prominent
Irish leader, implored the Chartists to send hundreds
of delegates to Dublin "to teach the Irish people their
rights." Without the Charter in Ireland, Repeal would
do the Irish little good because an Irish Parliament
would be a landlords' Parliament.[139] On the English
side, Ernest Jones strongly urged collaboration. Irish
residents in England who joined the Chartist ranks
"would carry the war into the enemy's camp." For them
"every blow struck in the metropolis or provinces of
England would have double the effect of a blow struck
in Ireland." They should realize that "the cause of
the English working classes is the cause of the Irish
people."[140]

Collaboration became widespread in 1848, in both
an overt and a covert manner. Before April 10 it was
largely out in the open. After that date, much of it
went underground or dissipated. The time around St.
Patrick's Day in Manchester provided a highlight for
fraternal feelings, an event Chartists called "the
marriage ceremony...between the working men of England
and those of Ireland."[141] In Leeds an Irish orator
asked his Chartist audience whether they would resist
Ireland's being put to the sword, and they answered him
with resounding cries of "We will!"[142] In Birmingham,
another Irish Confederate offered to spill the last
drop of his blood for the English Chartists and promised to find some cheap weapons for them if they had
none.[143] Meanwhile, the Fraternal Democrats added
Irish fraternization to their widespread concerns. In
an "Address to the People of Great Britain," starvation
in Ireland was described as the "anarchy...of middle
class and millionaire supremacy." While the Fraternal
Democrats still saw the struggle in Ireland as one of
"words", the "day of deeds" was coming. British workers were exhorted to help the Irish "win liberty for
both nations."[144] The organization pledged itself to
"cooperate with the people of Ireland against the
infamous government which alike oppresses both
nations."[145] In Dublin at the same time, the United
Irishman played up the same theme, but more vigorously.
In depicting the march of democracy around the world,
the newspaper of the Irish Confederates said that at

the upcoming demonstration of April 10, 300,000 English
Chartists "would have London in their hands."[146] Chartists could even take instruction on street fighting
from the pages of the United Irishman.[147]

More than anything else, collaboration really
meant that much more rich Irish oratory was brought
into the Chartist movement as it surged towards April
10. One classic example can serve to illustrate scores
of Irish speeches heard up and down the land in March
of 1848: An Irish barrister from Dublin named Dohney
held forth from a wagon at a Chartist meeting at Oldham
Edge. Before him was a steep, barren hillside covered
that day by Chartist sympathizers. Most of his audience consisted of respectably dressed working men, many
of them "of mature age". From time to time he looked
out upon a sea of umbrellas as rain mixed with hail
fell on the crowd.

Dohney began by describing himself as an Irish
Chartist and said he had come to England to find out
whether or not people there would "stand by and see the
Irish butchered." The audience responded with cries of
"no! no!" Thus reassured, Dohney asked whether he
could go back to Ireland and say that "if a charge of
cavalry were made along the streets of Dublin,...half a
million of men in Lancashire had sworn fealty to Ireland...." Would they swear to it upon their open hillside, "in the face of the day?" Would they say that
"their cause, and that of Ireland, were the same?"
Many in the crowd cried "yes," and one booming voice
invoked Feargus O'Connor: "Tell them that an Irishman
is our father in England."

Surely, Dohney insisted, it was no advantage to
the English people that "the Irish people should be
oppressed, should die of famine, and then be thrust
into the grave like dogs." Now, "when thrones were
crumbling", they all should make a bid for "Irish
freedom and English Chartism." Applause built up as
the speech reached its cresendo: "I am accredited to
say, on behalf of the Irish people, 'The Charter, the
whole Charter and nothing but the Charter.'" In return, Dohney asked for "Ireland, all Ireland and nothing but Ireland for the Irish!" Did they accept it?
Cries of "yes" and applause marked the end of the
oration.[148]

The Roman Catholic clergy would not have approved
of Dohney's speech. In fact, it was even claimed that

they withheld the sacrament from Irish Chartists until
they surrendered their Chartist membership cards.[149]
While disdaining any interference in "party politics,"
the clergy were "anxious" to prevent members of their
flocks from breaking the peace and being led into
"illegal and immoral" acts. Catholics were enjoined
to "refrain, for the present, from taking part in any
processions or promiscuous meetings where large bodies
of men assemble." Catholicism taught obedience to law
and respect for the civil authorities, so it was "sin-
ful" for Catholics to take part in prohibited, illegal
meetings.[150] There is no way of telling how influential these admonitions were.

    As with most important issues, collaboration with
Ireland's Confederates elicited differing responses
from the left and the right of the Chartist movement.
Some moral force Chartists said "so be it" when they
heard tales of how the Irish Confederates were prepared
with "the sword, the gun and the pike." This would do
for Ireland but not for England. Englishmen were to
rely upon "moral power only", regardless of what the
Irish were going to do.[151] On the other side of the
Chartist spectrum, the most militant physical force
Chartists found justification for belligerency in the
condition of Ireland, which some called the "Poland of
the West". They felt it was crass hypocrisy for the
government to be concerned over loss of life in case
civil strife broke out in England. The government was
not concerned about death in Ireland because they stood
by while millions were "consigned to premature graves
through starvation."[152]

    With the Irish eagerly supporting Chartism in
England, the upper and middle classes had something to
add to their fears over the influence of the French
Revolution of 1848 on British workers. The established
press was convinced that the Irish were behind the
thrust towards violence in the Chartist movement in the
spring of 1848. The Times saw the Chartists as "tools
in the hands of a gang of desperadoes." England had to
confront more than "simple Chartism." What they really
faced was a "ramification of the Irish conspiracy."[153]
The Times believed there were "surreptitious delegates"
at the Chartist Convention "in league with the sangui-
nary Dublin conspirators." They were out to "bully and
cajole" Chartist leaders, seeking to push them into an
émeute. These "traitors and rebels" hoped for French
aid and plotted "massacre and incendiarism...."[154] The
Irish were really responsible for the "bad...brutal...

language...and...atrocious schemes" issuing from Chartist ranks. What would a foreigner think if he read the speeches in journals? Because of this Irish influence he might think that "our Chartist population is the most savage in the world...."[155]

The radical _Weekly Dispatch_ shared these sentiments, expressing anger over the importation of "Celtic fury" into the "sober regions of the more calculating Saxon."[156] In March the _Weekly Dispatch_ had good reason to believe that the Irish were abusing "hospitality" in the worst way, by fomenting the wave of riots that struck London, Manchester, Glasgow and Edinburgh.[157]

The Broken Glass of March

The ominous spectre of an English revolution rose for the establishment in March, as violence broke forth on a small scale. In terms of death and destruction, the riots of March were mild affairs, milder, certainly, than the endemic disorders of the 18th century or early 19th century analysed by George Rudé.[158] But coming when they did, against a background of Chartist resurgence, Irish oratory and political earthquake in Europe, they were alarming for the men of property.

London around Trafalgar Square was the scene of tumult on March 6, when a demonstration against a proposed rise in the income tax was turned into a democratic rally.[159] The authorities had the original meeting cancelled, on the grounds that it violated a statute prohibiting open air meetings to petition the legislature occurring within a mile of Westminister Hall.[160] It was done too late, for the notices from the organizers to cancel the meeting did not circulate in time, and by one o'clock thousands had gathered.

G. W. M. Reynolds, an ardent republican and a democrat, leapt from the crowd and assumed leadership. Reynolds was a newcomer to the Chartist movement in 1848, an editor whose later and now scarcely remembered fame came from writing a long stream of sensational pulp novels. A report sent to the Home Office about him described Reynolds as "an avowed atheist and a scoffer...."[161] James Linton, the radical engraver, dismissed Reynolds as "the tin kettle at the mad mob's tail."[162]

31

Stirring speeches and some horseplay around the
fountains of Trafalgar Square marked the meeting, but
when the police came to break it up they were overwhelmed in a set of scuffles and forced to retreat. A
wooden fence around the Nelson pillar was broken up by
members of the crowd for weapons, which were used when
the police came back strongly reinforced. The police
carried the square, and fought several small scale
battles in the vicinity until nightfall. In the evening, a body marched towards Buckingham Palace, breaking
street lamps and looting a baker and publican of their
wares on the way. The guard at the palace turned out,
providing the discouraging sight of their gleaming
bayonets, which had the desired effect. The crowd
streamed back to Trafalgar Square where the police went
into them again, seeking ringleaders. Several were
arrested, including a boy conspicuous for his epau-
letted coat, who, upon seizure, began to cry. Most of
the participants were youthful. The Morning Chronicle
described the rowdy crowd as "blackguard boys," with
not "a full grown man amongst them."

The crowd seemed to have no political aim in view.
As they marched about they cheered individual policemen, sometimes with variations of "Vive la republique!"
Their spirit was high. Smashing glass was the chief
mischief of the more unruly, a practice that was kept
up here and there for several nights after the meeting.
One surgeon sought to protect his glass front by arranging his red, clear and blue medicinal bottles to represent the French republican flag, but to no avail.[163]

Punch was characteristically cynical over the
whole affair, wondering if the featured speaker was
related to a glazier. Reynolds' speech was "on the
necessity of abolishing everything, an uniting manking
in one great elastic Indian rubber band of universal
brotherhood." Punch also supplied some variations of
the French republican cry, claiming that "Weave lay
Republik!" and "Veeve ler publics!" had resounded.[164]

March riots elsewhere were similarly apolitical,
even if more violent. Glasgow had the worst of it.[165]
Unemployment was rife, particularly among railway
navvies and weavers. When several thousand poor assembled for a meal provided by a relief committee and
found it wretched, they marched on the city hall to
complain. When ordered to leave, they went on a ram-
page, smashing into shops, thirty, all told, looting
provision dealers, silversmiths and gunsmiths. Over

five hundred lamps were smashed and when all was over
an estimated 50,000 in injury and damage had been
done. Police, thousands of special constables, detachments of out-pensioners and large bodies of the military counterattacked at the height of the riot.
Shooting erupted after a line of out-pensioners were
stoned. Some of the old soldiers fired over the crowd,
but some fired into it. Five fell, two of them dead.
Later one of the corpses was placed on a board and
taken on a mournful procession through the streets.
Over one hundred persons were taken into custody, some
apprehended in nearby mining districts in possession of
guns, cheese, butter and ham. The press called the
whole affair an émeute, and once again a political
motive was hard to find. The newspapers thought the
demonstration was used as a cover for the operations
of common thieves and vagabonds.

Glass flew in Edinburgh as well, although the disturbance was on a much smaller scale than that in
Glasgow. A thousand lamps and many windows were shattered, until dragoons and pensioners dispersed the
crowd. There was some cost in injuries, but none in
lives.[166]

Manchester's riot was triggered by a protest of
the poor against the "labor test" of picking oakum as
a qualification to get relief.[167] Manchester was well
prepared when rioting came, but it still took truncheons and cutlasses to disperse the demonstrators.
Chartists wanted no blame for the riot, and repudiated
the rioters as "mischievous imps and lads."[168]
Attempts to turn out the factory hands were thwarted by
the police as reassuring reports came into the Home
Office describing the peaceful, "loyal and good" dispositions of the workers. Most workers in Manchester, as
well as workers in the rest of Lancashire and in Yorkshire, remained aloof from these troubles and remarkably peaceful.[169]

What marked their activity in the north in March
were large, enthusiastic meetings in the old, familiar
places for Chartist gatherings: Nottingham Forest,
Parsonage Green in Macclesfield, Oldham Edge, Peep
Green in Leeds, Paradise Square in Sheffield[170] and
several sites for camp meetings in the West Riding.
Many trains were filled with Chartists going to these
gatherings, many "uproarious" from local ales.[171]

33

Political oratory took on an edge in the north in March. Chartists were called upon to be "up and stirring" to "demand" what they had "long sought".[172] McDouall, speaking at Nottingham, exemplifies this militancy. He declared that if each town in Britain sent 25 delegates to London, and each village five, all armed with a musket each, they would establish the Charter and "go much further."[173] In Nottingham and elsewhere, Chartists spoke of the "rifle franchise."[174]

Faced with this oratory from resurgent Chartism in meetings being held up and down the land, as well as with the smashing of glass in riots, the government held to a firm line and took requisite action. The Home Office kept track of the erractic pulse of the agitation throughout, sifting reports from all corners of the country, noting where quiet prevailed and where militancy was particularly strident. For example, the Home Office learned that it was quiet in Salford, Coventry and Birmingham;[175] Liverpool had "excitement";[176] there was nothing new about Edinburgh that was not in the newspapers.[177] The forces of law and order, the police, special constables, magistrates and the army were carefully prepared to meet any challenge.[178]

The punishments meted out after a riot that broke out in London south of the Thames on March 13 indicated the government's determination. Of 15 rioters arrested and tried, 11 were sentenced, some to seven years' imprisonment, some to 14 years and the known thieves among them were transported to Australia.[179] An important point was raised by the prosecutor. He asked whether this criminal activity of the rioters was a result or a corollary of the political meeting that had preceded the riot. If a result, such meetings should not be permitted to continue, despite the importance of the constitutional rights of meeting and petitioning. Meetings of that sort would "excite alarm" and lead to criminal activity. The legal apparatus for repression hinged upon that interpretation.

The Home Secretary, Sir George Grey, called the March riots "serious", and worried about rioters going to gunsmiths' shops, but he was realistic. He found out that the numbers involved in these "disagreeable and troublesome" outbreaks small, composed mostly of "lads". Even so, he had the mounted police on the streets of London and the Life Guards' horses saddled just in case they were needed.[180] In Parliament, Grey called the outbreaks "slight" disturbances,[181] which was the same information he passed on to Queen Victoria. The monarch was thereby enabled to write to the King of Belgium that "our little riots here are mere nothings...."[182]

The public tried to be as confident, bolstered as they were by the press. The causes of the tumult were repeatedly interpreted in the newspapers. The stimulus of the new French Revolution was certainly one factor at play.[183] The Weekly Dispatch found it acted out in a "grotesque, disgusting and contemptible...parody." But there were major differences: the French uprising demolished a throne, while the English broke windows; the French overturned a dynasty, the English lampposts; the French expelled royal and noble families while the English rioters found lodgings in "the station house." In sum, Britain had only produced a "blind and bastard" imitation of a revolution.[184]

The Irish in England were singled out as another cause. The words of an Irish Confederate at Salford, who called for "the pike, the bayonet and the sword" were pointed out to show that the Irish in England were following the instructions of their leaders in Ireland.[185] Chartists were merely lending themselves to a "stupid conspiracy."[186]

Another cause of the tumult was singled out from all sides: the nefarious activities of the "criminal element". In the 19th century, people believed that there was a class or a race of criminals who were hopelessly beyond redemption. These evil folk had their own vile neighborhoods where they bred the next generation of thieves, pickpockets, shoplifters, prostitutes and con men, neighborhoods that the police had just begun to penetrate.[187] Big demonstrations brought them out, particularly in London. They hung on the fringes of meetings, looking for easy prey, and when meetings broke up they used disorganization to cover stealing, looting and plundering.

All classes and all Chartists disparaged these criminals, sometimes reaching heights of vituperation. They were the "scum" and "refuse" of society; the "riffraff"; "despicable looking characters"; "banditti"; a "rabble" consisting of "pickpockets, thieves and vagrants"; "mischief mongers"; "scoundrels"; "malefactors"; and "blackguards".

Glass shattered in March not because there were specific grievances, suffering or political discontent, according to the explanations in the press, but because this element became unleashed. The "Scotch malefactors" were responsible for the Glasgow riots, men who bore no resemblance at all to the "Parisian heroes." These "maurauders" had no objects in mind except "outrage and plunder."[188] Such "ruffians" were also the cause of the violence after the Trafalgar Square meeting. Several hundred of them were able to break loose from London meetings and, with a cry of "Let's make a smash", batter the defenses of shops. Hatchets, iron bars and hammers would flash as glass and wood yielded.[189] According to the Dispatch, their aim was not revolutionary at all, it was just to "enjoy a real St. Giles saturnalia."[190]

Another aspect of lawlessness was juvenile delinquency, a form of crime less understood in the 19th century. A very large proportion of those arrested in London for looting were between 13 and 20 years of age.[191]

Chartists did everything in their power to disassociate themselves from the criminal elements that the Manchester Guardian found lurking at every Chartist meeting, looking for a "favorable occasion" to ply their "professional abilities."[192] To an extent, the press helped them make the distinction. The Leeds Mercury stated that London meetings always drew a class "with whom it would be most unjust to confound with the Chartists."[193] The Glasgow Examiner decried the way criminals under arrest gave false working class occupations in court. They were not working men, the Examiner insisted, they were thieves. The Morning Chronicle pointed out that the majority at Chartist meetings were not thieves or a "rabble", but poor people who had the potential to be good citizens.[194]

Disassociating Chartism from crime was easier than separating Chartists from rioters and would-be revolutionaires. All through the spring and summer of 1848, moral force and mainstream Chartists were concerned over the public's readiness to make this identification. Leaders took pains to show that Chartists were peaceful and law abiding democrats who were engaged in a constitutional agitation aimed at a major constitutional change. Time and time again, they exhorted their audiences to be peaceful, orderly, disciplined, and controlled, so that their agitation would be

carried out in a "manly" manner. Chartist leaders followed the advice proffered by the Weekly Dispatch:
"Let every dog walk soberly when there is a cry of mad
dog."[195] McDouall, who made some of the most strident
speeches in March, let his hearers know that "he depre-
cated breaking windows, stealing watches and pilfer-
ing...."[196] Those who blamed him for helping to cause
the riots at Glasgow were all wrong, for "he would make
special care to have nothing to do with a riot."[197]
Harney insisted also that Chartists had nothing to do
with the March riots. The "thieves that law-created
hunger makes" had been at work. Chartists had
"winnowed...the chaff from the corn" and "vindicated
Democracy [sic] from violence and license" by disassociating themselves from riot. Harney cited an address
of the south Lancashire and Cheshire Chartists, which
declared: "Liberty is too sacred to be associated with
unmeaning violence...."[198]

     Disassociation from revolutionaries was the most
difficult task of all, given the rhetoric from the
meetings and in the National Convention. So many Chartist speeches were designed to play the game of 1830
once again. Moreover, it did not help that the authorities were receiving complaints from everywhere that
the French Revolution of 1848 was "a common and exciting topic among the working people."[199] George Jacob
Holyoake and many others tried to point out that this
enthusiasm for France "inspired them with pleasure,
but not with insurgency," something for which British
workers were "uninclined" and "unprepared".[200] He
could also have pointed out that so far none of the
most militant rhetoric either called for or led to any
specific steps for a revolution, and there were no
attempts to seek any aid from France.[201]

     Nothing the Chartists could say after the violence
of March could efface the identification of Chartism
and danger to property in the minds of those who had
property, or Chartism and revolution in the minds of
those who feared revolution. Every Chartist meeting
could be suspected of having its component of
"degraded" men ready to break loose, and so every Chartist meeting was feared. This partially explains the
mounting hysteria as the great meeting on Kennington
Common on April 10 approached. It also partially explains the resolute determination of Feargus O'Connor
and other leaders to make sure that peace prevailed.

The Chartist agitation in March had one focus: the presentation of the Chartist petition, now reputed to have almost 6,000,000 signatures. Delegates departed for the Chartist National Convention in London, a body of 44 representing 36 localities which met in the old Owenist meeting place, the John St. Institute. They left their home towns with great expectations. One delegate was brought to the railroad station in a procession, and pulled away as hats and handkerchiefs waved and shouts of "Do not return without the Charter" rang out.[202]

The National Convention got down to business on April 4, spending much of its time hearing reports of the condition and mood of the various constituencies. The rhetoric was militant but the actions of the Convention concentrated on handling the petition. Everybody looked ahead and worked towards the great day of decision, April 10, and the great meeting at Kennington Common.

April 10 may have been anticipated by the Conventioneers as a very unique and special day, but Chartist meetings on Kennington Common and government preparations for them were nothing new. In August, 1842, Sir James Graham, then the Home Secretary, considered processions from Chartist meetings at Kennington Common dangerous in light of the distrubed condition of the country. Graham at that time ordered the Metropolitan Police to intercept such movements and not permit them to advance over the bridges.[203]

Less than one month before April 10, 1848, on March 13, a large Chartist meeting took place on those very grounds and served as something of a dress rehearsal for April 10. Estimates of the number attending varied from 13,000 to 15,000. The government had a chance to unlimber its strength in nearly the same circumstances as they faced on April 10. Preparations were extensive: thousands of police, foot and horse, were posted in nearby buildings and over a thousand waited near the bridges with instructions not to let processions or combined bodies of men pass over the Thames. Other policemen waited in reserve at their stations. Special constables were enrolled in the tens of thousands and the military, under arms and ready, were not far away.

The rehearsal on March 13 was somewhat less peaceful than the actual performance on April 10. Some of

the lowest of the low haunted the meeting as thousands
strained to hear the Chartist orators, who stood in
wagons. A few commotions took place at the periphery
of the gathering, resulting in the plundering of several peripatetic provision dealers and some bakers'
carts. In addition, one pawnbroker's shop and a few
other small businesses were looted to the tune of
£1,000.[204] From a safe distance, the editor of the
Leeds Times summarized the whole situation under the
headline: "London in a Fright." He found the government's preparations "extraordinary" for what was,
except for a few disorderly acts, a remarkably "rational and peaceful" meeting.[205] A Morning Chronicle
reporter, in closer proximity, praised the "gentle,
though copious rain" which drowned the speeches of the
orators and washed an audience that had "an antipathy
to that process."[206] It was a dress rehearsal complete
even to the level of journalists' mockery.

Notes to Chapter One

[1]Thomas Frost, Forty Years' Recollections:
Literary and Political (London 1880), pp. 129-30.

[2]David Large, "London in the Year of Revolutions, 1848", in John Stevenson, ed., London in the Age
of Reform (Oxford 1977). Donald Read, "Chartism in
Manchester," in Asa Briggs, ed., Chartist Studies
(London 1959), p. 61, reported that in Manchester
alone, 84,000 operatives were working short time,
24,000 were unemployed and only 77,000 were working
full time. Karl Marx was sure that the world trade
crisis of 1847 had been the underlying cause of the
February Revolution in France. See Engels' introduction to Karl Marx, "The Class Struggles in France, 1848
to 1850," in Karl Marx and Frederick Engels, Selected
Works, Vol. 1 (Moscow 1962), p. 13.

[3]This introduction to Chartism must be kept
brief. Readers wishing more familiarity with the movement may wish to start with Edward Royle, Chartism,
Seminar Studies in History (London 1980). Those who
wish to update their information should consult David
Jones, Chartism and the Chartists (London and New York
1975). G. D. H. Cole's Chartist Portraits (New York
1965) will serve very well as an introduction, despite
the fact that it is really a collection of well joined
and extremely well written biographical sketches.
London in 1848 is very ably treated by David Large,
"London in the Year of Revolutions, 1848", particularly
pp. 179-80 for the condition of London Chartism. Most
recently, David Goodway, London Chartism, 1838-1848
(Cambridge 1982), has explored the history of the movement in great detail. He emphasizes its strength in
1848 on pp. 68-96. Joseph McCabe, Life and Letters of
George Jacob Holyoake (London 1908), describes six
groups of Chartists in operation before 1848 created
temporary unity: O'Connorite, O'Brien and friends,
Cooper and friends, Lovett and Collins ("Knowledge
Chartism"), Vincent and friends ("Teetotal Chartism")
and O'Neill and friends ("Christian Chartism"), p. 113.
Some indication of the upsurge in Chartist activity in
1848 can be gained by examining the Chartist material
in the Home Office papers. The bundle for 1847, H. O.
45/1826, "Chartist Disturbances in 1847", contains only
five items, but many large boxes of letters and papers
remain for 1848.

[4]The author traveled in the Republic of South Africa in 1979 and was struck by how the old arguments used against the Chartists were being used against the black majority.

[5]These other revolutions only received passing mention in Chartist sources. For a rare example, the Austrian rising was cited by John West in a speech reported in the Macclesfield Courier, April 8, 1848. For the impact of Eastern European revolutions in 1848, see B. G. Iványi, "The Working Classes of Britain and Eastern European Revolutions (1848)", The Slavonic and East European Review, Vol. 26, no. 66 (Nov. 1947). Only one figure east of the Elbe attracted much attention in Britain, Louis Kossuth, who many saw as a middle class liberal and Byronic hero. See F. B. Smith, "Great Britain and the Revolutions of 1848," Labour History (Australia), no. 33 (November 1977).

[6]J. T. Ward, Chartism (London 1973), p. 199.

[7]"The People of Salford to the French Revolutionists", Northern Star, March 18, 1848, p. 8; "The Irish and English Repealers of Manchester to the Sovereign People of France", Northern Star, March 25, 1848; "The Inhabitants of Burnley to the French People", Northern Star, April 1, 1848, p. 6; "The Halifax Chartists to the Republicans of France", Northern Star, April 1, 1848, p. 6; "Address of the People of Macclesfield to the People of France", Northern Star, April 8, 1848, p. 5.

[8]Northern Star, March 18, 1848, p. 8, also reported in the Manchester Guardian, March 15, 1848, p. 5; April 12, 1848, p. 5, speech of Wm. Donovan. The delegation of the National Charter Association to Paris came back with the same message, Northern Star, March 11, 1848, p. 5. Other Chartists claimed an English origin for French revolutionary principles, Manchester Guardian, March 15, 1848, p. 5. A few went so far as to say that the Prussians had obtained the People's Charter as well, Macclesfield Courier, April 15, 1848.

[9]Bradford Observer, March 16, 1848.

[10]Manchester Guardian, March 15, 1848, p. 5, reporting speeches of Salford Chartists.

[11] Manchester Guardian, March 15, 1848, p. 5, "Address of the People of Salford".

[12] Northern Star, April 1, 1848, p. 5, quoting a report from Dumfries.

[13] Manchester Guardian, March 15, 1848, quoting James Leach; Northern Star, April 8, 1848, quoting Julian Harney, p. 2.

[14] Manchester Guardian, March 15, 1848, p. 5.

[15] Manchester Guardian, March 15, 1848, quoting G. H. Smith.

[16] Manchester Guardian, March 15, 1848, p. 7, quoting a Chartist named Roberts.

[17] Northern Star, March 4, 1848, p. 1.

[18] Northern Star, May 13, 1848, p. 5.

[19] Manchester Guardian, March 15, 1848, p. 5, quoting John Flynn; Northern Star, March 18, 1848, p. 8.

[20] Northern Star, March 4, 1848, p. 1.

[21] Macclesfield Courier, April 15, 1848.

[22] Weekly Dispatch, March 12, 1848, p. 127; Northern Star, April 8, 1848, p. 2.

[23] Weekly Dispatch, March 12, 1848, p. 127.

[24] Weekly Dispatch, March 12, 1848, p. 125.

[25] Northern Star, March 4, 1848, p. 1.

[26] Northern Star, April 1, 1848, p. 4.

[27] Northern Star, April 8, 1848, p. 5. See also the Macclesfield Courier, April 15, 1848, the declaration of Yorkshire Chartists reported in the Leeds Mercury, March 18, 1848 and the Bradford Observer, March 16, 1848.

[28] Northern Star, April 29, 1848, p. 5. Also the Metropolitan Delegate Committee's resolution, reported in the Northern Star, March 4, 1848, p. 5.

[29] Northern Star, April 1, 1848.

[30] Weekly Dispatch, March 26, 1848.

[31] Northern Star, March 4, 1848, p. 4.

[32] Northern Star, March 25, 1848, p. 4.

[33] Northern Star, February 26, 1848, p. 4.

[34] Northern Star, April 1, 1848, p. 2, quoting William Howitt.

[35] Manchester Guardian, April 15, 1848, quoting John Nutall at Manchester.

[36] Northern Star, March 18, 1848, p. 4; also Macclesfield Courier, April 15, 1848.

[37] Northern Star, April 8, 1848, p. 1.

[38] Northern Star, April 1, 1848, p. 2. William Howitt was the author.

[39] Manchester Guardian, April 12, 1848, p. 5.

[40] Glasgow Examiner, March 11, 1848.

[41] Macclesfield Courier, April 8, 1848.

[42] Northern Star, March 11, 1848, p. 1. The speaker was Cuffay.

[43] Northern Star, April 8, 1848, p. 4. G. W. M. Reynolds, in the National Convention, stressed that lightly armed Parisians had carried out their "glorious" revolution in the face of 100,000 troops". Surely "the English people were equally brave, resolute [and] determined". Reported in the Weekly Dispatch, April 9, 1848, p. 180.

[44] Manchester Guardian, April 5, 1848, p. 5; April 15, 1848.

[45] Manchester Guardian, March 29, 1848, p. 5.

[46] Northern Star, April 1, 1848, p. 6, "Address of the Halifax Chartists to the Republicans of France."

[47] Manchester Guardian, March 15, 1848, p. 7.

43

[48] Northern Star, April 1, 1848, p. 8

[49] Northern Star, March 11, 1848, p. 4; Liverpool Journal, March 18, 1848, p. 2, quoting Edmund Jones.

[50] Morning Chronicle, April 8, 1848, p. 6.

[51] Northern Star, April 1, 1848, p. 2.

[52] Northern Star, April 8, 1848, p. 8.

[53] Weekly Dispatch, March 13, 1848, p. 141.

[54] Harney used this motif endlessly. For an example, Northern Star, April 8, 1848, p. 5.

[55] An example of this is in O'Connor's speech reported in the Northern Star of March 11, 1848, p. 1.

[56] Northern Star, April 8, 1848, p. 1.

[57] These were the favorite clichés of an Irishman in Lancashire named Doheney. See the Manchester Guardian, March 22, 1848, p. 6.

[58] Northern Star, March 4, 1848, p. 4. Also G. W. M. Reynolds at a public meeting reported in the Northern Star of March 11, 1848, p. 1 or Edward Pilling at Manchester, Manchester Guardian, March 15, 1848, p. 5.

[59] Northern Star, March 18, 1848, p. 5.

[60] Northern Star, March 4, 1848, p. 1.

[61] "Address from the National Convention to the Men of London," reported in the Northern Star of April 8, 1848, p. 1.

[62] Manchester Guardian, March 15, 1848, p. 5, speech of James Leach.

[63] Northern Star, April 29, 1848, p. 6.

[64] A slight variation of this was part of the "Address of the Irish and English Repealers of Manchester to the Sovereign People of France," reported in the Northern Star of March 25, 1848. Also the Manchester Guardian, March 22, 1848, p. 6; Leeds Mercury, April 8, 1848, p. 9.

[65] Leeds Mercury, April 8, 1848, supplement describing a large Chartist meeting.

[66] Placard: The South Lancashire and Cheshire Chartist Delegates to the People, Manchester, March 14, 1848, H.O. 45/2410 London.

[67] Manchester Guardian, March 15, 1848, p. 5.

[68] Northern Star, April 8, 1848, p. 1.

[69] Macclesfield Courier, May 20, 1848.

[70] For some examples, Northern Star, April 4, 1848, p. 7; March 4, 1848, p. 5.

[71] The Reasoner, Vol. 4 (1848), p. 233. The organization was the Democratic Committee for the observation of the French Revolution.

[72] "Address to the French People From the National Association, London", (London 1848). The skilled, well paid workers of the trade unions were much less concerned with the French Revolution of 1848 than the Chartist movement. But the Executive Committee of the National Association of United Trades did send an address to the president of the commission for workers in Paris. See the Northern Star, March 11, 1848, p. 2. Robert Owen, the famous philanthropist, spoke at length on the French Revolution in March. He had grave fears of an English revolution and felt that the government was "reposing on a barrel of gunpowder". See the Northern Star, March 4, 1848, p. 5; April 1, 1848, p. 3.

[73] William Lovett, Life and Struggles of William Lovett (London 1967 ed.), p. 276.

[74] Northern Star, March 18, 1848, p. 1.

[75] Staffordshire Mercury and Potteries Gazette, March 11, 1848, p. 4.

[76] Northern Star, April 1, 1848.

[77] Northern Star, April 8, 1848, p. 1.

[78] Hansard, Parliamentary Debates, Third Series, Vol. 98, p. 84.

[79] Northern Star, February 26, 1848, p. 1.

[80] Accounts of the Fraternal Democrats appear in Julius Braunthal, A History of the International (New York and Washington, 1967), Vol. 1; A. R. Schoyen, The Chartist Challenge: A Portrait of George Julian Harney (London 1958). An older and often quoted interpretation is Fiodor Rothstein, From Chartism to Labourism, Historical Sketches of the English Working Class Movement (London 1929); a newer analysis is in the sketches of Harney and Jones in E. Kandel, Marx und Engels und die ersten proletarischen Revolutionäre (Berlin 1965), a translation of recent Soviet contributions. Also Henry Weisser, "Chartist Internationalism, 1845-1848", The Historical Journal, Vol. 14, no. 1 (1971), pp. 49-66; British Working Class Movements and Europe, 1815-1848 (Manchester 1975), pp. 118-172.

[81] Many semantic and philosophical problems surround the use of the word revolution, as pointed out in Issac Kramnick, "Reflections on Revolution: Definition and Explanation in Recent Scholarship", History and Theory, Vol. 11, no. 1 (1972), pp. 26-53.

[82] Frank Gees Black and Renee Metivier Black, eds., The Harney Papers (Assen 1969), p. 240, Harney to Engels, March 30, 1846.

[83] Northern Star, March 4, 1848, p. 1; March 18, p. 5; March 25, 1848, p. 5; Schoyen, The Chartist Challenge, pp. 158-9.

[84] Northern Star, March 4, 1848, p. 4; March 18, 1848, p. 4; March 25, 1848, pp. 4-5.

[85] Northern Star, March 4, 1848, p. 1.

[86] Northern Star, March 4, 1848, p. 1.

[87] See in particular the "Address of the Fraternal Democrats to the People of Great Britain and Ireland", Northern Star, March 25, 1848, p. 5; "Address of the Fraternal Democrats to the People of Great Britain", Northern Star, April 1, 1848, p. 5.

[88] These views were often presented to justify Continental revolutions to moral force Chartists. Mazzini was noted for this approach.

[89] In March a new council for the Fraternal Democrats had to be elected. Schapper and Bauer, two important German members, were gone by then.

[90] It is reproduced in full on the front page of the Northern Star, March 4, 1848.

[91] A full report is in the Northern Star of March 11, 1848, p. 5. The Manchester Guardian, March 11, 1848, p. 4, also carried it.

[92] John Saville, Ernest Jones: Chartist (London 1952), p. 231; Schoyen, The Chartist Challenge, p. 159.

[93] Northern Star, March 11, 1848, p. 5, "Report of the Delegation to Paris".

[94] Northern Star, March 18, 1848, p. 5.

[95] Hansard, Parliamentary Debates, Third Series, Vols. 97 and 98; Annual Register, 1848, p. 50.

[96] Lawrence C. Jennings, France and Europe in 1848: A Study of French Foreign Affairs in Time of Crisis (Oxford 1973), pp. 49-50. See also Evelyn Ashley, The Life of Henry John Temple, Viscount Palmerston, 1841-1865, Vol. 1 (London 1876), pp. 87-8.

[97] Royal Archives (R. A. henceforth) Add. MSS J 68/2 Colonel Rowan to General Bowles, n.d., but probably March. Use of the Royal Archives was due to the gracious permission of her Majesty the Queen.

[98] W. Maude to Sir George Grey, Manchester, March 26, 1848, H.O. 2410, Part 1A.

[99] W. W. Weston to Sir George Grey, April 10, 1848, H.O. 45/2410, London.

[100] Quoted and denied in the Weekly Dispatch of April 30, 1848, p. 209. The French journal was the Commune.

[101] Northern Star, April 15, 1848, p. 8.

[102] Edwin Hodder, The Life and Work of the Seventh Earl of Shaftesbury (London 1886), Vol. 2, p. 238.

[103] Ashley, Life of Palmerston, Vol. 1, p. 81, from Palmerston to Lord Normanby, Feb. 28, 1848.

[104] For example, the Morning Chronicle editorial of April 7, 1848, p. 4.

[105] Staffordshire Mercury and Potteries' Gazette, April 8, 1848, p. 3. See also the Liverpool Journal, March 18, 1848, p. 2.

[106] Leeds Mercury, April 8, 1848, p. 4.

[107] The Times, April 6, 1848.

[108] Weekly Dispatch, April 23, 1848, editorial.

[109] Northern Star, April 1, 1848, p. 1

[110] Northern Star, March 25, 1848, p. 5.

[111] Northern Star, March 18, 1848, p. 4.

[112] Northern Star, April 8, 1848, p. 1.

[113] Northern Star, April 1, 1848, p. 4; April 8, 1848, p. 5.

[114] Northern Star, March 4, 1848, p. 1.

[115] Northern Star, March 4, 1848, p. 1, also reported in the Manchester Guardian of March 11, 1848, p. 4. See also the address of the "Inhabitants of Burnley to the French People", Northern Star, April 1, 1848, p. 6.

[116] Northern Star, March 11, 1848, p. 1.

[117] Northern Star, April 8, 1848, p. 1.

[118] Hodder, Life of Shaftesbury, pp. 238-41.

[119] Hansard, Parliamentary Debates, Vol. 97, pp. 336-8.

[120] James Gibson to Joseph Hume, May 3, 1848, Russell Papers, P.R.O. 30/22 7B.

[121] J. Fred Foster, Esq. to S. M. Phillipps, Manchester, March 8, 1848, H.O. 45/2410, Part 1a.

[122] Staffordshire Mercury, April 8, 1848, p. 3.

[123] *Morning Chronicle*, March 9, 1848, p. 4; also March 31, 1848, p. 4, editorial.

[124] A Fellow Labourer, "What the Chartists Are. A Letter to English Working Men", (London 1848), p. 4.

[125] *Northern Star*, March 11, 1848, p. 5.

[126] *Northern Star*, March 18, 1848, p. 5.

[127] *Northern Star*, March 11, 1848, p. 5.

[128] *Weekly Dispatch*, March 19, 1848, p. 134.

[129] *Northern Star*, April 1, 1848.

[130] Rachel O'Higgins, "The Irish Influence in the Chartist Movement," *Past and Present* no. 20 (November 1961), pp. 86-91.

[131] Robert Kee, *The Green Flag: A History of Irish Nationalism* (London 1972), p. 245.

[132] The members of Young Ireland were respectable, comfortable, middle class nationalists, whose oratory and editorials might make a thrilling romantic impression, even today, but it all seems to have meant little to the peasantry. Raymond Postgate claimed that not one in a hundred of the Irish peasants for whom they claimed to be speaking could understand them. Raymond Postgate, *Story of a Year: 1848* (London 1955), pp. 37 and 40. Also Kee, *The Green Flag*, p. 263.

[133] Kee, *The Green Flag*, pp. 263-70.

[134] Kee, *The Green Flag*, p. 270.

[135] Studies of human violence reveal that one of the most effective ways to lower the levels of resistance is to deprive people of sufficient calories, a technique employed by Nazi concentration camp officials. John Gunn, *Violence in Human Society* (Newton Abbot 1973), pp. 33-4.

[136] *Weekly Dispatch*, May 7, 1848, p. 228, quoting Captain O'Brien; also quoted in the *Northern Star*, May 6, 1848, p. 6. For an interpretation of the Irish role in London in 1848, see Goodway, *London Chartism 1838-1848*, pp. 61-67.

49

[137] The Times, April 10, 1848, p. 3, quoting the Liverpool Albion, speech of Matthew Somers.

[138] Weekly Dispatch, April 2, 1848, p. 9.

[139] Northern Star, May 6, 1848, p. 1; Manchester Guardian, April 12, 1848, p. 4.

[140] Morning Chronicle, April 3, 1848, p. 4.

[141] Northern Star, March 25, 1848, p. 5. There was a meeting at the Free Trade Hall, a soiree in Manchester Town Hall a day later and an Anglo-Irish camp meeting at Oldham Edge a day later.

[142] Leeds Mercury, April 8, 1848, supplement.

[143] Mayor of Birmingham to Dennis Le Marchant, April 12, 1848, H.O. 2410, Part 3, B-Z.

[144] Northern Star, April 1, 1848, p. 5.

[145] Northern Star, April 8, 1848, p. 5.

[146] This excerpt was read in the House of Lords. Hansard, Parliamentary Debates, Third Series, Vol. 98, p. 26.

[147] Northern Star, March 11, 1848, p. 8.

[148] Manchester Guardian, March 22, 1848, p. 6.

[149] O'Higgins, "The Irish Influence in the Chartist Movement", p. 89.

[150] Handbill signed by the Catholic clergy residing in Manchester and Salford, H.O. 45/2410, Part 1.

[151] Macclesfield Courier, May 20, 1848, from a report of a Chartist meeting in Macclesfield.

[152] Leeds Mercury, April 22, 1848, p. 8, from a speech at a West Riding Chartist meeting.

[153] The Times, April 10, 1848, p. 4.

[154] The Times, April 11, 1848, editorial.

[155] The Times, April 13, 1848, p. 4.

[156] *Weekly Dispatch*, April 9, 1848.

[157] *Weekly Dispatch*, April 9, 1848, p. 181; also, the editorial of April 2, 1848.

[158] George Rudé, *The Crowd in History* (New York 1964). Details of the March riots are found in Goodway, *London Chartism, 1838-1848*, pp. 111-16.

[159] *Annual Register*, March, 1848, pp. 35-6; *Morning Chronicle*, March 7, 1848, p. 7 and March 9, 1848, p. 7.

[160] 57 Geo. III, c. 19, according to the *Annual Register*, March, 1848, p. 35.

[161] W. W. Weston to Sir George Grey, H.O. 45/2410, London.

[162] William James Linton, *James Watson: A Memoir* (Manchester 1880), p. 65.

[163] *Morning Chronicle*, March 9, 1848, p. 7.

[164] *Punch*, Vol. 14, 1848, pp. 112-15.

[165] *Annual Register*, March, 1848, p. 37; *Morning Chronicle*, March 10, 1848, p. 3; *Glasgow Examiner*, March 11, 1848; John Stevenson, *Popular Disturbances in England, 1700-1870*, pp. 171, 175.

[166] *Morning Chronicle*, March 9, 1848, p. 7.

[167] Stevenson, *Popular Disturbances in England*, p. 267; *Annual Register*, March, 1848, p. 37; *Manchester Guardian*, March 11, 1848.

[168] Donald Read, "Chartism in Manchester", p. 63.

[169] Fred Foster to S. M. Philipps, March 8, 1848; W. Maude to Sir George Grey, March 26, 1848, H.O. 2410.

[170] Thomas Frost, "History of the Chartist Movement", serialized in the *Bradford Observer Budget* from June 5, 1886, onwards, chapter 9.

[171] *Manchester Guardian*, March 22, 1848, p. 6.

[172] *Bradford Observer*, March 23, 1848.

[173] *Weekly Dispatch*, March 26, 1848, p. 7. He added his hopes that they would never be driven to that extremity, typical of the kind of qualifying statement that Chartists used.

[174] *Northern Star*, April 1, 1848, p. 6, meeting in Dumfries.

[175] Charles Gibson to Sir George Grey, March 10, 1848, H.O. 45/2410, Part 1a; various letters in H.O. 45/2410 P.

[176] Letter to the Mayor of Liverpool signed by small businessmen, n.d. H.O. 45/2410, Part 1a.

[177] Sheriff of Edinburgh to Sir George Grey, March 8, 1848, H.O. 45/2410, Part 5, A-L.

[178] There are numerous letters pertaining to this in H.O. 45/2410, Part 1a. In particular, J. Fred Foster to Sir George Grey, March 12, 1848 and George Grey to the Earl of Derby, March 13, 1848.

[179] *Annual Register*, March, 1848, pp. 39, 48-9.

[180] G. P. Gooch, ed., *The Later Correspondence of Lord John Russell, 1840-1878* (London 1925), pp. 186-7.

[181] Hansard, *Parliamentary Debates*, Third Series, Vol. 98, p. 313.

[182] Theodore Martin, *The Life of His Royal Highness The Prince Consort*, 2nd ed., (London 1875), p. 28.

[183] For an example, the editorial of the *Leicester Journal*, March 10, 1848, p. 3.

[184] *Weekly Dispatch*, March 12, 1848, p. 125.

[185] *Manchester Guardian*, March 29, 1848, p. 6.

[186] *Morning Chronicle*, April 7, 1848, p. 4.

[187] J. J. Tobias, *Crime and Industrial Society in the Nineteenth Century* (London 1967), p. 11. He notes that London was particularly attractive to the "swell mob" in times of public disturbances "such as Chartist activities". (p. 72).

[188] Weekly Dispatch, March 12, 1848, p. 127; March 19, 1848, p. 133.

[189] Annual Register, March, 1848, p. 48; Weekly Dispatch, March 12, 1848, p. 127.

[190] Weekly Dispatch, April 16, 1848, p. 185.

[191] Annual Register, March, 1848, p. 48.

[192] Manchester Guardian, June 3, 1847, p. 7. Some Chartists went to the extreme of claiming that the police were encouraging "disgraceful persons" to commit plunder when Chartists met. (Weekly Dispatch, March 19, 1848, p. 141.) From the other side, there were rumors that money from the Irish Confederates and perhaps even French and American sources of funds were going into the pockets of the "pickpockets, thieves and vagrants" to create disorder. (Weekly Dispatch, June 11, 1848, p. 278.)

[193] Leeds Mercury, April 15, 1848, p. 4.

[194] Morning Chronicle, March 15, 1848, p. 4.

[195] Weekly Dispatch, June 11, 1848, p. 281.

[196] Weekly Dispatch, March 26, 1848, p. 151.

[197] Manchester Guardian, March 22, 1848, p. 6.

[198] Northern Star, March 18, 1848, p. 4.

[199] Lord Ashley to Mr. Anson, April 22, 1848, RA Add. MSS., C 56, Item 48.

[200] George Jacob Holyoake, Bygones Worth Remembering (London 1905), Vol. 1, p. 77. Also the speech of Joseph Barker in the Leeds Times, March 4, 1848, p. 5.

[201] Only one obscure letter in the Northern Star called for French aid. It was from someone named 'Gurth' in Dumfries. (Northern Star, April 1, 1848.) John Saville, "Chartism in the Year of Revolution: 1848", The Modern Quarterly (Winter 1952-3), p. 25, points out that despite all of their efforts, Chartists were identified with petty criminals, rioters, radicals, and foreign revolutionaries.

[202] *Northern Star*, April 8, 1848, p. 8.

[203] Sir James Graham to the Lord Mayor of London, August, 1842.

[204] *Annual Register*, March 1848, p. 39. David Large, "London in the Year of Revolutions, 1848", p. 184 and John Stevenson, *Popular Disturbances in England*, p. 270, have also called it a 'dress rehearsal'.

[205] *Leeds Times*, March 18, 1848, p. 3.

[206] *Morning Chronicle*, March 15, 1848, p. 4.

CHAPTER II

PREPARATIONS

The Reign of Fear

As April 10 loomed, leaders on both sides were
consumed with frantic preparations for the great confrontation. Before examining the government's elaborate response and the nature of the Chartist challenge
in detail, it is necessary to describe the fear that
was so pervasive until the tenth was over.

Fear of revolution was the core of the anxiety.
After all, there was something strange, mysterious,
unexpected and unpredictable about the insurrection in
France and the swift reappearance of the phenomenon in
many other European capitals. Who was to say, from
the perspective of the beginning of April, that it
might not happen in London as well? No matter how confident Englishmen might be over the stability of their
institutions, it was, in the words of the Annual Register, "impossible to view without alarm so immence a
multitude" as that which planned to gather on Kennington Common. Shocking events in Europe made it impossible for anyone to "pretend to guess what might be the
fortuitious results" of the Chartist assembly.[1] Several speakers in Parliament described the pervasive
alarm in the country. In the minds of some Members,
"excited mobs" of pillagers and plunderers "who had no
respect for the law" were just over the horizon.[2] The
period just before the tenth was marked by "universal
panic," wherein each man "made his house a castle", yet
"trembled for his windows," according to one magazine.[3]
The Leeds Mercury found the "degree of alarm" on the
part of the government and among people generally "such
as we do not remember to have been equaled." The state
of alarm came from the "uncertainty" surrounding the
causes of Continental revolutions, as well as the realization that "where combustibles exist a mere spark may
kindle a great conflagration."[4] The Times went further. "Common sense" pointed to "an indefined danger,"
according to the editorial of April 4. Common sense
also abhorred "the spectacle of one or two hundred
thousand men marching through a metropolis in military
array" or coming to the "door of the legislature" with
demands they professed to fight for. To allow such a
scene to take place was foolish, since "within fifty

days a dozen of the greatest cities of the world have
been revolutionized by exactly the same process."
Feargus O'Connor was seen by The Times as only "the
stalking horse" of a "bolder...less scrupulous party"
that was determined to carry arms that day contrary to
O'Connor's "pacific councils." The intended demonstration had, in short, a "perilous character."[5]

What The Times feared most was an accidental flash
of violence and an explosion from all the combustible
elements present. It did not regard the English "mob"
as "bloodthirsty," no matter how "wanton and destructive" it might be on occasion. Nor would it be armed
or allied to any foreign cause. "The danger," The
Times editorialized, was "in coincidence and combination." Even a demonstration by as few as 50,000 could
cause trouble if "some sudden sight of blood" or the
"rashness of some soldier or official" ignited the
"more violent leaders" of the Chartist Convention. A
new element would "come into play from Continental
examples" because the "prestige" of successful revolutions abroad would "embolden the assailant and unnerve
the defender." Just let "a few mischievous foreigners
show the way and the Irish Confederates follow the
lead; let pike and musket make their appearance" and
who could know the outcome?[6] There is irony in the
fact that these fears expressed in The Times were fully
shared by Feargus O'Connor!

Many whose politics were somewhere between that of
The Times and that of O'Connor shared their anxious
outlook. The radical Weekly Dispatch predicted "a very
serious affray," pointing to "a thousand ominous circumstances...."[7] Most ominous were the inflammatory
speeches of Harney, Jones and Cuffay on the one side,
and the massive preparations by the government on the
other. A collision seemed more than likely.[8] While
the Newcastle Chronicle thought there was "too much
alarm," a dangerous combination of European revolutions
and violent Chartist speeches was at play.[9]

Any impending tense confrontation can be expected
to have an aura of grisly rumors. So it was with April
10. A pamphlet described how violent Chartists planned
to fill both Houses with "armed ruffian bands," place
Members in restraint, appoint a provisional government
and proclaim a republic.[10] A workman wrote to the Home
Office informing the government that the Chartists
planned to make the capital "like Moscow" if they did
not obtain their Charter.[11] Grim scenes raced through

56

the popular imagination, such as London reduced to ashes, Buckingham Palace overrun by revolutionaries.[12] The Times cited a "manifesto" from the National Convention calling upon men in London, English and Irish, to begin the "demolition of the existing political system."[13] News vendors wrote to their publishers in anticipation of gore. "If the Chartists should gain the day...send me all that you can spare. Unless a few people are shot or sabred, there will be no interest in the proceedings," so do not send an oversupply.[14]

Contemporary letters readily reveal the widespread fears of the well born and the highly literate. The Dutchess of Bedford wrote to tell Lord John Russell that she had been "in an agony about you."[15] The wife of Colonel Phipps, advisor to Prince Albert, feared that the Chartists would "massacre" her husband.[16] Thomas Carlyle, distressed in general that so many nations were "deep in the quagmire of revolution," believed that there were "great miseries and confusions" in store for Britain.[17] Charles Kingsley wrote to his wife from London, asking her to send money so that he could buy religious tracts for the poor, "anything which may keep even one man from cutting his brother's throat...."[18] Meanwhile his publisher half jokingly told Mrs. Kingsley that she might hear of his shop being pillaged and he himself thrown into the Trafalgar Square fountains by the mob.[19]

Contemporary diaries reveal as much fear as contemporary letters. Lady Charlotte Guest was worried about bloodshed ensuing when "the starving met the troops" and the "implacable hate" that such a clash might engender. All of this caused her "many an anxious hour."[20] The Earl of Shaftesbury recorded that "we have yet a tumult in store...'Count no man happy before he be dead,' count no event small until it shall have passed." The Earl of Malmesbury wrote of the increasing alarm as April 10 approached, declaring that "everybody expects that the attack will be serious." Even the extensive precautions of the government "increased people's fears," so that "alarm" was "very general all over town."[22] Lord Broughton felt grave anxiety as separating from his wife and children on the fateful day, and was concerned that someone had mysteriously chalked his door. When he sat down in his office, he felt it "by no means improbable" that he should hear "discharges of musketry or cannon."[23]

Perhaps the aristocrat most fearful for England's fate was an exile at a whist table, a man who formerly controlled the destinies of east central Europe. Prince Clemens von Metternich predicted that of all the violent and destructive revolutions of 1848, an English one would be the worst. He maintained that Jacobinism had not shot its bolt in England, so the aristocracy and church still had immense revenues to become "the spoil of ravenous democracy." Russell himself recorded Metternich's gloomy prophesy.[24]

A few persons not at the center of government could see through the hysterical alarm and discount it. Matthew Arnold, for instance, wrote to his mother about the "ridiculous terror" of people in London. He found it "beyond belief."[25] Some others were so confident of the troops that they did not fear putting down "the violence of misguided men" with "force."[26] The press bolstered their views by attempting to show how hopeless the dreams of Chartist revolutionaries were. The Morning Chronicle insisted that the Chartist leaders knew that all of the higher and middle classes were against them, as well as "the best of the working class." Chartist leaders cannot "possibly deceive themselves" into believing that either police, or special constables or soldiers would take their side. There was no way that the Charter could be "forced down the throats" of the classes that did not adhere to those principles.[27] The Manchester Guardian was equally blunt: No matter what happened on the Continent, anyone "mad enough" to attempt an uprising in England would be "speedily put down" by the government, local authorities and the "well disposed" population.[28]

The Chartist threat actually brought forth a response not unlike that elicited by Dunkirk or the Blitz. April 10 was seen as an opportunity to bring out the "sterling qualities of the English character", which would not allow submission to a mob.[29] The Times, despite its fears of accidental conflagration, prophesied "a firm, peaceful, and almost majestic union of all classes in defense of constitutional liberty and order."[30] Nothing really pleases prophets more than to have their predictions come true, and this partially accounts for the jubilation after April 10.

The defensive spirit ensured the transformation of fear into an hysteria of assertion, to use F. C. Mather's phrase. The government was urged from all sides to resist staunchly. Groups of inhabitants and individuals called upon the government to prevent the meeting.[31] The police were urged to "deliver London from anarchy, bloodshed and pillage", and warned that the lower orders possessed "staves and stones" to use against them.[32] Lord John Russell received much advice to take a hard line. For example, C. E. Trevelyan urged him to arrest Jones and other Chartist leaders straight away if they could be apprehended for sedition under existing law, and if not, suspend Habeas Corpus. At the same time Trevelyan wanted a solemn declaration from Parliament to extoll British freedoms and express the loyalty of the overwhelming majority of the population, as well as their determination to put down disaffection. Above all, the government should appear active, confident and firm.[33] Prince Albert was of a similar mind when he wrote to the Prime Minister to urge him to prosecute the Chartist leaders because their oratory went "beyond all bounds."[34] Lord Palmerston, always practical, called for a step up in the manufacture of muskets and the formation of a volunteer corps.[35]

Londoners were resolved to sink their fears into resisting disturbance on April 10, remembering the broken windows and looted shops of March, and drawing inspiration from the patriotic pronouncements in the press. According to the Morning Chronicle, the country was "sound at heart, loyal, patriotic and steady" in their defense of British freedom. But the question was: would the government join them in this strong defensive spirit? The ministers had a "noble and seaworthy ship," but did they have "the seamanship to handle her?"[36] As The Times put it, the British government had so much more to defend than Continental governments, so it must certainly act decisively when the crisis came on April 10.[37] The Chronicle earnestly hoped that the government would not be "wanting in decision," because whenever "mobs have gained ascendancy in England" it was due to "the irresolution of the executive or the magistracy."[38]

Energy, dispatch, decisiveness, firmness, strength -- this is what alarmed subjects wanted from their Whig government. They got it all on April 10, with everything ultimately guaranteed by a thick red line under the command of Wellington.

The Confident Government

The nature of the leadership of the Whig government made it particularly well suited to face the fears
of revolution in 1848. Lord John Russell was a peculiar Prime Minister. He was an aristocrat of markedly
small physical stature, with a dry, pedantic manner, a
thin skin, a good education, a good intellect and pride
of lineage. Perhaps he was, as A. J. P. Taylor has
called him, the last great Whig and the first Liberal.[39]
He believed in ancient English liberty, for which one
of his illustrious ancestors died on the scaffold. At
the same time he was a reformer, one of the key men
responsible for the Reform Bill of 1832. He was also
something of a keen follower of the cold, harsh doctrines of political economy, and so he was instrumental
in introducing the New Poor Law of 1834, so hated by
the Chartists. He also had enough of reforming the
franchise, a stance which gained him the nickname of
"Finality Jack." Yet overall he believed in gradual
human progress within the context of civilization's
inexorable upward march. He exuded a vague, benevolent
deism, and his day to day style would be called "low
key" in contemporary America.

Chartists did not really upset him. He was too
intelligent and too phlegmatic and too well informed
to be carried away by the hysteria that perceived a
revolutionary presence amongst the champions of democracy. As F. C. Mather has stated, Russell's position
was that "he thought too little of Chartism" rather
than that he "feared it."[40] He tolerated the Chartist
agitation as the crisis of April 10 approached, a
"doveish" position which brought him into conflict with
the "hawks" such as the Duke of Wellington. The
"hawks" wanted nothing left to chance.[41] They wanted
to overwhelm. For his own part, Russell would have let
the Chartists come to Parliament with their petition,
but others prevailed upon him to have the Chartist procession stopped.[42]

Russell called upon military force reluctantly,
but he acknowledged that peaceful citizens deserved the
protection of professionals. After all, as he told the
House of Commons, whole communities ranging from twenty
to fifty thousand inhabitants had been subjected to
"commotion and disturbance" by "five or six hundred
boys between fifteen and twenty years of age...."[43]
This is how he dismissed the Chartist agitation of
March. A reassuring letter written to Prince Albert on

April 9 shows his confident outlook. Just in case the
Chartists "fire and draw their swords and use their
daggers," the military would come out. "I have no
doubt of their easy triumph over a London mob." He had
"every reason" to think that all would "pass off
quietly" without the use of the army, however, and this
would be best because loss of life would cause "a deep
and rankling resentment."[44] Russell expressed these
same views in a Cabinet meeting on the very eve of
April 10. Ironically, many Chartists went to bed that
night convinced that the government was dead set upon
their massacre.

The Prime Minister was only one of several government figures who took pains to reassure the royal
family. Colonel Phipps, a close advisor, told them to
expect "some disturbance," given the "present excited
state of the lowest classes," but thought that "they
will be easily suppressed."[45] For their own part, the
royal family seemed to have an outlook somewhere between the alarm of the propertied classes and the confidence of the Prime Minister. Victoria wrote to the
King of Belgium that although she "could almost fancy
we have gone back into the last century," meaning the
turmoil of the revolutionary era, "one must not be
nervous or alarmed at these movements...." She felt
required to "muster up courage to meet all the difficulties."[46] Prince Albert saw a confrontation coming
between "the Chartists combined with all evil [sic]
disposed people in the country" on the one hand, and
the government, bolstered by the law and the good sense
of the country on the other. He declared to Lord John
Russell that he did not "feel doubtful for a moment,
who will be found the stronger." What the Prince
feared was being "mortified" by a "commotion," since
Europeans regarded the stability of England as such an
important matter.[47] Russell continued to reassure the
royal family right through to the tenth, declaring that
"any mischief" would be the "act of individuals."
These "wicked" men were cowardly, and would be daunted
by the preparations.[48]

Nobody was more capable of reassuring Victoria and
Albert than the Duke of Wellington, and nobody was more
confident than he was over the government's ability to
prevent insurrection. The Duke was, after all, in
charge of military preparations. The Duke made efforts
to calm the fears of other worried members of society
as well. One lady reported that Wellington had advised

them to drive about as usual on the tenth, because there was not "the slightest danger to be apprehended."[49]

Wellington was not the key figure in the government's defense against the imagined storm. That person was the Home Secretary, Sir George Grey. Like Russell, he was admirably suited for his role on the tenth. Grey, a nephew of the great Reform Prime Minister, was a cool, calm, clear headed administrator, a man who could organize efficiently and remain unruffled and dignified at the helm in the best tradition of the stereotype of the English gentleman.[50] This calm deliberateness carried over into his presentations on the floor of the House of Commons. For Grey, as for Russell, historic British liberty was precious, yes, but it had its limits. The sacred rights of assembly, free speech and petitioning were not to go beyond the point where the populace would be terrified or the government overawed.[51] He, in his official capacity, would be the one to decide just when the limits of liberty had been crossed.

Like Russell, Grey was supremely confident of what would happen on April 10. Why should he think otherwise? All his many sources of information pointed to a peaceful conclusion. He had indirect communications with Ernest Jones and a delegation of Chartists from the National Convention; he had smooth and swift communications with authorities in the provinces; he had detailed reports from the police; and he could, like anyone else, read the debates of the Chartist Convention in the newspapers, to say nothing of listening to O'Connor's pacifism in the House. His conclusion, expressed in a letter to Russell on April 9, was that "the course which we have decided to take is right and will lead to a quiet termination of this business."[52] As it turned out, the events of April 10 made him the most popular man in the House of Commons and in the country.

Like all great matters, the Chartist challenge was debated in Parliament just before the Kennington Common meeting. It was there, on April 6 and 7, that the government had the opportunity to state its position, listen to objections, and more or less prepare the nation's representatives and peers for the drama to come.[53]

A member concerned about keeping Parliament from being overawed or intimidated raised the issue. Grey began his response by presenting a summary of the communication he had received from the Chartist National Convention, saying that a peaceful procession would bear the petition to Parliament. Grey then announced that the government had seen fit to issue a notice declaring the procession illegal and warning people to abstain from taking part. The notice also called upon subjects to give their assistance to the government in preserving the peace. An upset Feargus O'Connor rose to defend the procession, saying that it would be tranquil and had been long anticipated by his followers. Grey was simply "taking the people by surprise." O'Connor pointed out that the Chartists against whom the notice was directed had themselves "passed a resolution that every single man should...be a special constable." The Chartists would preserve the peace themselves and "take every individual into custody who violated the rights of property." For himself, O'Connor assured the House that he would be "unworthy of filling a seat" if he lent himself to any demonstration to overawe the House. The hundreds of thousands that planned to assemble "have no more notion of disturbing the peace than I have."

There was no question of O'Connor's peaceful predisposition. Grey gave him "full credit" for being the "last man" to encourage violation of the law. The point was that O'Connor could not be responsible for a great mass of people who might "inspire...terror and alarm" in the minds of "Her Majesty's loyal and peaceable subjects." A supporting speaker added that nobody could "undertake to answer for the conduct of 50,000 men marching through the streets.

O'Connor was not without at least a few supporters, most notably Hume and Wakley. They joined him in asking why notice was given so late, making it difficult to cancel the procession. Hume thought it was dangerous to interfere with a procession long planned. Wakley, interrupted by shouts of "oh, oh!", maintained that the people had been "allured into the supposition" that they could proceed. Grey's notice was published and distributed throughout the metropolis on the sixth of April. How could the Home Secretary say he had acted as quickly as possible? Surely the government knew of the planned procession long before the National Convention sent their message. As things stood, only four day's notice was given to cancel a demonstration planned by the Chartists for months in advance.

Another significant question to come up in the debate was whether the Kennington Common meeting would be prohibited as well as the procession to the doors of the House. Grey's response was masterful: He said it would depend entirely upon "the circumstances under which the meeting was held." If it terrorized inhabitants it would be illegal. So in Parliament the government was clear on the illegality of the procession and vague on the legality of the meeting, prompting objections that "collision and disturbance" might ensue on account of misunderstandings. Nevertheless, this position clearly enabled the government to hold options over allowing the meeting to go on, right up until its conclusion.

Other objections centered on the government's use of a statute against tumultuous assemblies accompanying petitions which was exhumed from the reign of Charles II. This was the legal basis for prohibiting the procession. Grey was asked whether or not the Bill of Rights of 1689 had repealed it. No, he responded, referring to a dictum of Lord Mansfield, the judge who presided at the trials for the Lord George Gordon riots. Grey went on to cite legal precedents that distinguished between mere petitioning and petitioning accompanied by tumultuous assemblies. The government sought to prevent only the latter variety, he insisted.

O'Connor responded by citing the peaceful nature of the planned Chartist procession once again, and wavered a bit in saying that it was not intended to come up to the doors of the House, but only over Westminster Bridge. A short time later he wavered again, sensing the government's determination. At last he hoped that the whole idea of the procession would be given up, and that the Chartists would support the government in efforts to preserve order. But the meeting would go on, regardless. Still, the prohibition of the procession struck him as unfair, because several petitions had been accompanied by large crowds in the recent past.

Very few rallied to the defense of the Chartist position. In fact, strong support came from the opposition benches, including a vigorous speech by Sir Robert Peel. The former Prime Minister said he was aware that in the past large numbers of persons had been permitted to approach the House, and he "rejoiced" in this right to petition. He thought indulgence was the best policy in most cases, but not at present, "considering the events...in foreign countries and... the excited state of the public mind at home...." He feared that a procession on the tenth might involve people being "accidentally excited to disturbances" whose consequences were "impossible to forsee." Therefore, he held that the government were "fully justified" in prohibiting it. They were, in short, doing their legal and humanitarian duty.

O'Connor even had some difficulty arranging a time for the discussion of the petition in the House, pleading that the document was "of great importance to some millions of the people," and therefore, should be taken up on the evening of the tenth. Russell gracefully refused to give up "certain business fixed for that day." but noted that a petition "so numerously signed" should have "early consideration." Early meant the following Friday.

It is fair to conclude from all of this that the government prepared the legislature for the confrontation with considerable skill. They were able to do so because the hysteria did not extend to the centre of government. Russell, Grey and Wellington were forewarned and forearmed, and took a steadfast and resolute pose. On the morrow of the great day, it became an heroic pose. The hysteria did them no harm, and they did very little to stop it, except for reassuring certain privileged persons privately, such as Victoria. As we shall see, the great fear of April 10 about the doggedly peaceful, legal and constitutional Chartists awarded Russell, Grey and Wellington rather easily earned laurels.

There was another advantage. With Russell, Grey and Wellington in charge of the situation, it was hardly possible that the government could act with rash, impulsive viciousness, a reaction that often comes from deep set fears. Reactions like that can trigger revolutionary potential. These men were masters of the wet blanket technique.

Mobilization

As the fateful day of April 10 drew near, government preparations intensified. It became mobilization.

At the center was the Home Secretary, presiding over a nationwide communications network which linked him to mayors, magistrates, military authorities and various departments of the central government. The flow of information in and out of the Home Office was swift and crucial. Grey was watchful, wary, cautious and firm as he tapped this extensive network for information. Police reports, spy reports, informers' tips, reports from mayors, letters from prominent citizens -- all flooded his desk in increasing numbers as April 10 approached. On the eve of the crisis, George Grey was the best informed man in England.

Questions shot out to the provinces: What were the Chartists up to here or there? What was the condition of the special constables in this or that region?[54] The 1,800 miles of the telegraph lines provided an important new tool for the government. It was as revolutionary for the police and the army in 1848 as the computer is today. Messages could travel to important centers almost instantaneously. Birmingham, Edinburgh, Glasgow, Newcastle, Sheffield, Newport, Liverpool, Leicester, Leeds, Bradford, Bristol and Manchester were amongst many places already linked by clacking wires.[55] While the telegraph was privately owned, the government could and did take it over in times of emergency. During one critical week in April, the government did so. This temporary nationalization meant that the government was assured a monopoly over instantaneous information. The companies were well compensated.[56] Could the telegraph be used by revolutionaries surreptitiously? Since officials of the companies were apprehensive that Chartists would send messages in cypher, they decreed that only known persons would be allowed to use cypher.[57] During the week of nationalization, superintendents of the stations were ordered to send no messages from anyone who did not have a note signed by George Grey specifically authorizing the bearer to use the telegraph system.[58] Nationalization also meant that the spread of false reports and rumors could be curtailed. Most of what came in from the provinces during the critical week were good messages. The country was generally quiet, watching and waiting to see what would happen in London. This swiftly gathered information goes a long way in explaining why Russell, Grey and their subordinates could be so calm and composed on April 10.[59]

The government used the telegraph and the post for a quiet, restrained mobilization of resources, and also to urge local officials to conform so that a united front could be maintained. For example, the mayor of Leeds received a letter encouraging the magistrates to "exercise the greatest vigilance and precaution to prevent any interruption of the public peace in the borough."[60] Ammunition in Norwich had to be safeguarded.[61] At the same time, Birmingham correspondents were informed that paramilitary associations "for the preservation of peace" were not encouraged.[62]

Arms were a particularly grave concern. The problem was to get weapons into the right hands and keep them out of the wrong ones. Muskets, bayonets, and cutlasses, sometimes disinterred from castles, were sent to police forces to be used in guarding key installations such as gaols and railroads.[63] Whole lists of gunmakers and pawnbrokers and their stocks were gathered by the Home Office, and these tradesmen were enjoined to hide their weapons and take the locks off of them.

The railroads were also critical and mobilized. They were a great advantage to the English government because police and troops could be rushed to danger spots with a speed hitherto unknown. In the past, a battalion could march from Manchester to London in 17 days; in 1848 they could reach London in nine hours. Moreover, there were 5,000 miles of track, putting Glasgow 13 hours from London. Railway companies disposed their own forces to protect and maintain their network during the crisis,[64] but even so, the government was careful to ensure that key locations were specially safeguarded.[65] The steam engine at sea was another technological breakthrough on the side of the government in 1848. Steam packets could bring troops from Ireland in 14 hours.[66] Furthermore, steam gunboats were ready at the Thames, and, if need be, sailors from Royal Navy ships in the port of London could lend a hand to the authorities.[67]

The front line of the government's forces was thick and blue. The police had high morale, and were proud of the fact that they had never required help from the military, a record they certainly did not want broken on April 10.[68] A total of 4,012 metropolitan policemen readied themselves to meet the Chartist challenge. Their depositions included 700 at Trafalgar Square, 600 at the Palace Yard and 500 at Vauxhall Gardens. Westminster Bridge had a detachment of 500, as did Waterloo Bridge. Blackfriars had 400, Vauxhall and Hungerford fewer. City of London police guarded Southwark and London bridges.[69] Mounted detachments were issued broadswords and pistols. The Thames police had several boats ready to cruise.

The second line of the government's forces was much thicker, and became the most significant and celebrated aspect of the whole mobilization in the eyes of contemporaries and historians. Every policeman on duty on April 10 was backed up by at least forty special constables. They were practical. They freed the police to withdraw from many areas and concentrate their numbers at key locations. Specials stayed behind, filling in for them as well as garrisoning important buildings and centers of communication. Most took over a specific beat when the police withdrew. If disturbance flared, they were to aid each other, and the quick ringing of church bells, the sound of alarm, would gather them around their appointed leaders.[70] In fact, their organization was marked by almost Teutonic planning. Each parish had an assembly point, where specials were divided into units. Some parishes had divisions, subdivisions and sections. Units were to function alone or in combination, depending on the circumstances.[71] A special force of London specials, composed of 2,000 of the "younger and more active" constables, were put directly under the inspectors of police to act as a "flying squad" to be used where most needed. Many retired captains and colonels saw service again at the head of divisions and subdivisions. Some old officers felt the need to make patriotic addresses, expressing their pride at the opportunity to lead loyal citizens against disturbers of the public peace. Cheers for the Queen and the constitution resounded in their assembly yards on the eve of the tenth.

A great ground swell of support for the regime could be seen in the eagerness with which volunteers came forth. It was like the first days of World War I. Even before a royal proclamation called for them, "respectable and patriotic" citizens formed themselves into bodies, acquired leaders and awaited the call.[72] The government was besieged with requests to arm the loyal with authority to keep the peace.[73] Lord John Russell was warned in early April that "the shopkeeping and other middle classes in London" were "calling out against the apathy and inaction of the Government." They wanted to be organized, gain proper officers and assembly points.[74] Many letters came in from parish churchwardens proclaiming the cheerful zeal of inhabitants to serve.[75]

All sorts of volunteers queued in long lines at police stations and magistrates' offices as April 10 approached. Corporate bodies had their ranks sworn from top to bottom. The whole Admiralty donned armbands, from the First Lord downwards. The same occurred at the Bank of England, the Temple, Lincoln's Inn, Grey's Inn, the Customs House, the East India Company, the Post Office and numerous other government offices. All sorts of clerks joined. So did the jobbers and stock brokers of the stock exchange, the entire fire brigade, members of the University Club, and the Common Councilmen of the City. Many workers showed up in the specials' ranks: hundreds of tanners and wool sorters from Bermondsey, the Thames coal heavers and lightermen, workers from the railway companies, some from building companies, some from breweries, and even over a thousand workers engaged in rebuilding the House of Commons. The House of Lords, far less geriatric than imagined, joined en masse and brought many of their sons out with them.[76] Servants from many of the great houses were sworn in, to the extent that fashionable society complained of their absence.[77] In Greville's words, "every gentleman in London has become a constable." One ex-special turned pamphlet writer described the "motley crew...jammed together at the Magistrate's office: Noblemen, tradesmen, and workmen thoroughly intermingled. No class stood apart. Grey-haired men and slim youths went side by side; coal-whippers and young dandies; literary men and those to whom books were unknown."[78]

The great surge of volunteers was a nationwide phenomenon. In Manchester, a force of 11,000 wore the white armband and carried staves. Many were young men from the warehouses; some were railway workers; some were mounted to patrol and communicate with distant outposts.[79] Up in Scotland, students served under titled captains, while the police drilled them in the evenings. In Norwich, all of the officers and servants of the gaol in Norwich Castle were sworn.[80] Even Rugby schoolboys modestly volunteered their services, "feeling that any assistance, however small, may not be entirely useless." They promised to muster 60 who were 17 years old or older in 10 minutes notice.[81] Many more examples from outside London can be cited to show that volunteering as a special was a fad far and wide, but the fact remains that local conditions did not cause it. All eyes were on London. The coming confrontation there brought them out.[82]

The many famous men mobilized as special constables were certainly not in the provinces. They included Robert Peel, the former Prime Minister, and William Gladstone, the future Prime Minister.[83] The Duke of Argyll found a curious looking special at one assembly point, and described him as "a short man with an immense nose, and small, cunning-looking eyes." This "ugly little man" was none other than Prince Louis Napoleon, who was destined for election as the first president of the French Republic.[84] On April 10 he was stationed near Trafalgar Square.[85] Forever after the Chartists referred to him as "King Constable," the "tyrant" who had aided the ruling classes in their "unholy war against the rights and liberties of the oppressed English people."[86] Why did exiled Louis Napoleon take up badge and truncheon? According to his biographers, it was due to political calculation. When someone asked him why he was on duty, Napoleon replied, "Sir, the peace of London must be preserved." In short, he wanted to project an image to his countrymen of standing for order by coming out against the Chartists. French revolutionary propagandists sympathized with Chartism, but great numbers of Frenchmen were already worn out with agitation and fearful of what they called "the mob." These Frenchmen appreciated his stance.[87]

How many were mobilized in London, famous and unknown? The legendary figure for special constables is 170,000, quoted in the Annual Register, and thereby passed on to many historians.[88] The Times put it at 200,000,[89] and other newspapers put it down to 150,000.[90] A recent historian, David Large, concluded that the exact number will never be known because the returns are too fragmentary. An even more recent historian, David Goodway, concludes that the legendary figure is another myth of 1848. He puts the number at only 80,000.[91] Considering that even greater variation exists in estimating the number of Chartist demonstrators on April 10, the day has to be a sad one for historians who quantify. There are no hard statistics to show respective strengths.

Give or take 50,000, the psychological advantage from having so many citizens excited by the opportunity of playing a loyal part in what was expected to be a great historical moment can never be underestimated.

No matter how ineffective they might have turned out
to be if called upon to fight, the ranks of the specials provided a massive show of force in defense of
British institutions. They were perceived as a wide
and deep citizens' moat that the Chartists dare not
cross.

The third line of the government's forces was
thick and red. A grand total of 8,148 regular soldiers
took up positions backing up the police and specials.[92]
Army logistics functioned smoothly as troops and equip-
ment were drawn into London. The Royal Horse Guards
came from Windsor; the 12th Lancers from Hounslow; the
Grenadier Guards from Chichester; the Coldstream Guards
from Windsor; the 63rd Regiment of Foot came in from
Chatham; the 62nd from Winchester; the 17th from Dover.
The 1st and 2nd Life Guards were already on hand in
London, as well as seven battalions of foot guards.
Four field batteries rumbled into the metropolis from
Woolwich, each consisting of three nine pounders and a
single 24 pound howitzer, making 16 guns in all. Every
kind of ammunition came with them, as well as entrench-
ing tools. The troops of artillerymen included the
rocket service and 1,000 of the Foot Artillery, armed
with rifles and ready to supplement the infantry.

The military took up positions at key locations,
but were deliberately kept out of sight as much as possible. They were close to all the strategic bridges
and in or near the major government offices. Somerset
House was packed with them. Two regiments stayed at
the Millbank Penitentiary, and 1,200 infantrymen waited
at the Deptford Dockyards. The Bank and Mansion House
had contingents of troops. So did Westminster Hall,
and riflemen took up stations on the top of the Houses
of Parliament. Buckingham Palace was heavily defended,
even though the royal family was no longer there.
Reinforcements of men and cannons waited at the Tower,
ready to move by land or water, and other reinforcements waited on Blackheath.[93] Guns had to be concealed
around Westminster Bridge and the approaches to Parliament.[94] The cavalry had to be kept close to these
points, which meant that stables were placed at the
army's disposal.[95] So were houses overlooking Westminster Bridge, with most of the people living in them
quite willing to welcome the redcoats.[96] To look after
the army's stomach, 10 to 15 days of rations, in the
form of salt pork, biscuits and spirits were stored at
various places, including the Tower of London.[97]

Even this thick red line was backed up by another line, although rather thiner. Retired servicemen, the Chelsea and Greenwich out-pensioners were called up and armed. A total of 1,290 were mustered and assigned to guard the Bank, the Mint and the Tower, among other places.[98] Sometimes they formed mixed detachments with special constables. Ninety-five out of every 100 were mustered for April 10, a remarkably high figure that undoubtedly denotes their great enthusiasm.[99] The marines and some sailors at a dozen naval stations were under arms for the tenth as well, and an order went out that all steam vessels be held in readiness to convey troops along the Thames when needed. Out in the surrounding counties, the yeomanry and the militia were armed and waiting to be called.[100] The Duke of Buckingham exemplifies the patriotism that April 10 called forth. Although he was almost bankrupt, he volunteered his corps of yeomanry for service anywhere, at his expense, and on the fateful day he himself awaited orders at the Carlton Club.[101]

Key public buildings had to be defended. Everywhere gates were closed, windows barricaded, and defenses looked after. The Bank of England became a veritable fortress. A breastwork of sandbags stood along the building's parapet wall, with loopholes for muskets. Each corner of the building had bullet-proof, sandbagged emplacements for muskets and small carronades, and sandbags sat on the roof as well. The windows were boarded up with timber pierced for musket fire. Throughout the tenth, spectators milled about to see these fortifications. Inside were casks of provisions brought in to help withstand a siege, a strong detachment of troops, armed pensioners and 500 clerks and servants sworn in as special constables, each of the latter armed with a brace of pistols, a musket and a cutlass.[102]

Other fortresses were prepared, including the East India House, Mansion House, the Guildhall, and the Customs House. The Post Office received 2,000 stand of arms, packed in boxes, for the use of its sworn clerks and officers. The Admiralty was supplied with staves, 500 muskets and bayonets, 500 cutlasses and over 2,000 rounds of ball cartridges. Marines mounted guard at the gates.[103] Wellington's home, Apsley House, was barricaded, and had ball proof shutters drawn over the windows.[104] Many were concerned over the defense of the Mint, whose clerks and porters were sworn in as special constables.[105] A detachment marched off to protect the small arms factory at Enfield, while weapons and ammunition were brought under the safe protection of the specials in the British Museum. Its director, Henry Ellis, was not so sure that the building was all that safe. He was sure that if the edifice were to be taken by "disaffected persons" it could become a "fortress...holding six thousand men."[106] For the last time in its history, the defenses of the Tower of London were prepared in earnest. Double sentries were everywhere, the gates were down, and nobody was allowed within except those who had important business inside. Outside, sappers and miners put up sandbags along the western entrance and all along the lower ramparts facing the river. Strong timber fortified the old stonework.[107]

Contemporaries noted elements of comic opera in the frantic martial preparations of civilians. Fraziers Magazine described the way "peaceful quill drivers," men who spent their ordinary days reading papers and talking of social events, suddenly appeared "with powder-flasks and belts," and concealed loaded pistols in their desks. Macaulay made the discovery that the real use of Blue Books was for barricading windows and forming loop-holes. In Greville's office Council Registers served the same purpose, while old, decorative guns were taken down to defend his building.[108] At the Foreign Office Palmerston was very apprehensive because the building was exposed on four sides. He wanted the police inside.[109] Palmerston himself commanded a motley garrison at the Foreign Office, consisting largely of clerks armed with cutlasses and old muskets that looked like borrowed stage properties.[110] Provisions were stored in many public buildings, and some of them had small detachments of sappers and miners armed with wet blankets to be used against incendiary fires.[111] Private preparations had their notes of ludicrousness as well. The Earl of Malmsbury had his five keepers arrive at his house armed with double barreled guns, and he claimed that many gentlemen had similarly filled their houses with "trusty men" for the tenth.[112]

No details escaped the government's attention. The police ordered merchants to cease selling powder and shot. Gunsmiths were asked to unscrew the barrels of their guns. The broken granite laid down to repair roads near Kennington Common was removed.[113] Paving authorities in the West End were asked to desist from road works temporarily so as not to supply missiles to

73

hurl against policemen and windows.[114] The docks were closed. The city prisons and gaols were guarded. Hospitals and churches became temporary barracks. Parks were closed. The Chartered Gas and Light Company agreed to put all the public lamps on half an hour earlier than usual in order to contribute to "greater security."[115]

The royal family's well being was a very important detail. They had to be out of London, but it was felt that even in Osborne on the Isle of Wight the Queen might be insufficiently protected. Precautions had to be taken lest revolutionaries ferry their way across the Solent.[116] James Graham, a former Home Secretary, did not like the idea. He thought the flight looked like cowardice, and was, according to Greville, "indicative of a sense of danger" that should "not be shown."[117] The Chartists eventually had a good laugh over their departure, with McDouall saying that it was "a cruelty to the Queen" to hurry her away to Osborne, out of fear that "Chartists would hurt a woman."[118]

Attention to public announcements was another important detail. Placards and handbills were everywhere. Westminster Bridge was plastered with notices calling upon the public not to loiter and to pass on at once.[119] Some privately produced handbills extolled the benefits of life in England and denied the Chartist contention that nothing had been done to relieve the working classes. Bread and other items specifically enumerated were not taxed. While other specific items were still taxed, "patient endurance" would make these impositions be repealed before long. Workers were warned of Chartist leaders whose "thirst for power" might be at the cost of their lives. Therefore, they should not "sanction" Chartist proceedings by being present at Kennington Common.[120]

The mobilization of the government's legal apparatus was another important matter. The laws against sedition and tumultuous assemblies which excited subjects to "terror and alarm" had been used against Chartists since 1839, and could be applied again on April 10 without any difficulties. But the prospect of a procession over Westminster Bridge to the doors of Parliament meant that an ancient weapon had to be dredged from the government's legal arsenal. A statute from the reign of Charles II came to hand, which declared that no persons may "repair" to the sovereign or the Houses of Parliament "upon pretense of presenting or delivering any petition or declaration" accompanied by "excessive numbers of people." Excessive was defined as anything over 10. A police placard announced that mere presence would willfully countenance prescribed proceedings, whether the procession or any meeting "calculated to excite terror and alarm." Therefore, anyone showing up was liable to punishment.[121]

Chartists became indignant over this on constitutional grounds. The revival of an act "long deemed obsolete" from the reign of a "libidinous tyrant" and virtually repealed by the Bill of Rights was outrageous.[122] They had a point. Greville recalled a conversation he had with Sir George Grey on April 5, when the Home Secretary alluded to the "doubtful" state of the law about processions.[123] Moreover, the Chartists had precedents on their side, most notably the two mile procession that brought in the great petition of 1842.[124]

The network of magistrates coordinated by the Home Secretary did not have these doubts made known to them. They, too, were mobilized for the tenth. One of them was to accompany each military detachment in order to give them the proper authority to unleash their firepower against civilians.[125] Other magistrates stayed on continuous duty at the principal courts.[126]

Magistrates, troops, specials and police were all mobilized into an overwhelming array of force. But how were they to be used? What were the strategic and tactical plans of the men in charge? A Home Office memorandum issued the day before the procession reveals the government's plans in detail.[127] These plans were formulated at the Cabinet level, on April 8 and 10, with Colonel Rowan and the Duke of Wellington present.[128] The decisions were passed down on Sunday to the Lord Mayor and the Commissioners of the City and Metropolitan police forces. They had an interview with Sir George Grey at the Home Office, who was breaking a lifelong habit by working on the Sabbath. There was also a meeting at the Mansion House where the plans were passed along to the Aldermen and other civic authorities.

Two overriding goals were set forth: first, no procession would be allowed to move from Kennington Common to Parliament bearing the petition; second, if possible a collision between the authorities and the demonstrators would be avoided.

A body of police were to be stationed near the Common. If the demonstrators were peaceful and unarmed, the police were to offer no opposition to the meeting. But if they formed a procession to take the petition to Parliament, the police would give them notice that the petition could only be sent with a very few. Forces on all of the bridges were to be ready to block any procession and thwart any attempt to force a crossing. At Blackfriars, strong detachments should oversee the passing of a lightly accompanied petition. Large numbers would have to be stopped, and it was expected that the police would be strong enough to resist attempts to force a passage. If not, the military would be massed nearby, and either a magistrate or a commander of the police could call for their assistance. On each of the other bridges, strong bodies of police, each with a magistrate, would be in place, similarly backed up by soldiers.

If all went according to plan, and the petition was north of the Thames without a collision having taken place, it was to be moved along quickly to Parliament. Meanwhile, the police would hold the bridges for one hour. Ordinary traffic could pass over them until the hour expired, but at the discretion of the men on the spot. They could stop all traffic if it seemed expedient to do so. Thereafter, if they still seemed peaceful, the Chartists would be allowed to go home over the bridges in small numbers. Westminster Bridge was an exception: it was to stay blocked. Police and specials would stay on street patrol in force to make sure that no new assemblages formed.

Behind these plans loomed a great historic figure, who emerged for one more moment of dramatic command at the advanced age of 78. The Duke of Wellington had offered his services and advice to the Whig government, and as a result he was placed in command of the military forces. He helped at formulating the strategy, although Colonel Rowan of the Metropolitan Police probably worked out most of it beforehand.[129] According to Greville, Wellington had no doubts but that he could "answer for keeping everything quiet" because there were "plenty of troops." What he thought necessary was that the government be "firm and vigorous." Greville observed that he was in a "prodigious state of excitement" once he had assumed his new command.[130]

On Sunday, the ninth, Wellington attended the Cabinet,
where he lent his firm, unflinching, assured support.
He entered while it was in progress, and bowed formally
two or three times. He said little, but each sentence
was pithy and incisive. Colonel Rowan's previous presentation had made many of the same points, but Wellington's authority gave weight to them. Of course,
everyone listened and looked on very respectfully. One
witness called this meeting a "regular council of war,
as on the eve of a great battle." Reports of the
enemy's movement, maps, plans of defense, contingency
plans, and notes on means of deployment all lent themselves to creating such an atmosphere.[131]

Wellington's attitudes towards handling the Chartists were crystal clear, if within the confines of the
military mind. He had remarked after the Newport
Rising of 1839, when 30 troops routed 6,000, that in
England "there is one thing always to be borne in
mind", and that was "whenever people do what they know
is wrong, and against the law, they become most terri-
bly frightened and are ready to run away."[132] When
Queen Victoria interviewed him to ask whether there was
any danger forseen for the tenth, he replied, "None,
Madam, if I am allowed to proceed with my precautionary
measures." The Queen replied that if he had to act
against the crowd she hoped he would be merciful. The
Duke replied that the greatest mercy in such a case was
energy and decision.[133] Nothing that actually happened
on the tenth changed his views. In supporting coercive
legislation in the Lords shortly thereafter, Wellington
denied that the throng was submissive to the law volun-
tarily on the tenth. Participants were peaceful
because they had to be, given the forces deployed
against them.[134]

It was Wellington who emphasized that troops must
be kept out of sight. As he told a Prussian observer,
"not a soldier or a piece of artillery shall you see
unless in actual need," and need meant a situation in
which the police were "overpowered or in danger."
Troops were not to do the work of the police and the
police were not to do the work of troops. The military
must never be "confounded" or "merged" with policemen.[135] Russell was of the same mind on this point,
and when in authority in the past he had always applied
this principle.[136]

Wellington and Rowan agreed that the deputation
with the petition should be detached from the assembly

as far away as possible from the centre of government, and moved along quickly. Wellington thought the government had the option to stop any procession at any point it wanted to.[137] He also wanted the parks clear with their gates shut, and the streets around Westminster clear as well.[138] To keep the military profile as low as possible, Wellington himself planned to dress as an ordinary gentleman on the tenth, and instructed his aides-de-camp to do likewise.[139] For the Duke, that meant an ordinary blue coat and a round hat.

The great precautionary mobilization was complete by the tenth. Parliament sat as usual, but the ministers gathered to wait out the day at No. 10 Downing Street. Lady John Russell was advised by Trevelyan to leave the vicinity, but she chose to go to Downing Street to be with her husband.[140] Trevelyan was concerned about the effect the sound of cannon would have upon her, but undoubtedly her husband was not, because he did not expect to hear any.

The Foxes Prepare

As April 10 drew near, Chartist enthusiasm reached a peak. The unfolding dramas on the Continent, the riots of March, the widespread meetings, the frantic preparations for the petition, and the gathering of the National Convention all generated intense excitement. Everything was focused on the tenth, the day that the Charter might well become the law of the land.

While threats, innuendoes and thinly veiled predictions of an English revolution were heard all over, the leaders in London came to urge more and more caution and restraint as the confrontation drew near.

Undeniably, there was a vocal minority of Chartists who said that this was the last petition, and that "other measures" would be adopted thereafter.[141] One orator declared that if the government refused to take up the petition, they should "walk to the palace, and if they could not find admission, let them make admission." Such Chartists were "prepared for the worst" and would fight "if they must."[142] The women were prepared also, "ready to take the place of the men who are cut down."[143]

At the National Convention several delegates acted as spokesmen for the more bellicose in their

constituencies. For example, the Edinburgh delegate
said that he represented Chartists who "were ready to
support their principles at the stake, in the dungeon,
or on the field." The Northampton delegate said that
if the petition failed, his constituents "would demand
its enactment at the point of the bayonet." G. W. M.
Reynolds represented Derby, and pointed out that
"recourse must be had to physical force" if the petition failed. He noted that London had only 5,000
troops, so the multitude of Chartists in London on
April 10 "would be more than strong enough to produce
a change in the government by eight o'clock on that
evening." Someone else suggested that the different
trades should assemble, "each individual carrying a
baton for his personal protection," and that they
should brook no interference from the police. A whole
group of Chartists made it known that if the government
shed any of their blood on April 10, they must be
avenged.[144]

This brave talk was not free from romantic melodrama. William Cuffay, the only Chartist of African
ancestry, drew criticisms from the chair for his
"extravagant expressions." Cuffay had said, among
other things, that "he spoke now as if he stood upon
the edge of the grave," for his life "was not worth an
hour's purchase." Despite the chairman's cautions,
the flow of melodrama continued: One Chartist declared
that it "was better to die at once than the slow,
lingering, horrible death of starvation." Another said
that "if only one man of them was left alive on Monday,
that man would...join in the procession." Yet another
said the government "were now on a mine," and if they
"let loose their minions of war upon the people" there
would be a dramatic response "from one end of the kingdom to another," a response so severe "as England might
never recover from."[145]

All of this romantic, inflammatory rhetoric from
the Convention was counteracted simultaneously by
advice from other Chartists, who urged that the movement remain calm and peaceful on the tenth in order to
avoid bloodshed. Some radical friends lent a hand to
these efforts, such as Thomas Slingsby Duncombe, the
M.P. who had presented the first petition to Parliament
in 1839. Duncombe pleaded with the militants not to
jeopardize "a good and just cause" by "extravagant
language and foolish threats." If they carried on in
that tone, they certainly risked a collision with the
authorities, to say nothing of retarding "progress" by

"disarming its best friends."[146] James Bronterre
O'Brien, the celebrated intellectual of the movement,
bade the Convention delegates to be cautious, saying
that he "would not move an inch against the law," as
long as there was still a chance of the law doing them
justice, and even if this chance were gone, he would
not move against the law until the people clearly had
a power greater than the law.[147]

     The advice to be peaceful became the official
position of the Convention, despite the romantic and
bellicose pronouncements of some of its members. The
Convention's "Address to the Shopkeepers, Tradesmen and
other Inhabitants of London," issued in early April,
states the pacifistic position unequivocally. The
Convention viewed "all attempts to create disturbance
and effect plunder" with "unmitigated abhorrence," and
pledged itself to adopt all means to "ensure order,
peace and good conduct" on the tenth.[148] Many in the
Convention fumed over the insinuations in The Times and
other papers that they were organizing a "physical outbreak," and felt compelled to issue a declaration
asserting "in the most positive terms" that they had
"no intention of breaking the law." The Chartist
demonstration would be "an unarmed moral demonstration"
only.[149] In an "Address to the Men of London," the
Convention declared it anticipated "a great peaceful
revolution" due to the "immense moral power" of the
people. The eyes of all Europe were on them and to
prove themselves worthy of such attention, they must
"legally, peacefully, but enthusiastically proceed."
The day and the hour "to strike the great moral blow"
was at hand.[150] Thomas Martin Wheeler, a quiet man
very close to O'Connor, was responsible for moving
pacifistic addresses in the Convention, while continuing to insist that the Kennington Common meeting must
be held. Wheeler was undoubtedly acting for
O'Connor.[151] Support for this position came in from
the provinces. For example, Manchester Chartists urged
peaceful preparations for the tenth in a handbill,
which stated: "Let every step you take be marked with
the dignity of manhood. Liberty is too sacred to be
associated with violence."[152]

     Public declarations were not the only means used
by the Convention to ensure peace on April 10. A delegation of three, G. W. M. Reynolds, Thomas Clark, and
W. P. Wilkinson went to the Home Office to see Sir
George Grey on April 7. Instead, after sitting for a
very long time in the waiting room, they got to see

the Undersecretary, Sir Dennis Le Marchant, the Attorney General and the Chief Magistrate of Bow Street. Le Marchant informed them that he did not recognize the National Convention. Eventually, the delegation left a message for Sir George Grey, assuring the government that the Convention "utterly" repudiated the idea of an armed assembly or armed procession. They would "entirely discountenance" any attempts to "create disorder or break the public peace" at the upcoming meeting. Any disturbances "assuredly will not be provoked nor encouraged on our part." They were dismissed with that "cold civility" that the English have developed to such a fine art.[153]

The same message came in to the government from other sources. Russell received two anonymous letters which "convinced" him that the Chartist leaders had renounced any thought of physical force. Russell thought that the reason for it was either the hopelessness of achieving success or sheer awe at the extent of government precautions.[154]

It was the message of the delegation of three that Grey brought to the House on April 7. A challenge came from another Member, who asked whether this meant that he acknowledged the body "by condescending to receive a letter" from their representatives. Grey assured him that the Chartist delegation "were not recognized as delegates of any National Convention." His office received them "only as persons coming from a meeting held in a certain house...."[155] Recognized or not, the National Convention had its peaceful message proclaimed in Parliament. Its official nonviolent policy was clear, despite the romantic effusions of some of its members.

The leaders of the National Charter Association were, in a way, trapped by the flooding tide of anticipation and enthusiasm which overtook them by April 10. They walked on a tightrope. Too much militancy on their part might trigger disorder and violent repression; too little would bring charges of cowardice and betrayal. Of those at the centre, the roles of Ernest Jones and George Julian Harney deserve scrutiny. It goes without saying that the part played by Feargus O'Connor has to command the greatest attention.

Viewed from the outside, Harney, Chartism's foremost internationalist and _enfant terrible_, was suspected as one of the more dangerous militants. The

radical Weekly Dispatch disparaged him by describing
how he was "tricked out in a red scarf with a tricolor
ribband across his breast" at a meeting of French
residents in London, and how "the English people" were
far from "these Julian Harneys, shamelessly bedizend
with foreign colors."156 Surely his leadership would
only "sully" the people's cause with "threats of violence."157 He might lure others to drastic deeds, but
his own spirit was so "cowardly" that he would be "the
last man in the mob to fire off a gun or use a pike...."
Harney had been "barking and snarling for years; and
while his vocation brings in the needful, he will continue to yelp until the crack of doom."158 Harney's
reputation was equally bad but less noticed in the respectable press.

Despite the bad reputation, Harney was a moderate
in the crisis of 1848. He had to be if he wished to
retain his position as editor of the Northern Star,
owned by O'Connor. As the day approached, Harney toed
the line for moderation. In early April he warned at a
meeting that there were two dangers to guard against at
Kennington Common: "rashness and weakness." A rash
act "might launch us, not into a revolution, but into a
row...." Such a circumstance would be "more fatal to
our character and moral standing than even to our persons." There must be no weakness either; Chartists
must present their just demands bravely, and prove "to
the world" that they would not "hug [their] fetters"
while "slaves of every other land were breaking
theirs."159 He wanted the Chartists "so strong in
numbers" on April 10 "that neither thieves nor policemen shall dare to disturb the peace."160

Ernest Jones had a highly visible role in 1848, to
the extent that many historians have linked him to
revolutionary activity. Jones was a middle class convert to Chartism, a lawyer by training. He was
destined to become the favorite English disciple of
Marx and Engels, a role which gained him lasting notoriety. He would much rather have earned fame from his
novels and poems, but only the most dogged Soviet
anthologists celebrate them today.

As a member of O'Connor's group, his behavior
became ambiguous as April 10 approached. The established press carried his more extravagant threats, and
regarded him as a dangerous incendiary. The Times
quoted him telling the Chartist National Convention
that if they did their duty "we shall have a St.

Patrick's Day in England for all the vermin will be driven out."[161] Jones was one of those who wanted to carry on with the banned procession to the House of Commons, provided that it was "peaceable and unarmed."[162] Nevertheless, if the police should prevent them from walking "peaceably," then they should "scatter the police before them like chaff before the wind."[163] He differed with O'Connor when the Irishman urged cancellation of the procession, declaring that they would "compromise their expressed condition and resolves" and "excite the contempt of their enemies" if they backed down. He for one was ready to "proceed with the procession in the teeth of every prohibition."[164]

Jones warned the government not to try physical force against them, "lest physical force be turned against" the government. What Jones repeatedly called for was a "bold physical front" on the part of the Chartist movement, because it would actually "prevent the necessity of physical action...." In a way, this might be seen as the Chartist equivalent of the argument and excuse used by modern sovereign nations who are locked in arms races. At any rate, Chartists must be "prepared for the worst." So they should go off with "military precision," led by "captains and officers," forming a veritable "army." Without such discipline, "they would be a mob."[165] Jones also called for simultaneous meetings everywhere on Monday noon, just in case there was a clash with the troops, in order that the forces of authority would be kept dispersed.[166]

In one celebrated flight of oratory, Jones acclaimed the readiness of Chartists to "charge down from the hills of Yorkshire, Lancashire, and the vales of Northamptonshire and plant the green flag of liberty in Downing Street." The men of the Midlands, the "manufacturers of Nottingham" and the "agriculturalists of the rural districts" were all prepared to aid the men of London on April 10. "All they asked for was the signal. When the brilliant rocket shot star-like into the heavens, the bold and the brave of their country would rise, and the corrupt of every class would sink.[167]

While some of his listeners waited for the rocket on April 9, Ernest Jones made contact with the authorities. A letter in the Russell papers reveals that he had contacts with Home Office agents who reported him frightened and eager to avoid accidental clashes. Jones was reported saying that if the meeting were allowed to take place the people would be satisfied and the affair brought off quietly. When an official asked him to pen a notice to abandon the procession, he refused to do so, claiming he could not control the demonstrators in such a manner. While in conference, the government's agents took advantage of the opportunity to impress Jones with the firm determination of the police to follow their orders next morning.[168] Jones left the meeting with no disposition to shoot any rockets on the following day.

Unlike Jones, Feargus O'Connor had not indulged in firey rhetoric before April 10. While he has often been accused of opportunistic wavering, inconsistency and erratic behavior in his leadership of the movement at crucial turning points in its history, it is difficult to pin this accusation on him over the crisis of April 10. He was firmly, clearly and unhesitatingly determined that the Chartists behave peacefully on that day, and bent all of his efforts towards that end. He warned Chartists not to jeopardize the success of the petition by "bluster, bravado or folly."[169] He expected every Chartist attending to be a "policeman" or his own "special constable."[170] Those who feared democracy anticipated a "disorderly mob" on April 10, and he was determined to prevent the thieves and pickpockets attending from causing any disturbance.[171] He did not anticipate that "a single pain [sic] of glass should be broken, nor any tumult caused...."[172] Feargus advised, "If you see a man breaking into a shop" on April 10, do not stop to hand him over to the police, but knock him down at once." Let the Chartists be guilty of no wrongful acts, but let them only display "good and orderly citizen-like conduct on this occasion."[173] If the peace were broken on that day, "the government, not the people, will be the aggressors." After all, the Convention had passed a unanimous resolution to respect property, peace, law and order.[174]

O'Connor was certainly laboring under heavy pressure in the early days of April. Pressure from the left came from younger, more militant Chartists who opposed his pacifistic stance. Defensively, O'Connor addressed his "Old Guards" in the movement, and bade them "ask the youngsters who would now fain take the command of our movement" where they were when O'Connor and other veteran leaders were in prison.[175] Those who said they were "tired of agitation" and demanded

84

revolutionary change were not around when the Old Guard had braved prosecution and the dungeon.[176] Feargus declared that it was absurd of them to boast that they could "make arrangements" in case a confrontation with the authorities came about. Could they make arrangements "with all the pickpockets and vagabonds of London, for whose actions they could not answer?..." These petty criminals would be the first to "create confusion and riot" if a clash with the authorities occurred.[177]

The vocal militants in the Convention made him angry, and embarrassed him in the House of Commons, where he was held responsible for whatever went on in the Chartist assembly. Exasperated, O'Connor bade the Convention, "...In the name of God...not to make him their scapegoat and laughing stock in the House of Commons" through "idle and foolish" pronouncements in the Convention.[178]

As we have seen, Feargus O'Connor, M.P., quite clearly stated in the House of Commons what the Chartists had in mind for the tenth. For himself, he was not going to be a "coward" and "shrink from the consequences" of the meeting and the presentation of the petition. As for the danger to his person, he considered that "when a man has brought others into a position where there is danger, he is bound to take...the lion's share of it."[179] Even so, the great variety of messages and threats that came to him served to weigh him with additional pressure.

They came from the authorities, fellow Members of the House, friends and enemies. O'Connor claimed that he had received "about 500 letters from members of the police force and other persons, warning him that he was especially marked out for slaughter."[180] When O'Connor brought up one example in the House of Commons, the allusion misfired. O'Connor claimed that Alderman Thompson said to him that he would "certainly be shot" if he appeared at Kennington Common. Thompson immediately rose to say that he did not furnish any such information.[181] Thomas Slingsby Duncombe's melodramatic warning was more tangible: "One false step," he wrote, "may seal the fate of millions."[182]

Millions aside, O'Connor was anxious that his own fate might well be sealed. Rumors brought by several persons that the government planned to shoot the leaders from certain windows on the way to Westminster did

nothing to allay his anxieties.[183] Neither did the
stories circulating in the press about what happened
during the Lord George Gordon riots, an episode undoubtedly brought forth to intimidate him. The Morning
Chronicle saw fit to "commend to the attention of Chartist leaders" the scene from the riots of 1780, when
Lord George Gordon presented a petition while a mob
howled outside of the House of Commons. General Murray
confronted Gordon with these words: "If only one of
your lawless followers enters, I shall consider rebellion as begun, and I will plunge my sword into your
heart as its promotor."[184] Feargus took note and made
out his will on the night of April 9.[185]

Another source of pressure for O'Connor was from
within. He felt terrible, physically, and was, indeed,
on the threshold of physical decline, a decade before
his death. In the editorial columns of the Northern
Star he described his "state of anxiety and excitement", induced by "working hard all day, eating but
little, and spending sleepless nights...." But, he
assured his readers, undoubtedly to counteract the
rumors that the bottle had made him its slave, "never
once resorting to any artificial means to sustain me in
the struggle."[186] By the time he got to Kennington
Common he complained that he had spent "six sleepless
nights" in the "service" of the people, and that his
"breast" was like a "coal of fire". He claimed that he
could "produce a certificate from a physician...that it
would be better for me if I were at this instant in
bed."[187]

Faced with all of these pressures, from Chartists
to his left, from polite society to his right, and from
within himself, Feargus O'Connor found some relief in
flying into melodrama, a style of escape often favored
by the Irish. His resolute determination to avoid
bloodshed was dressed up in the old green cloak of
blarney. Historians have been fooled by the cloak ever
since. The man of grandiloquent words and romantic
posturing was, underneath it all, much more of a
statesman than he has ever been given credit for.

Fault could and can be found with his patriarchal
patronizing: He called his followers "children," and
referred to himself as their "fond father."[188] "Large
as my family is," he declared in a remarkable similar-
ity to Elizabeth I facing the Armada, "you are all my
children," and "I love you better than I love my own
life."[189]

86

The image he projected of his own heroic death was
mocked by detractors after April 10, but it can be
interpreted as just another example of Victorian romanticism. He told his followers that "I would much
rather be taken a corpse from amidst that procession,
than dishonour myself, disgrace my country, and desert
you, by remaining away."[190] He also pledged that if he
were "stretched on the rack" he would "smile terror out
of countenance." O'Connor also defended his basic
peacekeeping role melodramatically: "...How should I
rest in my bed this night", he asked the throng at
Kennington Common, "if I were conscious that there were
widows awake mourning for their husbands slain?" He
wanted no act of his to jeopardize "the lives of thousands" and thereby "paralyse" the democratic cause.[191]
Can his sincerity be doubted on this?

Behind O'Connor's melodrama and behind the heroic
postures of many members of the Convention lay simple,
cold fear. Just as shopkeepers and peers shuddered at
the spectre of a mob unleashed, Chartists shuddered at
the thought of the establishment's powerful array of
force crashing into their unarmed ranks. One false
step, one nasty scene, one small collision could
unleash a flood of police, constables, troops and
artillery against them. There was the constraining
feeling that the movement walked a tightrope over an
abyss. Both sides in the confrontation approached the
fateful day with their own fears and trepidation. Only
the leaders of the government, well informed and secure
behind their thick defenses, could look on serenely.

Many Chartists shared the view that the authorities planned a Peterloo on a grander scale than in
1819. Thomas Frost feared that thousands on Kennington
Common might be challenged to disperse and refuse, and
that this would be a signal to begin a slaughter. His
own Chartist friends in Croyden expressed their apprehensions on the eve of the meeting by saying that the
government was out to provoke a collision deliberately.
So Frost urged them to give "no pretext for an attack."
If it came anyway, the government would be placed in
the wrong, as in the times of Charles I. Besides, Kennington Common was on the wrong side of the river for a
Chartist battlefield. Why risk taking arms for self
defense if they might only give the Whigs an excuse for
another Peterloo?[192] George Jacob Holyoake put it in a
sprightly fashion: Chartists concluded that the government wanted to "shoot down a number of the people
and then proclaim to Europe that they had 'saved

87

society' by murder...." While Holyoake knew that many
Chartists were ready to die for their country, they
would "serve it much better by dying without resistance
than dying with it." If any were killed in the procession, "their comrades should move quietly on."[193]
William Rider recalled his similar feelings in a letter
written long after the event: The government was
"arrayed in an attitude of brute force and panting for
the blood of the defenseless poor."[194] O'Connor also
had some fears that some of those in authority were
willing to bring about a collision of the military
against the unarmed Chartists. Therefore, he urged
Chartists not to play into the hands of their more militant enemies.[195] Feargus O'Connor appreciated an
overriding objective reality: they were utterly incapable of withstanding the armed forces of the government
on April 10.[196]

Rumors did not help. The word got out that the
government had hired men to cause a disturbance during
the meeting. There were also tales of stepped up
truncheon manufacture and rush orders for particularly
strong staves.[197] The unconcealed recruitment of constables added no small measure to Chartist anxieties.
One rumor had it that the government sent to the dockyards for a supply of "iron wood," wood purportedly as
hard as iron, and then put 30,000 people to work turning out staves from it for all those new constables.[198]
There were also rumors about the zeal of individual
citizens. Some shopkeepers were supposedly armed with
red hot pokers behind their shutters.[199] The Morning
Chronicle hinted that the police might have to be
called upon to protect the Chartists, given the
"present disposition of the London householders."[200]
Therefore, for many Chartists, April 10 loomed as the
day when they might be the victims, and not the shopkeepers, the aristocracy or the regime in general.

Amidst all of these rumors and fears, Chartists
made their contingency plans, at the same time that the
government made its own. Suppose the police occupied
Kennington Common? They would then meet at Blackheath,
four and a half miles away.[201] Suppose some unruly
Chartists disobeyed the directives of the Convention
and showed up armed? They would have marshalls functioning as Chartist special constables.[202] Suppose the
leaders were all shot down in the streets or swept into
prison? Harney proposed that the delegates should each
nominate their successors beforehand, and that they
should be elected immediately thereafter at simultaneous meetings.[203]

Even if they escaped the truncheons, staves, cutlasses, musket balls and cannon shot, what would happen
if their glorious petition were not accepted? Here was
the old dilemma of Chartism again, a replay of 1839 and
1842. A majority of the Convention decided on April 6
that in such an eventuality they would present a
national memorial to the Queen, calling for a dissolution of Parliament and the dismissal of ministers.
Meanwhile Chartists would continue to call simultaneous
meetings, in order to wear down the forces of authority.[204] The Convention would sit permanently and
become the focus of resistance.[205]

It was all brave talk. If the petition were rejected out of hand their bluff would be called. Their
other measures to make England a democracy had the
proverbial chance of a snowball in hell.

NOTES TO CHAPTER II

[1] Annual Register, April, 1848, p. 50. See also F. B. Smith, "Great Britain and the Revolutions of 1848", p. 65.

[2] Hansard, Parliamentary Debates, Third Series, Vol. 97, p. 1158; Vol. 98, p. 17.

[3] Fraser's Magazine, May 1848, p. 590.

[4] Leeds Mercury, April 15, 1848, p. 4.

[5] The Times, April 8, 1848, p. 4.

[6] The Times, April 10, editorial.

[7] Weekly Dispatch, April 9, 1848, p. 175.

[8] Weekly Dispatch, April 16, 1848, p. 187.

[9] Newcastle Chronicle, April 14, 1848, p. 4.

[10] A Conservative Reformer, "On the Disastrous Consequences which might have resulted had not the Government Adopted Precautionary and Preventative Measures Regarding the Late Expected Monster Meeting of the tenth of April, 1848" (London 1848).

[11] Anonymous letter, Mansfield, April 5, 1848, H.O. 45/2410, Part 3.

[12] Weekly Dispatch, April 16, 1848, p. 187, also various letters, H.O. 41/26.

[13] The Times, April 7, 1848, editorial.

[14] Quoted in the Weekly Dispatch, April 16, 1848.

[15] Dutchess of Bedford to Lord John Russell, April, 1848, Russell Papers, P.R.O. 30/22 7B.

[16] Colonel Phipps to Prince Albert, April 10, 1848, RA Add. MSS. C 56, item 21.

[17] Edwin W. Marrs, Jr., The Letters of Thomas Carlyle to His Brother Alexander, with Related Family Letters (Cambridge, Mass. 1968), p. 665.

[18] Charles Kingsley, Alton Locke, Tailor and Poet: An Autobiography, with a memoir by Thomas Hughes, p. xv.

[19] F. E. Kingsley, ed., Charles Kingsley: His Letters and Memories of His Life (Dondon 1894), Vol. 1, p. 116.

[20] The Earl of Bessborough, ed., Lady Charlotte Guest, Extracts from Her Journal, 1833-1852 (London 1952), p. 207.

[21] Hodder, The Life and Work of the Seventh Earl of Shaftesbury, p. 242.

[22] J. H. Harris, The Earl of Malmesbury, Memoirs of an Ex-Minister, an Autobiography, (London 1884), pp. 223-24.

[23] John Cam Hobhouse, Recollections of A Long Life, by Lord Broughton (London 1911), Vol. 6, 1841-1852, p. 215.

[24] Lord John Russell, Recollections and Suggestions, 1813-1873 (London 1875), p. 252.

[25] George W. E. Russell, Letters of Matthew Arnold, 1848-1888 (New York and London 1895), Vol. 1, p. 8.

[26] Edwin Hodder, The Life of Samuel Morley (London 1888), p. 80. Also Absalom Watkin, Extracts from His Journal, 1814-1856 (London 1920, p. 251.

[27] Morning Chronicle, April 7, 1848, p. 4.

[28] Manchester Guardian, April 8, 1848, p. 6. editorial.

[29] Morning Chronicle, April 7, 1848, p. 4. editorial.

[30] The Times, April 10, 1848.

[31] Inhabitants of Camberwell New Road to Sir George Grey, April 5, 1848, H.O. 45/2410, Part 5 A-L.

[32] W. L. W. Mason of Finsbury to the Police, March 11, 1848, H.O. 45/2410, Part 2.

[33]C. E. Trevelyan to Lord John Russell, April 4, 1848, Russell Papers, P.R.O. 30/22 7B.

[34]Prince Albert to Lord John Russell, April 10, 1848, RA Add. MSS C 16/47.

[35]Lord Palmerston to Lord John Russell, Russell Papers, P.R.O. 30/22 7B.

[36]Morning Chronicle, April 7, 1848, p. 4.

[37]The Times, April 7, 1848, editorial.

[38]Morning Chronicle, April 7, 1848, p. 4, editorial.

[39]A. J. P. Taylor, Essays in English History (London 1976), p. 68.

[40]F. C. Mather, Public Order in the Age of the Chartists (Manchester 1959).

[41]Stevenson, Popular Disturbances in England, 1700-1800, p. 269.

[42]Lord John Russell, Recollections and Suggestions, pp. 252-3.

[43]Hansard, Parliamentary Debates, Third Series, Vol. 97, p. 1179.

[44]Arthur Christopher Benson and Viscount Esher, The Letters of Queen Victoria: A Selection from Her Majesty's Correspondence between the years 1837 and 1861 (London 1907), Vol. 2, 1844-1853, contains this letter. The original is in RA Add. MSS. C 56, Item 14.

[45]Colonel Phipps to Prince Albert, April 9, 1848, RA Add. MSS C 56, Item 11.

[46]Martin, The Life of the Prince Consort, quoting Victoria to Leopold, March 11, 1848, p. 28.

[47]Prince Albert to Lord John Russell, April 10, 1848, RA Add. MSS C 56, Item 12.

[48]Lord John Russell to Queen Victoria, April 10, 1848, RA Add. MSS C 56/19.

[49]Harris, Memoirs of an Ex-Minister, p. 224.

[50] M. Creighton, Memoir of Sir George Grey, Bart. (Newcastle upon Tyne 1884), pp. 64-73; Mather, Public Order in the Age of the Chartists, p. 44.

[51] See the remarks of Grey and Russell on the Crown and Government Security Bill, Hansard, Parliamentary Debates, Third Series, Vol. 98, pp. 18-21.

[52] Spencer Walpole, The Life of Lord John Russell (London 1889), Vol. 2, p. 69.

[53] The debates quoted below are in Hansard, Parliamentary Debates, Third Series, Vol. 97, pp. 1353-1355; Vol. 98, pp. 4-20.

[54] H.O. 41/19.

[55] Among the other places were Colchester, Coventry, Derby, Durham, Dorchester, Darlington, Hull, Halifax, Peterborough, Rochdale, Slough, Strafford, Todmorden, Wolverhampton. H.O. 45/2410, Part 2, London.

[56] Use of the entire network and the employment of extra signal men for one week in April and a few occasional periods from March to May cost the government £500. Electric Telegraph Company to Sir George Grey, May 20, 1848, H.O. 45/2410, Part 2, London.

[57] Letter of the Secretary of the Midland Railway to the Electric Telegraph Company, April 8, 1848, H.O. 45/2410 London.

[58] Dennis Le Marchant, Letter to the Provosts, Mayors, Commanding Officers, April 9, 1848, H.O. 41/19.

[59] Admiral Sir C. Ogle to Lieut. Colonel Seymour, April 10, 1848, a letter reassuring the Queen. This point was not missed by David Large, "London in the Year of Revolutions, 1848", p. 188.

[60] Dennis L. Marchant to the Mayor of Leeds, April 8, 1848, H.O. 41/19.

[61] Philipps to the Mayor of Norwich, March 10, 1848, H.O. 41/19.

[62] Dennis Le Marchant to the Mayor of Birmingtham, March 24, 1848, H.O. 41/19.

[63] Dennis Le Marchant to the Visiting Justices, County Gaol, Leicester, April 8, 1848; George Grey to the Mayor of Manchester, March 14, 1848. The stores of Chester Castle yielded 500 cutlasses for Manchester's police.

[64] H.O. 45/2410, Part 5, AD-AL.

[65] D. Phillipps to the Mayor of Manchester, March 9, 1848, H.O. 41/10.

[66] Mather, Public Order in the Age of the Chartists, p. 161.

[67] Harris, Memoirs of an Ex-Minister, p. 224; Large, "London in the Year of Revolutions", p. 185.

[68] T. A. Critchley, A History of Police in England and Wales (London 1978 ed.), p. 100.

[69] Memorandum, W.O. 30/111.

[70] Bundle, 'The Chartist Riots, 1848', W.O. 30/111.

[71] St. George's Parish, the second largest in the metropolis, mustered 3,000 specials under the command of a Field Marshall, Lord Strafford. A duke, a viscount, an earl and several knights became captains of subdivisions in other parishes.

[72] Morning Chronicle, March 9, 1848. See Goodway, London Chartism, 1838-1848, pp. 71-2, 85-6, 129-133, 142-3 for more on the role of the specials in 1848.

[73] For example, the tradesmen of Kentish Town formed their own association, all ready to be sworn in. Thomas Green to Sir George Grey, April 18, 1848, H.O. 45/2410, Part 5, AD-AL. Also Charles Gibson to Sir George Grey, Salford, March 10, 1848, describing the "anxious desire to render the authorities every assistance in keeping the peace." In addition, R. Gladstone and D. Maude to Sir George Grey, Manchester, March 9, 1848, H.O. 45/2410, Part 1A.

[74] C. E. Trevelyan to Lord John Russell, April 4, 1848, Russell Papers, P.R.O. 30/22, 7B.

[75]Help in arming them sometimes came from private sources. Sir James Bathurst acquired a 1,000 staves for them in Marylebone and urged them to use the weapons without payment. Sir James Bathurst to D. Le Marchant, April 11, 1848.

[76]Smith, "Great Britain and the Revolutions of 1848", p. 77.

[77]Desmond McCarthy and Agatha Russell, eds., Lady John Russell: A Memoir (London 1910), p. 97.

[78]Charles C. F. Greville, The Greville Memoirs: A Journal of the Reigns of King George IV, King William IV, and Queen Victoria (London 1888), Vol. 6, p. 168; Anon., "A Letter From One of the Special Constables in London on the Late Occasion of their being Called Out to Keep the Peace", (London: William Pickering, 1848).

[79]Smith, "Great Britain and the Revolutions of 1848", pp. 48, 77-8; Mather, Public Order in the Age of the Chartists, pp. 84-5.

[80]Norwich Gaol, April 8, 1848, H.O. 41/19.

[81]Letter from Rugby Schoolboys, H.O. 45/2410, Part 2, London.

[82]For example, the Leeds Mercury, April 8, 1848, p. 5. In some places, such as the Pottery towns, more volunteers showed up than were needed, but magistrates were reluctant to turn them down. Mather, Public Order in the Age of the Chartists, p. 84.

[83]Gladstone had signed up as early as March 11, 1848, according to a laconic entry in his diary quoted by David Large, "London in the Year of Revolutions, 1848", p. 183.

[84]George Douglas, Eighth Duke of Argyll, Autobiography and Memoirs (London 1906), p. 304.

[85]Harris, Memoirs of An Ex-Minister, p. 225. Another witness, the American publisher Putnam, saw him near London Bridge. F. A. Simpson, The Rise of Louis Napoleon (London 1909), p. 278.

[86]Northern Star, June 17, 1848, p. 3.

[87]Simpson, The Rise of Louis Napoleon, p. 278; Robert Sencourt, Napoleon III: The Modern Emperor (London 1933), p. 95.

[88]Annual Register, April, 1848, p. 52. F. C. Mather takes this number in Public Order in the Age of the Chartists, p. 84, and cites Mark Hovell, The Chartist Movement (Manchester 1925 ed.). William L. Langer puts it at 150,000 in Political and Social Upheaveal 1832-1852 (New York, Evanston and London, 1969) 71; Stevenson, Popular Disturbances in England, 1700-1800, quotes press estimates ranging from 120,000 to 200,000 (p. 271).

[89]The Times, April 15, 1848, p. 4.

[90]Leeds Mercury, April 15, 1848, Supplement, p. 10. The Northern Star put the number of specials in the city alone at upwards of 70,000 persons.

[91]Large, "London in the Year of Revolutions, 1848", p. 188; Goodway, London Chartism, 1838-1848, pp. 74, 130-2.

[92]Large, "London in the Year of Revolutions, 1848", p. 189.

[93]Fraser's Magazine, May, 1848, p. 590.

[94]Colonel Fitzroy to Lord Fitzroy Somerset, RA Add. MSS C 56, Item 8.

[95]Lord Fitzroy Somerset to Sir Dennis Le Marchant, April 14, 1848, H.O. 45/2410, Part 2, London.

[96]Lord Fitzroy Somerset to Sir Dennis Le Marchant, April 14, 1848, H.O. 45/2410, Part 2, London; Geo. Wollett to Sir George Grey, April 7, 1848, H.O. 45/2410 Part 5, AD-AL.

[97]Large, "London in the Year of Revolutions, 1848", p. 189.

[98]Mather, Public Order in the Age of the Chartists, p. 152.

[99]W.O. 30/111.

[100]The Buckinghamshire and Middlesex yeomanry were under arms. Memorandum, April 8, 1848, W.O. 30/111.

[101] Note in W.O. 30/111 adted April 10.

[102] Northern Star, April 15, 1848, p. 6; Annual Register, April, 1848, p. 52; Leeds Mercury, April 15, 1848; William Smee to Sir George Grey, April 6, 1848, H.O. 45/2410, Part 5 AD-AL.

[103] Northern Star, April 15, 1848, p. 6.

[104] Bradford Observer, April 13, 1848.

[105] Dennis Le Marchant to the Master of the Mint, April 5, 1848, H.O. 41/26.

[106] Henry Ellis to Sir Dennis Le Marchant, April 9, 1848, H.O. 45/2410, Part 5.

[107] Leeds Mercury, April 15, 1848, p. 6.

[108] Greville, The Greville Memoirs, Vol. 6, p. 169.

[109] H. W. Addington to the Home Office, April 10, 1848, H.O. 45/2410 London.

[110] Herbert C. F. Bell, Lord Palmerston (London, New York, Toronto, 1936), p. 409.

[111] Anon., "Chartism," Fraser's Magazine, p. 590.

[112] Harris, Memoirs of an Ex-Minister, p. 225.

[113] Morning Chronicle, March 13, 1848, p. 3.

[114] Large, "London in the Year of Revolutions, 1848", p. 184.

[115] Chief inspector of the Chartered Gas Light Company to S. M. Philipps, April 7, 1848, H.O. 45/2410 London.

[116] Lord Palmerston to Lord John Russell, April 7, 1848, Russell Papers, P.R.O. 30/22 7B. Colonel Phipps to Prince Albert, April 9, 1848, RA Add. MSS C 56, Item 11.

[117] Greville, The Greville Memoirs, Vol. 6, p. 164.

[118] Northern Star, May 13, 1848, p. 3.

[119] Leeds Mercury, April 15, 1848, Supplement, p. 10.

[120] Anti-Chartist handbill, H.O. 45/2410, Part 5, A-L.

[121] Public Notice Placard from C. Rowan and R. Mayne, H.O. 45/2410, Part 2, London.

[122] Northern Star, April 15, 1848, Address of the Convention.

[123] Greville, The Greville Memoirs, Vol. 6, p. 164.

[124] Stevenson, Popular Disturbances in England, p. 269.

[125] Mather, Public Order in the Age of the Chartists, pp. 37-9, 73.

[126] Large, "London in the Year of Revolutions, 1848", p. 189.

[127] Memorandum, April 9, 1848, H.O. 41/26. Compare with Wellington's memorandum, April 5, 1848, W.O. 30/111. Also, George Grey to the Lord Mayor of London, April 9, 1848, H.O. 41/26.

[128] Hobhouse, Recollections of a Long Life, p. 214.

[129] Wellington wrote to Russell on April 6 saying that he had met with Colonel Rowan. Wellington to Lord John Russell, April 6, 1848, Russell Papers, P.R.O. 30/22 7B, Copy in W.O. 30/111.

[130] Greville, The Greville Memoirs, Vol. 6, p. 166.

[131] Muriel Wellesley, Wellington in Civil Life Through the Eyes of Those Who Knew Him (London 1939), p. 214; Hobhouse, Recollections of a Long Life, p. 214.

[132] Philip Henry, Fifth Earl of Stanhope, Notes of Conversations with the Duke of Wellington, 1831-1851 (Oxford 1938 ed.), p. 195.

[133] Bessborough, Lady Charlotte Guest, Extracts from Her Journal, 1833-1852, p. 210.

[134] Hansard, Parliamentary Debates, Third Series, Vol. 91, p. 500. He also wrote on April 5 that he expected "more serious disturbances of the public peace" after April 10. Memorandum, April 5, 1848, W.O. 30/81.

[135]Martin, Life of the Prince Consort, p. 174, quoting Chevalier Bunsen, who recalled Wellington's dictum.

[136]Rollo Russell, ed., Early Correspondence of Lord John Russell, 1805-1840 (London 1913), Vol. I, pp. 73-4.

[137]Wellington to Lord John Russell, April 6, 1848, Russell Papers, P.R.O. 30/22 7B, copy in W.O. 30/111. Russell received similar advice from others. C. E. Trevelyan advised Russell to "turn off" the stream of Chartists "at a distance" from Parliament and public offices. "Whitehall and Parliament street should be filled with special constables." C. E. Trevelyan to Lord John Russell, Russell Papers, P.R.O. 30/22 7B.

[138]Memorandum of the Duke of Wellington, April 5, 1848, W.O. 30/81; See also Large, "London in the Year of Revolutions, 1848", pp. 185-6.

[139]Wellesley, Wellington in Civil Life, p. 343.

[140]McCarthy and Russell, Lady John Russell, pp. 95-6.

[141]Weekly Dispatch, March 26, 1848, p. 151; Morning Chronicle, April 4, 1848, p. 7.

[142]Weekly Dispatch, April 9, 1848, p. 180. The speakers were first, Graspy, then Vernon. Also, Morning Chronicle, April 8, 1848, p. 6, speech of McCarthy.

[143]Northern Star, April 8, 1848, p. 5, at a meeting of the Fraternal Democrats, West speaking.

[144]Weekly Dispatch, April 9, 1848, p. 180, report of the National Convention.

[145]Morning Chronicle, report of the National Convention, April 8, 1848, p. 6.

[146]Letter of T. S. Duncombe, Northern Star, April 8, 1848, p. 1.

[147]Weekly Dispatch, April 9, 1848, p. 180. His speech drew a mixed response in the Convention, with some crying "oh, oh" and others "hear".

[148] Northern Star, April 8, 1848, p. 1.

[149] Morning Chronicle, April 8, 1848. The proclamation is dated April 7.

[150] Northern Star, April 8, 1848, p. 1.

[151] William Stevens, "A Memoir of Thomas Martin Wheeler, Founder of the Friend in Need Life and Sick Assurance Society, Domestic, Political and Industrial, with Extracts From His Letters, Speeches and Writings" (London 1862), p. 43.

[152] The Nonconformist, March 15, 1848, p. 171.

[153] G. W. M. Reynolds, Thomas Clark, W. P. Wilkinson to Sir George Grey, Waiting Room of the Home Office, April 7, 1848, H.O. 45/2410, Part 5 AD-AL; an account in the Morning Chronicle, April 8, 1848, p. 7. Also Creighton, Memoir of Sir George Grey, p. 66.

[154] Russell, Recollections and Suggestions, pp. 253-4.

[155] Hansard, Parliamentary Debates, Third Series, Vol. 98, p. 9. The questioner was R. H. Inglis.

[156] Weekly Dispatch, April 2, 1848, p. 157.

[157] Weekly Dispatch, April 9, 1848, p. 175.

[158] Weekly Dispatch, April 16, 1848, p. 186.

[159] Northern Star, April 8, 1848, p. 5.

[160] Northern Star, March 25, 1848, p. 5.

[161] The Times, April 10, 1848, p. 4.

[162] The Morning Chronicle, April 8, 1848, p. 6.

[163] Morning Chronicle, April 4, 1848, p. 7.

[164] Weekly Dispatch, April 16, 1848, p. 184.

[165] Morning Chronicle, April 3, 1848, p. 4.

[166] Morning Chronicle, April 8, 1848.

[167] Morning Chronicle, April 3, 1848, p. 4; Northern Star, April 8, 1848, p. 7.

[168]Sir George Grey to Lord John Russell, April 9, 1848, Russell Papers, P.R.O. 30/22 7B. The letter is reproduced in Walpole, The Life of Lord John Russell, p. 69. Reference to the meeting is also in Lord Spencer to General Bowles, April 10, 1848, RA Add. MSS. C 56, Item 16.

[169]Northern Star, April 8, 1848, p. 8; also Weekly Dispatch, reporting the Convention, April 16, 1848, p. 184.

[170]Northern Star, April 8, 1848, p. 1; also April 1, 1848, p. 1; Weekly Dispatch, April 16, 1848, p. 184.

[171]Northern Star, April 1, 1848, p. 1; Morning Chronicle, April 8, 1848, p. 6.

[172]Weekly Dispatch, April 9, 1848, p. 180; Morning Chronicle, April 8, 1848, p. 6.

[173]Northern Star, April 15, 1848, p. 7.

[174]Northern Star, April 8, 1848, p. 4.

[175]Northern Star, April 1, 1848, p. 1.

[176]Northern Star, April 8, 1848, p. 4.

[177]Weekly Dispatch, April 6, 1848, p. 184.

[178]Morning Chronicle, April 8, 1848, p. 6.

[179]Hansard, Parliamentary Debates, Third Series, Vol. 98, pp. 11-13. He repeated his remarks in Vol. 97, pp. 1354-5.

[180]Weekly Dispatch, April 16, 1848, p. 184.

[181]Hansard, Parliamentary Debates, Third Series, Vol. 98, p. 13 and 15.

[182]P. W. Kingsford, "Radical Dandy: Thomas Slingsby Duncombe, 1796-1861", History Today, no. 14 (1964), p. 404.

[183]Northern Star, April 15, 1848, p. 6. Alderman Humphrey allegedly informed O'Connor of this in the House of Commons.

[184] *Morning Chronicle,* editorial, April 7, 1848, p. 4; April 8, 1848, p. 6.

[185] Stevens, "A Memoir of Thomas Martin Wheeler", p. 44. William Rider claimed that O'Connor told him of making his will, explaining, "I do not expect to escape with my life this day."

[186] *Northern Star,* April 8, 1848, p. 8.

[187] *Northern Star,* April 15, 1848, p. 7. Thomas Wheeler wrote of how Feargus had already begun to sink in 1848 with an "overwrought brain." Stevens, "A Memoir of Thomas Martin Wheeler", p. 67.

[188] *Weekly Dispatch,* April 16, 1848, p. 184.

[189] *Northern Star,* April 15, 1848, p. 7.

[190] *Northern Star,* April 1, 1848, p. 1.

[191] *Northern Star,* April 15, 1848, p. 7. For a recent scholarly attempt to rehabilitate O'Connor up to 1842, see James Epstein, *The Lion of Freedom: Feargus O'Connor and the Chartist Movement, 1832-1842* (Gordon 1982).

[192] Frost, *Forty Years' Recollections,* pp. 135-7.

[193] Holyoake, *Bygones Worth Remembering,* pp. 78-9.

[194] Stevens, "A Memoir of Thomas Martin Wheeler", p. 44.

[195] *Morning Chronicle,* April 8, 1848, p. 6.

[196] *Weekly Dispatch,* April 16, 1848, p. 184.

[197] *Northern Star,* April 15, 1848, p. 8, reporting the Convention meeting of April 8.

[198] *Macclesfield Courier,* April 22, 1848. John West, a delegate to the Convention, reported this.

[199] Smith, "Great Britain and the Revolutions of 1848", p. 79.

[200] *Morning Chronicle,* April 7, 1848, p. 4.

[201] *The Times,* April 11, 1848.

[202]Large, "London in the Year of Revolutions, 1848", p. 191 and 207. He cites evidence that two armed men were actually ordered into a van on the tenth and disarmed by Chartists marshalls.

[203]Frost, History of the Chartist Movement, Chapter IX.

[204]Weekly Dispatch, April 9, 1848, p. 180.

[205]Northern Star, April 8, 1848, p. 8, Harney's remarks. Also p. 5.

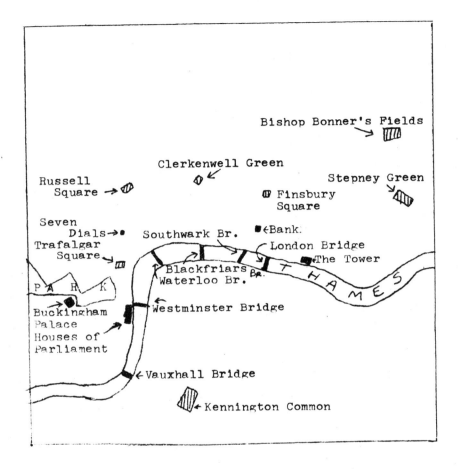

LONDON IN 1848

CHAPTER III

THE GREAT DAY

Onward and We Conquer
Backward and We Fall

(Motto of Feargus O'Connor)

Assembly

Trains at the Euston Square station of the London and North Western Railway disgorged large numbers of Chartists from distant locations, all eager to witness the drama of April 10. They came from Manchester, from Birmingham, Rochdale and Liverpool. Some even came from Edinburgh and Glasgow. On the way down to London, many huddled together in third class cars, drinking and singing lustily. One favorite had these words:

We'll march, We'll march,
Our tyrants' blood
Shall drench the thirsty land.[1]

How many of their descendants go to football games in a similar manner, but devoid of political purpose?

Those who stayed home in the provinces rivited their attention on London on April 10. Meetings were held up and down the land on and before the great day, but all eyes were on London, the center of the stage. Nevertheless, local authorities prepared for the worst, in imitation of the Home Office preparations for the metropolis. For example, Irish dragoons and troops of yeomanry were ready in Nottingham, backing up 1,500 special constables. They feared in particular for the safety of the gasworks.[2] In Leicester, authorities tried to put pensioners under arms and recruited specials.[3] In Leeds, a very large number of special constables were signed up and ready for action.[4] Great excitement was met with stern precautions in all the great centers: Manchester, Liverpool, Birmingham, Wolverhampton, Glasgow and Edinburgh.[5] In places where Chartism had been quiescent compared to 1839 or 1842, interest flared anew as April 10 approached. Newcastle was a case in point. Until the beginning of April, Chartism was hardly mentioned at all in the press, and when local leaders decided to call a rare meeting for the tenth, it was dismissed as a "little go" by the Gateshead Observer, staged so Newcastle Chartists would not be "behindhand."[6]

All of these provincial gatherings were peaceful, moral force demonstrations. As a Chartist speaker declared at a meeting of 10,000 in the forest near Nottingham, "They had met to show the government their moral power.... The sabre could not cut down an argument nor the bullet stop the progress of opinion."[7]

Telegraph messages clattered into the Home Office from the heavily prepared local authorities, before, during and after the provincial meetings on April 10, reporting the pervasive calm.[8] Once it was all over in the metropolis, the telegraph sent a set of 'all clear' messages from the Home Office back to various localities. So while police, special constables, troops and Chartists acted out miniature scenes of Kennington Common in a score of places, the one and only focus of everyone's attention remained London.

London itself had several foci until the great conversion on Kennington Common. Stepney Green at eight o'clock was the point of assembly for many Metropolitan Chartists, but towards nine there were only knots of apprehensive demonstrators present.[9] A deputation went to the Convention to see if any change in the arrangements had taken place, and they returned just before nine, bringing the word to proceed. At this point, things began to happen: a band appeared, and a large group of men following the flag of the Stepney Society of Cordwainers fell in behind it. Other groups of Chartists from the neighborhood joined, bringing their own banners, and soon a procession was off to Finsbury Square, four abreast. On the way, people from courts, alleys and side streets swelled the procession. At Finsbury Square, Chartists poured in from Clerkenwell Green, Russell Square and other assembly points. The Stepney Green band kept in front as the whole assemblage backtracked briefly and then surged towards London Bridge.

At Clerkenwell Green and other assembly points, the plainclothed police watched unobtrusively and noted what they saw. Inspector Mayne got terse reports promptly: Three thousand were at Clerkenwell Green, but no appearance of arms.[10]

Throughout their route to London Bridge, the Chartists tramped in an orderly manner, four abreast, tall
hats bobbing along. A flow of people walked on both
sides of the procession, looking in some places as
though they outnumbered those in the ranks. Although
banners proclaimed resoluteness, and Caps of Liberty
here and there served as reminders of the French Revolution, as did several women marching in tricolored
outfits, there was nothing along the whole peaceful
procession to cause alarm. Except for a few walking
sticks, Chartists bore nothing visible with which to
defend themselves. The shopkeepers north of the Thames
trusted them as long as they were moving off to the
other side of the river. Except for a few, the shops
were open and unprotected.

Where were the police, the specials and the military, the Chartists wondered as they approached the
bridge? From their departure at Finsbury Square all
the way to the river they had not seen the armed
officials of the law, except for a knot of special
constables in front of a building in Bishopsgate
Street, half hidden behind railings. Yet when the
Chartists spotted them, the marchers raised a friendly
cheer and nothing more. Would forces converge at
London Bridge and block their way? Fears and expectations gripped the procession as the head of the column
came to the span. No, the way was clear. The forces
of order stood aside and let them parade across to the
south of the Thames unmolested.

Other contingents of Chartists and the Irish
Repealers had Russell Square as their assembly point.
At nine o'clock, cordwainers, bricklayers and others
were to join the Irish Confederates. The cordwainers
arrived promptly, and in very good order. Men from
Westminster arrived next, many of them tailors and
artisans. All the while, unmarshalled spectators and
sympathizers poured into the square from several directions, from Tottenham Court Road, Grays Inn Lane, and
Holborn. They so filled the west side of the square
that there was some difficulty passing through. At
9:30, with a burst of cheers, the orange and green
banners carried by a column of Irish Confederates came
into the square. Soon the order to fall in was shouted
around and the combined procession marched out of the
square, people linked arm in arm, eight across, cordwainers leading the way. Their banner went before
them, proclaiming: "Liberty, Equality and Fraternity.
The Charter and No Surrender." Off they went, around

107

Bloomsbury Square and into Holborn. The Irish drew
hearty cheers in Holborn, what with their bright new
banners, the best banners to be seen the whole day.
Some were of green silk, fringed with orange. One had
the ancient Irish harp embossed in gold near its message: "Let Every Man Have His Own Country." Arm in
arm, eight across, they trooped towards Blackfriars
Bridge, Quiet spectators, mostly women, peered from the
upper windows of the shops. Spectators in the streets
were now quiet as well, and only a few feeble cheers
were given. The police, specials and military were out
of sight. What about the bridge? Would they be cut
off? No, they too went over without any check or hesitation.

In another group, Thomas Frost saw two lines of
police as he crossed Waterloo Bridge, and a glimpse
over the parapet near Somerset House revealed a dis-
mounted trooper of the Household Cavalry, one of the
very few soldiers seen by the Chartists that day. The
trooper scurried back to Somerset House when he knew he
was being observed.11

Once over the river, at Elephant and Castle, the
Chartists from Russell Square followed up those from
the East End towards the great rendezvous at Kennington
Common. Near the common the marchers could see that
the local inhabitants were less trusting than those
north of the river. The doors and windows of houses
and shops were tightly shut and many were barricaded.12

Thousands were already assembled to greet them.
They had arrived from nine o'clock onwards, choking the
streets nearby. Contingents from different Chartist
associations arrived from everywhere after nine, with
bands, flags and banners. Tricolors sprouted on the
common, most of them red, white and green, the old
Chartist colors, but many had French colors. Even an
American flag waved. Every slightly elevated part of
the common was filled with spectators seeking a good
view. So were the higher windows of houses overlooking
the green, where well dressed women anxiously surveyed
the Chartists assembling. Down on the common, marshalls with sashes in red, white and green took charge
of the contingents already there, dividing them up into
30 sections. Section leaders ranged their men six deep
around the edges of the common, a human wall to protect
the masses on the inside in case the authorities should
launch an incursion.

It was no mean task. Everybody had to be crammed into less than 20 acres of scanty and stunted vegetation surrounded by buildings on all sides. An unassuming Chartist named Thomas Martin Wheeler was responsible for much of the order and discipline operating on Kennington Common. He worked in O'Connor's shadow, and on his behalf. This general secretary of the N.C.A. was a loyal lieutenant and friend who never in his life repudiated his Irish leader. Wheeler "noiselessly" directed the various divisions at Kennington Common, and urged restraint everywhere. How much credit he must be given for maintaining peace and order that day is not clear, but certainly he must share O'Connor's laurels for making April 10 an almost bloodless day.[13]

All the while that the tramp of London's workers resounded on the way to Kennington Common, the Chartist National Convention deliberated in an excited state. They had a reply from Scotland Yard, in response to their message of April 9 to the Commissioners of the Police announcing a change in the route of their controversial procession. Scotland Yard flatly refused to let it take place, but would allow the petition to come forth in a proper manner, that is, escorted by only a few persons. At least it was some consolation that the Commissioners of Police had not flatly banned the meeting.

Feargus O'Connor's speech to the Convention was lengthy and repetitive, stressing again the fact of his own poor health, and the long history of his sacrifices for the people. He cited the "folly" of some persons out of the Convention and a few in it, an obvious slap at the militants who had indulged in empty but threatening oratory. O'Connor held them responsible for engendering the now all too obvious public opposition. He asked the militants to put themselves in the place of the government after the authorities heard them at their worst. Would they themselves escape the feeling that it was "their duty" to do everything to maintain the peace?

Clearly, O'Connor saw the handwriting on the wall, and was ready to abandon the procession before he reached the meeting and before his celebrated upcoming interview with the police. He warned the Convention that he would stop the procession by "physical force" if any Chartists attempted any kind of physical force themselves. If the government had forbidden the procession, "he would ask the people not to hold it."

Above all, Chartists had to be firm and resolute to "act temperately" so as not to "jeopardize their cause" through a collision with the authorities. After all, he could be lost, and with him his valuable advocacy of their cause in the House.

O'Connor no longer shared the hopes of so many of his followers that the Charter would be enacted that day, and he told them so. Consolingly, he wafted about the old hopes for the Charter becoming law some indefinite day in the future, the old, endless refrain that was heard in the movement since 1839. He asked his listeners to imagine another convention sitting, simultaneous meetings going on all over the country, and Feargus O'Connor dramatically holding up the House of Commons all the while with question after question on the Charter. But for today, April 10? No, not today.

When O'Connor finally finished, just before ten, the delegates formed their own part of the procession to Kennington Common. Two large horse drawn cars were ready for them. The first, festooned with Chartist tricolors of red, white and green, and drawn by four "beautifully caparisoned" Land Company farm horses, awaited the petition for the Charter, which was stored at the National Land Company Office, not far away. The second car was drawn by six horses and was capacious enough to take the principal members of the Convention as well as numerous journalists.[14] Its front bench was occupied by O'Connor, Doyle, McGrath, Ernest Jones, Wheeler, and Harney. All were O'Connor's lieutenants and all had been active members of the Fraternal Democrats. Banners ran all over both cars; the usual ones, including the points of the Charter, as well as some remarkable ones: "Speak with the Voice -- Not with the Musket;" "The Voice of the People is the Voice of God;" "The Voice of Knowledge would silence the Cannon's Roar;" "Live and Let Live." These are not the slogans from which revolutionaries draw inspiration. Two old slogans also decorating the van were more pointed: "The Charter and No Surrender;" "Liberty is worth living for and worth dying for." But even these were still far from calls to the barricades.

When the cars began to move, a cheer went up, and people fell in behind, eight across in the street, with others moving down the pavements. The procession from the Convention moved down and across the streets near the British Museum, stopping for a time in Holborn to load the petition. Five large rolls of paper, nine to

ten feet in circumference, were hoisted aboard the
first car and lashed into place, an impressive cargo,
each roll the size and shape of a bale of cotton. The
cars started up again and the procession continued down
to Blackfriars Bridge. All was cheerful as the column
marched in good spirits past open shops with not a
policeman in sight. At New Bridge Street they saw one.
When they crossed Blackfriars Bridge they saw two or
three hundred pensioners who had come on duty down on
the steamboat pier. The Chartists gave them a loud
cheer and on they went. A more serious display greeted
them on the other side of the bridge, where several
hundred police stood, stationed in line on the road.
Further on, they passed 50 mounted police, sheathed
cutlasses at their side. Beyond Blackfriars Road, the
shops were no longer open. Some were boarded up as if
awaiting a siege.

     At Elephant and Castle, more large bodies of work-
ers waited to join this part of the procession, and
together all went on to the common. There, in the
sunshine, the great meeting was coming together. What
greeted the eyes of those in the cab were trade union
flags, Irish flags, disciplined bodies wheeling and
marching into position, an almost military array cor-
doning the sides of the common, and thousands upon
thousands already assembled in loose throngs at the
centre. The lines parted, the cars rolled over the
green grass and thousands of feet pounded towards them,
thousands of bodies crowded around them and thousands
of voices roared a long, deafening, rolling, echoing
cheer for the petition, the leaders, the Charter, and
the hopes of all years past and all years to come. The
golden day and moment for Victorian democracy had at
last arrived.

     O'Connor and the delegates acknowledged the cheers
by waving their hats. The cars moved on, slowly pushing through the densely packed, orderly, good humored
crowds around them. One tall, brave man made his way
through the crowd towards the van without cheering. He
was a police inspector.

                 Behind The Thick Lines

     In the West End, while the Chartists had been
marching over the bridges, a rider attended only by his
groom trotted through the park towards the War Office.
He was dressed in a blue frock coat, white waistcoat

                         111

and black military trousers. He was 78 years old, and those who saw him canter up to the War Office noted that he seemed in better health and spirits than usual. He was the Duke of Wellington.[15]

The surprisingly vigorous old hero was in his element again. One observer declared that he was "alive again, like an old war horse at the sound of a trumpet."[16] Another said his "old eyes...sparkled," another said that "the fire of other years" glowed again. Here was a man about whom apocryphal stories and tales could grow into legend. April 10 provided a few. When asked when the troops would come into the situation, he is supposed to have replied, "not as long as a single constable is alive and on his legs."[17] This story does not fit with his tactical plan, of course. There may be more truth in another: Someone asked him, "Has Your Grace protected London Bridge?" "Done two hours ago!" he replied in his usual laconic, abrupt, factual manner. "And Blackfriars?" "Done two hours ago." "And Waterloo?" "Done, too!" The questions ranged up the whole Thames, with the Duke replying with ever decreasing patience. Finally, the questioner got to Richmond Bridge. "Richmond Bridge may go to the devil!"[18] Yet another story is that as the Chartists marched, the Duke calmly read a newspaper. An excited aide de camp burst in after a long gallop to tell the Duke about the Chartists' progress. "How far are they from the bridge?" he asked. When informed, he replied, "Tell me when they are within one quarter of a mile," and went back to his newspaper. Whether these tales are true or not, Wellington was certainly calm, assured, and undoubtedly pleased to serve his country once more.

From other vantage points, government officials and friends of authority gained reassurance when they heard what was not happening, although they did not carry on with the studied aplomb of the Iron Duke. At Number 10 Downing Street, Lord and Lady John Russell and Sir George Grey received a flow of reports. After one o'clock, they had no moments of apprehension.[19] At two o'clock, Grey left and walked about the crowds at Charing Cross, the hero of the day.[20] Colonel Phipps, out and about, noticed with pride how the police moved about in small bodies with a look of confidence and assured superiority. Yet he also saw "sufficient elements" capable of "mischief" if the "comprehensive... preparations" had not stood in their way. These were "small parties of desperate looking ruffians" who were

"ready to take advantage of any accident."[21] These
types were apparently not observed by the Earl of
Malmesbury, who noted how the "mob" was "the best behaved" he ever saw, with everyone walking about "as
safely and as quietly as on any other day." There was
"no excitement -- nothing but curiosity."[22]

     Others witnessed different aspects of the drama.
An observer at Picadilly wondered where the fashionable
carriages and other private vehicles had gone to, and
where were the gentlemen?[23] For some, it was ominous
to see patrols of mounted police and single files of
soldiers in ordinarily quiet streets.[24] Many people
remember what they saw while serving as special constables. Lord Lyttleton "walked up and down Pall Mall for
a long time with a blue stick and a crown badge" along
with other specials who ranged from Lords to the
ragged, but who were all "ready to die for their country." In fact, there were more specials parading the
street than all the other people put together.[25]

     Perhaps the most colorful of eyewitnesses on the
streets that day was the famous French romantic composer, Hector Berlioz. Early in the morning he had been
warned that England would be "engulfed like the rest of
Europe." What he observed led him to believe that
"your Chartist is a very decent sort of revolutionary."
Who was in the chair at their meeting? Berlioz wrote
that "the cannon, those eloquent orators and formidable
logicians whose arguments appeal so powerfully to the
masses, were in the chair. They were not required to
utter a word, their presence being enough to persuade
everybody of the inexpediency of revolution...."
Berlioz concluded that the Chartists "know as much
about starting a riot as the Italians about writing a
symphony."[26] The French composer knew as little about
Chartist intentions that day.

     Everywhere on the tenth, specials were on the
lookout for the dangerous foreign agitators everyone
had been warned about. Many men had shaved off their
"moustachios" for fear of being taken for a foreigner,
and for good reason.[27] As Lord Palmerston commented,
the specials of April 10 "had sworn to make an example
of any whiskered or bearded rioters" by having them
"mashed...to jelly."[28]

     Still, foreigners were perceived on the streets of
London in "unusual" numbers; many of them were said to
be "the best known and worst characters" from

113

revolutionary Paris.[29] The Times warned of "foreign propagandists in the metropolis, ready to manufacture a tragedy."[30] Rumor had it that the police were watching upwards of 500 who had slipped into England in order to aid the Chartist demonstration.[31] Some were sure that the Frenchmen lurking about would have sprung into action had the procession to the House been allowed.[32] They were observed in knots of 10 to 12, seeking to look inconspicuous.[33]

In this time of excitement, rumor and suspicion ran riot. Naturally, with France less than 30 miles from Dover, Frenchmen can always be observed in London. No clear evidence can be cited to show that those present on April 10 were linked to any sinister activity.

Actually, one shabbily dressed Frenchman stood out from the others on that day, and he remains anonymous. He took it upon himself to harangue a small crowd at Charing Cross in rather bad English. His message was that Englishmen ought to go to Paris to learn how to build barricades and fight for their liberty. At this point a butcher's boy interceded by knocking the Frenchman down. "Us don't want no barricades here or any of your French humbug," the boy was quoted as saying, in what became a very popular anecdote.[34]

For all the great fear of foreigners on April 10, and, for that matter, Chartist rioters and revolutionaries, there was very little to show for it behind or in front of the police lines.

The Meeting Itself

Meanwhile, on Kennington Common, the policeman reached O'Connor's van. He bore a message from Police Commissioner Mayne, who was waiting at the nearby Horne Tavern, an establishment completely taken over by policemen and military leaders for their headquarters. The inspector shouted his message: Commissioner Mayne wanted a brief word with O'Connor before the proceedings began. O'Connor alighted from the van immediately, along with McGrath, and the three men began to push through the crowd. O'Connor towered over those around him as he threaded his way, for he was one of the tallest men in the House of Commons. Suddenly the rumor spread like wildfire that he had been arrested. "They have got him!" was the cry. The crowd seethed forward in breathless excitement. Yet they did not block the progress of the three men and nobody made an attempt to abort the mission of the single policeman, who swayed through the throng like someone walking through a field of corn. In fact, some Chartists helped the three push through. If anything, this scene proves the peaceful disposition of the Chartist crowd that day.[35]

Police Commissioner Mayne's report of his meeting with O'Connor near Horne Tavern survives.[36] He told O'Connor, in no uncertain terms, that the petition could go to Parliament, but no body of persons in any procession or assemblage could go with it. O'Connor was eager to agree. Yes, the Commissioner had his word that there would be no procession across the bridges. O'Connor gave his hand on the point, a very ordinary thing for a gentleman to do. The petition should go in a cab. "I never saw a man more frightened than he was", Mayne reported, "and he would, I am sure, have promised me anything."

Many were thronged around them shouting, under the impression that the Chartist leader was being taken into custody. To quiet them down, O'Connor climbed on top of a cab standing nearby and declared that he was only giving the police a "friendly communication."

After this brief meeting near Horne Tavern, O'Connor and McGrath pushed back to their van on the common, amid thunderous shouts of joy and the waving of a sea of handkerchiefs. The roar of approval echoed out to the outer reaches of the mass. A victory of sorts had been won: O'Connor was not arrested; the meeting went on; and, above all, a potentially danger- ous flash point had been passed in safety.

Out in the crowd, Thomas Frost "breathed more freely" when he heard the terms of the arrangement announced. He thought that a majority of the audience around him were similarly grateful for being released from the "painful suspense" of not knowing the govern- ment's "ultimate intentions."[37]

The panorama before O'Connor would daunt any speaker before the age of electronic amplification. Just how many people were there will never be known. The bias of those hostile to the affair led them to minimize the number present. The Annual Register cited from 15,000 to 150,000, and quoted military estimates of from 23,000 to 33,000.[38] The Leeds Mercury declared

that only 20,000 to 25,000 people showed up out of a
metropolitan population of two million, indicating the
weakness of Chartism in the metropolis.[39] The Times
put the figure as low as 10,000, with 10,000 bystanders
in addition.[40] Some members of the establishment quoted
ridiculously low figures in their letters and diaries.
Palmerston, for example, wrote that the Chartists "did
not muster more than fifteen thousand on the common."[41]
The Earl of Shaftesbury put it at 13,000.[42] Perhaps
they got these estimates from Mayne's curious official
figure of 12,000.

Chartist estimates were, of course, much higher.
Even the hostile Weekly Dispatch put the number up,
citing from 50,000 to 200,000.[43] The Northern Star
quoted estimates of from 200,000 to 500,000, declaring
"from our experience there could not be less than a
quarter of a million persons present, on and around the
common alone."[44] Perhaps the best friendly source for
an estimate was Thomas Frost. He guessed that 150,000
were there, which tallied with the independent guess of
a bookseller friend of his. Frost claimed that the
"most impartial" journals came up with the same
figure.[45]

One recent historian, David Large, has given close
attention to this question. He measured Kennington
Common and came up with the figure of 13,640 square
yards and calculated that 54,560 persons were present,
on the basis of four persons per square yard.[46] Yet
might the density per square yard have been more?
Crowded meetings today sometimes vie with the underground in rush hour when it comes to minimizing space
per person.

One of the curious phenomena of April 10 was that
someone took a photograph of the meeting, which was put
away in the Royal Archives until very recently, when the
Sunday Times displayed it with the caption: "Found --
The World's First Crowd Photograph." Spaces do show up
in the background, but it is impossible to say at what
point in the meeting this remarkable picture was taken.

While the actual number participating on April 10
will always be a mystery, one aspect is certain: The
number present was less than the establishment had
anticipated. How many of them actually heard O'Connor
and the other speakers is another mystery. Certainly
not those lining the edges in a defensive cordon, who
were far from the van. The Irish Confederates were far

away, at the south-eastern corner. One group of Chartist leaders, including Harney, Reynolds and West, eventually left the gathering around O'Connor in order to address those crowds in the south-east, which they accomplished from a balcony of a house overlooking the common.

O'Connor was, as usual, the main speaker. But first one of his Irish lieutenants, Doyle, took the chair and warmed up the audience. He set the tone quickly:

> "I need not ask you to conduct yourselves with the greatest propriety; for recollect that on your good conduct this day, on your peaceful but firm demeanour, depends the success of one of the most glorious causes ever agitated by man."

He introduced Feargus, saying that not only would O'Connor give his own opinion and advice, but the opinion and advice of the National Convention as well.

O'Connor stood high on the van and began a long, rambling, repetitious speech in which he gave his best and his worst. His essential message came through at least three times: The Convention had received the news that the police would not permit the procession, and the Executive therefore was not going to permit it either, lest "you shall be brought into collision with an armed force." He was direct and clear on this point, with no wavering, no opportunism, no veiled meanings at all: "You will not walk in procession. You must go peaceably to your homes...." He used his old, familiar orator's ploy: All those who thought that the Convention acted wisely were to hold up their hands. A sea of arms and hands engulfed him, what the Northern Star called a "monster" show of hands. He did this twice in the speech. In another part of his oration he used melodramatic flourishes to hammer away at his message: He implored his hearers, "in the name of that great and good God who has this day blessed us with a splendid sunshine" not to "now destroy the cause I have so struggled for all my life..." by becoming disorderly and violent. He "counseled, enjoined," and declared that he "would go down on...[his]...knees to beseech" them to be peaceable and orderly. Such was his consistent theme throughout.

117

The content of the rest of his speech, inter-
spersed as it was between the reiteration of the main
message, was vintage O'Connor. He recapitulated his
family background and his career given over to sacrifices for the people, made vague allusions to the
glorious eventual triumph of the Charter, presented a
strong pitch for the wonders of the Land Plan, and took
a swipe at the "capitalists" who were "fed with the
blood that is in little children's bodies." There is
no point in quoting any of these sections, for they are
all found in so many of his other speeches and really
had nothing to do directly with the crisis at hand.

Besides these old topics and the main message, the
speech dwelt on the subject of the great leader's own
heroism and the prospects of his demise. This was
Feargus at his worst, maudlin melodrama and bathos.
Moreover, it was largely an extended, emotional repeti-
tion of what he had declared in the House of Commons
previously. He told the audience about all the threats
on his life, of "at least 100 letters" warning him that
his life would be sacrificed if he attended. But there
he was, and see, "my hand does not tremble." After
all, he had always sought "the lion's portion of the
popularity," so why should he not face up to "the
lion's share of the danger?" The old showman got his
applause on that line. He got cheers for this one:
"Yes, you are my children...this car is yours -- made
from your timber (referring to the origin of the wood
on a Land Plan farm); I am only your father and your
bailiff, but your honest father and your unpaid bailiff." He sounded more like the stereotyped Jewish
mother, however, when he cautioned them against disturbances by asking: "How would you feel if you were
conscious that you had been parties to my death?"

As for the Charter, no, they would not have it
today, but "so help me God, I will die upon the floor
of the House or get your rights for you." At the end
of the long oration the audience was given a foretaste
of this drama, for O'Connor appeared to be suffering
from "severe bodily pain" and "exhausted with the
effort of speaking." He descended from the van looking
extremely ill, and walked with difficulty, leaning on
two persons. Curtain on O'Connor.

The police watched all of these proceedings, noting that while he spoke more people left the meeting
than joined it. The policemen only spotted a few
foreigners, but they were taking no active part as

leaders. No arms were observed, not even bludgeons, so the officers of the law had no need to interfere.[47] One reporter from The Times noted some thieves' activities on the outskirts of the meeting that led to "slight and somewhat amusing episodes."[48]

Ernest Jones followed O'Connor. He gave the same message, but more succinctly. The audience was informed that they had the "honour of Great Britain" in their hands, "and you must not soil that honour...by a foolish collision or by bloodshed." Clearly, it was "useless" to attempt "a collision" because they had already gained their "point" by having the meeting. Jones called for more and more meetings, "day after day" in order to keep up the Chartist momentum. Considering how frequently Jones was cited in the established press as a dangerous revolutionary, his role on April 10 could stand as a sharp refutation. He himself was aware of the irony, asking his hearers to recollect that he was commonly called "a physical force Chartist."

Over by the Irish in the south-eastern corner, Harney, Reynolds and West carried on simultaneously with and after O'Connor's long speech across the way. Naturally, the main topic on that side of the common had to be Ireland, but the same O'Connorite message for peace, law and order came through clearly there as well.

G. W. M. Reynolds, also a dangerous man according to the established press, stated that their cause "would be injured by the least outrage," so the audience should consider themselves "special constables for the preservation of order." That was the means to display "that they could be trusted with self government." George Julian Harney, another sinister figure to newspapers like The Times, also exhorted demonstrators to "return home peaceably", but his speech was unlike the major addresses of O'Connor and Jones, in that it was laced with bitterness and disappointment over the cancellation of the procession. He said he would "never again be a party to calling upon the people to come to any meeting unarmed...." The authorities had responded with as much force as "if the French had landed at Dover" and were clearly out to "slaughter the people" that day. They were trapped south of the Thames, and could not possibly face the government's forces with any chance of success. Therefore, in calling off the procession they had retreated, but "only as the ablest generals had done," that is, to return another time. Meanwhile, their "discipline and order" would serve

119

them well in the continuation of the struggle. These
unique remarks added a note to April 10 that would be
picked up by others afterwards.

By about quarter to two the speeches were all
over. Termination of the meeting was marked by abrupt-
ness. The van containing the speakers was moved so
quickly that they crashed their shins. Three ordinary
cabs were drawn up, the great bales of the National
Petition were stashed securely and the Chartist Executive Committee, its only escort, were taken aboard.
The cabs wheeled away from the throng at a "rapid
pace", and nobody attempted to follow, much to the
relief of those escorting it. Banners and flags were
rolled up, and only a few figures here and there sought
to hold up the rapidly dispersing crowd with impromptu
harrangues. It was all over. Dreams of half a million
marching on Parliament, a collapse of government and
the transfer of power to the Conventioneers were shattered forever. It was neither death nor glory for
Chartist militants on April 10.

April 10 did not pass without some violence.
There were some cracked skulls and blood on the pavement, contrary to all the effusions about the utter
peacefulness of the event in the established press.[49]
It happened because dispersal routes across the bridges
were blocked by deep ranks of police on the south side
of the Thames. The police had advanced and cleared the
streets approaching the bridges, and intended to hold
these positions for an hour, in accordance with the
tactical plan. On all but one bridge there were no
serious problems. On all but one, small numbers of
Chartists were allowed to trickle over them and disperse north of the river. Violence broke out at Blackfriars Bridge, where a dense mass waited to go across.
As on the other spans, the police planned to let them
through in twos and threes at a time. But the Chartists at Blackfriars surged forward as pressure on
those in front built up from the crowds behind them.
Soon the Metropolitan Police were using their staves.
Beaten back, the Chartists came on again and again.
Stones filled the air. When the police rushed forward
and seized several who threw them, groups of Chartists
swarmed in to free them. Some specials joined the
fray, and several were "roughly handled," some losing
their staves and others having their hats broken. The
yelling and shouting was "deafening" according to one
eye witness. The police lines separated here and
there, and finally, with a great shout, a dense mass

120

pushed the police back across the bridge. Some of them were virtually lifted and carried backwards by the crowd, staves held high. So the unarmed Chartists were able to force a bridge on April 10. Once on the other side, though, the forces of law and order were able to overcome them, arresting many under the formidable intimidation of the police horse patrol, which was riding about with sabres drawn. On both sides of Blackfriars Bridge, bloody headed men limped and staggered away, helped by their friends. These men would never be able to share the common view of the peacefulness of the day. At any rate, by three o'clock, everything had subsided everywhere.

After the petition crossed to Parliament, Feargus O'Connor, happy to be alive, and happy that all of his followers were alive, called upon the Home Secretary. He announced to Grey that the meeting had unanimously resolved to give up the procession and disperse quietly. In private, Grey was delighted that the whole business had passed off quietly, and attributed the success exclusively to the vast precautions and not in any way to O'Connor's leadership. Still cautious, Grey kept his forces active and on the alert until late in the evening.[50]

The Prime Minister was similarly delighted and wrote to the Queen of how O'Connor was "pale and frightened" and "expressed the utmost thanks" to Mayne and "begged to shake Mr. Mayne by the hand." Russell also reported how Feargus O'Connor repeated the same scene in front of Sir George Grey, quoting him as having said "Not a man should be taken away" from the forces guarding the bridges. O'Connor was so eager to oblige that he expostulated that he understood the government's position and had sought to explain it to the Convention.[51]

It was sad that Grey and Russell did not see O'Connor's position. They only saw abject fright, and so the myth of April 10 was in the making before the day was over.

NOTES TO CHAPTER III

[1] Leeds Mercury, April 15, 1848. Bills had been posted in many towns prohibiting the Kennington Common meeting. According to the Leeds Mercury of April 8, 1848, they were all defaced.

[2] Peter Wyncoll, Nottingham Chartism (Nottingham 1966), p. 44.

[3] Alfred Temple Patterson, Radical Leicester: A History of Leicester, 1780-1850 (Leicester 1954), p. 357. He reports the response as "lukewarm".

[4] Leeds Mercury, April 15, 1848, p. 6.

[5] Weekly Dispatch, April 16, 1848, p. 187; Leeds Mercury, April 22, 1848, p. 8.

[6] Gateshead Observer, April 15, 1848, p. 3. See D. J. Rowe, "Some Aspects of Chartism on the Tyneside", International Review of Social History, Vol. 16, Part 1 (1971), p. 39.

[7] Wyncoll, Nottingham Chartism, p. 44. There was a more militant scene in Oldham, according to Hartley Bateson, A Centenary History of Oldham (Oldham 1949), p. 67.

[8] Numerous messages are in H.O. 45/2410 London.

[9] Unless otherwise noted, the entire account of the processions and the meeting are amalgamated from The Times, The Northern Star, and the Illustrated London News, April 11, 15 and 15, respectively. Whenever possible, facts have been checked against eye-witness accounts, the most notable of them in Frost, Forty Years' Recollections. In addition see the account of the April 10 meeting in Goodway, London Chartism, 1838-1848, pp. 129-142.

[10] Police Report, 8:45, April 10, H.O. 45/2410, Part 2, London.

[11] Frost, Forty Years' Recollections, p. 136. Also Robert Crowe, "The Reminiscences of a Chartist Tailor", Outlook (August 9, 1902), pp. 916-17.

[12] Annual Register, April, 1848, p. 51

[13]William Stevens, "A Memoir of Thomas Martin Wheeler", is a short hagiographic account, in which Wheeler is given full credit for foiling the "blood thirsty plans of the government to massacre the people." (p. 44). See also Ray Faherty, "The Memoir of Thomas Martin Wheeler, Owenite and Chartist", Society for the Study of Labour History Bulletin, no. 30 (Spring 1975).

[14]The Northern Star says the 'principal' members, whereas the Annual Register says that all the members sat in the second car. Annual Register, April, 1848, p. 52. The Times said the van could carry 50 persons.

[15]Leeds Mercury, April 15, 1848.

[16]"Chartism", Fraser's Magazine, p. 590.

[17]Wellesley, Wellington in Civil Life, p. 342.

[18]"Chartism", Fraser's Magazine, p. 591.

[19]Walpole, The Life of Lord John Russell, Vol. 2, p. 69.

[20]Creighton, Memoir of Sir George Grey, p. 74.

[21]Colonel Phipps to Prince Albert, April 10, 1848, RA Add. MSS C56 Item 21.

[22]Harris, Memoirs of an Ex-Minister, p. 225.

[23]Norman and Jeanne Mackenzie, Dickens: A Life, (Oxford 1979), p. 204.

[24]Leeds Mercury, April 15, 1848.

[25]Lord Lyttleton to Lady Lyttleton, n.d., RA Add. MSS C56 Item 31.

[26]David Cairns, ed., The Memoirs of Hector Berlioz (London 1969), p. 44.

[27]The Morning Chronicle recalled this phenomenon on May 3, 1848, p. 4.

[28]Ashley, Life of Palmerston, Vol. 1, pp. 93-4; J. P. T. Bury, "Great Britain and the Revolutions of 1848", in Francis Fejtö, ed., The Opening of an Era -- 1848: An Historical Symposium (London 1948, p. 186.

[29] Manchester Guardian, April 12, 1848, p. 4.

[30] The Times, April 8, 1848, p. 4.

[31] Weekly Dispatch, April 16, 1848, editorial, p. 193, quoting the Paris correspondent of The Times.

[32] Sir B. Hall to Dr. Meyer, April 11, 1848, RA Add MSS C56, Item 32.

[33] Colonel Phipps to Prince Albert, April 10, 1848, RA Add MSS C56, Item 21.

[34] Sir B. Hall to Dr. Meyer, April 11, 1848; Lord John Russell to Prince Albert, April 11, 1848, RA Add MSS C 56, Items 32 and 28. Morning Chronicle, May 3, 1848, p. 4.

[35] The account in various newspapers is corroborated by Frost, Forty Years' Recollections, p. 138. Also, Annual Register, April, 1848, p. 52.

[36] Report of J. W. Mayne and His Meeting with Feargus O'Connor, 11:45, April 10, 1848, H.O. 45/2410, Part 2, London.

[37] Frost, Forty Years' Recollections, p. 138.

[38] Annual Register, April, 1848, p. 52.

[39] Leeds Mercury, April 15, 1848, p. 4.

[40] The Times, April 11, 1848.

[41] Ashley, Life of Palmerston, Vol. 1, p. 80.

[42] Hodder, Life of Shaftesbury, p. 243.

[43] Weekly Dispatch, April 16, 1848, p. 184.

[44] Northern Star, April 15, 1848, p. 6.

[45] Frost, Forty Years' Recollections, p. 139; History of the Chartist Movement, Chapter X.

[46] Large, "London in the Year of Revolutions, 1848", p. 192.

[47] Police Report, April 10, 1848, 12:45 a.m., H.O. 45/2410, Part 2, London.

[48] The Times, April 11, 1848, p. 6.

[49] Accounts are in the Northern Star, April 15, 1848, p. 7, claiming police brutality; Weekly Register, April, 1848, p. 53; Frost, Forty Years' Recollections, pp. 140-1.

[50] George Grey to the Marquess of Salisbury, April 10, 1848, H.O. 41/19.

[51] Lord John Russell to the Queen, April 10, 1848, RA Add MSS C 56, Item 19.

CHAPTER IV

THE AFTERMATH

Relief, Euphoria and Congratulation

When the great day had come and gone peacefully
there was a great outpouring of relieved and congratulatory feelings from many quarters. The tension had
been so high that when it was removed many sailed into
euphoria. The Home Office papers contain sheafs of
jubilant letters from high and low. They repeat one
another: thanks were expressed to the government; the
day showed a great victory for the constitution, law
and order; the zeal of all classes was applauded.[1]

At the highest levels of government these feelings
freely flowed. Queen Victoria, who had been informed
of the outcome as early as 2:00 p.m. via telegraph,
wrote to Prince Leopold to laud the loyalty of the
people and declare that she thanked God that the Chartist meeting had turned out to be a complete failure.
The populace, she reported, was indignant over the way
their peace had been "interfered with" by "such wanton
and worthless men."[2] Soon thereafter Victoria heard
from the Dutchess of Kent, who assured the Queen that
the "happy result" of 10 April would have "a very
salutary effect" on the Continent.[3] Around the same
time Prince Albert wrote to Lord John Russell, congratulating him because 10 April "terminated gloriously for
England!"[4] The Queen and the Prince Consort declared
that they felt the "warmth of feeling" with which
people "rallied around the throne," and they were
"anxious...to acknowledge it, in some way."[5] Prince
Albert had received a note from Colonel Phipps, his
secretary, who was overjoyed at how London "magnifi-
cently" displayed "the power of loyalty and sound constitutional feeling...over any attempt at republican
demonstration." Phipps assured the Prince that the
Queen needed "no other protection" than the "steady
hands and willing spirits" that he had seen at work in
London that day.[6] Albert responded to Phipps by declaring: "What a glorious day...for England!... How
mightily will this tell all over the world."[7] Eventually Victoria was able to convey her sense of relief
and satisfaction in a speech from the throne. "The
strength of our institutions," she proclaimed, "has
been tried, and has not been found wanting." Under
them, her subjects were entitled to "the enjoyment of

that temperate freedom which they so justly value."
Her subjects knew the advantages of "order and security" and would not allow "the promoters of pillage and
confusion" any success with their "wicked designs."[8]

Sir George Grey's note to Wellington was more
reserved. After all, how else could one write to the
Iron Duke? Grey expressed his awareness that it was
"a matter of satisfaction" that the troops did not have
to see service.[9] Grey was less reserved in a printed
circular letter that went around to various participants on the side of authority. He told of his "grati-
fying duty" in informing the Queen about the "loyal and
constitutional spirit" of the "great body" of Londoners
during the "recent apprehensions of a disturbance of
the public peace."[10]

Grey was one of three public figures to have a
flood of congratulations wash over him. The other two
taking bows were Lord John Russell and the Duke of
Wellington. When Grey rose in the House of Commons, he
could not say a word because of the loud cheers. Lord
Broughton could recall nothing similar happening in all
of his experience in Parliament.[11] When the aged Iron
Duke appeared in the Lords, a similar ovation broke
out.[12] Lord and Lady John Russell had "visits and congratulations without end."[13] All three of these
"heroes of peace and order" were overwhelmed by messages from home and abroad.[14] Perhaps most touching
for Grey was a letter from his old tutor, who praised
his "prudence and firmness" which "changed our general
feeling of alarm and sad forebodings" into "confidence,
security and thankfulness."[15] Russell's "habitual self
confidence" was cited by others similarly.[16] Of course,
it is easier to be prudent, firm and self-confident
when you hold all of the powerful cards and have been
shown your opponents' hand. Contemporaries of the
three heroes of April 10 were not aware of the realities behind the situation. They were sure, as the Earl
of Malmesbury wrote, that "serious consequences would
have ensued" if the Duke and the government had not
taken their "extraordinary precautions."[17] In the end,
Russell took the lion's share of the credit for himself, by writing: "With the valuable aid and assistance of the Duke of Wellington, I reduced the Chartists
to insignificance."[18] Grey, for his part, acted like
an applauded conductor: he called upon the orchestra
to take a bow. In the Commons he stated that "nothing
could have been more praiseworthy or meritorious" than
the "spirit" and "cordial cooperation in the

maintenance of order and peace" on the part of "the great body of the population of the metropolis."[19]

In public and in private, the themes of joyous relief were sounded again and again. Amongst the people of property, hysterias of fear suddenly gave way to euphorias of self-congratulation. On the afternoon of the tenth, some were "full of glee" in announcing that it was "all over!"[20] They stressed class cooperation, the "zealous" manner in which all society, "from the highest peer to the humblest mechanic" participated in "the promotion of order."[21] Some in the House of Lords singled out the middle classes of London for special praise.[22] Many expressed their thanks that no clash had taken place, because, in the words of Lord Denman, "collisions" would have produced "angry feelings."[23] There was also some rather smug satisfaction that the right to petition had not been interfered with, a right which nonetheless must be exercised in a proper "constitutional manner."[24] Contankerous Colonel Sibthorp was not entirely happy that April 10 had come and gone so peacefully. He had wanted to see those Chartists intending to disturb the peace "dragged into and ducked" in the Thames. No, he "would not say drowned...." But he wanted them "sent home in their wet clothes as a punishment for their daring."[25]

God was thanked privately and publicly. Lady Charlotte Guest confided to her journal of her "gratitude to God for our present safety" when other nations were "in such an awful state of confusion and anarchy."[26] The Earl of Shaftesbury's diary contains the question, "How shall we sufficiently praise God...?" Shaftesbury had written, early on that fateful day: "We are in the hands of God.... 'Except the Lord keep the city, the watchman waketh but in vain.'" By nightfall, he exulted, "Surely the glory must be to Him 'who stilleth the raging of the sea, and the madness of the people.'"[27] The Earl of Arundel ascribed the deliverance similarly in the House of Commons, declaring that England owed its safety "not to an arm of flesh, or to any human wisdom and firmness, but to the blessing of Almighty God."[28] Once again, as so often in history, God was perceived on the side of the larger armed forces.

The press was filled with expressions of relief and congratulation simultaneously, serving to focus and to form public opinion about April 10 up and down the land. "A Te Deum of fervent gratitude to the great

129

Disposer of events rose from tens of thousands of
family altars," declared an editorial in the Leeds
Mercury, when it became clear that nobody was "mad...
enough to kindle the flames of civil strife." The
"unruffled tranquility" of April 10 was actually a
"more honorable and happier omen to England than many
victories." What the day showed was the "loyalty" of
Londoners in their "determination to put down" disturbers of the peace. Moreover, it was good to see
the government doing its duty with "equal wisdom,
temper and firmness."[29] The Manchester Guardian
extolled the virtues of the day in much the same tone,
noting how "all classes, from the nobility to the
honest workmen in the large establishments," had "vied
with each other" in defending British institutions and
the "good order of society."[30] The press also gave
publicity to the Poor Man's Friend Society's efforts
to raise a subscription "in deep gratitude to Almighty
God for his goodness in preserving...this realm from
the horrors of anarchy...."[31]

Shortly after the events of April's great demonstration, amid relief and congratulation, the meaning
and significance of the day was expounded far and wide.
For many, April 10 was one of the most glorious days in
English history.[32] The Manchester Guardian expected it
to produce "lasting and beneficial" effects "upon the
destinies and interests" of Britain.[33] The Times
expected April 10 to be "long remembered as a great
field day of the British Constitution," the day in
which the British Empire "had its share in the European
crisis."[34] The Prince Consort put the point tersely:
"We had our revolution yesterday and it ended in
smoke."[35] Many saw the day as more important than days
of glorious military victories.[36] England's ageing,
trenchant, forceful Foreign Secretary, Lord Palmerston,
coined a memorable phrase for April 10: It was the
"Waterloo of peace and order."[37]

What, specifically, had made this day such a
glorious Waterloo? British institutions, law and order
had all been safeguarded and confirmed as good. Yet
April 10 was particularly glorious, as the Manchester
Guardian put it, not so much because of the efforts of
the government, but through "the acts of the people."[38]
Clearly, the day had shown, according to the Leicester
Journal and The Times, "the confidence of the British
public in their existing institutions."[39] As Sir
George Grey wrote exultantly to the Lord Mayor of
London, they could rely upon the "loyal and zealous

cooperation" of the "great body" of London's inhabitants in "upholding the supremacy of the law."[40] Similarly, Lord John Russell assured the Queen that "the friends of law and order are inspired with fresh confidence" as a result of April 10.[41] Colonel Rowan, the Commissioner of the Metropolitan Police, felt the same way. He found it "difficult...to overestimate the good" that came from such a "display of loyalty and excellent feeling."[42] The Annual Register put its stamp on this view, thereby influencing countless historians. It declared that it was "not the troops, nor even the police" that "put down" the "dangerous assemblage." It was the "zealous and almost unanimous determination of all classes" that did it.[43]

The repetitiousness of emphasis on all classes was significant in itself. It was common to depict the defenders of British institutions as ranging "from the nobility to the honest workman."[44] The message was that all classes of Britons were on the same side on April 10.[48]

The revelation of the weakness of the Chartist revolutionary threat at the very height of their agitation was also greatly significant. According to Colonel Rowan, the Chartists had "done their utmost" to be formidable, and had met a "signal failure."[46] Blackwoods magazine intoned that "for the first time for a hundred and sixty years, Revolution [sic] walked our streets" but came to nothing.[47] The Leicester Journal pointed out how "provincial demagogues" had assured their "innocent dupes" that a revolution would be had "without fail before sunset."[48] For The Times, the "signal of unconstitutional menace, of violence, of insurrection, of revolution" was flashed in the streets on April 10, but it was "despised" by the "loyal metropolis." In short, when the Chartists and Confederates "fished for a revolution" they "caught a snub."[49] In actuality, the Chartist threat of revolution did not even exist on April 10 but this view comes only from historical research. It was not a view shared by contemporaries, with the exception of those at the centre of government.

In the immediate afterglow of triumph, the established press was not nearly as hostile to the Chartist cause as afterwards. The Times found the "main body" of Chartists "in general, peaceful subjects," but ardent radical reformers. Unfortunately, some belonged to a "gang of desperados" who knew "how easily...the

131

trick had been done" elsewhere.[50] The Leicester
Journal went so far as to declare the points of the
Charter "honest and allowable doctrines" and the
triumph of April 10 as not really a triumph over Chartism but over its violent fringe and the Dublin conspirators.[51] The Leeds Mercury called for reconciliation: "Let all resentment be forgot; let all idea of
carrying the Charter on a...revolutionary tide be
abandoned." Instead, "reasonable demands, met by
reasonable concessions" would improve British institutions.[52] The tone of the press was soon to change.

Much of the jubilation over 10 April came from
assessing its wholesome effects in all directions: on
the Chartists, the Irish and throughout Europe. A few
days after the event, George Grey noted the good
"general effect" anticipated for subsequent Chartist
meetings.[53] The Manchester Guardian remarked upon how
"marvelously chastened and subdued" Chartism seemed
after the "ridiculous failure of the London demonstration."[54] Palmerston expected the Chartists to "lie by
for the present" because they had seen most of London
arrayed against them,[55] and Greville found Chartists
"crestfallen" and "conscious of the contemptible figure
they cut." He wrote that "nobody cares" about their
forthcoming meetings and bluster.[56]

From Dublin reports came to Sir George Grey that
the events of April 10 would "throw a great damp" on
the activities of the Confederates.[57] Palmerston was
sure that "a good and calming effect" would result for
the "Sister Island."[58] Greville was sure also, and
added that April 10 would help to keep Smith O'Brien,
the firey patriot, in "doleful dumps."[59] Lady John
Russell admitted privately that Ireland was "the weight
that almost crushes John," so she hoped that "this
triumph of the good cause" would have a beneficial
effect on "unhappy, misguided Ireland."[60]

The significance of April 10 abroad was not a
point missed by contemporaries or by modern historians.
Lord John Russell stressed the point that British influence abroad would be heightened in a letter to the
Queen.[61] He soon received letters from Paris confirm-
ing this assumption. Lady Abercromby wrote to say that
"all eyes" had been "turned to London" with great
apprehension before April 10. Thereafter people seemed
"to breathe more freely" once they knew of the "good
sense and the good feelings" of British people. The
rest of the world had an "excellent example" of what

"constitutional government" really meant.[62] According to the Leicester Journal, foreigners "yet in the vortex of change" could look to stable England for inspiration.[63] Prince Albert hoped that the events of April 10 would be "read with advantage" on the Continent,[64] a point Greville felt assured about, according to the entry in his diary for April 13. Greville expected "a vast effect in all foreign countries" when Europeans realized "how solid" the British "foundation" was.[65] Two days later, after hearing from the British ambassador in Paris, Greville could exult that April 10 "has astonished and disappointed the French more than they care to admit...."[66]

The hindsight of historians has not altered this interpretation of the effects of April 10 abroad. Elie Halévy found the "confidence of the Parisian middle class" restored by it.[67] Raymond Postgate, in his dated and sketchy account of 1848, mentioned how revolutionary forces abroad had been marking time, waiting for England to proceed.[68] More recently, David Large noted how the event was calculated to raise British prestige abroad and wipe out impressions of "feebleness."[69]

From all of these reactions, it is clear that a great pendulum of feeling swung on April 10. Why did so many hysterical fears change in one day into a gush of congratulations amidst great trumpeting of national pride? Basically, the very height of the rejoicing indicated the depth of the fears. April 10 overcame the fear that the mysterious epidemic of revolution abroad would strike England. The release was sudden and seemingly total, hence the volatile reaction. David Large quotes The Times description of the "meteoric, unsteady condition of the public mind" in April,[70] and observes himself that nothing justified the "hysteria" because nothing was intended by the Chartists. But there was more to the situation than an unsteady public mind. Thrones that lasted for centuries were being toppled. Powerful figures such as Louis Philippe, Metternich and the King of Prussia were in flight or cowering. Hasty explanations of why revolution ran like a plague were not satisfying. The establishment had to witness what they perceived as the death of revolution in the streets of London before they could transmute their guilt and dread into soaring euphoria.

Harriet Martineau's sharp radical mind was able to see through the psychological realities of April's reactions. She recalled an aristocratic lady in her autobiography whose "strain of exultation" after April 10 struck her as "vulgar." Before the tenth, that same anonymous lady had written to her in a "terrible panic," imploring Miss Martineau to use her "power over the working classes" to "bring them to reason." Now, after Kennington Common, the lady was as insolent in her triumph, by gleefully belittling the Chartists, "as she had been abject when in fear...."[71]

Wealth, comfort, good food and amusement can lead to deep fear when these things are enjoyed while millions go hungry, especially at a time when the tricolor waved anew.

England Is Different

The events of April 10 seemed to confirm a deeply and resolutely held conviction about England: English history lay outside the patterns of European history. In short, England was different. This essential conviction had bolstered the morale of the middle and upper classes as the thrones of Europe collapsed during the time that the Chartists built their agitation to its culmination in April.

The established press had been filled with editorials evoking this theme of England's uniqueness all through March and early April. The Leeds Mercury stated the proposition in classic terms:

> England, of all the countries of Europe is the most secure against internal convulsion. She is so, not from the strength of her army, the business of her middle classes, or her happy insular position, but from the...freedom she already enjoys, and from that capacity for peaceful progress in improvement and reform.... She is so, further, from the solid sense and right feeling of her people....[72]

The Morning Chronicle saw the country's "foundations" so "deeply and broadly" laid that England could "defy the storms that howl around it."[73] The press spelled out specifics: Britain had a free press, the Continent fettered presses; the middle classes were loyal in Britain, whereas they were revolutionary on the

134

Continent because of unmet grievances.[74] Britain had ways to reform constitutionally, but Continental states did not. The very rights and liberties demanded by Continental revolutionaries in 1848 were rights already enjoyed in England, namely freedom of the press, the right of meeting and petitioning, popular representation, responsibility of ministers, taxation by representatives, religious liberty, free trade and trial by jury.[75]

While some "exasperation and suffering" amongst the English people was undeniable, there was no outrage from the "meanness and vices" of the monarch; no "venality in the ministers;" no "scandalous traffic... in the emoluments of office;" and no "debauchery and profligacy" in the aristocracy; and no "systematic corruption in the executive government...." These had been problems in the France of Louis Philippe.[76]

Above all, England was superior because the voice of the people prevailed, and not just the voice of a ruler.[77] Since the "community" was satisfied in England, alterations would come peacefully and not in the "hurricane of revolutions.[78] The very nature of the population was different also, more "calm, considerate and self-possessed" than Continental populations, and without their "morbid ferocity."[79]

Everywhere in England there were signs of peaceful progress, improvement and reform, so it would be "silly and wicked" to take to the barricades.[80] Despite some "ills" or "grievances", England was emphatically the "land of liberty", and, as the established press intoned, there was "no analogy" between Britain and the Continental states in 1848.[81]

When April 10 came and went, confirmation of this analysis was at hand.[82] England had experienced just "a slight wiff" of the "violent storm" that had burst upon Europe.[83] This is precisely why April 10 had such a profound psychological effect on the middle and upper classes, to say nothing of its effect on the writing of British history ever since.

These themes in the press were almost identical with sentiments freely expressed at the highest levels of government. The Prime Minister declared in Parliament that England "had no need to enter on any bloody or doubtful struggle" to gain improvements. England could rely upon "the constant and peaceful progress of

human affairs...towards perfection."[84] In his memoirs
Russell wrote that April 10 gave him "fresh proof that
the people of England were satisfied" with their government and "did not wish to be instructed by their
neighbors...." They could do without the "liberty"
enjoyed under Robbespierre and the "order" established
by Napoleon.[85] Behind this staunch Whig interpretation
of English history was a deep personal pride on
Russell's part. He had played a major role in both the
passing of the Reform Bill of 1832 and the repeal of
the Corn Laws in 1846. The events of 1848 seemed to
confirm the wisdom of these reforms.

Parliament was not short of Whigs, Tories and
radicals who shared his interpretations and went on to
stress their own particular viewpoints: The Marquess
of Northampton praised the spirit of the middle classes; Joseph Hume found the middle classes "peaceful and
fond of order;" R. H. Inglis praised the loyalty of
British troops; Molesworth observed how the people of
England were attached to their institutions because no
class was privileged at the expense of another since
the Corn Laws were swept away. Most of these points
were presented in tandem with comparisons between Britain and the Continental states.[86] Yet the message
throughout was the same: England was different and
England was better.

More than any other group, the special constables
of April 10 were singled out as the best example of why
this was so. They received the highest praise. They
had saved the day, and they were the people: militant,
armed, resolute, restrained and loyal. According to
The Times, they had volunteered "with great inconven-
ience and some little risk" in order to face "an
insulting threat of revolutionary violence." Every
peaceful citizen could be reassured by this fact.[87]
Palmerston expressed his zeal for them by telling how
"the streets were swarming with them...men of all classes and ranks blended together in defense of law and
property.[88] The Lord Mayor of London received the
congratulations of the Home Secretary, who praised the
"men of all classes" who had come forward with "promp-
titude and zeal." Their role, Grey wrote, "affords the
strongest ground for confidence in the maintenance of
public peace and order."[89] Numbers counted. The Times
compared its estimate of 150,000 special constables to
its estimate of 10,000 demonstrators and concluded that
those who were "disposed to bully and intimidate the
Legislature" by carrying "a pike against it" were

outnumbered by 15 to 1. The 15 were "picked and trustworthy men," truncheons at the ready, who "could procure vouchers to their respectability".[90] The Illustrated London News hailed their role as "the noble stand of the 'Army of Order'."[91] Sir Erskine May declared that "the assembling of this force...was the noblest example of the strength of a constitutional government to be found in history."[92] In Parliament, Grey praised them liberally, again stressing the theme of "all classes" as participants.[93] Little children even played at a game called 'specials'.[94] Finally, the Annual Register sanctified the theme for almost all future historians with the pronouncement that when disaffection arose, the "loyal and well-disposed" came forward and demonstrated support for the regime with their numbers.[95]

Charles Dickens would do no "special constabling" on April 10, because, as he wrote in private letters, "there was rather an epidemic in that wise abroad." Dickens perceived that behind the fears and rumors about Chartists, the government was out to "make the most of such things for their own purpose." The government knew "better than anybody" how "little vitality" there was in them.[96] Dickens nonetheless created the most famous reflection in literature of the theme that England was different. His Mr. Podsnap informed a foreign gentleman that the British constitution had been bestowed by Providence: "This island was blest, sir, to the direct exclusion of such other countries as...as there may happen to be."[97]

Another great figure of Victorian literature deserves mention because her response was so atypical. While George Eliot was fervently enthusiastic about the French Revolution, she had no hopes for any such movement in England because the British "working classes are eminently inferior" to the French. In Britain "selfish radicalism" and "brute sensuality" was the rule, in contrast to the "electrified" French minds. The "slow progress of political reform", inferior to revolution, "is all that we are fit for at present."[98]

No Chartist shared Eliot's strikingly unique opinions, but their response to the proposition that England was different from the Continent is remarkable in its own way. Most Chartists concurred with the proposition enthusiastically. Both mainstream Chartists behind O'Connor and moral force Chartists behind O'Brien, Lovett, Cooper, Hetherington or Watson, all refused to draw clear analogies between themselves and French revolutionaries largely because they, too, saw England as distinct and different from Continental states. This factor goes a long way in helping to explain why there was no large body of Chartist revolutionaries in 1848.

According to the Northern Star, England was different from the Continent because Englishmen could meet, speak their minds, enjoy a free press, and petition. Foreigners needed revolutions to gain these blessings, and that was precisely what 1848 was all about on the Continent.[99] Chartists noted how the French erected barricades, which "might be well enough" for France, but "they did not want them here", because they had a superior "moral power" in Britain that would triumph without the need for armed insurrection.[100] George Jacob Holyoake was sure that they could not do well at creating barricades anyway, because, unlike the Parisians, most Englishmen had not seen military service, and had no experience with arms.[101] But they did have many peaceful, progressive experiences through the use of freedom of speech and assembly that they could draw upon. This point was emphasized by William Lovett in appealing to the middle classes to grant the suffrage to British workers. Why should the populations of Germany, Austria and Prussia, "just freed from the reigns of despotism," have the new right to vote while advanced British workers were denied it?[102]

O'Connor and his lieutenants were in full accord with moral force Chartists on this point. In fact, it was impossible to tell how O'Connor differed from the Tories, Whigs, Liberals and radicals when he rose in the House of Commons to declare: "I am satisfied that among the mass there is a conviction that they enjoy a greater degree of rational liberty than is accorded to any other people in Europe...."[103] Of course, O'Connor's hopes for the future in 1848 were all tied up with the Land Plan. This scheme was "a good solid system," the first "in the history of nations," and it was operable in England because workers used their freedom of speech and public meeting.[104] Men in other countries "were not so much prepared to use their liberty as the English."[105]

Ernest Jones also found British workers superior. They were sound political economists and social reformers, who were seeking power through the Charter as a means to an end. Therefore, "revolution has no terror

here, and life and property will be secure."[105] Peter
Murray McDouall used his leader's own words when he
declared that the working people of England "were the
best instructed people in politics in the world."[107]

The point that British workers were superior to
French workers was carried in the established press as
well. For example, the Morning Chronicle observed that
"the simplest doctrines of political economy are
unknown" amongst French workers, which was certainly
not the case amongst the "higher order of mechanics in
England and Scotland."[108] The Chartist Executive
wanted this point stressed as much as possible, in
order to get away from their identification with French
revolutionists, an identification that many in power
undoubtedly found useful. French revolutionists, Chartists maintained, were unlike them. French workers
were violent because they did not have the "political
education" enjoyed by all of those peaceful, mature
British workers.[109]

A few dissenting voices rose from Chartist ranks
to deny this emphasis. A letter in the Northern Star
complained that from reading many newspapers "one would
be apt to think that the French had everything to
struggle for, and we nothing." The writer went on to
complain of job discrimination, punishment for sedition,
and other limitations on freedom of speech.[110] The
Star also published commentaries on the French Revolution by William Howitt, who admitted that there indeed
were differences between France and England, notably
that the government left the "safety valve of popular
complaint" open in Britain, so that British democrats
could "throw off [their] wrath in talk and newspaper
declamation" while the oppressors could go on burdening
them.[111]

Such dissent was exceptional. Moral force Chartism and O'Connorite Chartism was at one with the
establishment in proclaiming that England was different.

Ridicule

The nasty side of the feelings of relief, congratulation and euphoria soon revealed itself in the form
of ridicule. The great Chartist petition was scalded
with ridicule in and out of the House of Commons, and

this, as much as anything else, devastated the spirit of Chartists in 1848.

A select committee of the House of Commons reported that out of the 5,706,000 signatures, only 1,975,496 were genuine. Thirteen clerks worked on it for more than 17 hours to arrive at the conclusion that 3,730,504 signatures were bogus. To this day, the method of counting and how they determined what was genuine remains a mystery. Even the weight was called into question. Chartists boasted of a five ton petition, but it only turned out to be five hundred-weight.[112] Unfortunately for historians enamored with the powers of the computer, the 1848 petition was quickly destroyed.

Popular graffiti had left its sad scars. Victorian clerks would never repeat what the Weekly Dispatch called the "obscene and disgusting words,...the very coarsest words, of the most vulgar and disgraceful meaning" that they found "in most unholy abundance, along with "cant phrases and gross ribaldry.[113] The Times had visions of tribes of men named "pugnose... longnose...flatnose...snooks...and Fubbs."[114] Several signed it "no cheese," but Punch thought "no bread" would have been a more truthful signature.[115] Famous people had their names forged: the Duke of Wellington 19 times; Colonel Sibthrop at least a dozen times; Lord John Russell, Sir Robert Peel, the Queen, and Prince Albert appeared frequently among many other well known names.[116] Only one of the reputed signers, irascible Colonel Sibthorp, rose in Parliament to deny his adherence by saying: "I should be one of the last to disgrace my family, myself, and the constituency" by signing.[117]

One angry member of the select committee, Cripps, took it upon himself to expose the petition to ridicule in the House of Commons, and thereby set the tone for society and the press. Cripps called it a "ribald mass of obscenity and impiety," with "disgusting" language throughout, having words at which "the vilest strumpet in the street would blush to name." It was a disgrace and could never be read in the House. Cripps regretted that such "blasphemy and obscenity" had caused the government so much "uneasiness" and "expense."[118]

Heavy attacks bore down upon O'Connor, the petition's only champion in the House. He tried to deny the committee's findings, saying that he did not believe that 13 clerks could have counted the signatures in that time, and suggesting that enemies of the popular cause had forged signatures. In a more feeble argument, he asked how it was possible for him "in the nature of things" to examine the petition beforehand. He had never seen any part of it until he observed the sheets rolled up in the House of Commons.[119]

These remarks drew a rejoinder from Hume, who was ordinarily a radical ally of the popular cause in the House of Commons. He maintained that every member was responsible for the petitions he presented, and the reprehensible scene before them "discredits the right of petitioning."[120] Hume had a point. O'Connor should have diverted at least some of the executive energies of the Chartist organization to checking signatures before submitting the petition. Here, anyway, it is impossible to defend his leadership.

O'Connor's clash with Cripps was severe. At one point Cripps said he was more than willing to "throw ridicule and obloquy upon the hon. Gentleman who presented it." This was too much for O'Connor, who abruptly left the House, cryptically remarking that he would have the matter "explained elsewhere."[121] Cripps received a challenge to a duel, and this was too much for the House. Both men were scolded for their intemperateness, and both yielded to the desires of other Members to smooth the matter out. For a brief time in this imbroglio, O'Connor was subject to arrest because he was ordered to the House by the Speaker in order to forestall any violence between the men.

All of this went on three days after the Kennington Common meeting, and indicates how highly pitched emotions were on all sides. In this atmosphere, the question of how the petition had gotten millions of false signatures began to find answers. Lord John Russell thought it was "obvious at a glance" that "large strings of names" had been written by one person.[122] Cripps offered evidence that people were paid to sign, and that many women had signed, at the rate of 8,200 for every 100,000 names.[123] These revelations in Parliament were amplified by letters that poured into the Home Office. One informant declared that Land Company shareholders were signed up automatically, including men "who do not even know what it means."[124] One minister wrote that nearly all of his politically inactive parishioners signed, despite the fact that none of them appeared to be Chartists. What

happened was that two Chartist emmisaries had arrived
in the parish, informing the inhabitants that they were
collecting names for a petition "to get men more work
and food." Men, women, children and even babies were
signed up.[125] Tradesmen reported that their shop boys
signed it, and not necessarily once. One of them was
especially insistent that the public mind and foreign
nations be "disabused" of the Chartists' numerical
boasts.[126] One notorious center for forging signatures
was a shoemaker's shop in Manchester. There, on the
open pages of the petition, were the names of the local
Anglican incumbent and several respectable tradesmen,
who "would as soon have thought of signing their own
death warrants as such a petition." For good measure,
some dead men's names and emigrants' names were added
as well.[127] In some places intimidation had been at
play. A workman reported to the Home Office that
"hundreds of persons" had signed the petition in Mansfield out of fear. He wrote that he himself had been
"threatened with death" for refusing to sign.[128]

Chartists themselves looked for the causes of the
false signatures. The printer of the Northern Star
said that many were the work of "idle boys." One of
the lads in his shop admitted signing it every time he
passed a place where it was available, declaring:
"Wasn't it a jolly lark?"[129] More widespread were the
accusations that the "enemies of the people" and paid
police agents had sedulously undermined the voice of
the people by their wicked espionage. Richard Pilling,
a Manchester Chartist leader, suggested that the government clerks themselves had forged the silly signatures.[130]

Chartists defended their petition as best they
could amidst the roars of scornful laughter. Chartist
groups from various localities protested that at least
their segments of the whole were substantially genuine.
Ernest Jones maintained that notwithstanding the
exposé, the document was "an important manifestation of
the public feeling."[131] Indeed it was, particularly
when population figures are brought into play. One of
the criticisms that Cripps had raised in the House was
that all the males in England above 15 did not exceed
seven million. This point can be turned against the
government's case easily, for even if there were only
1,975,496 bona fide signers, this sum was at least
twice the electorate of the House of Commons.[132] This
very respectable sum was more than that received in
the great petition of 1839 and almost two-thirds of

the number on the 1842 petition, and neither of the
two previous petitions received such scrutiny.[133] The
sympathetic Nonconformist put the Chartists' case succinctly: "After every reduction" had been made, the
remaining signatures were "sufficiently numerous" to
warrant the "respectful consideration of Parliament."[134]
These signatures did tap and display the vast reserves
of disaffection in England in 1847-8, as well as the
strength of faith in democracy, no matter how hard the
petition's critics tried to laugh it out of existence.

Ridicule gave polite society an excuse to dismiss
the whole petition at one fell swoop, despite the
almost two million genuine signatures. The Prime Minister did so, expressing his hopes that people would no
longer "be gulled by the leaders of...[the]...Conven-
tion" who had "so grossly deceived them." These men
were, after all, "false to the country, traitors to the
Queen and rebels to their God...."[135] Greville
recorded in his gossipy diaries that "ridicule and disgrace" now enveloped all of the Chartist movement.[136]
This was true, because the press carried the theme with
a vengeance. The Weekly Dispatch was most bitter in
its denunciations: The "ferocious monster" of a petition turned out to be nothing but a "scarecrow" once
its "rags and mask" had been stripped away.[137] With
all the "forgeries, nicknames and obscenities" affixed,
"fraud, fabrication and humbug" had been meted out to
the Chartist Convention, who in turn "had the impudence
to palm such a cheat on the public...." Such "swind-
ling practices" degraded the cause of the people.[138]

Like the petition, Feargus O'Connor was a prime
target for ridicule. The story of Feargus O'Connor as
the frightened, pale, cowardly, cringing, overawed
Irish bufoon spread. The version enshrined in the
Annual Register has been picked up by many historians.

How did it originate? Certainly O'Connor's physical condition and the strain of the situation played
its legitimate part. The sharp snap back from fear on
the part of the upper and middle classes played a part
also, because when we are fearful of something unneces-
sarily, we are apt to mock and ridicule the person or
thing that formerly frightened us. Many were hysteric-
ally fearful of what the Chartists would do, or would
blunder into in April 10. When it was all over, there
stood Feargus O'Connor as a target for ridicule,
because human fears, as well as human hopes, are so
easily personified. Many possibly projected their own

self-ridicule at being so alarmed over nothing out at O'Connor. In other words, ridiculing him relieved the unconscious need for self-ridicule, if that is not too much of a digression into the realms of psychohistory.

Besides, frightened Feargus, the cowardly lion, made a good story. Good stories gain something in the telling, as any veteran of the pubs of Dublin knows. By the time the tale got to the Earl of Malmsbury's memoirs, O'Connor was "pale as ashes" and "trembling from head to foot" when he spoke to Commissioner Mayne. When he learned of the government's plans, according to Malmsbury, O'Connor gushed with relief, saying, "in a delighted tone", that Mayne was his "best friend". O'Connor tried to grasp Mayne's hand, declaring: "I'll do anything you like." Malmsbury wrote that he then turned to Chartists nearby and shouted: "Fools! I always said you were fools...you are a parcel of fools. Mr. Mayne is the best friend I have in the world." Malmesbury concluded that this was all a "ridiculous exhibition."139 Actually, it was a ridiculous account, but it became a common one.

O'Connor the buffoon emerged from story after story by relieved contemporaries. Lord Palmerston passed on his own variation: "Feargus was frightened out of his wits and was made the happiest man in England at being told that the procession could not pass the bridges."140 Greville added flourishes to the scene of O'Connor calling on Grey at the Home Office after the meeting: O'Connor thanked the government for its "leniency" and said that the Convention would not have been as lenient if it had "gotten the upper hand." O'Connor also said, in Greville's tale, that he was not going back to the Chartist meeting because "he had his toes trodden on till he was lame, and his pocket picked...."141 Lady John Russell told how that "abject blusterer" came "pale and haggard and almost crying" to speak with Grey.142 Her husband retold the tale of O'Connor calling his followers fools in his recollections, but this time O'Connor was purported to have made the declaration at the van, when confronted with the policeman's summons, and not near the tavern, after meeting with Mayne.143 O'Connor's version, presented in the House, was that he feared the people would molest the policeman who came for him, and so he said that he would "knock down the first man that touched" the officer, and bade them "give the policeman plenty of room." The House jeered at his account.144

No holds were barred in vituperating O'Connor
after April 10. To the Duke of Argyll, he was the
"vapouring fool" who "flinched."[145] John Arthur Roebuck, a radical, said the Chartists "have made a pretty
hash of it. Feargus O'Connor is a rogue, a liar and a
coward -- a precious compound!"[146]

This vituperation, and these stories, so laced
with abuse, ridicule and the hilarity that follows
release from anxiety, made the image of O'Connor at
Kennington Common for history. The image is part of
what John Saville has called the "absurd lumber to be
got rid of" in thinking about 1848 in England.[147]

O'Connor needs to be defended. First of all, he
was sick and worn out before the meeting. Why should
he not look pale? Secondly, he sealed a bargain with
Commissioner Mayne with a handshake, a perfectly normal
thing to do, but which has been seen as groveling
eagerness to submit to authority. Third, he did have
a bargain: the police wanted no meeting and no procession originally. Feargus got his meeting and the
police got an agreement for no procession. Here was
another compromise in English history, something that
was not simply a victory for authority as it is all too
commonly presented. Fourth, under the circumstances,
what was wrong with being frightened? O'Connor knew
some of the more militant Chartists and he knew the
kinds of ruffians that hung about any large London
meetings. Everywhere around these potentially volatile
elements, anonymous in the crowd, the government had
poured its precautionary might. A spark could produce
a death-dealing explosion. Some victories for democracy came from such explosions on the Continent, temporarily, at least, but corpses came from them too.
Besides, there was a very real possibility that one of
the corpses might be that of a particularly large Irish
gentleman. The innocent, unarmed throng on the common,
many of them females, some of them children, were
candidates for slaughter as well. Peterloo was just 29
years before 1848. O'Connor had sense enough to see
that the government's preparations boded hideous violence for these people should they be unleashed. Must
this man be mocked through the ages because he had
fear? Under such circumstances, fear was the health-
iest and most sanest emotion to have.

Moreover, from his brawls and battles in politics,
when he used words and when he used his fists, we know
that O'Connor was not a coward. Remember that when

145

insulted by Cripps, his response was to challenge
Cripps to a duel. Besides being archaic, duels were
dangerous, and cowards did not invite them. What is
more, he would never have been trusted, followed and
admired by millions of British workers for so long if
he had been as cowardly as he was described in polite
society and the established press.

Above all, what did he expect to get out of the
whole show on April 10? Certainly not revolution, and
not even the Charter. Commissioner Mayne did not
frighten him out of the planned procession when they
met near Horne Tavern, a story that has made the rounds
ever since. O'Connor had sense enough to know that it
was too dangerous to proceed, had already given up the
plans to proceed, and was sincerely grateful to have
the police flatly forbid what he did not want to
happen. He had told the convention in the morning that
if the police forbad it, he would not try it.

So the day was a victory in a sense for Feargus
O'Connor, just as it was for the authorities. Both he
and the authorities were determined to curb Chartist
violence, to avoid bloodshed and protect property.
Where they differed was over holding the meeting, and
in this O'Connor had his way.

Myths Take Shape

O'Connor's version of his role on April 10
appeared in the Northern Star for the rest of the
spring. It stressed his own personal danger and the
dangers of the tense situation on the common, where a
single policeman in disguise or a footpad could have
caused a row and unleashed all of the forces of authority against the unarmed Chartists. O'Connor emphasized
that Chartists had gained a victory on April 10 by
defiantly holding their meeting and focusing the attention of the whole nation on the Charter. For a time,
"men and women and children of all ranks" talked constantly "about the Charter and the Charter only." He
claimed great credit for himself "that no blood was
shed."[148]

He got some credit elsewhere as well, in the first
flush of relief after April 10, before the tales of
O'Connor the frightened buffoon spread from society to
all of the established press. The Leeds Mercury com-
mended his "prudence" and "energetic employment of his

146

influence" in keeping the Chartists "out of harm's
way" by getting them to abandon the procession. The
Mercury believed that if Jones or Harney had been in
charge instead of O'Connor, "the streets of London
might have been deluged with blood."[149] Even the
Weekly Dispatch wrote positively of his leadership on
that day,[150] and the Illustrated London News praised
his "discretion."[151]

Many Chartists went along with his interpretation of April 10, to the extent that they addressed a
"Memorial of Congratulation" to him for preventing the
"slaughter of unarmed multitudes."[152] The fact that
violence had not broken out, despite the scene at
Blackfriars Bridge, became the basis of a Chartist
celebration of April 10 as something of a victory.
Many had their own myth of April 10 at play, which saw
the government planning a massacre. As William Dixon
assured the Convention the very next day, "the foul and
infamous government" had intended, "on the slightest
pretext" to "shed the blood of an unoffending
people."[153] Even Chartists who did not suspect the
government of such sinister plans felt that a victory
had been gained by avoiding a collision while maintaining a "bold front."[154] As Ernest Jones put it, the
government's display of force had "afforded Chartists
the opportunity of displaying...their courage,...their
self-command,...and...their love of peace and order.
..."[155] John West was convinced that the Chartists had
"awed" the Whigs.[156] Chartists outside of the metropolis picked up the theme: James Leach in Macclesfield
declared that if London's Chartist leaders "had been a
hair-brained [sic] set of men, London would...have been
a scene of bloodshed."[157] A Glasgow Chartist called it
"a great, glorious but bloodless victory...."[158]

Some members of the Convention were not so sure on
April 11. A long discussion "of a very warm character"
ensued, wherein some militants registered their dis-
approval. But a majority of the delegates supported
the "prudential proceedings" of their leaders on April
10, and embodied these sentiments in an address to the
people of Britain, drafted by Ernest Jones. "The first
victory is gained!", it announced, because "the courage
of the men of London" had been "tested". It went on to
call for more efforts, in a rather strained tone.[159]

The peacefulness of the Chartists and the powerful
preparations of the government on April 10 are incon-
trovertible facts. But did the latter cause the

147

former? In other words, would the Chartists have been peaceful if the government had not prepared for conflict so overwhelmingly? The Chartists said yes, emphatically. The preparations were unnecessary. The Nonconformist took their side, insisting that they "would have shrunk from the use of physical force" even if their success had been probable.[160] The government said no, equally emphatically. The Duke of Wellington clearly stated the government's view a few days after the event in the house of Lords. He duly noted how large numbers of persons met and dispersed without "the exercise of force" on April 10, but stressed that this was not "out of submission to the law." It was submission to force:

> Was not the whole population of the town, civil as well as military, under arms? Were there not several hundred thousand persons embodied as constables?...Were there not thousands of troops under arms? and were there not thousands of police in readiness to act if need be? Can it be said, then, that it was respect for the law which prevented any outrage being committed by these persons?[161]

Going beyond the key question of whether the preparations were necessary at all, were they necessary on such a gigantic scale? Before and after the confrontation, a curious suspicion lingered that the government had overprepared. Seeing all of it going on around him on April 9, Greville remarked, "It is either very sublime or very ridiculous."[162] After the event, polite society found it to be the former extreme and Chartists the latter. O'Connor wondered why the authorities should take all the credit since he had the Convention accept his recommendation that the procession should not pass over the bridges. He saw that as the crucial decision of the day.[163] On the morning after, Gladstone's secretary, Sir Stafford Northcote, was also somewhat uneasy about all of the preparations as the muskets and bayonets in his office were being taken away. But, he concluded, "it was better to err on the side of over caution."[164] An article in Fraser's Magazine noted sarcastically that with all the preparations made against the Chartists, they must be "too formidable to be any longer put beyond the pale of political discussion." The article went on to observe that Wellington "made his depositions about as he would have done for a city in a state of seige", and that

these preparations themselves created alarm.165 This
point was brought up in the House of Commons also, when
Hume declared that the preparations "only had the
effect of creating an alarm which was altogether unnecessary."166

Grey met the criticisms of governmental overpreparation in Parliament by maintaining that doing it
openly "gave confidence to the loyal" and "struck with
terror" those who "might have been disposed to create
confusion."167 Grey was undoubtedly encouraged to face
his critics by a private letter from his old tutor, who
quoted Captain Cook saying that "Preventive measures
are always invidious, because when most successful their
necessity is least apparent."168 Grey was backed by
The Times, which seemed to sense some uneasiness at the
disproportion between cause and effect. An editorial
carefully listed the dangers of conflagration on the
tenth, in order "to justify preparation," and explained
that the government had resolved to be "on the safe
side." While this policy risked a "degree of ridicule,"
it would have a great "moral effect" for all of
Europe.169

Knowing that the government were not in a state of
alarm themselves, these indications of contemporary
awareness of overpreparation point to an interesting
conclusion: To a considerable degree, massive preparations were intended to gain a public relations victory
at home and influence abroad. The government was
highly successful in this, at the expense of tens of
thousands of unarmed, peaceful Chartists.

The government was helped by the swiftly spread-
ing standard myth of April 10. A word was applied to
the Chartist demonstration that has stuck until the
present day: It was a "fiasco". Greville stated it
succinctly: He rejoiced that a great "defensive
demonstration" had taken place, and that a "memorable
lesson" had been given to the "disaffected" as well as
to the "loyal" at home, and to the whole world beyond.
Faced with it, the Chartist demonstration became a
"ludicrous farce." April 10 demonstrated for all time
that when "sedition and rebellion hold up their heads
in this country, they will instantly be met with the
most vigorous resistance."170

A vigorous chorus of scorn and derision underlined
the standard myth. To Justin McCarthy, the Chartist
demonstration was "utterly ridiculous."171 To the Earl

149

of Malmesbury it was "very absurd."[172] Matthew Arnold
wrote of how the "braggarts...gave up at once...at
seeing the preparations...."[173] James Burn wrote of
the "intended émeute" being "as contemptible as its
leaders."[174]

In politics the most savage attacks often come
from close quarters, as any veteran of left wing or
right wing or church politics is apt to recognize.
For the Chartists, the bitterness of the radical Weekly
Dispatch over April 10 was exceptional. It depicted
Chartism's "fire eating heroes" sneaking out of their
procession "without so much as looking a policeman in
the face..." after they had vowed to spill their blood,
to be shot at the head of the procession and "shed the
last drop of their blood in their Land Company's adver-
tising van."[175] Rather than "die on the floor of the
House, Feargus O'Connor has preferred to snore out its
debates on the benches."[176] Parisian demonstrations
were a "subject of thrilling emotion," but Chartist
demonstrations "fell flat as humbugs."[177] What, after
all, had the Convention done, besides aim at a "chaotic
demonstration of drums, trumpets and thunder?" Did
they work for proper voter registration? What had all
of their assemblies and activities ended in but "banners, beer and bluster, flags, folly and fustian, meetings, musterings, marching and dispersion?"[178]
O'Connor, Harney and Jones had "spoiled Chartism," and
"ruined it," so no matter how they tried to "vamp it
up". Henceforth, "anything that smells of Chartism
positively stinks in the nostrils of men."[179] For the
time being, Chartism had "sunk below the privilege of
discussion."[180]

Some Chartists were overwhelmed by the onslaught
of the myth of April 10 and dropped out of the movement. Some vowed to be peaceful no longer and looked
for weapons. Still others sought collaboration with
the powerful and influential middle classes. A large
number tried to continue on and keep up the momentum of
agitation in mainstream Chartism. Probably all of them
were more cynical after April 10, in the same spirit as
that of a Leeds Chartist who learned that churchmen
were preparing prayers of thanksgiving that all had
passed off quietly on the tenth: "If the people had
been slain by thousands and hundreds of thousands...the
Church would have prepared a prayer thanking God that
they had been able to put them down."[181]

The National Convention, in their address to the men of London in early April, predicted that "the tenth of April shall be a day memorable in the annals of political agitation."[182] Indeed it was, but not in the way that they had imagined.

NOTES TO CHAPTER IV

[1]Many letters are in H.O. 41/26, 41/19.

[2]Queen Victoria to Prince Leopold, April 11, 1848, RA Add. MSS Y 93/27.

[3]Dutchess of Kent to Queen Victoria, RA Add. MSS Z 129/124.

[4]Prince Albert to Lord John Russell, RA Add. MSS C 16/49.

[5]Prince Albert to Lord John Russell, RA Add. MSS C 16/50.

[6]Colonel Phipps to Prince Albert, April 10, 1848, RA Add. MSS C 56, Item 21.

[7]Martin, Life of the Prince Consort, p. 34.

[8]Creighton, Memoir of Sir George Grey, p. 74.

[9]George Grey to the Duke of Wellington, April 12, 1848, H.O. 45/2410, London.

[10]Printed circular letter of George Grey, April 12, 1848, H.O. 45/2410, London.

[11]Hobhouse, Recollections of a Long Life, Vol. 6, p. 216. He wrote that Grey was cheered "as if we owed our safety to him."

[12]The Times, April 11, 1848, p. 6.

[13]Walpole, The Life of Lord John Russell, Vol. 2, p. 69. McCarthy and Russell, Lady John Russell, p. 99.

[14]Gooch, The Later Correspondence of Lord John Russell, contains many such letters.

[15]Letter from Rev. J. Endell Tyler, M. Creighton, Memoir of Sir George Grey, p. 74.

[16]Gooch, The Later Correspondence of Lord John Russell, p. xxiii.

[17]Harris, Memoirs of an Ex-Minister, p. 226.

[18] Russell, Recollections and Suggestions, p. 423.

[19] Hansard, Parliamentary Debates, Third Series, Vol. 98, p. 165.

[20] Hobhouse, Recollections of a Long Life, p. 216.

[21] Greville, The Greville Memoirs, Vol. 6, p. 169; Harris, Memoirs of an Ex-Minister, p. 226.

[22] Hansard, Parliamentary Debates, Third Series, Vol. 98, p. 72, speech of the Marquess of Northampton.

[23] Hansard, Parliamentary Debates, Third Series, Vol. 98, p. 279.

[24] Hansard, Parliamentary Debates, Third Series, Vol. 98, p. 70.

[25] Hansard, Parliamentary Debates, Third Series, Vol. 98, p. 158.

[26] Bessborough, Lady Charlotte Guest, p. 210.

[27] Hodder, Life of Shaftesbury, Vol. 2, pp. 242-3.

[28] Hansard, Parliamentary Debates, Third Series, Vol. 98, p. 290.

[29] Leeds Mercury, April 15, 1848, p. 4.

[30] Manchester Guardian, April 12, 1848, p. 4.

[31] Poor Man's Friend Society Circular for Private Circulation, RA Add. MSS C 56, Item 47.

[32] For example, the letter of Sir B. Hall to Dr. Meyer, April 11, 1848, RA Add. MSS C 56, Item 32.

[33] Manchester Guardian, April 12, 1848, p. 4.

[34] The Times, April 11, 1848, editorial.

[35] Martin, The Life of the Prince Consort, p. 34.

[36] Hobhouse, Recollections of a Long Life, p. 217, quoting Lionel Rothschild.

[37] Ashley, Life of Palmerston, Vol. 1, p. 93, quoting Palmerston to Normanby, April 11, 1848.

[38] Manchester Guardian, April 12, 1848, p. 4; also the Leeds Mercury, April 15, 1848, p. 4.

[39] Leicester Journal, April 14, 1848, p. 4; The Times, April 11, 1848, editorial.

[40] Sir George Grey to the Lord Mayor of London, April 17, 1848, H.O. 41/26.

[41] Lord John Russell to Queen Victoria, April, 1848, RA Add. MSS D 17/60.

[42] Colonel C. Rowan to General Bowles, April 11, 1848, RA Add. MSS C 56, Item 30.

[43] Annual Register, April, 1848, p. 53.

[44] Manchester Guardian, April 8, 1848, p. 6.

[45] For examples, Sir B. Hall to Dr. Meyer, April 11, 1848, RA Add. MSS C 56, Item 32.

[46] Colonel Rowan to General Bowles, April 11, 1848, RA Add. MSS C 56, Item 30.

[47] Blackwoods Edinburgh Magazine, June, 1848, p. 654.

[48] Leicester Journal, April 14, 1848, p. 4.

[49] The Times, April 11, 1848, editorial.

[50] The Times, April 15, 1848, p. 4; April 11, 1848, editorial.

[51] Leicester Journal, April 14, 1848, p. 4.

[52] Leeds Mercury, April 15, 1848, p. 4.

[53] Sir George Grey to Prince Albert, April 13, 1848, RA Add MSS C 56, Item 34.

[54] Manchester Guardian, April 15, 1848.

[55] Ashley, Life of Lord Palmerston, Vol. 1, p. 93, Palmerston to Normanby, April 11, 1848.

[56] Greville, The Greville Memoirs, Vol. 6, p. 170.

[57] T. B. Horsfall to Sir George Grey, April 12, 1848, RA Add MSS C 56, Item 37. Also Sir R. Routh to C. E. Trevelyan, Dublin, April 12, 1848, claiming that April 10 had an "excellent effect" in Dublin. Russell Papers, P.R.O. 30/22 7B.

[58] Ashley, Life of Lord Palmerston, Vol. 1, p. 93, Palmerston to Normanby, April 11, 1848.

[59] Greville, The Greville Memoirs, Vol. 6, p. 170.

[60] McCarthy and Russell, Lady John Russell, p. 99, Lady John Russell to Lady Mary Abercromby, April 13, 1848.

[61] Lord John Russell to Queen Victoria, April 10, 1848, RA Add. MSS C 56, Item 19.

[62] Lady Mary Abercromby to Lord John Russell, Turin, April 19, 1848; also Michael Chevalier to G. R. Partu, April 16, 1848, Russell Papers, P.R.O. 30/22 &B.

[63] Leicester Journal, April 14, 1848. Also, Manchester Guardian, April 12, 1848, p. 4; Identical phrases were in The Times editorial for April 11.

[64] Martin, Life of the Prince Consort, p. 34.

[65] Greville, The Greville Memoirs, Vol. 6, p. 169.

[66] Greville, The Greville Memoirs, Vol. 6, p. 170.

[67] Elie Halevy, A History of the English People in the Nineteenth Century, Vol. 4, Victorian Years, 1841-1895 (London 1951 ed.), pp. 246-7.

[68] Postgate, Story of a Year: 1848, p. 107.

[69] Large, "London in the Year of Revolutions, 1848", p. 187.

[70] Large, "London in the Year of Revolutions, 1848", p. 187. He quotes The Times of April 12, 1848.

[71] Maria Weston Chapman, ed., Harriet Martineau's Autobiography, Vol. 2 (London 1877, p. 297, 299-300.

[72] Leeds Mercury, April 8, 1848, p. 4.

[73] Morning Chronicle, February 29, 1848, p. 5.

[74] Morning Chronicle, March 27, 1848, p. 4 and April 7, 1848, p. 4.

[75] Leeds Mercury, April 8, 1848, p. 4; Morning Chronicle, April 3, 1848, p. 4; Liverpool Journal, March 18, 1848, p. 2, col. 5; [Mary Atkinson Maurice] "The Chartist's Friend," by the Author of 'Aids to Development', (London, B. Wertheim, Aldine Chambers, 1848), p. 10.

[76] Illustrated London News, April 1, 1848, p. 207.

[77] Glasgow Examiner, March 25, 1848.

[78] Liverpool Journal, March 18, 1848, p. 2.

[79] Leeds Times, March 18, 1848, p. 4; Similar sentiments in the Leeds Mercury led to praise of the "solid sense" and "right feeling" of Britons. (April 8, 1848, p. 4.)

[80] Leeds Mercury, April 8, 1848, p. 4; Lloyd's Weekly London Newspaper, March 26, 1848, p. 7.

[81] Glasgow Examiner, March 25, 1848.

[82] For a few examples of the many statements of confirmation, Staffordshire Mercury, April 15, p. 3; The Newcastle Chronicle, April 14, 1848, p. 4.

[83] Illustrated London News, April 15, 1848, p. 164.

[84] Hansard, Parliamentary Debates, Third Series, Vol. 98, p. 58.

[85] Russell, Recollections and Suggestions, pp. 254-5.

[86] Hansard, Parliamentary Debates, Third Series, Vol. 98, pp. 72, 93, 290; Vol. 97, p. 1174. See also the letter of the Duke of Bedford to Russell, quoted in Walpole, The Life of Lord John Russell, Vol. 2, p. 70; a letter from the Prince Consort to his stepmother, June 7, 1848, quoted in Martin, The Life of the Prince Consort, p. 75.

[87] The Times, April 5, 1848, p. 4.

[88] Ashley, The Life of Viscount Palmerston, Vol. 1, p. 80.

[89] Sir George Grey to the Lord Mayor of London, April 13, 1848, H.O. 41/26.

[90] The Times, April 11, 1848, editorial.

[91] Illustrated London News, April 15, 1848, p. 244.

[92] Creighton, Memoir of Sir George Grey, p. 68.

[93] Hansard, Parliamentary Debates, Third Series, Vol. 97, p. 460.

[94] Anon., "A Letter from one of the Special Constables...", p. 1.

[95] Annual Register, April, 1848, p. 59.

[96] Norman and Jeanne Mackenzie, Dickens: A Life (Oxford 1979), p. 204.

[97] Quoted in a similar context by F. B. Smith, "The View from Britain I, Tumults Abroad, Stability at Home", in Eugene Kamenka and F. B. Smith, eds., Intellectuals and Revolution: Socialism and the Experience of 1848 (London 1979), p. 120.

[98] Gordon S. Haigt, The George Eliot Letters, Vol. 1, p. 254, quoting a letter of George Eliot to John Sibree, March 8, 1848.

[99] Northern Star, February 26, 1848, p. 1, O'Connor's editorial; March 11, 1848, speech of Doyle at the Clerkenwell Green meeting; May 20, 1848, p. 1, O'Connor's editorial.

[100] Macclesfield Courier, May 20, 1848, speech of Thomas Webb.

[101] Holyoake, Bygones Worth Remembering, p. 77.

[102] William Lovett, "Justice Safer than Expediency: An Appeal to the Middle Classes on the Question of Suffrage" (1848), p. 5. This position was strongly endorsed in the Weekly Dispatch. See the issues of March 12, 1848, p. 125; March 19, 1848, p. 133; April 30, 1848, p. 205; May 7, 1848, p. 217; July 2, 1848, p. 313.

[103] Hansard, Parliamentary Debates, Third Series, Vol. 98, p. 17.

[104] Northern Star, April 29, 1848, p. 5.

[105] The problem of the Provisional Government in France in dealing with unemployment should not happen in England, because the Land Plan "would not leave a single man in England unemployed." Weekly Dispatch, April 30, 1848, p. 206, quoting a speech of his in Nottingham.

[106] Northern Star, July 1, 1848, p. 1. Letter from Ernest Jones.

[107] Manchester Guardian, August 9, 1848, p. 3.

[108] Morning Chronicle, March 4, 1848, p. 4.

[109] Northern Star, June 17, 1848, p. 8, Letter of the Executive Committee to the People.

[110] Northern Star, March 11, 1848, p. 2.

[111] Northern Star, April 1, 1848, p. 2.

[112] The debate on the petition is in Hansard, Parliamentary Debates, Third Series, Vol. 98, pp. 284-94.

[113] Weekly Dispatch, April 16, 1848, Annual Register, April, 1848, p. 54.

[114] The Times, April 14, 1848, p. 4.

[115] Punch, 1848, p. 168.

[116] Annual Register, April, 1848, p. 54.

[117] Hansard, Parliamentary Debates, Third Series, Vol. 98, p. 293.

[118] Hansard, Parliamentary Debates, Third Series, Vol. 98, pp. 291-2.

[119] Hansard, Parliamentary Debates, Third Series, Vol. 98, pp. 286 and p. 292.

[120] Hansard, Parliamentary Debates, Third Series, Vol. 98, p. 294.

[121] Hansard, Parliamentary Debates, Third Series, Vol. 98, p. 291.

[122] Hansard, Parliamentary Debates, Third Series, Vol. 98, p. 288.

[123] Hansard, Parliamentary Debates, Third Series, Vol. 98, pp. 290-1.

[124] Rev. Henry Moule to Earl Grey, April 13, 1848, H.O. 45/2410, Part 2, London.

[125] Rev. E. Williams to Sir George Grey, April 10, 1848, H.O. 45/2410, Part 2, London.

[126] J. H. Mann to Sir George Grey, April 12, 1848, H.O. 45/2410, Part 2, London.

[127] Manchester Guardian, April 19, 1848, p. 7.

[128] Anonymous letter from a working man, Mansfield, April 15, 1848, H.O. 45/2410, Part 3, B-Z.

[129] Thomas Frost, Forty Years' Recollections, p. 133.

[130] Manchester Guardian, April 19, 1848.

[131] Leeds Mercury, April 22, 1848, p. 8.

[132] F. B. Smith, "Great Britain and the Revolutions of 1848", p. 79.

[133] Large, "London in the Year of Revolutions, 1848", p. 192.

[134] Nonconformist, April 19, 1848, p. 274.

[135] Hansard, Parliamentary Debates, Third Series, Vol. 98, p. 287 and 289.

[136] Greville, The Greville Memoirs, Vol. 6, p. 170.

[137] Weekly Dispatch, April 23, 1848, p. 197.

[138] Weekly Dispatch, April 16, 1848, p. 193.

[139] Harris, Memoirs of an Ex-Minister, pp. 225-6.

[140]Ashley, The Life of Viscount Palmerston, Vol. 1, p. 80.

[141]Greville, The Greville Memoirs, Vol. 6, p. 170.

[142]McCarthy and Russell, Lady John Russell: A Memoir, p. 97, Lady John Russell to Lady Mary Abercromby, April 10, 1848.

[143]Russell, Recollections and Suggestions, p. 254.

[144]Hansard, Parliamentary Debates, Third Series, Vol. 98, p. 156.

[145]Douglas, Autobiography and Memoirs, p. 304.

[146]Robert Eadon Leader, ed., Life and Letters of John Arthur Roebuck, with Chapters of Autobiography (London and New York 1897), p. 203.

[147]In Saville's words, he was not the "eccentric Irish bufoon, imposing his demagoguery upon the deluded masses..." and he needs to be treated with the "analytical respect he deserves as the leader of a massive political movement...." John Saville, "Some Aspects of Chartism in Decline", Society for the Study of Labour History Bulletin, no. 20 (Spring 1970), p. 16. For a recent rehabilitation of O'Connor up to 1842, see Epstein, The Lion of Freedom: Feargus O'Connor and the Chartist Movement, 1832-1842.

[148]These viewpoints are repetitiously presented in the Northern Star, particularly in the issues of April 15, 1848, pp. 1, 2 and 7; April 29, 1848, pp. 1 and 5; May 20, 1848, p. 4. Also Weekly Dispatch, April 30, 1848, p. 206.

[149]Leeds Mercury, April 15, 1848, p. 4.

[150]Weekly Dispatch, April 16, 1848, p. 187.

[151]Illustrated London News, April 15, 1848, p. 239.

[152]Northern Star, May 6, 1848, p. 4.

[153]Northern Star, April 15, 1848, p. 7.

[154]Leeds Mercury, April 15, 1848, p. 6.

[155] Northern Star, May 20, 1848, p. 1.

[156] Macclesfield Courier, April 22, 1848.

[157] Macclesfield Courier, April 15, 1848.

[158] Northern Star, April 29, 1848, p. 5.

[159] Northern Star, April 15, 1848, p. 7.

[160] Nonconformist, April 19, 1848, p. 274.

[161] Hansard, Parliamentary Debates, Third Series, Vol. 98, p. 500.

[162] Greville, Greville Memoirs, Vol. 6, p. 168.

[163] Hansard, Parliamentary Debates, Third Series, Vol. 98, p. 166.

[164] Andrew Lang, Life, Letters and Diaries of Sir Stafford Northcote, First Earl of Iddesleigh (Edinburgh and London 1891), p. 52.

[165] "Chartism", Fraser's Magazine, p. 591.

[166] Hansard, Parliamentary Debates, Third Series, Vol. 98, p. 157.

[167] Hansard, Parliamentary Debates, Third Series, Vol. 98, p. 166.

[168] Creighton, Memoir of Sir George Grey, p. 75.

[169] The Times, April 10, 1848, editorial.

[170] Greville, Greville Memoirs, Vol. 6, p. 169.

[171] Justin McCarthy, M.P., Reminiscences, Vol. 2 (London 1899), p. 262.

[172] Malmesbury, Memoirs of an Ex-Minister, p. 225.

[173] Howard Foster Lowry, The Letters of Matthew Arnold to Arthur Hugh Clough (London and New York 1932), p. 79.

[174] James Burn, The Autobiography of a Beggar Boy (London 1882), p. 139.

[175] Weekly Dispatch, April 23, 1848, pp. 192-3.

[176] Weekly Dispatch, April 16, 1848, p. 181.

[177] Weekly Dispatch, April 30, 1848, p. 209, also pril 23, 1848, p. 193.

[178] Weekly Dispatch, April 23, 1848, p. 192.

[179] Weekly Dispatch, April 16, 1848, p. 187.

[180] Weekly Dispatch, April 23, 1848, p. 197.

[181] Leeds Mercury, April 22, 1848, p. 8.

[182] Northern Star, April 8, 1848, p. 1.

CHAPTER V

THE SECOND STAGE: APRIL TO JUNE

A Counter Revolution Takes Shape

At the same time that the Chartists were assembling their petition, the government prepared two new legal instruments to repress potential disorder. Both went into the statute books after April 10, and can be regarded as major steps in a counter revolution against the Chartist drive for democracy in England in 1848.

The first, the Crown and Government Security Act, was better known as the "Gagging Act".[1] It was in its second reading on the very evening of April 10, and by the summer its punishments were falling upon English and Irish dissidents. This act created a new offense, treason-felony, subject to the punishment of seven years' imprisonment to transportation for life. The act was designed to bridge the gap between sedition, a misdemeanor, and treason, punishable by death. Treason-felony, in the words of the statute, meant "open and advised speaking," with seditious intent, of treasonable matters, specifically "compassing, imagining and levying war against the Sovereign." This measure also brought punishments in Britain and Ireland into uniformity.[2]

While this act has been cited for its application to Ireland, and it certainly brought howls from Smith O'Brien, the Irish leader in the House, there is no doubt from the debates in Parliament that the Chartist challenge figured substantially in its passage by an overwhelming majority.[3] Russell defended it by declaring that it would not impose any restrictions on the "free, full and indisputable right" of "deliberating upon every political matter." But it could interfere with the so-called Chartist 'monster' meetings. These were not for political discussion, Lord Brougham pointed out in the Lords. They were too large for discussion and only served as "exhibitions of physical force." The Duke of Wellington agreed, referring, on the evening of April 10, to the great "grievance" that the metropolis had suffered, with its inhabitants alarmed and trade and business paralysed. The Duke thought meetings should be limited to a proper size for discussion and the kind of meetings seen on the tenth prohibited. Furthermore, as Robert Peel insisted

163

in the Commons eight days later, neither O'Connor nor anyone else could possibly control "excited...tens of thousands" no matter what peaceful disposition he might have. Peel thought peace was kept on the tenth not so much from O'Connor's leadership or the nature of his followers but from the sacrifices of the citizens and the expensive use of government forces. From the far right, Colonel Sibthorp responsed to complaints of the bill's stringency by regretting "that it was not ten times stronger."

O'Connor opposed the measure as best he could, with some help from the radicals. He argued that the proceedings of April 10 should convince everyone that such a measure was unnecessary. O'Connor claimed he had "always told the working classes that the Constitution...was worth living for, and worth dying for...." Freedom of speech had "always enabled the people to bring a moral force to bear upon the government," but "once gag the people", by putting "fetters upon the free expression of public opinion", there would then be "an end to the boast of the British Constitution." O'Connor feared, quite correctly, that the Gagging Act would encourage secret societies, something he unequivocally opposed. The government should not care about the noise of Chartist extremists, as he did not care "what any Mr. Tomfool said." This bill would remove "the safety valve...through which their folly would pass harmlessly away." It was all to no avail.

Outside of Parliament, Chartists found some support for their opposition in the established press. For instance, the Morning Chronicle thought the bill was based on the principles of those countries where "despotism reigned not a month ago."[4] The Illustrated London News found no need for it as long as there were "special constables enough to coerce and quench Chartism."[5] Chartists were livid about it. Samuel Kydd found the bill "as bad as any law of Louis XIV".[6] William Lovett defiantly stated that "no gagging law, however severe,...will silence...the public voice."[7]

The second instrument of repression passed after April 10 was the notorious and controversial Alien Act. It was a harsh measure: any alien who had come to Britain since 1845 could be deported simply on the basis of a written, signed statement against him in the hands of the authorities. Lords Lieutenants or the Secretary of State were empowered to deport aliens without trial, and could hold them in jail without bail

164

pending deportation.[8] There were some mitigating
features: Aliens resident for over three years and
members of diplomatic households were excluded and it
was temporary, lasting for one year only. In actual
practice, the Alien Act was never applied to anyone.[9]

Even so, it had a repressive effect. There was a
howl inside and outside of Parliament against it, particularly from the society that felt most threatened,
the Fraternal Democrats. In Parliament, various speakers objected to the arbitrariness of the measure, citing the manner in which the accused need not be
confronted openly or be given a public trial. Moreover, a hostile or malignant informer, or a "despotic
and tyrannical government" might cause the banishment
of a foreigner unjustly.[10] Grey defended the government's position, saying that Britain had a right to
protest itself against "apostles" of republican principles, meaning Frenchmen operating in England or Ireland. As the Marquess of Lansdowne explained, the
measure was aimed at those who would abuse hospitality
by creating "distrust" of the British government. Any
kind of alien could come to Britain, "monarchical,
constitutional or republican, but he had to obey the
laws of England while a guest, meaning the laws against
sedition.

To what extent was the bill aimed at Irish collaboration with French republicans and to what extent was
it directed against Chartist internationalism in
London? It is difficult to determine this, because
suspected activity in both Dublin and London provided
impetus to pass the act. The prospect of Irish conspirators forging links with French republicans to wage
"civil disturbance and civil war" was certainly a major
concern in the minds of some Members. Nevertheless,
Lord Beaumont saw "the empty boasting of two or three
hundred harebrained individuals" in Ireland as insufficient grounds for such an act.

For some Members, April 10 had shown that there
was little to fear from aliens in the metropolis, but
for others in both Houses, fear of foreigners in London
remained pronounced. The Marquess of Landsdowne passed
on the rumor that 40,000 to 50,000 foreigners waited
for an opportunity to help overthrow the British monarchy. The Duke of Bedford offered no figures, but
said that "a great number" were in London, many of whom
were "the worst characters of France", men determined
to "raise sedition and disturbance in England."

According to various other speakers, "desperate characters" from abroad, including some revolutionary veterans, mingled with British crowds and incited them to violence, or fraternized with delegates of the Chartist National Convention. Frenchmen were cited in nearly all cases, but one Member of the House of Commons mentioned Germans as well, aliens who "entertained wild and anti-social opinions". Events on the Continent had shown how even a small number of them could produce "great confusion and bloodshed", so it was vital to be able to get them out of the country quickly.

These arguments did not go down uncontested. Lord Brougham found the rumor of 50,000 Frenchmen ready to aid an English revolution "without the shadow of a foundation" and Landsdowne, who made the assertion, had to admit that he did not know if the rumor were true. A few other speakers found the idea of foreigners leading Englishmen into sedition ridiculous. As Hume put it, a "Frenchman or a German" standing up to "advocate revolution" at a British meeting would only receive "hissings and hootings." It would be as rational a belief to think that "a bevy of ourangoutangs [sic] should visit the country on a like mission." Besides, the Lamartine government refused to send any republican missionaries to England or Ireland.

To prove that the contagion of dangerous exiles existed, the Earl of Malmesbury actually read part of a speech by George Julian Harney, purported to declare the willingness of foreigners to assist in a struggle in England. This, too, was challenged, but not in a manner that gave any credit to Harney. Lord Denman said he would not pay much attention to "vapouring threats" from such individuals because their "monotonous ravings" were "hardly worth the notice of any reasonable man."

Outside of Parliament, the debate on the Alien Bill was carried on in the established press. For example, the Morning Chronicle argued that if the Alien Act were necessary for Ireland, "let it be confined to Ireland." There was no point in depriving "all the respectable foreigners who visit England" of the "protection of the law" just because some of the Young Ireland group "talked loosely and foolishly of fraternizing with Frenchmen...."[11] On the other hand, The Times found it necessary because of all of the "plots, treasons, secret and open armaments" going on.[12]

166

Eventually, an overwhelming majority in both Houses sided with The Times as the bill became law.

While the influence of the Fraternal Democrats on the passage of the Alien Act remains debatable, the influence of that law on them is quite clear. The Fraternal Democrats were positive that the act was "levelled against this association", and sought to banish "any 'foreigner' suspected of cherishing democratic principles." Henceforth, England would be a refuge "only for the enemies of liberty" and those "privileged 'foreigners' living in luxurious idleness...." They felt that there should be a law to deport Prince Albert and Louis Philippe instead. Clearly, this was an act that was a "deliberate attempt to obstruct the progress of mankind's fraternity...."13

Unquestionably, it obstructed the progress of the Fraternal Democrats. By the end of April Harney complained that the association was "disorganized," in large measure because the threat of prosecution had cost them their regular meeting place.14 To reorganize, they dissolved themselves in early May, thereby releasing their "foreign brethren" from the obligations of membership, and, they hoped, from the grasp of the Alien Act. They then reconstituted themselves with an exclusively British membership, and pledged to continue as a "Foreign Affairs Committee," meeting openly and publicly as before, but taking special precautions against spies.15

To some extent, the plight of the Fraternal Democrats became an issue in the movement at large. At a well attended West Riding meeting, Daniel Lightowler, a Bradford Chartist, laughed at the way the government was frightened of "a few bearded men walking about the streets of London." The proper application of the Alien Act, he maintained, was to have Prince Albert go first; the "ex-king of France" to go next; Guizot next; and all the other aliens who had been "burdens" on the country.16 Such humor, though undoubtedly appreciated, could not efface the hard fact that repression, through the Alien Act, a measure never applied in any court of law, effectively smothered Chartist internationalism for the rest of 1848.

The Fraternal Democrats were victims of a backlash against all phases of Chartism that followed April 10. Backlash is a word that became familiar during recent civil rights struggles in the United States, and

denotes a sharp reaction against militancy. In April
and May, after a brief period of euphoria, a vigorous
backlash built up against Chartism from a variety of
sources, and for a time it seemed to push the government towards repression.

Backlash can be sensed in the harsh editorial comments about Chartism in The Times in late April:
Workers were "wasting their time" listening to the
"rabid trash of sedition mongers", and "fooling away
their money" by contributing to the Chartist movement.
The six points were "an imputent humbug" and militant
Chartist oratory was "a gratuitious outrage."[17] Some
attacks were scurrilous, such as Punch changing "universal suffrage and vote by ballot" into "universal
suffering and vote by bullet."[18] In May, Fraser's
Magazine offered this insight on Chartism's relations
with the press:

> A newspaper reporter's idea of a Chartist
> is, that every pickpocket and every
> drunken man...taken up immediately before
> or after a public meeting of the working
> classes, is a Chartist, and he puts it in
> his paper accordingly.[19]

Chartism had lost the propaganda war. The middle class
press was almost universally hostile to the movement
after April 10.[20]

Backlash can also be perceived in the spate of
pamphlets that appeared after April 10, which generally
derided Chartism and linked it to revolutionaries
abroad.[21] One pamphlet called the Chartist National
Assembly "A French Chartist abortion" that contained "a
few demagogues" who represent "five millions of 'Pug-
noses!'". The Chartists, it went on, "imitate the
French in everything." They would have had revolution
if the government were not so well prepared on the
tenth, so they should not take so much credit for their
peaceful behavior on that day.[22] Many pamphleteers
focused their scorn on the old French revolutionary
slogan of 'Liberty, Equality, Fraternity', sometimes
using the threadbare analogy of a country compared with
a family in order to illustrate the dictum that some
should rule and some should obey.[23] Lecturers went
about making these same points. One of them, Charles
Knight, was particularly indignant over the way Chartists expropriated the term 'the people' for themselves.

The 'people', Knight insisted, meant more than just labor and much more than just Chartists.[24]

The fears that had been relieved by April 10 resurfaced again, and account for much of this reaction. For example, in May the Prince Consort wrote to Baron Stockmar about the "incredible" organization of the Chartists, and how they might be successful in a "coup de main" if they all threw themselves at a key point.[25] Only six days after Kennington Common, Queen Victoria wrote an anxious letter to the Prime Minister, complaining that "there is so much inflammable matter all around us that it makes one tremble."[26] In late April the Voice of the People raised the spectre of the violent wing of the Chartists as the "avowed disciples of communism and socialism". These Chartists would divide land and property, and abolish the right of inheritance.[27]

Backlash and fear also can be seen in the zealous letters arriving at the Home Office. Local functionaries wrote to describe seditious speeches, lament Chartists meeting on Sunday and to report arming and drilling here and there.[28] One correspondent went so far as to suggest that the government make a misdemeanor out of attending a political meeting not in a person's own parish, or, if a freeholder, out of his county. This way, "political incendiaries" could be confined to their own localities, where the constitutional rights of meeting and petitioning would stand. Peers and Members of Parliament were to be excepted, of course.[29]

Grey was not ready to move in April. He was cautious and watchful. The Home Office temporized in responding to alarmed correspondents. Exact words of seditious speeches were solicited. Problems of authenticating seditious language were noted. When supplied with particulars, the Home Office was inclined to declare that it was "not expedient" to take up legal proceedings at that time. But all the correspondents were thanked for their information, since it was very important for the Home Office to know what was going on.[30]

Caution extended to the question of the safety of the royal family in April. When Prince Albert wanted to speak to a group of workers in Exeter, Russell warned him against it, saying that Chartists might interrupt him, and probably fearing that they might do more than that. But the Prince Consort's Teutonic enthusiasm had centered on the plight of the workers for the time being, as a result of April 10, and he wanted to express his "immense interest" in the "welfare and comfort of the working classes." In this way he would show that "the Royal family are not merely living upon the earnings of the people...."[31]

Backlash occurred here and there in the provinces in late April on the initiative of local authorities. A handbill in Leeds signed by a Chartist, who was described as "a most inflammatory and seditious character", brought forth a reward of £10 for anyone who could identify the printer.[32] The Warwickshire Yeomanry readied themselves in case they had to march to Birmingham to face "treasonable movements". Manchester forces were prepared to put down "any émeute that might break out."[33] In Liverpool, the police broke into an iron monger's establishment without a warrant. The place was run by a so-called "Dr." Reynolds, who sold knives advertised "to cut bacon or anything you like." Swords, pistols, guns and bayonets were also for sale in his store. The magistrate involved had to declare reluctantly that the police had exceeded their duty, and cautioned them not to enter dwellings without proper authority. He also recognized "circumstances of great extenuation", given the arming and drilling in the area. He found it disgusting that the very people who threatened to burn Liverpool down and entice loyal workers to arm for bloodshed should raise a howl at "the slightest infraction of the law" when it affected them.[34] This magistrate was ready for the counter-revolution.

May: The Chartist Reaction and Reorganization

Chartist activity for the remainder of April in the aftermath of the tenth provides a very mixed picture. Much energy went into justifying April 10, or questioning it, and into dealing with the scorn and ridicule for the petition, O'Connor and the movement in general. Energy also went into electing delegates to the National Assembly, successor to the National Convention. Chartists met in simultaneous meetings on Good Friday, April 21, in order to elect delegates for the new body. In some places in the provinces attendance was good; in others it was poor. London had one of the best gatherings, with from 14,000 to 16,000 attending at Bonner's Fields, near Bethnal Green.[35]

As Linton complained, an organization devoted to equal electoral districts had very unequal ones for its own legislative bodies.[36]

Scottish Chartists were the most militant in late April. A great meeting in Glasgow, amidst tricolors, heard reports on a new, 500 man "National Guard" which was to be equipped by a Birmingham gun manufacturer who offered to sell guns and bayonets to them at only 12s 6d each, wholesale. The meeting resolved to order one for each member of the new "National Guard".[37] Naturally, the Home Office kept well informed about these developments.[38] In Aberdeen, thousands marched for two consecutive nights, in connection with electing a delegate to the National Assembly and voting for their own "National Guard".[39]

Elsewhere Chartist activity in the last two-thirds of April was more subdued, but not without flashes of militancy here and there. The Home Office received reports of pike making and threatening language in Bradford; arming and drilling in Barnsley; a militant camp meeting held near Rochdale.[40] London had another demonstration led by Cochrane, this time against the workings of the Poor Law. He held forth from a van in Leicester Square and proceeded to Trafalgar Square to speak again. The police cut into his audience by moving bystanders along. Cochrane had his own petition on the subject, which he delivered to the Home Office. Needless to say, George Grey was not at hand to receive it.[41]

Otherwise, Chartists marked time for the rest of April. The Prime Minister thought they were "declining in numbers and mischief."[42] While Leeds Chartists displayed disunity,[43] Liverpool Chartists and Irishmen "settled down to a perfect calm", according to one reporter, busy "following their usual occupations peaceably."[44]

Regardless of conditions in their immediate environment, Chartists still had a focus for their hopes in London, as they looked forward to the opening of their National Assembly on May 1. It dissolved in less than two weeks, on May 13. Throughout the short span of its existence, the National Assembly worked in an atmosphere hardly conducive to productive deliberations. Outside was the great roar of middle and upper class scorn for them. Inside, bitter wrangles errupted from frustrated, disappointed men sincerely seeking the ideals of democracy, social equality, and economic

amelioration. Anyone familiar with radical Protestant-
ism in the 17th century or, for that matter, with the
recent history of the Labour Party in Britain or the
Democratic Party in the United States may have more
empathy for the Chartist National Assembly of 1848.
Idealists on the left so often seem to have a morbid
determination to attack each other in the name of some
greater good for mankind, usually to the benefit of
their real but ideologically distant enemies.

Assemblymen wrangled over a wide spectrum of
issues: whether or not to prepare another petition;
how members should be elected; whether or not to continue supporting Feargus O'Connor; over what kind of
lecturers should tour the country; whether or not to
seek collaboration with middle class reform movements;
whether or not to arm and form a national guard; over
the way to reorganize; over O'Connor's leadership; and,
of course, whether or not this or that delegate should
be seated. Physical force versus moral force, that
tried and true Chartist debating issue, similar to
predestination versus free will or grace versus works
among Christians as an historic source of divisiveness
and unending argument, was given another full airing.
On the whole, the National Assembly was a sad, turgid
affair, what with its motions, counter motions, and
very fulsome speeches. It would go too far to join one
delegate who, in his disgust with the debates, summed
up the assembly as "a standing disgrace" attended by "a
set of washerwomen."[45] The Chartist delegates were in
a difficult position, casting about for some means to
accomplish what had not been brought about even by the
combined effect of the French breeze, the monster petition and the great meeting of April 10.[46]

What did they hit upon? Some wanted heroic withdrawl from tobacco and spirits, excisable articles,
until the Charter was the law of the land. Others
wanted less heroic withdrawls from the banks, hoping
that economic chaos would come about and make the
Charter the law of the land. Finally, they agreed to
go ahead with the plan to send a memorial to Queen
Victoria, following an ancient constitutional practice.
Approaching her as "faithful subjects", Chartists
planned to ask her to dismiss her ministers and replace
them with leaders who would make the Charter the law of
the land. This would enable England to avoid any
chance of enduring "extremities" seen on the Continent
in 1848. Victoria was informed, as a Tudor monarch
might be informed, that she was laboring under

172

"misapprehensions" about the dispositions of her subjects from "the false statements of her advisors". The
Queen was reassured that there was no feeling of "hostility" towards her "in any factory, workshop or mine."
Hostility was directed at "the present system of government". The majority of the British people looked to
the throne for the redress of grievances, "seeing that
both Parliament and Ministers have treated the People's
petitions with neglect."

A Chartist delegation, which included McDouall and
Jones, was designated to present the memorial in a
"respectful" manner, but in the end they never delivered it. Even so, this Chartist recourse to such an
archaic constitutional form is a singular testimony to
their desperation in May.[47]

The ferocity of the debates also points up their
desperation, from the reports of constituents' feelings
to the shouting contests on the floor over O'connor's
role. O'Connor's leadership was called into question,
particularly over whether his determination to carry
through with the Land Plan sacrificed the greater
interests of Chartism.[48] O'Connor himself was absent,
busy in Parliament and busy at the Land Company office.
Moreover, he informed the staff of the Northern Star
that they could either continue to work for the newspaper or sit in the National Assembly. Harney stayed
with the Star and Jones joined the assembly.

The overall militancy of the delegates is hard to
determine. Some called for a national guard and shooting clubs, declaring that submission was more of an
evil than insurrection. Others decried the image of
Chartists as "bloodthirsty anarchists" being created by
their fellow delegates. The militancy of the constituencies they reported upon is similarly difficult to
assess. Some delegates thought Chartists were "not so
lively" in their areas as they had been in 1839, and
others were either alarmed or pleased about the excessive excitement in their localities. The assembly
itself has some excitement when someone in the
strangers' gallery threw a large lead rifle ball in
their midst. They had allowed the general public to
observe from a gallery, at the price of one penny per
day,[49] but after this incident, there was increasing
indignation over undue influence from Londoners in the
gallery.[50] But London was not Paris, as almost everyone knew by then, rifle balls notwithstanding.

173

In fact, Paris and the whole Continent were more or less forgotten as the National Assembly churned on. Few analogies with France were drawn, even for the physical force versus moral force rhetorical exercises. Issues tended to be internecine, such as whether to replace the "National Charter Association" with the "Chartist National Association" or why it was that lecturers sent to Scotland were unable to hold forth "from absolute drunkenness."[51]

If anything, delegates began to see that the French Revolution of 1848 was a two edged sword that was now beginning to cut against them. As the government readied its counter revolution, some delegates asked why "the attaining of new franchises and privileges" on the Continent "ought to deprive them of any of the old rights and privileges which belonged to Britons?" The French breeze was beginning to blow the wrong way.

Despite all of the turgid debates and bitter recrimination, Chartism emerged from the National Assembly substantially reorganized in order to sustain an agitation in the face of mounting repression.

All of Britain was divided into districts, and each district was formed from a union of contiguous localities. Localities were divided into wards and classes, with ten men forming a class and ten classes a ward. The reorganization was designed to call out large bodies of Chartists on short notice without alerting the authorities. A message would travel from the national executive to the leaders of Chartist districts. District leaders would summons the leaders of localities, who would in turn inform the leaders of wards, who would inform the leaders of the classes. Class leaders were to complete the process by getting the word to the nine other men in their group. The class leaders were enjoined to "make themselves acquainted" with the residences of their class members.[52]

What models did this plan of organization have? Some claimed that it was based on the United Irishmen; others found similarities with the Chartist insurrectionary committees of 1839. Still others compared it to Continental secret societies, although Thomas Frost denied that there was any basis for such a comparison. The Chartist arrangement, according to Frost, did not have the hallmarks of European secret societies, specifically the oaths of secrecy, oaths of fidelity, initiation ceremonies, secret symbols, passwords or hand grips.[53] Instead, the organization of Methodism was probably very influential.

Many contemporaries and historians have assumed that the reorganization marked a commitment to insurrection. Certainly men could now be swiftly and secretly summoned by word of mouth, forgoing the usual Chartist means to assemble meetings, placards and newspaper announcements. There was also a significant shift towards more militant leadership in the results of the elections to the new Chartist Executive. The Land Company crowd, including O'Connor, was shunted aside, allowing Samuel Kydd, James Leach, Peter Murray McDouall and Ernest Jones to take over. Yet it is important to bear in mind that O'Connor supported the reorganization, and that Ernest Jones may have had other plans for Chartism that fell far short of taking to the barricades.

For a very brief time, between the National Assembly and his arrest in early June, actually less than a month, Ernest Jones was clearly the most important national leader of Chartism. In all of the hubub of the National Assembly, Jones tried to put forth this reorganization, and finally got it through. What he wanted was a sustained Chartist activity, "enrolling, preparing...keeping up...a continuous Chartist agitation" so that the government would have "no rest" and the "Whig exchequer" would become empty from taking "precautionary measures".[54]

This was the post April 10 strategy of Jones and many O'Connorites -- to wear the government down. It was in operation until June. Did it make any sense? Given the fact that middle class taxpayers and the school of political economy abhorred needless public expenses, yes. Pressure from meeting after meeting, simultaneous demonstrations, large processions and rallies might have been effective in forcing at least some concessions before too long. Judging by comments in the established press, this was an area of vulnerability. The Times found the April 10 demonstration an expensive disruption, both in the cost of maintaining law and order and in terms of resultant losses in business and trade. An editorial warned that "if we are threatened with another" Chartist demonstration of that sort, "it will be time to think of some cheaper, less troublesome, and more summary way of suppressing

the nuisance."[55] The Leeds Mercury complained of how
the agitation hurt trade in its area, and warned that
if it kept up, the forces of authority would have to
be numerous and active, "for all of which the public
will have to pay a heavy bill."[56] The Manchester
Guardian published a letter from a special constable
complaining of the cost of Chartism. He calculated
what one day's demonstration cost "the peaceable and
orderly portion of the community", and came up with
the sum of £5,585, even omitting many indirect costs.[57]
Everything the authorities thought was necessary to
confront a Chartist demonstration: special constables,
police on overtime pay,[58] cabs, pensioners, troops,
loss of wages, loss of business, all cost the rate-
payers money. The step-up of the government's repressive counter offensive in May and June undoubtedly had
much to do with the desire to cut costs by crushing
Chartism quickly. The Chartist movement was not solid
enough or broad enough to carry on with Jones' strategy
of wearing the government down. Instead, Chartism was
worn down and driven underground.

    It was the only idea to come forth from the ran-
corous National Assembly that had at least a chance.
That body had its own serious financial problems in
simply existing, as numbers and support dwindled
rapidly towards mid-May. The name "National Mockery",
picked up from one of its disgruntled members, came to
be used for it regularly in the established press.
Ernest Jones defended the body, along with the violent
language that many delegates used. Jones said it gave
voice to "the manly indignation of a long-oppressed
people."[59]

    Another viewpoint can be had by way of an histori-
cal comparison. Germany had its Frankfort Parliament
in 1848, which debated the fate of the nation while the
King of Prussia gathered his forces to impose the fate
of Germany. While the Chartist National Assembly was
certainly unlike the Frankfort Parliament in several
important respects, it did sit and argue while Sir
George Grey, in his own English way, husbanded his
forces for his own very English counterrevolution.

            Militancy and Counterrevolution in May:
                    Bradford and London

    In May many Chartists presented the "bold front"
so desired by Ernest Jones. Reports flooded into the

Home Office about marching, drilling and arming. A center of such activity was Bradford in Yorkshire. Bradford had substantial numbers of unemployed and desperate woolcombers, hard hit by the introduction of machinery over the years. They were "Chartists to a man", one informer declared, "and believe that the Charter would find them plenty of good work and good wages if it became the law of the land."[60] Bradford even had a Chartist mayor, said to be similar to the Lord Mayor of London described by Dickens in Barnaby Rudge. The mayor sat with arms folded as Chartists met, armed secretly, and drilled at midnight.

A conspicuous leader emerged from among these Bradford Chartists. He was by no means a moral force, education oriented Chartist in the style of William Lovett, nor was he an O'Connorite, enmeshed in the N.C.A. and the Land Plan. He was part of the new left of Chartism that surfaced in 1848, Chartists who forced their way to the forefront after April 10. These new left leaders were less known, less articulate, more militant, more provincial and more determined. They put action before speeches. The leader in Bradford became something of a folk hero, under that old, heroic name from English history, Watt Tyler. He was a blacksmith named Issac Jefferson, "ferocious looking", according to the authorities. He took an oath that he was not going to shave his beard until the Charter became the law of the land. Beards did not become ordinary in England until after the Crimean War, so Watt Tyler looked very conspicuous, marching through the thoroughfares with a green velvet cap and his great black beard. At his forge he struck pikes and knives without concealment, and no one dared interfere.[61] Justices of the Peace had reports that armed men guarded his forge every night.[62]

Shopkeepers quailed when Chartists approached. Chartists insisted that shops post their handbills. One who refused was deprived of all of his customers because a cordon of Chartists soon formed to block his doorway. Others were pressured into joining the movement or at least making contributions to it.

Bradford Chartists called the force that drilled with arms their 'National Guard', and rumor had it that they were out to enroll a million men in industrial England for a march on London. They would give the government but one choice: The Charter or a republic.[63]

177

They marched in military style, with captains in red and green caps and the men divided into sections and companies. Their flags were tricolors, and their banners bore more trenchant inscriptions than those flown at Kennington Common: "More Pigs and Less Parsons"; "Down With the Aristocracy"; "England Free or a Desert".

They marched on Sundays and at night. One night in late May they appeared in a particularly menacing manner to watching police constables. They had staves, six feet in length, and were being put through "military evolutions" by an "ancient soldier". When a policeman sought to find out the drillmaster's name, several Chartists began to scuffle with him. The policeman's cries of help brought police reinforcements, who had been massed and waiting, from one direction, and a flurry of stones and brickbats from the other. The next night the Chartists marched out again, 200 strong, in regular regimental step. Rumors circulated that other Chartists were assembled at various points, ready for action if the police made another foray. For the time being they did not.[64]

In daylight the marching Chartists of Bradford looked less awesome, at least to a reporter of the Bradford Observer, who did his own observing from his office window. Their drum was a tin can, played by a youth, and the fifer was the ancient soldier. "There was no lack of good humor about these poor fellows," the reporter wrote, for "they seemed to amuse themselves by marching à la militaire", and by "hearing their feet fall to the ground with the noise of a regular regimental step."[65]

At the Home Office, Sir George Grey was not at all amused. In May the government abandoned temporizing and began to urge provincial authorities to move against the Chartists. Messages informed mayors and magistrates that George Grey "thinks it most desirable" that "persons drilling should be arrested and punished."[66] The Home Office reminded officials of the specific point of law which could be brought to bear: "The marching of great numbers of persons in military array...in such a manner as to strike terror into the peaceable inhabitants and...excite...fears that property may be invaded is illegal...." Magistrates should have no hesitation about applying this law. They should first proclaim it, and if drilling continued, they should apprehend two or three ringleaders, with

178

care so that no riot "or serious breach of the public peace" should occur. "No time should be lost."[67] The Home Office also requested an investigation of a suspicious order for 5,000 muskets sent from Bradford.[68]

Justices and police in and near Bradford were alarmed. They were certain that Chartism was increasing rapidly as an armed force and that any outbreak in England or Ireland would cause Bradford Chartists to rise.[69] They feared making arrests because any such moves would "inevitably cause a collision". The special constables were "afraid to act" without the military. Chartist scouts were everywhere, watching the magistrates, police and special constables. There were some streets so controlled by armed Chartists that "the police dare not venture" into them without military support. The justices called for troops and the suspending of the Poor Law's provisions forbidding outdoor relief, coercion mixed with conciliation.[70]

Bradford was not the only trouble spot for the Home Office in May. Leicester was in an uproar over a Poor Law ruling. Police were stoned by the recipients and had to call in the pensioners as reinforcements. A hand to hand struggle ensued, with truncheons flailing and men dropping to the ground. Finally, the pensioners advanced with fixed bayonets, and this scattered the rioters. These brawls were henceforth called the "Bastille Riots' in Leicester. Although many Chartists condemned the riots, they were held responsible for them nonetheless. Offended moral force Chartists angrily demanded an investigation of police brutality towards the rioters. Leicester soon quieted down, but not without a legacy of bitterness.[71]

Manchester saw some large Chartist meetings in conjunction with Irish Confederates in late May. Police, special constables and the military went forth to curtail them, resulting in some violence. Mounted police were stoned, one horse was stabbed, and some pavement was pulled up before truncheons and cutlasses cleared the streets.[72]

Other places were calm. Birmingham gained Grey's "satisfaction" for its "improved tone of public feeling." It was no longer necessary to keep a spy, euphemistically called "a reporter", at the meetings in People's Hall.[73] Nearby, in the Black Country, there were many meetings, but peace prevailed.[74]

179

At the end of May, full scale repression was ready to strike in Bradford. A new mayor, the magistrates, special constables, extra police, the yeomanry and troops were gathered to impose their authority by force. The Bradford Observer described the "state of siege" in the town: Police appeared on the streets with cutlasses instead of staves; troops of the line, infantry and cavalry, as well as local yeomanry, were all quartered in the town; special constables were on regular duty; shops had their shutters drawn. A magistrate read the riot act, and both he and a military officer spoke to the shopkeepers, who responded with cheers.

When the authorities struck they did so in force: a 1,000 men launched a sweep against a Chartist neighborhood. The police and magistrates were in front, 500 specials were in the center and two divisions of infantry and cavalry brought up the rear.[75] They were out to arrest the Chartist leaders living on Manchester road, and to search the vicinity for arms. Large numbers of Chartists blocked their way, and soon a furious street battle was underway, cutlasses and staves on the one side, bludgeons and stones on the other. The police and specials were forced back in confusion, many of them badly wounded. For a time, their retreat blocked the assault of the military, but once the dragoons got to the front the Chartists gave way quickly. One eyewitness recalled that the "horse soldiers" dashed up the street "with drawn swords slashing in all directions."[76] In the ensuing rout, 18 Chartists were arrested, one of whom struggled to the last, dagger in hand.[77]

London had its own struggles in late May. London Chartists arranged almost nightly meetings and demonstrations, their version of keeping up a 'bold front', which was no mean feat of organization in such a huge area that really consisted of many towns.[78] Some of the inspiration for these meetings came from sympathy for the recently convicted Irish patriot, John Mitchell, who received a long sentence of transportation. Throughout the month the police thwarted the Chartists with determination, which led to several confrontations.

At the outset of one such affair, on May 29, Chartists met at Clerkenwell Green late in the afternoon and tramped four abreast to 12 abreast to Finsbury Square. Others came from Stepney Green and the parade milled through Leicester Square on the way to Trafalgar Square.

John Frost heard that a Chartist named Fussell had started the march by calling out "fall in!" Frost also learned that when Fussell was asked whether anything more than a demonstration was planned, he replied, mysteriously, "I don't know; we shall see." Frost concluded that nothing more was aimed at than a testing of the new organization.[79] It was impressive. Speeches were short and nothing was announced about the meeting publicly. The police found it difficult to get their reporters close enough quickly enough to record what was being said.[80]

Russell and Grey were so troubled by the affair that they sat up until after midnight to make sure that it all ended quietly. The next day the police proclaimed such meetings illegal, and the government put magistrates, specials and Life Guards on the alert.

The next night, May 30, an assembly appeared on Clerkenwell Green once again. The police marched forward in the middle of someone's speech, mounted officers in the lead, and pushed the meeting out of existence. For the following night, the police were again fully prepared, and posted a notice against tumultuous assemblages and processions. Five thousand of them were ready to move in on any Chartist assembly, and they were backed up by three squadrons of Horse Guards now newly posted in Clerkenwell and Finsbury. Furthermore, the whole fire brigade was alerted on account of rumors that Chartists intended to become incendiaries. Some special constables were called out as well, but most were just on alert.

The uncompromising use and show of force worked: Chartist leaders did not appear and the police dominated the quiet streets. The next night it was the same. Once more Chartist leaders did not appear, although knots of would-be demonstrators raised a slight commotion before they were dispersed by the overwhelming numbers of police.[81]

Sustained repression seemed to be working in London, as the efforts to wear down the authorities with wave after wave of meetings appeared to falter by the end of May. A Chartist from the provinces may have caught the mood of the times when he complained that he was "weary of walking up and down the streets" when he could have been more "usefully" employed for the cause elsewhere.[82]

Chartism's June Days

The February Revolution went sour in France in June, as a rising of the working class sections of Paris was brutally crushed by the republican forces of General Cavignac. Marx called these 'June Days' "a fight for the preservation or annihilation of the bourgeois order."[83] Marx, Engels, Harney and others saw the revelation of the class struggle in all its naked glory in Paris. For Chartists in general, news of the 'June Days' was a bitter disappointment, setting forth the worrisome thought that a republic under universal manhood suffrage might not end oppression after all.[84] Chartism had its own June Days to contend with, its own struggles with repressive forces. Here again, in its own peculiar, insular and singular way, English history seemed to move with the rhythms of the Continent.

In April the government had prevented the procession from Kennington Common; in May meetings, processions, arming and drilling were suppressed in many places; in June they went further. They were ready to move against speakers, prosecuting them for sedition. This holder operation was designed to repress Chartism by eliminating its leaders, a policy of decapitation proven successful in 1839 and 1842, the two other years when a powerful Chartist presence seemed to threaten the stability of the state.

A flurry of recommendations went out from the Home Office in June: get accurate reports of seditious language; if any speeches make reference to an organized and armed resistance, have a reporter take down the words; speeches calling upon the people to arm and organize in order to change the law cannot be permitted; if clear evidence can be obtained against the speakers, they ought to be apprehended.[85] Skilled reporters were dispatched by the Home Office to several cities and towns. All of these directives had one aim in view. The English counterrevolution was out to remove Chartism's militant leaders.

Grey outlined his steps for the benefit of the Queen: Since Chartist meetings of a "formidable character" were expected in June, the police had orders to prevent all processions in London, as well as meetings

182

held at unacceptable hours or under situations that might cause undue alarm. Those who drilled or made violent speeches were to be arrested.[86] The Prime Minister concurred, expressing encouragement for repression, but pointing out the need to have an accurate reporter at work whenever a move was made to apprehend a seditious speaker.[87] Despite ongoing disturbances and rumors of disturbances to come, Grey expected "that the arrest of the leaders will produce a beneficial effect."[88]

If this were not enough, the government had reserves in its legal arsenal to call upon in order to crush the reorganized National Charter Association. Strong laws against corresponding societies had been enacted decades ago. A law of 1799 banned all associations consisting of separate divisions, each with its own officers. A law of 1817 prohibited societies which elected delegates to confer with other clubs.[89]

The Home Office checked with the Attorney General and Solicitor General to see if prosecution of the National Charter Association could proceed. The legal experts came to the conclusion that the reorganized Chartist society was in fact an unlawful confederacy. The government never had to use the laws against corresponding societies in 1848, however, because the other repressive statutes deployed against Chartism were sufficient in themselves.[90]

At the same time the government monitored arms production and distribution to make sure that the Chartists were not stockpiling weapons. The destinations of firearms sent from Birmingham were investigated to make sure that they were "legitimately disposed of" by sales to "persons of character".[91] London pawnbrokers and retail arms dealers were surveyed to see how many guns, pistols, swords and daggers they sold to "mechanics and labourers...believed to be...Chartists".[92]

As a result of these efforts, Grey was able to write to Victoria to reassure her that only "to a certain extent" were the Chartists armed, but there were no massive arms purchases by Chartist groups. The government's investigations led to the conclusion that large, suspicious orders placed in Birmingham were for arms destined for the Continent.[93]

Pressure intensified against Chartist meetings everywhere. Magistrates at Manchester prohibited them in mid-June, and were backed up by Grey at the Home Office.[94] A hard line was laid down to the magistrates at Bradford and many other places: All meetings "calculated to excite terror and alarm...ought no longer to be allowed."[95]

Chartists took evasive action. When a meeting was prohibited, they might hold it an hour later and claim that it was a different meeting.[96] Or they might take their meetings out of the towns, to the hillsides, heaths, and moors, where no ordinary citizens could possibly fall into terror or alarm. What could the government do then? Bradford magistrates pondered this problem and queried Grey. The Home Office replied by advising them to "abstain from any direct interference" if the meeting was a considerable distance from town and if no breach of the peace resulted from it. But magistrates should gather accurate information nonetheless, "and take proceedings against any parties whose speeches are of a treasonable or seditious character."[97]

An examination of one of these great outdoor meetings can serve as an illustration of the atmosphere and the tension from repression outside of London during the month of June. Thousands of Chartists gathered at Toftshaw Moor in the vicinity of Bradford in mid-June.[98] Chartist hymns provided a prelude. Suddenly, two solitary riders approached the throng, magistrates from the neighborhood. Apprehensions spread. Were they going to stop the meeting? Slowly, one of the magistrates made his way to the hustings. As he came close to the platform, somebody shouted, "Throw him off!" From the platform came the pleas of Chartist leaders not to molest him. The magistrate on horseback turned to the crowd and told them that if the meeting were peaceful and orderly, and if no attempt were made to march into Bradford, nobody would interfere with it. But they could have no processions with flags, banners or music marching into Bradford. A cry came from someone in the crowd: "We will have them!" Another voice added: "Very well sir, and what right have you to interfere with us?" The magistrate replied that he had a simple duty to perform, "and that was to inform them that "we are determined you shall not go through the town in procession." That duty, he insisted, "will be discharged with kindness if we can, but if not, we shall do it firmly and fearlessly...." One of the

184

leaders on the hustings proclaimed his agreement, and the magistrate wheeled about to go. Some in the crowd joked with him as he departed, asking if he wanted them to escort him home, "if he felt apprehensive of any personal danger." The magistrate smiled, said "no, thank you," and rode off.

The meeting continued, on a low key at first, with one orator declaring that "the Chartists did not intend any breach of the peace...." Later on, several speakers took a much more militant line and received a markedly warmer reception. Mitchell the martyr, the "blood thirsty Whig government" and the prospects of a "Republic of Yorkshire and Lancashire" brought loud cheers. These speakers called for arms, and declared that the shopkeepers never felt safer than when they were protected by "the National Guards of Bradford."

A commotion errupted in one part of the audience in the midst of these flights of oratory. Someone was observed taking notes, and he was jostled and roughly forced down to the hustings. The crowd thought he was a government informer, an agent who could testify in court with the kind of accurate notes demanded of late by the Home Office. But he turned out to be merely a newspaper reporter.

Most of those present headed towards an area on the outskirts of Bradford, Broomfields, for dispersal once the meeting was over. A substantial minority marched towards Bradford itself, banners flying, and in direct defiance of the magistrate's orders. They got within the town, but when they came to the top of George Street they could see before them an array of force. The magistrates had called out several hundred special constables and the military, and there they stood, blocking the street, staves and truncheons at the ready. The Chartists bolted. Flags and banners were furled instantaneously, as the alleys and cross streets echoed with the sound of running feet. The special constables surged forward to seize the banners, and after a few minutes of scuffling they gained some.

Their adrenalin up, the specials and the military turned their attention to the bulk of the audience which had arrived at Broomfields. Trumpets blew, infantry and cavalry advanced. The crowd scattered but reformed again. The magistrate came forward and remonstrated with them to go home, but they paid little attention to him. Next the specials advanced, along with the artillery. For dramatic effect, one of the artillerymen ignited his match. With more effort on the part of the law's forces, the rest of the Chartists were finally dispersed.

The next day some of the Chartists came to the courthouse to ask for their banners, and got one of them back at the price of listening to a lecture. They were advised to make children's pinafores out of their banner. Some were not returned because of the "objectionable" mottoes on them.

The special constables had their own meeting, which produced a resolution that was passed on to the magistrates. It declared that "the time had come for more energetic measures than had been hitherto pursued...." Both sides were militant in June.

At nearby Blackstone Edge, in the hills separating Lancashire and Yorkshire, Bradford Chartists met again and gave free reign to their own feelings of outrage.[99] For them, the days of speeches and petitions were over, as well as the times they had "begged, and prayed, and crouched, and crawled like dogs...." It was now time that "this accursed system should come to a speedy end." If people were organized throughout England the way they were in Bradford, where a "civil war" was going on, there would be no need for further speeches. The bitterness of these Chartists is indicated by the remarks of one of their leaders, George White, about Lord John Russell:

> Lord John Russell, the poor little hop-o'-my-thumb, was going to put them all down. God help his little carcass;... they defied him; and if he did not mind his knitting, they would put him and the whole crew down.

Policemen in plain clothes listened and noted White's remarks. One of them, disguised as a drover, was discovered and "roughly handled" by members of the crowd. He fled to a stable for refuge, and George White, the very Chartist who fulminated against Russell and the accursed system, interceded between the crowd and the policeman. The Leeds Mercury observed that it "required all of Mr. White's exertions to save [the policeman] from further violence." This vignette may serve as an illustration of the difference between

186

Chartist rhetoric and Chartist deeds. The man who railed against the system came to protect the system's agent who was there in order to incriminate him.

London Chartists did not have lonely hillsides to meet upon. Just as the June Days for France were Parisian, Chartism's June Days saw a culmination of demonstration and repression in London. Despite the suppression of the Clerkenwell Green meetings in late May, Chartists rallied again in early June, as they continued to carry out Ernest Jones' tactics to force concessions.

They were having no small effect in wearing down the patience of the authorities and the establishment. The Prince Consort and the Queen were upset.[100] Greville wrote at great length about the impact of the ongoing agitation. According to his diary, the military were "so savage" that officers wondered if they would be able to restrain their men if a collision took place. Clergymen and doctors, Greville claimed, were saying that discontent had increased considerably since April 10. The ongoing meetings were an "evil", besides being a "great bore". Many people, Greville reported, were willing to have a "severe chastisement" applied in the form of troops opening fire on the mob, because they were "provoked to death with these continued alarms." Greville himself thought it "impossible not to feel alarm when we consider the vast amount of the population as compared with any repressive power we possess."[101] At the same time, Lady Charlotte Guest wondered when the "volcano" would explode.[102]

The fears that had built up for April 10 had returned once more, stimulated by the new organization of the Chartists and another spate of rumors about a Chartist insurrection. Ernest Jones' plan to organize and agitate incessantly was beginning to bear fruit, as an editorial in the hostile Weekly Dispatch indicates:

> The pillars of our own solid empire have
> been shaken. The tenth of April, like
> the Ides of March, has come, but its
> effects have not yet gone. Nay, it seems
> as if it were only now that they were be-
> ginning to develop themselves. Without
> placard, advertisement, beacon or fire or
> any of the ordinary means of producing
> combined action, simultaneous and dis-
> orderly meetings of the rabble have been

held in many disaffected districts,
creating feelings of insecurity....
Organized mobs are drilled to the
measured tread of military array,
and habituated, little by little, to
encounter the constabulary....[103]

In early June the newspapers regularly carried
news of swearing in special constables, arming pensioners and troop movements.[104] The press also called for
more repression. The Manchester Guardian urged "vigor
and determination" to end the Chartist meetings, "considering the hardships which tumultuous assemblages
inflict upon the orderly and well disposed portion of
the community."[105] Physical force meetings were "fla-
grant humbugs" anyway, run by "professional agitators"
and thronged by thieves and Irish "noisy braggarts".
"Steady, hard-working people" would stay away from them
anyway. It was all part of an "artificial agitation".[106] The Leeds Mercury was convinced that Chartists met "less to discuss than to intimidate...."
They were really "the worst enemies" of reform because
they discouraged the true "advocates of progressive
improvement", the "sincere reformers", from doing anything at this time.[107] Many letters from local inhabitants to the Home Office underscored the encouragement
for repression found in the press in June.[108]

June 4 was perhaps the most violent day in England
in 1848. There were two important simultaneous meetings in London, at Bonner's Fields and Bethnal Green in
Hackney. Both meetings ended in considerable violence
between the dispersing demonstrators and the police,
many of whom were badly injured by stones.[109]

Ernest Jones gave one of his standard, rousing
speeches at the Bonner's Fields meeting, a speech not
dissimilar from scores of others he had made since
February. Two days later, the government struck.
Warrants for the arrest of Jones and five other speakers for sedition were issued, and Jones was apprehended
in Manchester a few days later.[110] He had anticipated
his arrest, and melodramatically pleaded that "people
would not risk their valuable lives to save him"
because he was determined to carry on the fight against
the government in a court of law. The circumstances of
his arrest were far from heroic. He emerged "not quite
dressed" from a bedroom he shared with a "Mrs. H.", who
had accompanied him to a Chartist meeting the previous
night.[111]

Whit Monday, June 12, was April 10 all over again
in many respects. Chartists promised to have massive
simultaneous meetings all over as a protest against
repression and arrest. There were rumors that a rising
was planned, circulating even among Chartists, but
there is no evidence for it.[112] In fact, Peter
McDouall, who was suspected of conspiratorial leadership by some, contacted the authorities to assert the
right of public meeting and promise that the Chartists
would meet and disperse peacefully if the police did
not molest them. McDouall wrote to Grey in the name of
the Executive Committee of the National Charter Association, pledging the "most peaceable and orderly" proceedings. Moreover, the Chartists were willing to
furnish Grey with any further information he might want
about their "peaceful...objects". The Home Secretary
was reminded that they were "exercising the great constitutional right of meeting in public to discuss their
grievances."[113]

The government had mobilized once again. Over
5,000 troops, the same ones that took positions for
April 10, took new positions for June 12, in the east
end of London instead of the west end.[114] Wellington
came to the fore once more. He wanted the parks closed
again and offered numerous technical suggestions, including specific instructions on how to attack barricades and narrow, fortified streets. For his own part,
Wellington did not expect barricades to go up in
England, but he noted that Chartist leaders had "given
much attention to what was passing abroad." Still,
"under the existing circumstances", he wrote, "I don't
think the Chartists in England are disposed to attack
at all!" If they became armed, they might.[115]

On the twelfth, Bonner's Fields, the Kennington
Common of that day, was occupied. Sixteen hundred
police, plus 100 mounted police, 500 pensioners and a
detachment of the Horse Guards ensured that the Chartist meeting would not be held. The meeting was
scheduled for noon, but the leaders did not show up.
McDouall sought out the magistrate and asked him
whether the government would stop the meeting. The
answer was simply, "Yes, sir."

At Bonner's Fields the police had something of a
holiday, as they sprawled on the grass, eating and
drinking the provisions of itinerant vendors. They
were interrupted by a heavy rain, but not by any
Chartists. Only groups of women and boys with a

sprinkling of men ever showed up for the meeting. It
all ended with the police standing about in a drenching
rain by themselves. This was London's tranquil contrast to the June Days in Paris.[116]

June 12, 1848, an uncelebrated and largely forgotten date, was a turning point for the democratic
challenge of 1848, in a manner that April 10 was a
turning point. Mass agitation had been driven away by
a powerful counterrevolutionary repression. Some
leaders, including the most important one of all, Jones,
were already facing trial. For many Chartists, April
10 was the day to give up and leave the movement, and
for many others June 12 was the day to do so. Yet for
some, June 12 meant that they had to go underground,
plotting and arming for a violent physical revolution
in earnest at last.[117]

Mainstream Chartists, largely unsupported by the
established press, were left to howl their protests
against the impairment of the constitutional freedoms
to meet and to speak as well as against the brutalities
attendant upon repression. The Northern Star railed
against the way processions and meetings were being
shut off; how the police and specials created disturbances themselves, and how many of the charges of drilling and training were trumped up. The Star printed a
list of meetings broken up by police forces, and
recounted how Chartists resisted by throwing stones,
brickbats and ginger beer bottles. How could the press
have it both ways, by claiming that Chartism was dead
after April 10 and then announce "the existence of a
vast Chartist conspiracy of the most dangerous character?"[118]

Class war was at hand, the editorials of the Star
declared in June. The Whigs had proclaimed "a war of
the rich against the poor", and armed one class against
the other.[119] Harney found his particular enemies at
work, the middle classes. They had a hostility to
Chartism "of the deadliest character" and were against
it "to a man", despite some semi-collaborating "shopo-
crats". The middle classes wanted a Chartist clash
with the police and military as "an excuse for an
indiscriminate and wholesale butchery." What did they
say? "Shoot the dogs! Grapeshot them! Why are not
the leaders transported? Hang the rascals!" Such came
from the "fool tongues" of the "jury class" in June.[120]

Chartists with a less developed sense of class
consciousness than Harney could also see the handwriting on the walls. They had the firm conviction that
their rights were slipping away, one by one, as the
government moved against Chartism. "What concession
would they want next?" they asked. In June "local
fools" had sent "soldiers to parade the streets and
break into...houses". What right did they have to
break in searching for pikes? Couldn't a poor man have
the right to have a pike when a rich man had his gun?
Some went so far as to proclaim their conviction that
the government was plotting ways and means to "murder
the leading men in the Chartist ranks."[121] Samuel
Kydd, a very active national leader in 1848, described
all of this as a "reign of terror. So close has our
political atmosphere become that we are almost suffo-
cated."[122]

Chartists raised the cry of police brutality. The
Executive Committee of the National Charter Association
complained to Lord John Russell about it. The police,
they contended, were the real disturbers of the peace,
not the Chartists. Policemen sent "idle boys" to Chartist meetings "to break windows on a given signal",
acts that served to "justify an attack" on an otherwise
peaceful meeting. At other times, the police waited in
ambush until meetings were in the process of dispersal,
and then launched an "onslaught" that "paid no regard..
to...age, sex or condition." In short, the Executive
Committee feared that the people were being "bludgeoned
out of their right of meeting."[123]

Complaints also came into the Home Office. One of
many letters declared that "no savages in the world
could have been more brutal" than the police breaking
up a Chartist meeting. "The swearing...was awful", the
correspondent continued. An old man on tottering legs"
was knocked down and violently beaten. Another person
was struck in the face while holding an infant. An
innocent office clerk who happened by was first struck
by a policeman and then felled with his head ripped
open by the cutlass of a horse policeman. The correspondent pleaded not for the Chartists, but for the
innocent people of his neighborhood.[124] There were
many complaints of drunken policemen waylaying people
recklessly in the streets, flailing away indiscriminately with their truncheons. According to Thomas
Frost, one innocent victim died of a fractured skull
as a result.[125] In one neighborhood, local inhabitants
formed a committee to gather evidence on police

191

brutality and sought to raise funds for police victims. The police rejected their charges and got up their own subscription for wounded policemen.[126]

Brutality aside, the police were arresting and dispersing Chartists effectively in the battles of June, which decided whether or not the Chartist agitation would continue to have mass meetings. From the well known leaders to the unknown demonstrators who struck policemen, Chartists arrested at the Bonner's Fields meeting were tried and sentenced.[127] Even Feargus O'Connor, M.P. had a taste of June's repression. It happened when he arrived at Loughborough railroad station to greet a crowd of his supporters. They had hoped to march in a procession with him, but found a troop of dragoons waiting at the station instead. When O'Connor arrived the magistrates took him aside for a private interview, at which time they handed him a proclamation prohibiting the procession. Undoubtedly with a strong sense of déja vu, O'Connor mounted a table, read the proclamation and said that under these circumstances it would be better if he just caught the next train, which he did.[128]

As repression surged in England in June, a very different scene went on at Buckingham Palace. The Queen received a loyal declaration from Lancashire operatives thanking her for royal assent to the Ten Hours Bill.[129] Victoria was also occupied by considering 900 prize essays on the Sabbath by working men, introduced by a cheerful note describing them as "an example no other nation can parallel", for they "exhibit British Labourers [sic] as men of prayer, who convey to the footstool of God the great interests of this vast Empire."[130] Did Victoria realize that for every worker who submitted one of these pious essays, several thousand had signed the Charter?

At any rate, her government's policies seemed to be working well by the end of June. The ever handy laws of the realm had removed some leaders, and would soon remove others; Bradford and London had been swept clear and there were many signs that Chartism was subsiding rapidly.[131] The Weekly Dispatch summed up how the Chartist situation was under control: "The police are active...the Guards do not fraternize with the blackguards..." and the more extreme leaders not already caught will soon be arrested and "lugged to Botany."[132]

NOTES TO CHAPTER V

[1]The Statutes of the United Kingdom of Great Britain and Ireland, 11 and 12 Victoria, 1847-8, Vol. 89, c 2.

[2]For the "Gagging Act", see Large, "London in the Year of Revolutions, 1848", p. 208; Mather, Public Order in the Age of the Chartists, p. 33; Creighton, Memoir of Sir George Grey, p. 67; Lord Campbell to Lord John Russell, April 1, 1848, Russell Papers, P.R.O. 30/22 1B; Reynolds' Political Instructor, January 26, 1850, p. 94; Greville, Greville Memoirs, Vol. 6, pp. 170-1.

[3]The debates are in Hansard, Parliamentary Debates, Third Series, Vol. 98, pp. 19-22, 54, 70-4, 157, 229, 375-8, 454, 463-8.

[4]Morning Chronicle, April 8, 1848, p. 6.

[5]Illustrated London News, April 15, 1848, p. 240. By contrast, there was support for it in the Manchester Guardian, April 8, 1848, p. 6.

[6]Northern Star, May 13, 1848, p. 2.

[7]William Lovett, "Justice Safter than Expediency: An Appeal to the Middle Classes on the Question of the Suffrage", p. 7.

[8]The Statutes of the United Kingdom of Great Britain and Ireland, 11 and 12 Victoria, 1847-8, Vol. 89, c 20.

[9]Creighton, Memoir of Sir George Grey, pp. 76-7.

[10]Hansard, Parliamentary Debates, Third Series, Vol. 98, pp. 138, 264-80, 560-1, 580-584.

[11]Morning Chronicle, May 3, 1848, p. 4.

[12]The Times, April 12, 1848, editorial.

[13]Northern Star, May 6, 1848, p. 8; April 22, 1848, p. 5; Similar sentiments are found in resolutions passed at a public meeting reported in the April 22 issue.

[14] *Northern Star*, April 29, 1848, p. 8.

[15] *Northern Star*, May 6, 1848, p. 8.

[16] *Northern Star*, April 29, 1848, p. 7; Also reported in the *Bradford Observer*, April 27, 1848. For other comments on the Alien Act, the *Weekly Dispatch*, June 18, 1848, p. 293, Samuel Kydd at the National Convention, *Northern Star*, April 15, 1848, p. 8.

[17] *The Times*, April 13, 1848, p. 4.

[18] Quoted in Robert Crowe, "The Reminiscences of a Chartist Tailor", *The Outlook* (August 9, 1902), p. 918.

[19] "Chartism", *Fraser's Magazine*, p. 579.

[20] Stevenson, *Popular Disturbances in England, 1700-1870*, p. 269. Saville cited the press for helping to "paralyse the political will to victory" on the part of the Chartists. Saville, "Chartism in the Year of Revolution: 1848", p. 26.

[21] Some examples are: [J. Allport] A Friend to the Working Man, "The Chartists; or, Liberty, Equality and Fraternity" (London 1848); The Pimlico Hermit, "An Appeal to the Chartists Proper, in a Series of Letters, Shewing in What Manner the People's Charter May be Rendered Worthy of Being Made a Reality", 2nd ed., Letter I (London: McGowan and Co. 1848).

[22] A Fellow Labourer, "What the Chartists Are...", pp. 6-7, 11.

[23] [Maurice], "The Chartist's Friend...", p. 5.

[24] Charles Knight, *Passages of a Working Life During Half a Century: with a Prelude of Early Reminiscences*, Vol. 3 (London 1865), pp. 88-92.

[25] Martin, *The Life of the Prince Consort*, p. 42, Prince Albert to Baron Stockmar, May 6, 1848.

[26] Benson and Esher, *The Letters of Queen Victoria*, p. 201, Queen Victoria to Lord John Russell, April 16, 1848.

[27] *Voice of the People*, April 29, 1848, p. 18.

194

[28] Mayor of Birmingham to Denis Le Marchant, April 12, 1848, H.O. 2410, Part 3, B-Z. Denis Le Marchant to Rev. L. J. Mills, April 20, 1848 (reply) H.O. 41/19.

[29] J. H. Mann to Sir George Grey, April 12, 1848, H.O. 2410.

[30] Denis Le Marchant to the Mayor of Birmingham, April 11, April 14, 1848; Denis Le Marchant to D. Maude, April 20, 1848, H.O. 41/19.

[31] Prince Albert to Lord Ashley, April 23, 1848; Lord John Russell to Prince Albert, April 27, 1848; Prince Albert to Lord John Russell, April 29, 1848, RA Add. MSS C 56, Items 50, 55 and 56.

[32] Leeds Mercury, April 15, 1848, Supplement, "State of Public Feeling in Leeds", p. 6. The Chartist who signed was Joseph Barker.

[33] Leeds Mercury, April 22, 1848, p. 8.

[34] Weekly Dispatch, April 30, 1848, p. 209.

[35] Large, "London in the Year of Revolutions, 1848", pp. 193-4.

[36] Linton, James Watson, A Memoir, p. 51. He claimed that 3,000 men elected three members for London and 100,000 elected only one at Halifax.

[37] Leeds Mercury, April 22, 1848, p. 8.

[38] J. Patterson to Sir Goerge Grey, April 20, 1848, H.O. 45/2410, Part 5, AD-AL.

[39] Annual Register, April, 1848, p. 59.

[40] Denis Le Marchant to the Mayor of Bradford, May 4, 1848, also various letters about Barnsley, H.O. 41/19. Weekly Dispatch, April 30, 1848, p. 206.

[41] Annual Register, April, 1848, p. 59.

[42] Lord John Russell to Prince Albert, April 22, 1848, RA Add MSS C 56, Item 49.

[43] Leeds Mercury, April 15, 1848, p. 10.

[44] Leeds Mercury, April 22, 1848, p. 8.

[45] Northern Star, May 7, 1848, p. 228.

[46] For some of the debates in the National Assembly, see the Northern Star of May 6, 1848, p. 2; May 13, 1848, pp. 2-3; Weekly Dispatch, May 7, 1848, p. 228.

[47] For the memorial, Northern Star, May 20, 1848, p. 1; June 3, 1848, p. 1; Leeds Mercury, April 22, 1848, p. 8.

[48] Jones, Chartism and the Chartists, p. 71.

[49] Weekly Dispatch, May 7, 1848, p. 228.

[50] Northern Star, May 13, 1848, p. 2.

[51] Weekly Dispatch, May 7, 1848, p. 228.

[52] For the reorganization of May, see Frost, Forty Years' Recollections, p. 144; History of the Chartist Movement, Chapter X, and the National Charter Association, "Plan of Organization for the National Charter Association of Great Britain and Ireland, Adopted by the National Assembly, May 1848, to Obtain the Speedy Enactment of the People's Charter", (Manchester: Livsey, 1848).

[53] Thomas Frost, The Secret Societies of the European Revolution, 1776-1876, 2 vols. (London 1876), Vol. 1, p. xi.

[54] Northern Star, May 20, 1848, p. 1.

[55] The Times, April 11, 1848, editorial.

[56] Leeds Mercury, April 15, 1848, p. 4.

[57] Manchester Guardian, June 3, 1848, p. 8.

[58] Police had the advantage of extra pay when they were on duty on account of Chartist meetings, and, in addition, they could put in for "admissions and expenses" at public houses. Mr. Wray, Receivor's Office to Sir Denis Le Marchant, May 11, 1848, H.O. 45/2410, Part 2, London.

[59] David Large, "London in the Year of Revolutions: 1848", p. 194, mentions that it cost approximately 300 per week to keep 100 men sitting in a

National Assembly. See the Morning Chronicle, May 15, 1848, p. 3 for an example of the use of the phrase "national mockery". Jones' remarks are in his address to his constituents in the Northern Star of May 20, 1848. His constituents were in Halifax.

[60] L. L. Bins to Sir George Grey, May 25, 1848, H.O. 45/2410, Part 4, AB-AC.

[61] Ibid.

[62] West Riding Justices of the Peace to Sir George Grey, May 19, 1848, H.O. 45/2410, Part 4, AB-AC.

[63] Joseph Pollard, J.P., to Sir George Grey, May 20, 1848; L. L. Bins to Sir George Grey, May 25, 1848; West Riding Justices of the Peace to Sir George Grey, May 19, 1848, H.O. 45/2410, Part 4, AB-AC.

[64] Bradford Observer, May 22, 1848, p. 2.

[65] Bradford Observer, May 25, 1848.

[66] H. Waddington to B. Ferrand, Bingly, May 25, 1848; H. Waddington to Wm. Ellis, May 25, 1848, H.O. 41/19. The statute cited was 60 Geo. 3, c 1.

[67] H. Waddington to R. Barr, Clerk to the Justices, Leeds, May 27, 1848; H. Waddington to the Mayor and Magistrates acting at Bradford, May 25, 1848, H.O. 41/19. For the time being, the government continued to temporize about the use of words. Magistrates at Worksop received Grey's message that it was inadvisable to take steps against the authors of a particularly offensive placard unless its display manifested a disturbance of the public peace. Denis Le Marchant to Henry Owen, Clerk to the Justices at Worksop, May 6, 1848, H.O. 41/19.

[68] H. Waddington to the Mayor of Bradford, May 23, 1848, H.O. 41/19.

[69] Rod Mulligan to Sir George Grey, May 5, 1848, H.O. 45/2410, Part 4, AB-AC.

[70] West Riding Justices of the Peace to Sir George Grey, May 19, 1848, H.O. 2410, Part 4, AB-AC.

[71] Patterson, Radical Leicester, pp. 360-1.

[72]Watkin, Extracts from His Journal, pp. 252-5; meetings are mentioned in Mather, Public Order in the Age of the Chartists, p. 152.

[73]Denis Le Marchant to the Mayor of Birmingham, May 10, 1848; Various other letters, H.O. 41/10.

[74]George J. Barnsley, The Working Class Movement in the Black Country, 1750 to 1867 (Wolverhampton 1977), pp. 146-9.

[75]Bradford Observer, June 1, 1848.

[76]Wilson, "Struggles of an Old Chartist", p. 11.

[77]Jones, Chartism and the Chartists, pp. 158-9, quoting The Times of May 31, 1848.

[78]For London's diversity, Iowerth Prothero, "Chartism in London", Past and Present, no. 44 (August 1969), p. 88.

[79]Frost, Forty Years' Recollections, p. 146.

[80]Large, "Chartism in the Year of Revolutions: 1848", pp. 196-7.

[81]Annual Register, May, 1848, pp. 73-4.

[82]Northern Star, May 13, 1848, p. 3.

[83]Marx, "The Class Struggles in France, 1848 to 1850", p. 56.

[84]For an analysis of the impact of the June Days on Chartism, see the section "Tricolour at Half Mast" in the next chapter.

[85]Waddington to the Mayor and Magistrates acting at Bradford, June 6, 1848; Waddington to the Mayor of Liverpool, June 7, 1848; Waddington to the Mayor and Magistrates of Birmingham, June 12, 1848; Waddington to Thomas Marshall, Barnsley, June 8, 1848. One letter in June, Waddington to Colonel Rolleston, June 23, 1848, backed away from prosecuting speeches, on the grounds that no riot or conflict occurred at the scene, which was Nottingham. H.O. 41/19.

[86]Sir George Grey to the Queen, June 4, 1848, RA Add MSS C 56, Item 86.

[87] Lord John Russell to the Queen, June 1, 1848, RA Add MSS C 56, Item 84.

[88] Sir George Grey to the Queen, June 5, 1848, RA Add MSS C 56, Item 93.

[89] F. C. Mather, ed., Chartism and Society: An Anthology of Documents (London 1980), p. 176.

[90] Mather notes that historians have credited the government with liberality for not using these statutes. Mather thinks "this was probably the result less of the government's scruples than of the success of other methods of handling the emergency." Mather, Chartism and Society, p. 176.

[91] Government Memorandum, June, 1848, H.O. 45/2410, Part 2.

[92] Metropolitan Police Report, H.O. 45/2410, Part 2.

[93] Ibid.

[94] Waddington to the Mayor of Manchester, June 12, 1848, H.O. 41/19; Watkin, Extracts From His Journal, pp. 254-5.

[95] Waddington to the Mayor and Magistrates of Bradford, June 1, 1848, H.O. 41/19.

[96] Northern Star, June 14, 1848, p. 6.

[97] Waddington to the Mayor and Magistrates of Bradford, June 14, 1848, H.O. 45/2410, AB-AC.

[98] A full account is in the Leeds Mercury of June 17, 1848, p. 10, from which this description has been taken.

[99] Leeds Mercury, June 17, 1848, p. 4.

[100] Martin, Life of the Prince Consort, p. 76, The Prince Consort to his stepmother, June 7, 1848, p. 76; Large, "London in the Year of Revolutions, 1848", p. 209.

[101] Greville, The Greville Memoirs, Vol. 6, pp. 194-7.

[102]Bessborough, Lady Charlotte Guest, p. 125.

[103]Weekly Dispatch, June 11, 1848, p. 277.

[104]Annual Register, June, 1848, p. 80 notes this.

[105]Manchester Guardian, June 14, 1848, p. 4.

[106]Manchester Guardian, June 3, 1848, p. 7.

[107]Leeds Mercury, June 17, 1848, p. 4.

[108]For example, Proprietors and Inhabitants around Bonner's Fields to Sir George Grey, June, 1848, H.O. 45/2410, London.

[109]Large, "London in the Year of Revolutions, 1848", p. 198, Goodway, London Chartism, 1838-1848, pp. 119-122.

[110]The others were Fussell, Sharpe, Williams, Vernon and Looney. John Saville regards the arrest of Jones as a turning point in 1848, marking the beginning of what he calls the third and last phase of Chartism in 1848. Saville, "Chartism in the year of Revolution: 1848", p. 30.

[111]Manchester Guardian, June 10, 1848, p. 10.

[112]Thomas Frost was told in some detail by a stranger that plans for an insurrection were afoot for Whit Monday. McDouall was mentioned as a liaison between the Chartist executive and a secret revolutionary committee. The stranger said that at the last moment McDouall learned that their arrests were pending and so he cancelled the plans for a rising. Recently David Goodway has pointed out that Frost was incorrect, and that insurrectionary plans went ahead only after June 12. David Goodway, "Chartism in London", Society for the Study of Labour History Bulletin, no. 20 (Spring 1970), p. 15. Goodway is correct, but Frost himself mentioned this about the incident: "I afterwards had reason to believe that they were not so prepared for a conflict as Rose [the stranger] represented them to be." Frost, Forty Years' Recollections, p. 162.

[113]Peter Murray McDouall and John McCrea of the Executive Committee to Sir George Grey, June 8, 1848, H.O. 45/2410, London; Large, "London in the Year of Revolutions, 1848, p. 199.

200

[114]Mather, Public Order in the Age of the Char-tists, p. 163. Greville, The Greville Memoirs, Vol. 6, p. 197, noted the massive preparations.

[115]Wellington was particularly impatient with the formalities of the law required before troops could open up on insurgents. He was also impatient with the subjects' right to bear arms and drill, and adamantly opposed to the formation of any national guard in Britain. Wellington to Lord Anglesey, June 17, 1848, W.O. 30/81.

[116]Annual Register, June, 1848, p. 80; Large, "London in the Year of Revolutions, 1848", p. 200.

[117]Two historians have noted the effect of the June Days of Chartism. Saville, "Chartism in the Year of Revolution: 1848", p. 30, and Large, "London in the Year of Revolutions, 1848", p. 200. See also Good-way, London Chartism, pp. 142-143.

[118]Northern Star, June 10, 1848, editorial, p. 4 and the list of meetings, p. 6.

[119]Northern Star, June 17, 1848, p. 4.

[120]Northern Star, June 17, 1848, p. 3, editorial of L'Ami du Peuple.

[121]Leeds Mercury, June 17, 1848, p. 4, quoting various Chartist speakers.

[122]Saville, "Chartism in the Year of Revolution: 1848", p. 32, quoting the Northern Star of August 5, 1848.

[123]Executive Committee of the National Charter Association to Lord John Russell, June 6, 1848, H.O. 45/2410, London.

[124]William Higgins to the Home Office, June 5, 1848, H.O. 45/2410, London. There are many letters of the same sort in these papers. A meeting of the Female Chartist Association at Leicester called for a defense fund to prosecute special constables guilty of brutal attacks. Manchester Guardian, June 3, 1848, p. 8.

[125]Frost, Forty Years' Recollections, p. 151.

[126] Large, "London in the Year of Revolutions, 1848", p. 199. Also letter of July 4, 1848, of the inhabitants near Bonner's Fields declaring that the police no longer had the respect of the inhabitants. H.O. 45/2410, London.

[127] Annual Register, June, 1848, p. 80.

[128] Northern Star, June 17, 1848, p. 6, taken from the Daily News.

[129] Lancashire Operatives Address, June 12, 1848, RA Add MSS C 56, Item 98.

[130] D. F. Oakly to the Queen, RA Add MSS C 56, Item 103.

[131] Charles Grey to the Marquess of Londonderry, June 24, 1848, H.O. 41/19.

[132] Weekly Dispatch, June 18, 1848, p. 293.

CHAPTER VI

OPTIONS

The Option of Gradualism

One aspect of the aftermath of the April 10 confrontation was a backlash of repression. Another
aspect was the search for alternative means of reform
on the part of a variety of reformers. At the very
same time that the government added to its legal
arsenal and began to drive the Chartists underground by
prohibiting their meetings, individuals and groups
deeply concerned about the deprivation and anger of
British workers set out in several directions for further reform. Chartists were at a crossroads by the end
of June, and those on the right and center were faced
with the dilemma of accepting or rejecting gradualism
in place of the Charter. This, too, was a significant
feature of challenge and response in England in 1848.

The Times blamed the French Revolution of 1848 for
setting all kinds of reformers in motion. "Reform
jumped up like a Jack in the Box", an editorial
declared, "Some liked reform for its own sake; others
wished a little reform to prevent a greater." The
Times complained of how "sensible and strong minded
men" became "afraid of a republic", and so felt that
"something must be done."[1] The Leeds Mercury, by contrast, wished that "reasonable demands" could be met
with "reasonable concessions" in order to "improve our
institutions and keep our people united." But Chartists need to give up the idea of carrying their six
points "on a kind of revolutionary tide."[2] "Happily,
the men of violence" were a "paltry faction", and the
people of England were ready for timely concessions.[3]

One thrust of radical reform in 1848 was the
"Little Charter" movement or the "Household Suffrage"
movement. Jospeh Hume was its leader, and the program
called for the ballot, triennial Parliaments, electoral
districts with more equality, the abolition of the
Members' property qualifications, suffrage for the
rate-paying householders and all sub-tennants who opted
to pay their own rates.[4] Cobden and Bright supported
it,[5] and again hopes turned to enlisting the working
classes as they had been enlisted to help pass the
great Reform Bill of 1832. Meanwhile, Joseph Sturge

and Thomas Attwood sought to reactivate the two class alliance in Birmingham.[6]

Courtship of working class leaders had mixed success. Harney saw it as another way to use the workers to foster middle class aims, in particular the shift of more of the tax burden from the bourgeois to the aristocracy. O'Connor wrangled bitterly with Cobden and Hume in the House over it. Other Chartists, such as Henry Vincent and Abel Heywood, drifted towards it,[7] and by the end of 1848, even Henry Hetherington, that old stalwart supporter of universal suffrage, was willing to go along.[8] Here and there at Chartist meetings, all the while the tide of repression went against the movement, emisaries showed up from the "Little Charter" radicals.[9] For many Chartists, collaboration was a tempting way out, more tempting than the desperate alternatives of violence or giving up on politics. But it meant surrendering the most important goal of Chartism, democracy's universal manhood suffrage.

Collaboration with the middle classes was always a difficult and divisive proposition for Chartists, a theme running through the history of the movement before and after 1848. The middle classes were tempting as allies for some Chartists because they had obviously growing influence and power in British society. On the other hand, they had a sinister reputation for using the working classes for their own ends exclusively. Nonetheless, an ideal opportunity for 1848 was perceived by the Weekly Dispatch: "If the Chartists come short of the Charter, the middle classes will extend their views beyond the Reform Bill -- a fair compromise...."[10]

Harney bitterly rejected this lure of gradualism in 1848. He felt the "Little Charter" movement would create "two classes of working men", one of which the middle classes would call "enlightened and peaceful" and the other the "Chartist distructives."[11]

The very name of the Charter was a point of contention. Many Chartists insisted on keeping it in any political activity, while many middle class leaders were put off by its association with mobs and riots, an association inculcated so regularly in the press.[12] The right wing Chartists were apt to seek collaboration in the summer of 1848, since their temporary cooperation with O'Connor's mainstream movement had broken amidst the bitter recriminations following April 10.

The more important Chartists in this grouping included
William Lovett, Henry Hetherington, W. J. Linton,
Thomas Cooper, Bronterre O'Brien, James Watson and
G. J. Holyoake.[13]

The celebrated veterans were no longer young men.
Hetherington was 56; Watson 49; Lovett 48 and O'Brien
44.[14] Lovett was not as active as he had been in previous years,[15] and Watson's special crusade, which
never got very far, was for republicanism.[16] Thomas
Cooper had prospered as a wide ranging lecturer, and
had become a ratepaying householder. He boasted that
he was "so thoroughly separated from O'Connor and his
party" that he was "entirely kept out of the 'Tenth of
April' trouble, and all the other troubles of the year
1848." Cooper continued to see England along the lines
of his friend Mazzini, the hero of Italian nationalism,
who emphasized freedoms already existing in Britain.[17]

These anti-O'Connorite, right wing, moral force
Chartists did tactically support the mainstream of the
movement until April 10. On that day they were out
with everyone else, resolved, of course, on strictly
peaceful behavior. In the aftermath of April 10,
Lovett and his friends formed yet another organization,
the People's Charter Union. In fact, on the very day
of Kennington Common, its first officers were elected,
and some of its members went out with notebooks to
record instances of police brutality.[18] Thereafter,
cooperation with the National Charter Association
ceased.

The People's Charter Union stressed using strictly
peaceful and legal means to acquire democratic goals, a
task seen as "no class work", but "the business and
duty of all".[19] Nothing much came of the People's
Charter Union, so Lovett launched yet another organization in 1848 with the same ends in view, but with a
more innocuous name, The People's League. This society
championed the points of the Charter, reduced government spending, the abolition of all customs and excise
taxes, the application of a progressive property tax,
and a reduction of government spending. The organization had the same old Lovettite formulae: It was
opposed to "every description of outrage and violence";
It would succeed through "moral courage" and "intelligence". Although support for the Charter was pledged,
a striking qualifying phrase showed that the organization was willing to pay a price for middle class
collaboration. The Charter would be sought "with such

alterations and amendments...as appear necessary.[20]
The possibility of allowing the Charter's partial dimu-
nition did not sit well with some of the members, who
made it an issue of contention.

Even Lovett described the response to the People's
League as "lukewarm".[21] At best, a few hundred people
showed up for its initial meetings and some support
came from the Nonconformist.[22] Attempts to lure the
household suffrage radicals, particularly Hume and
Cobden, failed, and O'Connorites opposed the People's
League in a particularly nasty manner by disrupting its
meetings. With exchequer almost bankrupt, the organization limped along until its dissolution in 1849.[23]

The "Schoolmaster of Chartism", its foremost
theorist, James Bronterre O'Brien, was even less effective than Lovett in 1848. He opposed O'Connor's Land
Plan and was willing to join the right wing in moderate
proposals. Like so many older Chartist leaders, a stay
in prison had encouraged him to eschew the use of any
form of physical force. At public meetings in 1848,
O'Brien's views brought hisses, boos and groans. Discouraged, he effectually moved out of Chartism and
spent the rest of 1848 as a spectator.[24]

There were several other varieties of reformers in
1848 who were not spread along the axis of right wing
Chartist and middle class radical collaboration. The
Owenists were still active, supporting peaceful reform
and dreading any revolutionary activity. They continued to dream of a socialist utopia in 1848.[25] A number
of literary figures offered reforms as well. Most of
them are little known in this century, something that
cannot be said of Harriet Martineau and Charles
Kingsley. Harriet Martineau actually agreed with some
Chartist views, but disagreed with others. She contributed to a short-lived periodical called the "Voice
of the People" in 1848, a journal primarily designed to
head off Chartist violence.[26]

Christian socialism was engendered by the
events of 1848. Their basic message was traditional,
whatever new teachings they imparted to the Anglican
establishment: Men's hearts could not be changed by an
Act of Parliament; the true Reformer's Guide was the
Bible; only Jesus could free them in the end. Charles
Kingsley, only 29 in 1848, emerged to lead the movement along with F. D. Maurice. They had been unable to
make up their minds about the Kennington Common

demonstration as it approached. Neither participated on either side, although Maurice offered his services as a special constable, only to be turned down because he was a clergyman.[27] A noted discussion group that met at Maurice's home was divided about it, the touchstone being willingness to enroll as a special. As it turned out, a majority donned the white armband on the tenth, and at least a few openly sided with the Chartists.[28]

Kingsley himself had genuine sympathy for Chartism. When he wrote to his wife to describe a Chartist meeting he remarked on the "courtesy,...eloquence,... the brilliant, nervous, well chosen language" and the "deep and simple earnestness...and moderation" displayed by the Chartists, men wrongly called "fools and knaves" and men "refused the rights which are bestowed on every profligate flop."[29] His approach to the Chartists was marked by the attractive ploys of a skilled clergyman. When he spoke at a Chartist meeting he dramtically announced: "I am a Church of England parson," paused in a long, theatrical manner, and added, "and a Chartist!" He claimed that the much maligned petition still had "a right to fair play, a patient hearing, and honorable and courteous answer." One of his favorite gambits was to claim that the Charter did not go far enough, that legislative reform was not social reform. He found "the devil's spirit" in the violent Chartists who uttered "bloodthirsty threats of revenge." Diabolical Chartism would justify the claims of Chartism's enemies and "disgust and cripple" the movement's friends. Nobody should defile the Chartist cause with "blasphemy, beastliness and blood."[30]

Kingsley and Maurice put their essential message on placards "to speak a word for God" among the workers. The placards proclaimed that the Charter was not bad "if the men who use it are not bad;" Yet the Charter would not free ·men from slavery to the stomach, the pocket and "one's own temper." But Jesus could.[31] Kingsley hoped that such placards and cheap publications would win over the workers to Christian socialism. He wrote under the name of Parson Lot and produced a variety tracts, articles and other polemical works.[32] Of all the literary output of the Christian socialists, only one novel, Kingsley's Alton Locke, has more or less withstood the test of time. John Saville called it "the literary version of what the middle class called the 'lesson' of 1848", and a "travesty" of what really happened.[33] Indeed, in Alton

Locke April 10 is sketched on one page of warped and distorted history.[34]

Other Christian leaders sought to solve the Chartist 'problem' without the 'socialism' of Kinglsey and Maurice. Building a new church in a Chartist stronghold was the solution for some.[35] Still others, such as the dissenting ministers writing in the Nonconformist, were able to offer the Chartists the comforting thought that "the greatest and most radical innovator who ever came into the world was Jesus Christ."[36]

Others concentrated on the economic aspects rather than the spiritual aspects posed by the Chartist challenge. The economic plight of the British workers became a fashionable topic, a cause of philanthropists, novelists, and the public spirited in general. The urgency of economic amelioration was a point grasped by a wide variety of people as the events of 1848 unfolded. Many non-Chartists had great sympathy for their plight.[37] Even The Times said that "if Chartism is to be effectively and permanently kept down, it must be by measures of social improvement -- not merely by demonstrations of power.[38] There was no doubt but that the agitations of 1848 had an economic root. As the Leeds Mercury put it, distress was followed by discontent, "even among the most patient and sensible population in the world."[39] A former special constable wrote that "poverty was at the root of Chartism."[40] Greville observed that Britain had "an enormous overgrown population", with a "vast proportion" in "undeniable misery and distress", who were "soured and exasperated by their sufferings." This was why workers were in a combustible state.[41]

The obvious solution was employment. The successful outcome of April 10, wrote Lady Charlotte Guest, "must not lull us into security" and lead to forgetting the duty of doing something "for our unemployed".[42] Many were convinced, in the words of one of Joseph Hume's correspondents, that Chartists really wanted "remunerating employment." With "work and fair wages", the population would be "content, peaceable and happy."[43] Prince Albert found "work for the suffering and unemployed" as a necessary corollary to repressing agitation. While he did not want French style "national workshops", he did want the government to do something in order to "help the working classes over the present moment of distress."[44]

Others would not invoke government responsibility.
The hard line of political economy can be discerned in
many of these observations. The Illustrated London
News urged everyone "to ameliorate the condition of the
poor..." on an individual basis, "each in his own
sphere."[45] Others offered the nostrum of more free
trade measures,[46] or more equitable taxation.[47] The
Leeds Mercury declared that it was "not possible" for
government "to give men...food...clothing...employment
...or wages."[48] Spencer Walpole stated the essence of
this spirit some time later, while writing on 1848:
"The first function of government is the preservation
of order", and people "cannot be allowed to destroy
property and imperil life because they happen to be
starving."[49]

Ironically, the man who many Chartists saw planning their slaughter, Commissioner Rowan of the Metropolitan Police, did not share the hard line of political economy. "I wish to God", he wrote shortly after
April 10, "it were possible for the government to do
something towards employing...people...." He suggested public works and warned that "unless something
can be done...we shall not be tranquil."[50]

Emigration was advanced again. A new emigration
scheme was moved in the House of Commons,[51] and scores
of former Chartists headed for the wide open spaces or
urban opportunities in the New World. As Lovett put
it, "thousands of the most enterprising and thought-
ful", the men whose skills and economy had accumulated
the means to emigrate, "shook from their feet the dust
of their unjust and ungrateful country...."[52]

It has become axiomatic in American history that
1848 enriched the United States with vigorous immigrants from the revolutionary struggles in Central
Europe. The Chartist contribution to these human
resources should not be overlooked.

Outside of packing up for the world's frontiers,
how did Chartists respond to the propertied classes'
concerns for their economic condition? One common
attitude was to deny that the middle classes cared at
all.[53] The old anger at the divergence of income
between rich and poor was always on the surface. A
Leeds Chartist, for example, denied that it was the
will of God that people should suffer so. The problem
came from the "drones" living on "the earnings of the
industrious millions".[54] It was in the oldest style

209

of radicalism to declare, in the words of an Ashton Chartist, that "there would always be rich and poor", but it was unjust that "one man should be living on the coarsest food" while another lived in "idleness and luxury" at the expense of the "industrious classes."[55] Actually, such simple words describe the basic, deep feeling of economic injustice that launched the Chartist movement in the first place.

Newer Chartist responses to the economic question involved insisting on exclusive dealing, that is, Chartist patrons would only shop at pro-Chartist stores. Some highly paid, highly skilled Trade Unionists had another tactic: agitation for protection to stem the flow of cheap foreign goods into Britain.[56]

Regardless of the nature of the proposal or the response to it, 1848 was a year when friends and foes of Chartism and Chartists themselves looked below the surface of politics to the economic conditions below. Peace and plenty were ever so closely linked in the popular mind, as were disruption and poverty.

Tricolor At Half Mast

Chartists at the crossroads at the end of June no longer had the French breeze behind them. In fact, it blew against them from June onwards, stiffly against those who sought an English insurrection.

Enthusiasm for the French Republic actually subsided for most Chartists after April 10. Before Kennington Common, meeting after meeting, address after address and speech after speech were given over to French affairs. After April 10, attention for France was scanty by comparison. For example, the debates of the Chartist National Assembly made little or no mention of any Continental matters. Here and there some speakers might go on with the same clichés,[57] and certainly the Fraternal Democrats kept on with a running commentary about France,[58] but for these Chartist internationalists as well as for mainstream Chartists, French affairs became keenly disappointing.

The June Days in France appalled Chartists. Harney found the "spectacles" of that month "calculated to almost break the hearts" of those who had hailed the revolution in February "as the dawn of democratic freedom, happiness and glory."[59] O'Connor responded to the

butchery of June by declaring, more or less, that he
had been right all along. When the French Revolution
of 1848 had broken out, he editorialized in July, "we
joined not in the shout of triumph", but said "wait
until we see the reward...in Labour's [sic] share of
the victory." The June Days showed, as "all previous
physical revolutions" had shown, that in the end
labor's "most perfidious enemies" gained power. It
was clear to him that labor's victory in February was
"applied to the benefit of capital". Why had not the
French workers learned from "our revolution of 1832,
whimsically called the Reform Bill?" It paralleled the
"bloody onslaught of the middle classes" upon the
"deluded and betrayed labourers of Paris...."[60]
William Lovett was more temperate over the June Days
in France. He decried the "selfish impatience" of the
middle classes in refusing temporary relief to the
working class, but also put some blame on the "crude
and startling" propositions of French communists and
socialists against property.[61]

Chartists were now clearly on the defensive over
the course of the French Revolution. Ernest Jones
found The Times and other opponents using "the anarchy
reigning in France" against the cause of democracy at
home.[62] Jones saw the June Days as a time when the
"Republican Despots" crushed the "Republican Democrats".[63] To use such terms at the opening of 1848
would have been unthinkable. At that time, a republic
under manhood suffrage was a vision which, if established, would bring all good things to the masses.
Now, according to an editorial in the Northern Star
probably written by Harney, "The 'Republic' is a mere
name -- a sham -- a mockery -- a delusion -- and a
snare.... Despotism -- the despotism of force...reigns
in Paris as in St. Petersburg."[64] Harney was furious.
Henceforth, he declared, "there is no longer ground for
compromise". In the future, France must have either a
despotism or "the Red Republic." This marked a new
stage in his ideological development, a stage frequently noted by Marxist writers.[65] Harney went on and on
about the lessons of the French Revolution of 1848,
filling columns of the Northern Star right through
until the end of the year and beyond.[66] Yet how many
British workers or Chartist leaders followed his repetitious analyses week by week? There is the feeling
that he trumpeted for the Red Republic in something of
a vacuum. At least he provided numerous dissertation
topics for European history graduate students in the
Soviet Union.

The reaction of the Weekly Dispatch to the carnage of June is enlightening. By the summer the Dispatch supported household suffrage and a working class alliance with the middle class.[67] Bad news from France really became grist in the mill to use against physical force Chartism. For example, an editorial in July explained that "one physical force revolution", even if carried out in a "just cause" would invariably "bring on an attempt at another." Violence "can only terminate in the destruction of constitutional government" and the sacrifice of freedom for order.[68] According to its editorials, republican France had made freedom mean "only universal suffrage and no victuals...." Fraternity became "fraternity in plunder"; liberty, "liberty to starve"; and equality was equality in wretchedness alone.[69] The bourgeoisie reigned now, and if Chartists and Repealers sought to take the "short cut of the pike", similar results would inevitably ensue.[70]

These views were widely shared by a broad spectrum of political opinion, from right wing Chartists to ultra Tories. If anyone doubted that all revolutions everywhere were of no lasting good, let him look to the example of France in 1848. As the Bradford Observer put it, there was no need for theories in dealing with the physical force threat in England because "we have a great fact" to appeal to, "the example and present condition of Paris."[71]

All of this discouraged the interest of most Chartists in France in the late spring and summer. But no matter how little interest they showed, Frenchmen supposedly at work in the Chartist movement continued to arouse concern. Foreigners were observed at joint meetings of Chartists and Irish Confederates in the summer, applauding the most violent statements.[72] A police report passed on the rumor that 400 Frenchmen, who dared not be observed in the Chartist movement, were ready to join an insurrection in London.[73] Individuals were watched: the Mayor of Manchester was advised by the Home Office that if one particular Frenchman should advertise any political lectures he should be informed "that the government has the power to send him out of England."[74] Letters continued to come in to the Home Office suggesting that Chartists were in league with "French communists", and therefore ready to overthrow "every existing institution" for "the sake of plunder and licentiousness".[75]

Feargus O'Connor was very perceptive about how the ongoing fears of Frenchmen in England and disparagement of their revolution could be used against the Chartist cause. He saw the French Revolution as a two edged sword in 1848, appreciating the "hope and exultation" that came with the initial excitement, and how the "party of progress" could thereby develop "a new phase of the movement". But on the other hand, the French Revolution roused "all the fears,...the energies" of the "dominant party in England".[76] O'Connor traced the government's reactions: As long as the French Revolution looked promising for the French working class, the government in England tolerated "the fiercest political agitation ever known in this country." But as soon as the "dominion of the middle classes" was assured in France "by the power of the sword", then England's rulers, "emboldened by the failure of France", cracked down on the Chartists. Enthusiastic Chartists who had been tolerated were tolerated no longer. "Tyrannical measured, abetted by the middle-class representatives in the House, were taken in England to accomplish the same ends as military repression accomplished in France.[77] So Feargus O'Connor actually linked the fate of Chartism with the fate of the French republic, and with Irish Repeal as well. To him, French butcheries, English courts sentencing Chartists and Irish coercion were all part of a European "reign of tyranny".[78]

Even so, much of the denunciation of the French Revolution of 1848 coming from nearly all quarters was similar to his own criticisms of it in purpose. It sought to discourage angry Chartists from any imitation through insurrection. Anti-Chartist handbills proclaimed: "Remain quiet and this country must be the manufactory of the world! What good has the revolution done France?"[79] Did Chartists think that the Charter would bring employment and better wages in the end, asked an editorial in the Staffordshire Mercury? "Look at France" where a republic and universal suffrage existed and the misery of French workmen was pronounced.[80] To Arthur Somerville, who has been called a working class reactionary propagandist, events in France proved his point about revolutions, that they must "by logical necessity" lead from chaos to military despotism. He was angry at how liberal newspapers had been so enthusiastic over it at the outset, thereby "inflaming the Chartist mind".[81] Pamphleteers carried on in the same vein: "Utopian patriots" proclaim a republic, "ferocious brigands" carry it on, and a "military dictator" terminates it.[82]

213

Any Chartist bold or brave or desperate enough to try for barricades in England in the summer of 1848 faced not only the opposition of the police, the specials and the army. He also had to sail against the French breeze. Yet some men carried on towards the revolution despite everything that stood in their way, physical or ideological.

The Option Of Violence

At the crossroads in late June, while the right wing of Chartism sought middle class cooperation, the extreme left wing sought armed insurrection. A substantial number of Chartists ceased debating either option and quietly left the movement, most of them never to be heard of in history again once their names ceased to appear in the closely printed columns of the Northern Star.[83] Many others turned inward and joined O'Connor in concentrating on the Land Plan. Two more model villages were opened in June, Snig's End and Minster Lovell. The Land Plan still had hope.

On the extreme left, a number of angry, desperate and generally only locally known Chartists decided to give real revolution a try. These were the men who had enough of petitioning, meeting and peacefully demonstrating. They sought to meet the government's repressive force with force of their own.

Members of Chartism's extreme left in the summer of 1848 tended to be younger men who had never undergone the sobering chastisement of incarceration, a bitter experience that many of the leaders of both center and left had endured before 1848. The men of the new left of Chartism did not edit newspapers, or make funded campaigns around the country, or dream of sitting in the House of Commons. Instead they accumulated the instruments of death in their grim habitations: pikes, pistols, muskets, cartridges.

Something of a classic pattern of revolutionary development came into play in the late spring and summer. As repression forced Chartists out of the movement or underground, active resistance was taken up by those furthest on the left. When the steps they called for became increasingly extreme, more and more dropped away. So it seems that the armed zealots who plotted in July and August of 1848 did so on behalf of a smaller but uncompromising following.

214

How small? The question is not whether armed
Chartists were ready to rise. Some surely were eager
and prepared to go behind barricades. But how numerous
were they and what kind of support did they have behind
them? We shall never really know. Clouds of secrecy
and misinformation cover their activities. It seems
that people on the left today wish to believe that the
revolutionists had a vast body of support, and people
on the right might dismiss them as they were dismissed
by the establishment in 1848, as a small group of
desperadoes out of touch with the overwhelming majority
of British workers. Surely the truth must be somewhere
in between these positions.

This is one of the most perplexing problems in
Chartist historiography. Historians of all persuasions
concur that the attempt to penetrate the clouds around
Chartist conspiracies in 1848 is extremely difficult.
D. J. Rowe notes that there has been "much academic
discussion of the extent and significance of...revolu-
tionary plotting within Chartism", and expects more,
but thinks it "unlikely" that any "useful conclusions"
can ever be drawn because of "the very nature of the
evidence on the subject."[84] David Jones concludes that
the "character and scale of Chartist violence still
baffle the historian" because sources, particularly of
critical meetings and arms clubs, are "inevitably thin
on the ground."[85] John Saville also points out difficulties, noting how troublesome it is to disentangle
militant efforts from attempts of police spies and
agents provocateurs to bring on "premature and abortive
action." Moreover, "exaggeration and downright lying"
get in the way of trial evidence.[86] F. C. Mather
describes such evidence as "tainted".[87] Thomis and
Holt, in Threats of Revolution in Britain, 1789-1848,
provide this insight: "A popular rising cannot be
openly planned because it is illegal, but if it is
secretly planned it can never be popular." On the
other hand, David Goodway found considerable support
for insurrection in London and believes that Thomas
Frost was not a good witness to the events.[88]

The high tensions of the times add to the problems. Excited men, sometimes over-stimulated by the
bottle, exaggerated facts or invented rumors. Many
were Irish conspirators, many were in relative isola-
tion, and some were paid on the basis of what they
could dredge up for the authorities.

The most lurid and detailed reports arriving at
the Home Office in June emanated from the work of a
single spy, a man named Davis. George Davis had a
secondhand shop in Greenwich and joined the Chartist
movement in order to betray them for money. He became
a Metropolitan Council Delegate, sold guns to them and
used violent language against the Queen to ingratiate
himself.[89] Davis described extremely violent Chartists
and their plans in lurid detail: Chartists planned to
get several bags of unslacked, finely powdered lime,
and when the police were drawn up against them they
hoped to dash it in their eyes. Another plan called
for an attack on the police stations at midnight, when
they were supposed to be lightly guarded. After knocking at the doors, Chartists would swarm in and kill
everyone there.[90] Davis also reported on schemes to
purchase vitriol, an attractive substance for Chartist
revolutionaries because it was cheap and could be put
into small phials to throw among the police and military.[91] Davis's reports indicated that the revolutionary plotters had the greatest confidence in their
ability to rise on a certain select day. Davis implied
that he could not report on exactly what day it was,
because only a few leaders knew of it.[92] They would
only inform others of the day of the rising on its eve,
when the armed followers would be gathered.[93] Davis
informed the Home Office that the leaders of this
"conspiracy" were armed with pistols and life preserv-
ers and dealt with Irish Confederates who were moving
between London and Dublin. In all of this, Davis made
sure to insert incidents to prove how dangerous his
profession was: He quoted Chartists saying that if
they found a spy among them "they are determined to
assassinate him on the spot."[94] He also recounted how
at one meeting a Chartist pulled out a knife and said,
"he would stab any one [sic] found to be a spy to the
heart."[95]

Other informants besides Davis were lurid. A
bookseller who had been at a closed Chartist meeting
reported a secret plot to assassinate Lord John
Russell. One Chartist allegedly brandished a knife and
said, "So help me God I should like to put that into
Lord John Russell."[96] Another informant's husband over-
heard Chartists sitting near him while having breakfast. He heard them plotting to burn London down and
attack the police. The informant concluded with "May
the Allmighty frustrate their wickedness...."[97] A
"humble mechanic" wrote in to tell what he heard
secondhand from a Chartist friend. Four hundred of

them had pistols and other weapons, and they intended
to use them on Whit Monday. Since he was "a lover of
my country and Constitution", he had done his duty by
informing Sir George Grey.[98] A man named Reading
reported Chartists plotting a rising "to take the
government by surprise." Reading had hopes of joining
the Chartists as a spy, and told of his plans to gain
selection as a delegate from the Charter Coffee House
at Hatton Gardens, "where the greatest confidence" was
placed in him. He had observed many "bludgeons of a
most formidable nature", pistols and knives, leading
him to the conclusion that arming was being carried on
to a "great extent".[99] The wife of a publican in
Holborn provided the interesting information that the
only Chartists with money to spend that she had seen
were McDouall, McCrea "and one or two others of their
leaders."[100] Another letter described a Chartist
shooting club that departed early in the morning for
target practice.[101] The Mayor of Nottingham reported
the information he received that Chartists had threatened "private assassination", and said "d..n them, they
are afraid of fire." These remarks were "uttered in a
savage and resolute tone by parties unknown", the mayor
wrote.[102]

Up until the summer, such fragmentary evidence,
much of it from questionable sources, provides almost
all the information available about Chartist activity
aimed at revolution. Chartists themselves hardly ever
gave out details about the nature of whatever armed
preparations were going on except in the form of
rumors. Many called for arming openly, as a constitutional right, but little was ever said about specific
plans to use the arms, except to form a 'National
Guard'. Such items as the news about a "human telegraph" included in a speech was exceptional. It was
to consist of a man posted at every half mile between
Bradford and Halifax to communicate what was going
on.[103]

There are enduring beliefs that Whit Monday, June
12, or June 16 or June 18 was designated for a rising.
Davis reported McDouall as the key figure involved.
He was supposed to have called it off at the last
minute.[104] Thomas Frost passed on hearsay information
that June 12 was fixed for a rising, a fact recently
cited as mistaken by one historian.[105] Actually, Frost
qualified his supposition later on: "I afterwards had
reason to believe that they were not so prepared for a
conflict as Rose [his informant] represented them to

be."[106] In August the situation became far less ambiguous.

So much of the problem of finding out what was transpiring stems from the fact that the extreme left of Chartism met in secret clubs in the summer. Some members were armed to the teeth. Muskets and pikes could be acquired from the leaders, sometimes on an installment plan, 6 d a week for a musket and 3 d per week for a pike.[107] Thomas Frost tells of asking a young Welshman about arms. He produced a pike from his closet and declared, "I can't say much about rifles, but there are hundreds of these in the hands of men who won't hesitate to use them when the time comes." Frost described this example of what John Mitchell called "the queen of weapons" as roughly finished with a staff of less than five feet in length.[108] The Weekly Dispatch was alarmed at the silent but "very rapid" spread of armed secret clubs "all over England".[109]

The atmosphere in these militant secret clubs must have produced a severe psychological strain. Rumors, whispers, false names and fears of apprehension all contributed to it. Some clubs even held their conferences in the dark, the participants clutching their weapons, lookouts searching for the police.[110] On the several occasions when rumors of a rising were mooted about, men would sit up and wait in their separate lonely abodes, clutching their weapons, waiting for their leader's signal that never came.[111]

Elsewhere in the same localities the police and soldiers sat up as well, and that is precisely why the signals never came. The police struck first because their agents had permeated the extreme left's clubs. Money bought the services of willing spies, some of them hard pressed by unemployment and some of them willing social deviants. This was perhaps the worst aspect of Chartism underground, the paranoia and well founded suspicions about spies. F. C. Mather has studied the use of spies throughout the Chartist period extensively. He found them to be "persons of no great standing, intelligence or moral integrity."[112] They usually ingratiated themselves in Chartist organizations and then offered themselves for hire to the authorities. They often functioned as agents provocateurs, with the dual purpose of gaining the confidence of the Chartists and leading them into activities which they could report back to the police for pay.

The worst, most notorious spy of all was Powell, who was responsible for much of the evidence brought against the Chartist plotters of August. He suggested all sorts of violent and vicious schemes to Chartist conspirators and then became the star witness against them.[113]

Thomas Frost had experiences with more prosaic and inept spies in 1848. One was the coachman of a conservative gentleman, and another was a well dressed young man who spoke enthusiastically of revolution and wanted to know the strength of the Croyden Chartists, Frost's group, and how ready they were for an uprising. Frost never saw him before and never saw him again.[114]

Thomas Cooper had indirect contact with schemers who may have been spies. An old friend told him that he knew a young man who had a chemical compound that could burn stone. Conspirators planned to burn London down with it. Cooper managed to get some of the substance and demonstrate its uselessness on stone. He left his friend with a strong admonition to avoid agents provocateurs.[115]

The Weekly Dispatch was convinced that "there is not one of the cabals which has not one member, at least, in the pay of the constabulary." The result was that the "wild, honest" Chartists were "regularly sold by their own most intimate friends."[116] The infiltration of spies became so pernicious that Samuel Kydd urged Chartists to invite government reporters to their meetings. He felt his freedom from arrest had been due to reporters, because spies would have perverted his remarks.[117]

It was a vicious cycle: the government forbad open agitation, thereby fostering secret clubs; the clubs hatched violent plans and rumors of these plans led the public to demand more repression. The Weekly Dispatch was correct in declaring that the Home Office, well supplied with funds for spies, "can never fail... to out-general an underhand plot."[118]

Public opinion was generally behind the government, thinking that their steps were, to quote the usual adjectives, "judicious, effectual, watchful, quiet" and "adroit".[119] The press urged the government on to even more repression, as when the Leeds Mercury expressed hopes that "a strict watch" would be kept over leaders liberated on bail and all others suspected

of "machinations against the peace of society." The
Mercury was convinced that Chartist clubs "meditated
the most atrocious and wicked designs."[120] The Weekly
Dispatch gave a warning to the conspirators that if "a
panic comes over the middle classes" about "the stability of the nation", they would be "strung up like
onions."[121]

     Under the circumstances prevailing in the summer
of 1848, it would appear that the extreme left had
little hope for success unless they could count on
massive and widespread support. The frustrating questions remain: How much working class backing did they
really have and how much combustible human material lay
at hand awaiting an insurrection? Two avenues of
inquiry can lead somewhat closer to the answers. The
conflicts of the summer, examined in some detail, will
shed some light. So will an analysis of the rhetoric
and the disputes over physical force in the open,
public agitation after April 10.

          Physical Force Rhetoric And Its Reception

     The rhetoric of the physical force Chartists in
1848 deserves analysis. Many contemporaries and many
historians have applied the blanket generalization that
many Chartists called for a revolution and let it go at
that. How did they call for revolution? What justification did they give for their more militant utter-
ances? To what degree was deliberate ambiguity
employed? How were these expressions received? To
what extent were they disputed?

     Politics has always has its slogans. Those of the
physical force Chartists were strung through their
speeches and emblazoned on banners, over and over
again. Typical banners read: "He that has no sword,
let him sell his garment and buy one; It is better to
die by the sword than to perish with hunger; We will
conquer or die; The oppressed shall go free in defiance
of oppressors; Britons strike home; England free or a
desert; Woe to the tyrants who obstruct our way to
freedom; Man to be free has only to will it; The Charter and down with the aristocracy; The Charter with
peace or a republic." Such banners came out for meeting after meeting, and reporters came to note particular ones that reappeared regularly.

There was nothing new about their messages. In
the tense years of early Chartism similar banners had
flown. Similar catch phrases had been used also.
Chartists had long pledged that they would use legal
and constitutional means to get their rights, but if
spurned "more direct means" would be used. What could
be more violent than the speeches of J. R. Stephens or
Richard Oastler in 1838 and 1839? An often quoted
sample from Stephens' oratory will suffice as an illustration. This sectarian Methodist preacher called for
"war to the knife" against Poor Law authorities:

> If the musket and the pistol, the sword
> and the pike were of no avail, let the
> women take the scissors, the child the
> pin or needle. If all failed, then the
> firebrand -- aye, the firebrand, I
> repeat.[122]

In 1848 speakers addressing crowds in the north
were the ones most likely to come forth with blood and
thunder speeches rivaling those of 1839. George Webber
speaking to thousands at remote Toftshaw Moor in June
can serve as one of many such examples. He demanded
"fair and manly combat" with the "blood-thirsty government", letting the "God of Battles" decide the outcome.
He called upon "all men who felt the glow of patriotism" to arm and "erect barricades". A flag staff with
a dagger at its top stood nearby, approximating a pike,
and Webber, grabbing it, shouted that "he would like to
behold the sun of heaven" shining on "the magnificent
spectacle" of "five hundred thousand men with instruments such as this."[123] George White, who shared the
platform with Webber, added humor:

> The middle classes used toothpicks to
> remove what stuck in their teeth after
> a good dinner; and it was the duty of
> every one of the working classes to
> provide themselves with toothpicks but
> of a rather larger size, to enable
> them to remove the obstructions in their
> way of getting a good dinner too.[124]

There was much more than blatant calls for judgement from the God of Battles in physical force rhetoric.
The more sophisticated speeches contained reasoned
arguments for calling Chartists to arms. Chartists
frequently cited their constitutional right to bear
arms, referring to Blackstone and other authorities.

Arming was described as a duty to protect against oppression.[125] Militants maintained that the best way to prevent revolution and to preserve human life was to arm the masses.[126] The government simply would not dare move against such a formidable array. Furthermore, governments had always conceded "when people had a musket in their hand [sic]". Chartists had to show that they had the strength to compel the acceptance of the petition by force before Parliament would pass it into law. While the government might scorn the petitions of defenseless men, they could not treat the petitions of armed men that way. With the Charter a law, revolution was absolutely out of the question.[127]

Chartists were also called to arms to protect themselves from the violence of the government. The "bloody government", according to John West, was making extensive preparations for "slaughtering the people."[128] Chartists argued that since the other classes were "physically prepared" to oppress them, why should not the workers "be prepared to drive back and repel all invaders of their rights and liberties?"[129] Let those who prohibited meetings, denied freedom of speech, broke into homes and gaoled freeborn Englishmen beware the people armed in defense of their rights.

Militant Chartists saw no sense in going on with moral force demonstrations when their enemies assumed a "physical attitude" towards them. Besides, had moral force ever achieved freedom anywhere? Had it not always been acquired through the use or the threat of physical force?[130] After all, physical force had led King John to sign the Magna Carta, so what should prevent the people from pursuing a "similar course" now?[131] "Tyranny" and "aristocracy" had been "kept up" by physical force over the centuries, and only physical force or the threat of it could destroy their power to "rob the working man of his rights."[132]

Impatience with the constitutional agitation marked physical force oratory. For example, George White had heard "too much talking." He thought Chartists were becoming "soft", and looked to democrats abroad as if they did not have "the pluck of a goose". Foreign democrats would say to them, "Oh, you are an English Chartist are you? Bring out a chair and the gentleman will give us a speech."[133] Many physical force Chartists declared they were through with agitating as long as the results were "mere froth".[134] They had enough of resolutions and enough of "black and white" petitions.[135]

No matter how impatient militants may have been, much of physical force oratory in 1848 was qualified, just as it had been in previous years. The spellbinders were adept at the old dodge of making an inflammatory statement and then taking all or part of it back later on in their discourses. A reporter for the Macclesfield Courier caught on to the technique. As he listened to speakers who were "more violent than usual" at a Chartist meeting in May, he realized that "they all put such qualifications to their statements that before concluding they had unsaid every word that they had said."[136] The advantage of this tactic was that they got cheers for militancy and, they hoped, the protection of their disclaimers should they be arrested. Harney, for instance, would issue blood stirring threats and barely disguised evocations of revolutionary effort and end with something like this: "Whether it was physical force, or whether it was moral force, he wanted no man to spill his blood who could obtain his rights without it."[137] A reporter from the Manchester Guardian aptly described this kind of oratory, replete with well cheered hints, as the "usual half menacing" kind.[138]

One way to qualify physical force statements was to urge a revolutionary step, such as sending deputies to London with muskets under their coats, and then quickly add hopes that "they would not be driven to that extremity."[139] Another way was to hope that there would be no "premature outbreak" while arming.[140] Moreover, definitions of revolution could be stretched when a Chartist orator was accused of advocating one. He could say he meant an important change.[141] Ernest Jones defended himself by saying that he regarded slavery emancipation as a revolution, and the Reform Bill of 1832, although the "trickery of the Whigs" had made it "abortive". Under pressure, Jones would not define revolution as "insurrection".[142]

Ernest Jones has been cited by David Jones for doing feats on the verbal highwire in 1848.[143] Indeed he did. In one sentence he said that people would ask for a republic if they were refused the Charter. In the next, that the men of London were as good as the men of Paris. In the next, that by showing a "bold physical front", Chartists would "prevent the necessity for physical action". In the next, that he did not believe it was necessary to "strike a single blow".[144]

223

Perhaps the most typical of the qualifying statements of 1848 was one or another variation of this non sequitor:

> Physical force could not be carried out
> until the united voice of the people
> proclaimed that the time was come for
> it and then there would be no need to
> resort to it.[145]

Punch had its own version of how physical force orators added qualifications, given in its description of "the model agitator":

> He excites the people to arm themselves
> for the worst, but he begs they will
> use no weapons. His talk is incendiary,
> his advice nothing but gunpowder, and
> yet he hopes that no explosion will take
> place. He is an arsenal wishing to pass
> for a Chapel or a baby-linen warehouse.[146]

The blurred nature of much physical force oratory complemented the unclear distinction between moral force and physical force Chartism. While there was no doubt about the position of those on either the right or the extreme left, the dichotemy of moral force and physical force was artificial for many Chartists in the center, as they themselves realized. An Ernest Jones aptly put it, "every man,...except a coward, was both a physical and moral force man, according to the circumstances."[147] One delegate to the National Convention said his constituents were moral force men who would "soon be converted into physical force man."[148] Many Chartists said they were "not particular" about the means, only the goals mattered.[149] Many wanted "moral force to be tried to the last", but wanted "another species of force" applied if peaceful measures failed.[150]

How attractive was the physical force position to the ordinary workers who attended Chartist meetings? It is a difficult question. There is some evidence of support for it, and some evidence for opposition. Sometimes speakers at large meetings called for a show of hands to indicate who the physical force advocates were. Some meetings displayed clear majorities, conditioned, of course, by the manner in which the speaker led up to his question.[151] On occasions moral force Chartists tried the same tactic, which sometimes led to

disappointment.[152] Some meetings were described as
"tame and spiritless" until addressed by a physical
force advocate, who would animate the assembly and
bring on bursts of heavy applause.[153]

  The readiness of the physical force advocates to
engage in at least verbal combat was never in doubt
because they readily interrupted meetings. For
example, when the chairman of a Salford Chartist meeting said it was folly to break the law and that moral
power was sufficient to gain Chartist ends, cries of
"We must not trust to that! We have trusted that too
long!" and "No! No!" rent the air.[154] They booed and
hissed as well, thereby making the "loud disapprobation" reported so often, as when a Manchester Chartist
told a London audience that "the people of this country
were not in a fighting posture."[155]

  As might be expected, meetings were most raucous
when speakers from both sides held forth. The sessions
of the National Assembly were a case in point. Leeds
had one delegate for physical force and one for moral
force, leading one local Chartist to ask, "What are the
constituents to do when their leaders are at logger-
heads?"[156] Leicester also had a schism, resulting in
the secession of the physical force minority to form
their own organization of a few hundred members.[157]
Such schisms happened elsewhere as well.[158]

  A rough indication of the physical and moral force
division at the National Convention can be gained from
constituency reports. They reveal that Chartist
localities did not rule out physical force by almost
four to one. Geography seems to have played no part
in determining stance, because constituencies espousing
either kind of force were scattered. Some appeals for
moral force were clear. For example, the delegate from
Exeter urged the Convention not to "throw aside the
majesty and dignity" of the Charter's moral power. On
the other hand, only few of the appeals for physical
force from constituencies were unequivocal. Edinburgh's delegate brought such a message, saying that
Chartists he represented were ready to support the
Charter "at the stake, in the dungeon or on the field."
Another example was the message from Wigan, where Chartists "would rather go to work and resort to physical
force at once, than remain in their present deplorable
position." These reports were exceptional because most
pronouncements on physical force were unclear and

qualified. One response, from the Chartists of Lancaster, was unabashedly honest: They were "ready to join in extreme measures", but only "if there existed any probability of success" and "not otherwise."[159]

The willingness of Convention delegates to countenance the possibility of using physical force as well as the popularity of physical force speakers at so many meetings goes against a fundamental point stressed by Chartist leaders at the center and right, namely that physical force Chartists were but a small minority of the movement.

The established press stressed this point as well. Physical force Chartists were "a mere handful", according to the Leeds Mercury.[160] The Manchester Guardian described them as "a very small minority".[161] The Times called them "an insignificant and powerless faction".[162] Fraser's Magazine made the distinction between the "good" Chartists and the "bad" Chartists, and found the latter to be small in numbers.[163] The Nonconformist thought that the "just demands" of the working class had been confounded by "a few excited and injudicious mob orators".[164]

Once again, the Weekly Dispatch exceeded all of the other newspapers in scorning the most militant Chartists. They were the "mean, cowardly, farcical... champions of anarchy". Chartists who went along with "these Duffys and Cuffays and Mitchells and Joneses", men of "big words and mean thoughts", were "dupes" of "bog trotting thugs" and "fustian ranting Chartists".[165] How could the industrious workers of England be represented by so many of these "wretched brawlers" at their National Convention and National Assembly? The Weekly Dispatch answered by finding Chartist elections a travesty of democracy. According to the Dispatch, Chartists should never complain of how Members of Parliament are chosen if their own representatives were so ill-chosen. The Chartist delegates were "voted into office...at small hole-and-corner meetings...without notice or preparation, by mere handfuls of hobbledehoys and their sweethearts...."[166] The outrageous and over-represented physical force minority alienated the middle classes from Chartism,[167] and, what was worse, their activities invited a crackdown from the government that would take away everyone's liberty. They turned public sympathy against reform and allowed oppression to be "called a necessity". The old right of public meeting came to be confounded in the public

mind with "riot, robbery and disorder."[168] The "oligarchs" were delighted with Chartism "run riot", with
prudent leaders deserted and "every spouter with blood
and fire in his mouth cheered to the echo!" In short,
"Reform was made Chartism, Chartism was made revolution, revolution was made incendiarism and communism...." What is more, the "oligarchs" could "point to
the very words which established the fearful identity"
coming from "the mouths of those who had come forward
to lead the people."[169] They would have their reward
in the gaols, hulks and gallows.[170]

By June, leaders of mainstream Chartism added
their own warnings to those on the extreme left. The
Executive Committee of the National Charter Association
issued an open letter in June calling for organization
only, and urged Chartists not to "make secret preparations" or be "led into secret organization...." All
"concerted plans, signs or conspiracies" were dangerous.[171] The signers of this letter included Ernest
Jones, Peter Murray McDouall, Samuel Kydd and James
Leach. That these men, who were all singled out by the
establishment as being dangerous revolutionaries,
should be so negative towards plotting has great significance.

This point was underlined again in July, when
Ernest Jones wrote an open letter calling for law and
order in Chartist demonstrations, pointing out that
there was "a vast difference between courage and violence." A "truly brave people" were never "disorderly"
and had "sufficient energy to prevent disorder in
others."[172] O'Connor denounced physical force consist-
ently all through the year. "My children", he wrote in
the Northern Star in June, "do not make jackasses of
yourselves by cheering every fool who tells you that he
has his pike and rifle at home while he never saw a
pike nor a rifle in his life."[173] The O'Connorites by
the summer of 1848 had by and large taken up the old
moral force position of Lovett's group. Philip
McGrath, one of O'Connor's closest associates, proclaimed: "Violent measures were not suited to...the
British mind,..." and therefore Chartists ought to rely
upon lectures, public meetings and a legal system of
organization.[174] Even in troubled Bradford, the Chartist Council disclaimed any responsibility for injuring
persons or property.[175]

What can be concluded from this analysis of rhetoric about physical force? Certainly the men who armed and plotted in secret clubs in the summer faced considerable opposition from the mainstream of the movement, to say nothing of the right wing, the radicals and the public in general. Once again Ernest Jones and some of his colleagues emerge as figures calling for a determined, threatening agitation, but an agitation that did not extend to the point where rhetoric became action. Their exhortations to arms and threats of revolution were usually qualified. Still, there is more evidence of enthusiasm for a violent solution among the rank and file than the mainstream Chartists would care to admit. But it seems that relatively few were ready to go beyond enthusiasm. By the end of June, physical force Chartists, moral force Chartists and mainstream Chartists all lacked sufficient support for their differing and conflicting programs. In 1848 as before, Chartism suffered from its divisions. Those who had made their decision to go ahead alone on the extreme left were no longer concerned about rhetoric or arguing. They wanted action.

NOTES TO CHAPTER VI

[1]The Times, July 8, 1848, p. 5.

[2]Leeds Mercury, April 15, 1848, p. 4.

[3]Leeds Mercury, May 6, 1848, p. 4.

[4]Simon Maccoby, English Radicalism, Vol. 3, 1832-1852 (London 1935), po. 284-9.

[5]Donald Read, Cobden and Bright: A Victorian Political Partnership (London 1967), p. 80. Cobden did not object to universal manhood suffrage.

[6]Steven Hobhouse, Joseph Sturge, His Life and Work (London 119), p. 85.

[7]Manchester Guardian, May 3, 1848, p. 6.

[8]Large, "London in the Year of Revolutions, 1848", p. 195.

[9]Weekly Dispatch, May 7, 1848, pp. 219 and 221; April 30, p. 206; May 21, p. 245.

[10]Weekly Dispatch, April 30, 1848, p. 205; Also May 7, 1848; Leeds Mercury, April 22, 1848, p. 8.

[11]Northern Star, May 6, 1848, p. 1.

[12]Many Chartists tried to sell the Charter to the middle classes. See P. M. McDouall, "The Charter, What it Means! The Chartists, What They Want! Explained in an Address to the Middle Classes of Great Britain" (London 1848).

[13]Holyoake claims he was suspected of being a Whig in disguise in the north, so he bought a pike, tipped it with a cork and brought it to London as a sample of northern Chartist arguments. McCabe, Life and Letters of George Jacob Holyoake, p. 142.

[14]Smith, "Great Britain and the Revolutions of 1848", p. 74.

[15]Lovett and his groups had met at the National Hall. Others, including Watson and Hetherington, operated out of the John Street Institution. Just

before news of the French Revolution arrived, he had been especially honored for his services to democracy by a public dinner and gifts. Lovett, Life and Struggles, p. 278.

[16]Linton, James Watson: A Memoir, pp. 56-7.

[17]Cooper wrote that he shunned the "monster meetings" and avoided all the "violence and failure" of that year. Thomas Cooper, The Life of Thomas Cooper, Written by Himself (London 1882), pp. 302-3, 311.

[18]Jones, Chartism and the Chartists, p. 185; Large, "London in the Year of Revolutions, 1848", pp. 194-5, notes the cooperation of moral force Chartists up until April 10. Also Edward Royle, Victorian Infidels: The Origins of the British Secularist Movement, 1791-1866 (Manchester 1974), p. 137.

[19]Handbill: "Objects and Rules of the People's Charter Union, H.O. 45/2410 London.

[20]Handbill: Proposal for Forming a People's League, Lovett Collection, p. 288.

[21]Lovett, Life and Struggles, p. 284.

[22]Nonconformist, May 10, 1848, p. 335; July 26, 1848, p. 550.

[23]For the People's League, Lovett, Life and Struggles, po. 280-92; Lovett Papers, Vol. 1, "Forms of Petitions in Favour of Universal Suffrage..."; Vol. II, p. 289, "The People's League for Obtaining Manhood Suffrage".

[24]For O'Brien in 1848, see Alfred Plummer, Bronterre: A Political Biography of Bronterre O'Brien, 1804-1864 (London 1971), pp. 188-92. Also Schoyen, The Chartist Challenge, pp. 163-5.

[25]The Reasoner, Vol. 4, 1848, pp. 232-3 contains Owen's proclamation on the French Revolution.

[26]Chapman, Harriet Martineau's Autobiography, Vol. 2, pp. 298-9; Knight, Passages of a Working Life, p. 88.

[27] John Saville, "The Christian Socialists of 1848", in John Saville, ed., Democracy and the Labour Movement: Essays in Honour of Dona Torr (London 1954), p. 136.

[28] Hughes, "Memoir", preface to Alton Locke, p. xiv.

[29] Hughes, "Memoir", preface to Alton Locke, p. xx.

[30] Hughes, "Memoir", preface to Alton Locke, p. xvi-xix, quoting Parson Lot's Letters to the Chartists, no. 1.

[31] Kingsley, Charles Kingsley: His Letters and Memories of His Life, Vol. I, p. 118.

[32] Among them were The Christian Socialist, Politics for the People, Journal of Association.

[33] Saville, "The Christian Socialists of 1848", p. 157.

[34] Kingsley, Alton Locke, p. 361.

[35] C. Stella Davies, A History of Macclesfield (Manchester 1961), p. 318.

[36] Nonconformist, April 19, 1848, p. 275.

[37] For example, Samuel Morley, who wrote: "I am far removed from being a Chartist, but I have the deepest sympathy for the working classes who are suffering an amount of misery which deserves more consideration." Hodder, Life of Samuel Morley, p. 80.

[38] The Times, April 22, 1848.

[39] Leeds Mercury, April 8, 1848, p. 4.

[40] Anon., "A Letter from one of the Special Constables...", p. 10.

[41] Greville, The Greville Memoirs, Vol. 6, p. 195.

[42] Bessborough, Lady Charlotte Guest, p. 210.

[43] James Gibson to Joseph Hume, May 3, 1848, Russell Papers, P.R.O. 30/22 7B.

231

[44] Prince Albert to Lord John Russell, RA Add MSS 16/47 and draft RA Add MSS C 56, Item 12.

[45] Illustrated London News, April 1, 1848, p. 207.

[46] Anon., "How to Disarm the Chartists", Blackwood's Edinburgh Magazine, Vol. 63, no. 392 (June 1848), p. 655.

[47] Representation of Merchants, Tradesmen and other inhabitants of Liverpool to the Mayor of Liverpool, H.O. 45/2410, Part 1 a.

[48] Leeds Mercury, April 8, 1848, p. 4. The Manchester Guardian noted that despite suffering, workers in the area were too intelligent to mitigate their suffering by breaking the law. Manchester Guardian, April 12, 1848, p. 4.

[49] Walpole, The Life of Lord John Russell, Vol. 1, p. 88.

[50] Colonel Rowan to General Bowles (Master of the Household), April, 1848, RA Add MSS C 56, Item 30.

[51] Smith, "Great Britain and the Revolutions of 1848", p. 84; Jones, Chartism and the Chartists, p. 117.

[52] Lovett, Life and Struggles of William Lovett, p. 291.

[53] The speech of Robert Anderson reported in the Manchester Guardian of April 22, 1848, p. 8, is typical. He saw the middle classes blind to British poverty while they expressed concern over the Poles and Russians.

[54] Leeds Mercury, April 22, 1848, p. 8. The speaker was named Shaw.

[55] Manchester Guardian, May 17, 1848, p. 8.

[56] Weekly Dispatch, April 30, 1848, p. 212. A report of the Aggregate Trades of the Metropolis noted plans for the formation of a "Labour Protection Board".

[57] Some examples are Issac Dawson at Middleton, Manchester Guardian, May 17, 1848; Other Chartist meetings reported in the Manchester Guardian, May 3,

1848, p. 6; June 14, 1848, p. 6; Gifford's speech, April 22, 1848, p. 8; Northern Star, May 20, 1848, p. 6, speech of McCrae; John Bezer reported in the Weekly Dispatch, August 20, 1848, p. 397; John Shackleton, Weekly Dispatch, April 29, 1848, p. 7; editorials in Weekly Dispatch, May 7, 1848, p. 221; June 18, 1848, p. 293.

[58]The very first inklings of coming disappointment were alluded to by Harney even before the meeting at Kennington Common. As early as March 25 the Fraternal Democrats were upset at a "menacing manifestation" of an "ill-advised portion of the National Guard." Northern Star, March 25, 1848, p. 4. The French elections of May produced an assembly that was too conservative for Harney and his friends. From Harney's point of view, the proletarians' "social emancipation" depended principally on having men of their own class as lawmakers". Northern Star, May 27, 1848, p. 3, an editorial by L'Ami du Peuple, Harney's pen name. O'Connor reflected disillusionment in May, saying that it was clear to him that the French people were not prepared for the Charter as the English people were on account of his leadership. Northern Star, May 13, 1848, p. 5; also p. 1; May 20, 1848, p. 1.

[59]Northern Star, June 17, 1848, p. 3.

[60]Northern Star, July 1, 1848, p. 4. One Chartist declared that the lesson from the June Days in France was simply that the middle classes could not be trusted. Northern Star, July 8, 1848, p. 2.

[61]Lovett, Life and Struggles, pp. 276-7.

[62]Northern Star, July 1, 1848. Jones made the point that only labor could properly legislate for labor.

[63]Northern Star, July 1, 1848, p. 1.

[64]Northern Star, July 8, 1848, p. 4.

[65]Harney now challenged the Chartist orthodoxy that states with universal suffrage would not have oppression and that insurrection against such states was unjustifiable. Henceforth, the red flag struck down in Paris in June would be the "flag of the proletarians throughout Europe." Northern Star, July 8, 1848, p. 6.

233

[66]Some of his lengthier pieces can be found in the Northern Star: June 10, 1848, p. 3; September 2, 1848, p. 1; September 9, 1848, p. 5; September 16, 1848, p. 4; September 23, 1848, p. 5; September 30, 1848, p. 5; October 21, 1848, p. 5; October 28, 1848, p. 5; November 4, 1848, p. 5; November 11, 1848, p. 3; November 18, 1848, p. 5; December 2, 1848, p. 5; December 9, 1848, p. 6.

[67]The Dispatch touted itself as the "companion to the artisan" which was also found "beneath many a thatched roof" in secluded hamlets. Several leading moral force Chartists of the right wing had some stake in the publication's success. See the quotation from 'John Bull' in the Weekly Dispatch of April 23, 1848, p. 197.

[68]Weekly Dispatch, July 2, 1848, p. 313. An editorial pointed out that training private citizens to bear arms wrecked democracy, as the French example showed.

[69]Weekly Dispatch, July 2, 1848, p. 313.

[70]Weekly Dispatch, April 23, 1848, p. 197.

[71]Bradford Observer, September 14, 1848, p. 4.

[72]Weekly Dispatch, August 20, 1848, p. 399.

[73]Police Report, August 14, 1848, from an informant named Ritchie, H.O. 45/2410, Part 2, London.

[74]Henry Waddington to the Mayor of Manchester, July 22, 1848. Waddington to the Mayor of Bristol, July 22 and July 27, 1848, H.O. 41/19.

[75]J. H. Mathiason to Sir George Grey, April 17, 1848, H.O. 45/2410, Part 5 AD-AL. A meeting of 400 to 500 in late April aroused suspicions on the part of the police that French "communist missionaries" were at work. Metropolitan Police Report, April 24, 1848, H.O. 45/2410 Part 5 AD-AL. Several of the delegates at the Chartist National Assembly were suspected of having come over from France, where they hitherto resided "for many years", and were presumably eager to foist Parisian fashions in politics on their fellow members. J. Patterson to the Home Office, May 20, 1848, H.O. 45/2410, Part 5 AD-AL.

[76] *Northern Star*, May 20, 1848, p. 4.

[77] *Northern Star*, September 9, 1848, p. 1.

[78] *Northern Star*, July 15, 1848, p. 1.

[79] Handbill, H.O. 45/2410, Part 5 A-L.

[80] *Staffordshire Mercury*, April 15, 1848, p. 3.

[81] Alexander Somerville, *Conservative Science of Nations, Being the First Complete Narrative of Somerville's Dilligent Hope in the Service of Public Safety in Britain* (Montreal and Toronto 1860), p. 222.

[82] A Fellow Labourer, "What the Chartists Are", p. 4.

[83] David Jones notes how some former leaders were reduced to "quiet cynicism" and how others "set off for Kansas City." *Chartism and the Chartists*, p. 168. Donald Read, "Chartism in Manchester", p. 64, observes that some who had remained "faithful to the movement during its weakest period, from 1842 to 1846, now began to give up."

[84] Rowe, "Some Aspects of Chartism on the Tyneside", p. 36.

[85] Jones, *Chartism and the Chartists*, p. 153.

[86] Saville, "Chartism in the Year of Revolution: 1848", p. 30.

[87] Mather, *Public Order in the Age of the Chartists*, p. 215.

[88] Malcolm I. Thomis and Peter Holt, *Threats of Revolution in Britain, 1789-1848* (London 1977), p. 116. Goodway, *London Chartism, 1838-1848*, pp. 86-96, 228-9, 266. Goodway also thinks it is wrong to emphasize the role of William Cuffay as leader. He found Payne, Mullens, John Rose, Brewster and James Barrett as the true leaders.

[89] Mather, *Chartism and Society*, p. 168.

[90] Metropolitan Police Report, June 14, 1848, H.O. 45/2410, Part 2, London.

[91]Ibid.

[92]Metropolitan Police Report, June 1, 1848, H.O. 45/2410, London.

[93]Metropolitan Police Report, June 10, 1848, H.O. 45/2410, London.

[94]Metropolitan Police Report, June 12, 1848, H.O. 45/2410, London.

[95]Metropolitan Police Report, June 11, 1848, H.O. 45/2410, London.

[96]Mr. Taylor to the Home Office, June 21, 1848, H.O. 45/2410, London.

[97]A. Evans to Sir George Grey, June 9, 1848; Also William Jones to Sir George Grey, June 15, 1848, H.O. 45/2410, London.

[98]P. Palmer to Sir George Grey, June 12, 1848, H.O. 45/2410, London.

[99]R. Reading to R. Mayne, June 12, 1848, H.O. 45/2410, London.

[100]Metropolitan Police Report, June 13, 1848, H.O. 45/2410, London.

[101]Edwin Patchett to Sir George Grey, May 31, 1848, H.O. 45/2410, Part 3.

[102]Mayor of Nottingham to Sir George Grey, June 7, 1848, H.O. 45/2410, Part 3; Also Waddington to the Mayor of Nottingham, June 8, 1848, H.O. 41/19.

[103]Leeds Mercury, June 17, 1848, p. 4.

[104]Mather, Chartism and Society, pp. 168-9.

[105]Goodway, "Chartism in London", pp. 14-15.

[106]Frost, Forty Years' Recollections, p. 162.

[107]From the indictment of Maxwell Bryson, Weekly Dispatch, August 27, 1848, p. 411.

[108]Frost, Forty Years' Recollections, p. 147. Frost also commented upon the cheapness of rifles,

12 s., mentioning that people scoffed at such a low price.

[109] _Weekly Dispatch_, August 20, 1848, p. 397.

[110] "Chartist Meetings, Speeches and Trials of July 26-August 25, 1848", Coll. Misc. 208, The British Library of Political and Economic Science.

[111] _Leeds Mercury_, August 19, 1848, p. 11.

[112] Mather, _Public Order in the Age of the Chartists_, p. 204.

[113] Powell was, according to Thomas Frost, "as horrible a miscreant as the mind can conceive". He constantly suggested "projects of conflagration and slaughter". Among other things, Powell set about interesting Chartist conspirators in making caltrops, spiked pieces of wood designed to be scattered in the streets in order to lame cavalry horses. _Frost, Forty Years' Recollections_, p. 150; Smith, "Great Britain and the Revolutions of 1848", p. 81, calls him "psychopathic".

[114] Frost, _Forty Years' Recollections_, p. 149.

[115] Cooper, _Life of Thomas Cooper_, pp. 303-11.

[116] _Weekly Dispatch_, August 20, 1848, p. 397.

[117] Mather, _Public Order in the Age of the Chartists_, p. 192.

[118] _Weekly Dispatch_, August 20, 1848, p. 397.

[119] _Annual Register_, August, 1848, p. 103; _Weekly Dispatch_, August 20, 1848, p. 397; _Leeds Mercury_, August 19, 1848, p. 11.

[120] _Leeds Mercury_, August 19, 1848, p. 4.

[121] _Weekly Dispatch_, August 20, 1848, p. 397.

[122] Quoted in Rowe, "Some Aspects of Chartism on the Tyneside", p. 19. It is often quoted elsewhere. See Cole, _Chartist Portraits_, for a biographical sketch of Stephens.

[123] _Leeds Mercury_, June 17, 1848, p. 4.

[124] Ibid.

[125] A good example of this view is in the speech of John Shaw at Barnsley reported in the Leeds Mercury of May 27, 1848, p. 10.

[126] Leeds Mercury, April 22, 1848, pp. 8 and 12; Also speeches at a Chartist meeting reported in the Macclesfield Courier, April 15, 1848.

[127] This line of argument was in many speeches. A good example was that of William Dixon, reported in the Weekly Dispatch, April 2, 1848, p. 159.

[128] Macclesfield Courier, April 22, 1848; Ernest Jones in the Northern Star, April 8, 1848, p. 8; Leeds Mercury, June 17, 1848, p. 4, speech of George White.

[129] Leeds Mercury, April 22, 1848, p. 8.

[130] Leeds Mercury, April 22, 1848, p. 12; Letter from John Mackay, Northern Star, March 25, 1848.

[131] Manchester Guardian, April 12, 1848, p. 5.

[132] Manchester Guardian, April 22, 1848, p. 7, quoting a letter by a Chartist named Nutall.

[133] Leeds Mercury, June 17, 1848, p. 4.

[134] Leeds Mercury, April 22, 1848, p. 8.

[135] Weekly Dispatch, April 2, 1848, p. 159.

[136] Macclesfield Courier, May 27, 1848, p. 2.

[137] Weekly Dispatch, April 9, 1848, p. 180.

[138] Manchester Guardian, March 29, 1848, p. 6.

[139] Weekly Dispatch, March 26, 1848, McDouall at a Chartist meeting in Nottingham.

[140] Leeds Mercury, June 17, 1848, p. 4.

[141] For example, John West's remarks reported in the Macclesfield Courier, April 8, 1848.

[142] Northern Star, April 29, 1848, p. 6.

[143] Jones, Chartism and the Chartists, p. 150.

[144] Northern Star, April 8, 1848, p. 7.

[145] Manchester Guardian, May 17, 1848, James Leach at a Chartist camp meeting.

[146] Punch, 1848, p. 130.

[147] Manchester Guardian, June 10, 1848, p. 9.

[148] Northern Star, April 8, 1848, p. 8. The delegate was David Thomas.

[149] Northern Star, March 25, 1848.

[150] Northern Star, May 6, 1848, p. 7, speech of Lightowler; Leeds Mercury, June 17, 1848, p. 4, speech of George Weber.

[151] John Shaw at a Leeds meeting got a unanimous show of hands after he taunted a previous moral force speaker. Leeds Mercury, April 22, 1848, p. 12.

[152] Leeds Mercury, April 22, 1848, p. 8.

[153] Leeds Mercury, June 17, 1848, p. 4.

[154] Weekly Dispatch, April 2, 1848, p. 159.

[155] Northern Star, April 1, 1848, p. 8.

[156] Leeds Mercury, April 22, 1848, p. 5.

[157] Patterson, Radical Leicester, p. 362.

[158] Sometimes the physical force Chartists were the recipients of disapprobation at public meetings. There is a good example of this at a Chartist meeting reported in the Leeds Mercury of May 6, 1848, p. 4. When physical force advocates claimed a good number of adherents in a given locality, moral force Chartists might withdraw from the whole movement.

[159] These conclusions are based on reports of the National Convention in the Northern Star of April 8, p. 1 and the Morning Chronicle, April 4 and 5, 1848, p. 3.

160 Leeds Mercury, April 8, 1848, p. 4. The Leeds Mercury found the physical force Chartists insane; their plots "crazy"; and their plans for a civil war "madness". (August 19, 1848, p. 4; April 15, 1848, p. 4.)

161 Manchester Guardian, April 12, 1848, p. 4.

162 The Times, April 10, 1848, p. 4.

163 Anon., "Chartism", Fraser's Magazine, May, 1848, p. 579.

164 Nonconformist, May 17, 1848, p. 335. These Chartists were described as trying to make "roast beef and plumb pudding everywhere abundant...as by magic... from pikes and...blood."

165 Weekly Dispatch, May 7, 1848, p. 229; Also March 12, 1848, p. 127; Sept. 24, 1848, p. 457, which stated that violent Chartism and "Irish Thugee" were "utterly insignificant" in their seditious efforts against "the stability of this stalwart and indestructible empire"; Also June 4, 1848, p. 270.

166 Weekly Dispatch, April 23, 1848, p. 192; also May 14, 1848, p. 233.

167 Weekly Dispatch, May 7, 1848, p. 221; March 12, 1848, p. 125; Leeds Mercury, April 15, 1848, p. 4; April 8, 1848, p. 4.

168 Weekly Dispatch, April 16, 1848, p. 185; Bradford Observer, August 24, 1848, editorial.

169 Weekly Dispatch, April 16, 1848, p. 185; Also March 12, 1848, p. 125. The Nonconformist held similar views, declaring that the "physical force agitators" offended "more seriously against progress than against law", by halting the "reform spirit" and giving "plausible excuse for repressive measures." Nonconformist, August 30, 1848, p. 654. They alienated "thousands of intelligent and respectable men from their cause." Nonconformist, April 19, 1848, p. 275.

170 Weekly Dispatch, July 16, 1848, p. 337; March 12, 1848, p. 125; July 30, 1848, p. 367; August 20, 1848, p. 397; Also remarks against revolution, July 2, 1848, p. 313.

240

[171] *Northern Star*, June 17, 1848, p. 8.

[172] *Northern Star*, July 1, 1848, p. 1.

[173] *Northern Star*, June 17, 1848, p. 1.

[174] Quoted in Saville, "Chartism in the Year of Revolution: 1848", p. 32.

[175] Handbill, H.O. 45/2410, Part 4 AB-AC. The Lancashire and Cheshire Chartist Delegates proclaimed that liberty was "too sacred to be associated with unmeaning violence." "The South Lancashire and Cheshire Chartist Delegates to the People", Manchester, March 14, 1848, H.O. 45/2410, London. See also speeches at a Leeds meeting reported in the *Leeds Mercury*, April 15, 1848, Supplement, p. 6.

CHAPTER VII

THE THIRD STAGE: FROM THE SUMMER TO THE FALL

> Come, all lovers of Sedition for its own
>   delightful sake;
> Come, all disaffected rascals, a disturb-
>   ance let us make;
> Come, at midnight let us meet, ye revolu-
>   tionary crew,
> With no purpose in particular but rioting
>   in view.
> Whilst in almost every capital of Europe
>   there's a row,
> Brother vagabonds, shall we alone continue
>   quiet now?
>
> (A clipping from <u>Punch</u> in
> the Royal Archives, C56/95)

The Short, Cool Summer

Unrelenting repression continued throughout the summer. The same orders rang out from the Home Office: Meetings that caused terror and alarm were to be stopped;[1] Chartist processions could not go on;[2] orators whose speeches were deemed "highly seditious and dangerous" were to be arrested.[3] If there were any "lawless proceedings" the authorities were ordered to interfere and bring the offenders to justice swiftly.[4] If certain designated individuals used seditious language, "the law must be put in force."[5] Arms shipments and particularly suspicious individuals continued under scrutiny.[6] Pike making, arms sold in Birmingham and purchasers of muskets were vigorously investigated.[7]

New orders rang out with the old. From April to July, the government had been moving on the offensive, adding to the pressure of repression, and more steps were taken in the summer: The authorities systematically broke into private meetings and private dwellings to search for arms. The Home Office encouraged magistrates to authorize breaking into "any building" to arrest "parties believed to be there for an unlawful purpose."[8] Breaking and entering could be justified as a search for arms, and when found weapons could be confiscated. Grey interpreted the law to enable magistrates to seize arms that they had "good reason to

243

believe are intended to be used against the government".[9]

Zeal led to excesses. The police burst into a meeting of the People's Charter Union in August. These staunch moral force Chartists would be the last of all the Chartists in the world to have any violent plans. They met at an inn, whose keeper became indignant when the police intruded, expostulating that the meeting was entirely peaceful. The magistrates defended the police presence in uniform, declaring that if they had not intruded, the speakers would have been in favor of physical force. The authorities were entirely unaware of how far Lovett, Hetherington, Holyoake, Linton, O'Brien and Watson were from the barricades.[10]

Despite the step up in repression, the Home Office still imposed some limitations: Supplying the police with firearms would "only be allowed as a temporary measure under circumstances of great and urgent danger", and once the danger passed, "those arms should be laid aside."[11] The same was true for giving cutlasses to specials[12] and magistrates themselves could only bear arms "in cases of absolute necessity."[13]

All through the summer of 1848, rumors of impending insurrection flew about. The London militants were going to attack the police and burn public buildings.[14] Their counterparts in Lancashire and Yorkshire were going to create a republic embracing the two counties.[15] In Lincoln, Chartists were ready to cooperate in an outbreak when they heard of successes elsewhere.[16] Chartists were out to blow up buildings in Bolton.[17] In Bradford the gas works and water works and public buildings were going to be blown up or burned. Bradford Chartists were only waiting for an uprising in Manchester.[18] At Hinchley "creditable witnesses" assured the authorities that a revolutionary conspiracy existed.[19] In Ashton, rumor had it that the principal streets would be barricaded and the major factories burned down. Manchester was also targeted for arson, but for the purpose of creating confusion so that banks could be pillaged.[20] Suspicious characters who had been discharged from the army without pensions were drilling armed Chartists. One of them, named McKee, was supposedly Inspector General of the Chartist Armed Forces, and the author of a small booklet on drilling.[21]

Throughout the summer, the suspicion that Irish conspirators were behind Chartist plans for insurrection continued to prevail. The Irish Confederates were hiding behind the mask of Chartism, waiting for a signal from Dublin to rise. So far, they involved themselves in "experimental émeutes", lined up English criminal elements in their pay, spread disaffection among the Irish regiments in the army and sought to play upon the sympathies of Irishmen in the constabulary.[22]

The Home Office continued to keep an eye on the Irish. The mayor of Liverpool was cautioned about the Irish clubs in the city and urged to take steps against them.[23] The mayor of Bolton was warned that Sir George Grey had information that Irish Confederates were meeting there "under circumstances which appear to show great organization" and "bore a military character." The mayor should investigate and provide more information.[24] The police continued to shadow Irish suspects. For example, an Irish Confederate named Churchill was expected to arrive from France, "where he has been taking an active part in the revolutionary movement".[25] Suspicious Irishmen arriving from New York were watched as well.[26]

Bradford and the Black Country had its share of Irish fraternization in the summer of 1848. A placard of the Bradford National Charter Association urged support of the Irish Repealers, explaining that "we are brought to a condition infinitely worse than any other population with the exception of our starving and plundered Irish brethren."[27] Meanwhile the magistrates were keeping their eye on a Joe Grady, head of the Irish Confederates of Bradford, who told an informer that he was out to keep Bradford Chartists "up to the mark" so that the government would be prevented from sending any more troops to Ireland.[28] In the Black Country, which had a large number of Irish immigrants, Confederates united with the Walsall Chartists to form a club which met regularly.[29]

The Irish helped continue the struggle in Bradford, which went on in the summer in spite of all the forces that the authorities had massed in the area. In July, Watt Tyler, the bearded Chartist blacksmith, was finally caught by the police, but only temporarily. When he shouted for help, hundreds rushed to his assistance, hooting and yelling, and firing stones and brickbats at the police. They cuffed and kicked the police, pinned their arms back, ripped their clothes and knocked their hats off. Women were at the forefront. Finally, the men in blue broke and ran, while Watt Tyler broke free.[30] Later the military joined the police in a sweep to arrest the ringleaders of the foray, capturing some of them.

Shortly thereafter the police and special constables prevented a Chartist meeting by occupying the meeting place. The Chartists switched the locale to the outskirts, and when the magistrate rode towards them to declare its prohibition he was greeted by a shower of stones, one of which struck him on the side of the head. The military advanced on the meeting place as the riot act was read and soon the field was cleared.[31]

In July one vigorous physical force orator in Bradford urged every Chartist to have his pike "and give his enemies sixteen inches of steel." The Charter was "too moderate" for him, for they "ought now to insist on a republic by forcible means." He boasted that he had opened a pike store, saying he could be visited daily to purchase arms. The police visited, found he had given the wrong address, and really lived at another house in the neighborhood. There they found only an old matress bed, a table and a chair. He had absconded.[32]

Ashton under Lyne became another Bradford in August. Many of Ashton's Chartists had formed up into a military organization, their National Guard, which prepared for a nationwide rising. They armed, drilled and worked on such details as where to place barricades, how to seize magistrates, where to fire on the military with cannon.[33] As groups of Chartists marched through the borough armed with pikes and guns on the night of August 14, close to midnight, an altercation with a policeman led to a shooting incident. A policeman named Bright was killed, another was wounded in the thigh with a pike. The magistrates had more police, specials and soldiers on the street in short order. All "suspicious looking people" were taken into custody, a total of 18. Magistrates held out free pardon for those who would give evidence about the "lowish built man" who killed Bright.[34]

Rumor flew that Ashton's clash was a premature outbreak of what was supposed to be a national general rising on the fifteenth of August. How much fire was

there amidst the smoke? London extremists were surely
up to something. They were busily meeting behind
closed doors. One historian, David Goodway, has traced
16 meetings between July 20 and August 15, with 20 to
40 persons present at each.[35] Another historian,
Edward Royle, estimates that all told, 1,000 men were
involved in London, many of them Irish.[36] Police
reports tell of suspicious meetings at the Orange Tree
Public House. At one meeting, each of those present
were to get four to six confidential men in line who
were willing to "turn out at a moment's notice." Their
purpose was to erect barricades and do "any other
desperate work that might be required of them."
Cuffay, the Mulatto Chartist, was the only fairly well
known figure present. A medical student or surgeon
named Mullins, a little known, uncompromising advocate
of physical force, was undoubtedly more important than
Cuffay in these conspiratorial activities.[37]

A Chartist source of information on the August
conspiracy is John Frost's Forty Years' Recollections,
from which Raymond Postgate drew so much for his Story
of A Year: 1848. How good a source is Frost? Frost
was a minor man of letters in the 19th century, an
active Chartist and radical. His writings on the movement tend to be balanced and judicious, free from the
bitter acrimony that mark the pages of that well known
and often quoted historian of Chartism, R. G. Gammage.
What is more, Frost was careful to hesitate and be
conditional if the evidence warranted such treatment.
His own attitude towards an insurrection was that it
was hopeless, owing to the unpreparedness of the conspirators. He kept aloof from the conspiracy, resolv-
ing that he would not be "compromised" by it,[38] but he
kept his ears open. His account is the most detailed
and objective of any that exist.

Frost thought that a secret committee of seven men
was preparing for an insurrection in London. Frost
could not fathom what connections the committee had
with the Chartist Executive, if any, but McDouall, who
was on the Executive, was mentioned by some of the
conspirators with whom Frost conferred. Cuffay,
Ritchie, Lacey, Fay, Rose and Mullins were members.
The role of Judas was taken by a man called Johnson,
who was actually Powell, the spy, nicknamed "the Welsh
novice". Cuffay was a tailor, Ritchie a plasterer,
Lacey and Fay were shoemakers, Rose was a currier and
Mullins was either a medical student or a surgeon.
Cuffay was a now and again accountant for the Land

Company, known to his associates for his quiet ways, humor and hard work at his trade. Frost thought that his involvement with a revolutionary conspiracy unfortunate, particularly since Cuffay himself was apparently convinced of the "hopelessness" of the undertaking as the summer passed. Yet his "younger and more reckless colleagues would not hear of its abandonment", and Cuffay's pride, or honor or fears of being called a coward kept him at it, against his better judgement, in Frost's view.[39]

The plan was to rise on the fifteenth of August. Frost heard later that it was to begin at Seven Dials, because the location was excellent for errecting barricades fairly close to the seat of government. The streets were narrow and radiated to many directions. Forst's information was second hand, hearsay really, and he confessed that the hints he received were "vague and imperfect".[40]

Eventually, to quote Frost again, "the conspiracy burst in smoke, without so much as a spark."[41] The reason was that the police cracked down immediately before the plan went into effect, while many key insurrectionists were assembled like sitting ducks at the Orange Tree pub in Bloomsbury, presumably waiting for signals from leaders outside. An inspector strode in with a drawn cutlass in his right hand and a pistol in his left. Those seated opposite the doorway could see at least a dozen similarly armed men behind him. There was a stir: Could they resist? Could they flee? The barked command that the first one to move would be shot down ended the instant of restless hesitation. The men and the room were searched, yielding an odd assortment of weapons, including a sword, a complete pike, several pikeheads, pistols, a rusty bayonet and shoemakers' knives. Everyone was trooped away under arrest.[42]

Elsewhere in the metropolis, the scene was repeated. Three hundred policemen converged on the Angel Tavern in Webber Street, Blackfriars. The commander and a picked group burst in dramatically with drawn swords, and demanded that they all surrender. Again the flash of movement and hesitation, resolved by the commander's threat: "If any man offers the least resistance, I will run him through! A large force surrounds this house!" Fourteen Chartists were hauled away from the Angel Tavern, and the arms seized there included three cornered daggers, spear heads, and

tow balls in addition to the usual weapons. One Chartist had literally sat upon a cache of 75 rounds of
ball cartridges. Several other simultaneous police
strikes interrupted similar meetings elsewhere in the
metropolis. One Chartist casulty occurred when a
suspect jumped out of a window and broke his leg. In
all, 26 Chartists were committed for felony without
bail.[43]

Meanwhile, at Seven Dials, a curious scene took
place, according to Frost's sources of information.
About 150 men stood about in groups at the street
corners, or around the doorways of public houses. A
man approached just after the arrests at the Orange
Tree and spoke briefly to a worker in a low voice.
The worker had a pickaxe and he and his companions had
been seriously contemplating a loose stone in the
pavement when the messenger arrived. Almost simultaneously, a large group of policemen appeared and assembled in readiness. The messenger quickly moved from
group to group, and as he did so they dissolved. Some
went into public houses and some disappeared alone
down the narrow streets. In almost no time at all,
the police could see only a tenth of whose who had been
there before.[44]

The ringleaders were rounded up, one by one.
Ritchie, Lacey and Fay were taken at their lodgings.[45]
So was Cuffay, who reputedly ignored warnings to flee
so that it could not be said that he abandoned his
London associates. Mullins escaped for a time, but
they found him at a house in Southwark, along with some
cartridges and a grenade. He was dressed as a woman,
but the disguise failed.[46]

The force that the London conspirators saw was
but the tip of the iceberg. The government had planned
well, aided as they were by informants, shorthand
reporters and spies. The military were ready once
more, as they had been on April 10 and June 12. Buckingham Palace, the Tower, the Mint and the Bank of
England were garrisoned again, and those still in the
barracks were waiting to move to the scenes of
trouble.[47]

The crackdown was nationwide. The police swept
into the Chartist clubs in Manchester, Liverpool,
Birmingham, Bradford, Edinburgh, Bolton and Ashton.[48]
In the north their catch was bountiful. George White
and George Weber, the two outspoken West Riding

militants, were caught in Manchester, where they were presumably preparing a northern rising. They were two of 46 prisoners taken in Lancashire alone as 300 police backed up by the Royal Irish dragoons stormed all of the Chartist clubs at one fell swoop.[49]

The crackdown was carried out even in the quieter areas. R. G. Gammage, the historian of the movement, was followed wherever he went in a peaceful rural area, and was eventually arrested when he refused a police command to stop speaking at a meeting.[50]

During the time that the conspiracies developed, Ernest Jones continued to urge Chartists to show a respect for life and property.[51] His advice was not given solely through open statements in the Northern Star. When Thomas Frost came into contact with an insurrectionary club, he received a letter from Jones advising him not to "compromise" himself with revolutionists, whose failure Jones predicted.[52]

Until his trial in July, Jones had been in the mainstream of a movement which appeared to wane rapidly all through the summer. Complaints against apathy appeared in the Northern Star, such as, "Men of London and Britain, why so sullenly stand with folded arms...?"[53] The Chartist Executive began to teeter on bankruptcy, complaining that they had not received "the encouragement or pecuniary support requisite for our sustenance and utility as a public body."[54]

Repression seemed to be working very well, and had strong support from the press, which reached new heights of hostility towards Chartism over the summer. The example of how Chartism fell in the estimation of The Times can serve as an illustration of this. In April an editorial declared that "we respect" the Charter, and would say "not a word" against the Convention, except to castigate the violent members who would "bully" Parliament.[55] By late August, The Times had this to say about Chartism:

> Who would suppose that in the midst of this rich metropolis, and in the great manufacturing towns of the north of England, there are small knots of pot-house conspirators, who hold nightly meetings, with the avowed intention of reducing Liverpool, Manchester and London to ashes?

A consciousness of their own degraded
condition and vicious existence renders
industry and its results hateful in their
eyes. ...They are enemies of the human
race...if they cannot build up they can
destroy; if they cannot raise themselves
they can reduce others. It is impossible
to despise them too much....

Chartism in its present form is not
a political but a criminal question.
Burglary and arson are not yet out of
date. Chartism is a compound of the two,
with murder superadded. Modern Chartism
has but three points -- fire raising,
bloodshed and plunder.

It is an insult to the common sense
of the public to suggest [that the schemes
of these] miscreants [could have been successful.] It is no easy task to cut off
the water pipes, set fire to London at
various points, overpower the police and
the military, plunder the houses, murder
the inhabitants, and reduce the town to
ashes.

Modern Chartism is a crusade against
the savings bank, the cottage and the
shop.[56]

Punch had its own kind of vituperation for the
forlorn Chartist plotters, spiteful glee. Words were
put in Cuffay's mouth: "I think we could have piked
the Cabinet; cut the throats of the police; shut up
the two Houses of Parliament and proclaimed a British
republic."[57]

By the end of the summer all Chartists were
identified with terrorism, to judge by such comments
in the press, a reputation which was undoubtedly a
factor in the movement's rapid demise. Benjamin
Wilson, an old Chartist from Salterhebble who had
worked for many years at various unskilled jobs, had
different views about the nature of some of the Chartist plotters of 1848. He recalled in particular a
friend who was moulding bullets in his cellar. He was
a poor man with a wife and five children dependent upon
him and he could not find any work.[58] Like so many

251

of the summer plotters, Wilson's friend was a desperate
man working for a hopeless cause.

The Loyal Forces Reconsidered

There is a ghost-like quality about the Chartist
militia that marched and drilled at night in the north
and an eerie atmosphere surrounding the clubs of the
urban plotters. The actual strength of Chartist forces
committed to leading or joining an insurrection will
always remain a mystery and a topic of debate or specu-
lation. Even if the most extreme estimates of their
readiness, strength and numbers were taken at face
value, would it really have made any difference? If
there had been twice as many clubs, twice as many
national guard organizations, and many more comings and
goings of this or that shadowy leader, could any of
this change the outcome in 1848? It certainly does not
seem so, providing that the forces supporting the government remained loyal. For a revolution to succeed
anywhere in 1848, some portion of the forces of authority had to be divided in sympathy. Such was the case
on the Continent, where successful revolutions were
brought about through the help of a militia or military
units that had gone over to the revolutionary side.

How sympathetic towards the Chartist cause were
the soldiers and specials confronting it? This is
really a more important dimension of the situation than
speculations about the numbers of armed Chartist revolutionaries. A close look at Chartist relations with
the army and a reconsideration of the role of the
special constables is necessary. The possibility of
any defection on their part needs to be explored.

The role of the British army was obviously of
great significance in 1848 in its role of backing up
the police with its potential overwhelming fire power
in confrontations. On the Continent the troops
wavered, which was a point not lost on the Chartists
because the press had emphasized it. According to the
Weekly Dispatch, all of the revolutions were decided by
the army. In France, the army had not been "vanquish-
ed", it had only been "convinced". Moreover, with a
large standing army the norm in French history, many
old soldiers had been available to help rear the barricades and take the first determined steps that "decided
the fate of revolution".[59] Harney professed similar
views in the Northern Star.[60]

With such an example in mind, winning over the soldiers became a conscious goal of militant Chartism. Ernest Jones addressed an open letter to British soldiers, urging each not to be "a tool of faction" or "a blind instrument of vengeance." They should feel that they were "part of the people", and the people in turn should "elevate" the soldier's position and "remedy" his grievances. Jones assured soldiers that these were not just his opinions, but "the prevailing sentiments of the British Chartists."[61] Another open letter in the Northern Star put the matter more bluntly. It was written by John H. Mackay, described as "an old campaigner". He urged the soldiers into "coalescing with the people, like the soldiers of France." Since they sprang from the people, they, too, had good reasons for disaffection. Mackay ended his message in stirring fashion: When the "death knell of despotism" sounded in Britain as it had on the Continent, the "toiling millions assembled in their might" would "rise en masse" to demand their "undoubted birthright" of freedom. At that time, the soldiers of Britain had the opportunity to "prove to the world" that they were "truly worthy of being called the defenders...[of their]...country."[62]

This message came from speakers' platforms as well. At one meeting the audience was urged "to mix amongst the soldiers" and "to treat them as men and brothers, and not shun them as heretofore." After all, they were not like the police, "who would sell their birthright for a mess of pottage."[63] At a large meeting in early April, Ernest Jones declared that "the soldiers were the friends of the working classes", and "the Charter would be the finest thing in the world for the soldier."[64] Some Chartist meetings concluded by giving three cheers for the army.

Chartists tried to encourage themselves with optimism that the troops would come over to their side.[65] As one Chartist put it, "the army was composed of the working men", so they would not "cut their brother's throats." There was more "sympathy" between the soldiers and the people than between the soldiers and their officers.[66] McDouall stated that he was not afraid of the soldiers because they were "their brethren".[67] The Female Chartist Association at Leicester expressed their optimism rather uniquely: "The soldiers would never attack them, for they loved women."[68]

Chartists made efforts to give substance to their optimism about the army by seizing on any shred of evidence showing fraternization. Ernest Jones told the National Assembly of how troops in Glasgow had slipped a friendly note to the Chartists.[69] Others recounted trivial incidents of friendliness when troops encountered civilians.[70] More to the point was the act of soldiers signing the petition. One meeting featured the announcement that a great number of Grenadier Guards had signed it.[71] Gammage records that one company left 37 signatures on a copy of the petition before leaving Hull for Ireland.[72]

The military authorities were concerned over this phenomenon, as indicated by reports in the War Office. In one instance, the authorities were informed that three privates of the Grenadier Guards had signed the petition as it lay upon the stonework of Westminster Bridge.[73]

Outside of several soldiers' signatures on petitions, there are only a very few indications of troops taking a friendly attitude towards Chartism. A police report recorded a scene of fraternization at a drinking establishment near Seven Dials in the summer. When a Chartist offered his hopes to the soldier "lads" that they would not "interfere" at a coming demonstration, a soldier replied: "There is little fear of that.... If we are called out and ordered to fire, we shall fire over your heads."[74] A conversation from a drinking establishment does not provide very strong evidence for the soldiers' disinclination to shoot the Chartists. But some soldiers were concerned over such a prospect, because a group of Roman Catholic soldiers went to their priests and asked whether they had to fire into the crowds if ordered to do so. The priests did their duty to Caesar by telling them to do their duty as soldiers.[75]

Chartist optimism about fraternization with the army was all in vain. There were no defections in 1848, and the establishment did not expect any. For example, the Earl of Malmesbury wrote that all depended upon "the fidelity of the troops" and he was sure that the soldiers were "perfectly loyal" as well as "furious" at Chartist attempts to "disturb the peace."[76] The Duke of Richmond took the same line in the House of Lords by declaring that anyone who feared that the soldiers might yield to "an undisciplined mob" knew "very little of the British army."[77] Radicals were similarly convinced, as editorials in the Weekly Dispatch clearly indicate.[78] George Eliot had no expectations of a revolution in England because "our military have no notion of fraternizing". Soldiers, in Eliot's view, were "as mere a brute force as a battering ram" and the British aristocracy had "firm hold of them."[79]

Frederick Engels had some interesting observations as well on the role of armies, presented in his introduction to Karl Marx's The Class Struggles in France from 1848 to 1859. In viewing the era after 1848 on the Continent, when the bourgeois had "thrown in their lot with the government", street fighting in the style of 1848 seemed obsolete to Engels. This was in large measure due to the fact that the troops no longer vacillated and civic militias were no longer at hand to join the revolutionaries. After 1848, Engels pointed out, the soldier "no longer saw...'the people' behind the barricades. Instead, he saw "rebels, agitators, levellers" and "the scum of society" and was willing to shoot them down at the state's bidding.[80] It can be argued that for England the situation Engels described existed before 1848. The bourgeois had thrown in their lot with the government and nearly all the soldiers apparently took the would-be Chartist revolutionaries at the establishment's worst estimate of them.

Engels also pointed out the technological advances made after 1848 that gave armies incomparable advantages over insurgents, developments such as small calibre breachloading rifles, percussion shells, dynamite cartridges, and the rebuilding of capitals with broad avenues. After 1848, a well equipped army could blow up barricades, blow through walls and fire much more accurately than in the days of grape shot, round shot and the pick axe.[81] Here again it can be argued that England was in the lead in gaining military advantages over insurgents. The steam engine, either in troop transports, in gunboats or on troop trains, gave the government enormous advantages in 1848, particularly since the movement and concentration of forces was facilitated by instantaneous telegraphic communications.

Failing to gain defections from the British army, the Chartists tried to deal with the need to have organized military support by forming their own civic guard, or national guard, and here again the inspiration of the French Revolution of 1848 was manifest.

Many places came to have their contingents of a Chartist 'National Guard' by the summer, including Edinburgh, Aberdeen, Ashton-under-Lyne, and Bradford.[82] Calling themselves 'national guards' added lustre to groups of Chartists mustering for drill, but there is little evidence of any professional military bearing in these organizations, except for the occasional appearance of an ex-soldier as drill master.

Did that other force in the field against revolution in England, the special constables, take the role of a civic militia? Actually the special constables were much older as a force than any national guard anywhere. They represented the modern continuation of the ancient responsibilities of the whole adult male population to repress disturbances. Just as the sheriff of Medieval England could call up the posse comitatus, two or more magistrates could swear in the specials when local police forces deemed inadequate. Either the county rate or the borough rate paid them.[83]

We have seen how their role was celebrated as the visible demonstration of the loyalty of all people to the British way of life in 1848. Is this another myth of 1848? How loyal were they? Did they really represent "all classes" or did they represent the middle classes in a class conflict with the working classes?

Certainly most of the men who guarded the shops, warehouses, banks and streets from mob violence were not aware of how their role would be elevated into the great and grand defense of the historic institutions and laws of Britain. They were simply protecting property and persons in their immediate vicinity from disorder. Riots in March, what with their smashed pawnshops, looted food stores, broken street lamps, pillaged silversmiths and gunsmiths, had been a lesson. Most of those who wore the white badge or armband and carried the truncheon on April 10 and thereafter were probably preoccupied with preventing similar acts from happening in their immediate vicinities.[84] Their eyes were sharp for suspicious characters, and their ears were cocked for the sounds of shouting and breaking glass nearby. It is likely that most of the specials on April 10 came nowhere near realizing that they were participating in what would be heralded ever thereafter as a glorious moment in English history, the Waterloo of peace and order. Speakers in Parliament and editorial writers had to point to their halos' glow before they basked in radiance.

Most special constables did not perceive of themselves as participants in the front line of a class confrontation either. They came to stand for the new power, numbers and self-confidence of the middle classes. Despite all the talk of "all classes" being represented, the most eager special constables do seem to have been drawn from the clerks, shopkeepers, professionals and businessmen, the very people who would sing the praises of Britain in the profitable high noon of Victoria's reign. Viewing them this way, it can be argued that something of a class conflict loomed on April 10 not entirely unlike the General Strike of 1926. The language of class conflict was disguised to an extent. "Well affected" citizens were enrolled to show the "disaffected" that "there was a power in society...sufficient to put them down."[85]

Most of them were not defending everything in Britain, a point picked up by the Weekly Dispatch: They were "defending no rotten boroughs and rotten privileges; they were thinking of their homes, families or properties." But now, the Dispatch observed, they were being "claimed as supporters, through thick and thin, of the state of things as it exists."[86]

The nature of working class participation as special constables has a strong bearing upon the description of April 10 and other confrontations of 1848 as class conflicts. The working class special constables were celebrated endlessly in a manner to deny the existence of a class confrontation in 1848. For example, the establishment's Poor Man's Friend Society praised those from the "industrious and laboring population" who had donned the white arm band "as supporters of constitutional order." They had set "a brilliant and admirable example to Great Britain and the world."[87] A correspondent of Prince Albert added that they were "a sight to be proud of", something "to make one thank God that one lived in such a country, and under such a government."[88] The sight was also welcomed in the press. The Times saw it as a demonstration that "the relations between employer and employed...still rest...on a generous feeling of mutual support."[89]

Of all the workers involved on April 10, the coal-whippers of the Thames were singled out for special adulation, perhaps because they were so undeniably proletarian. The Morning Chronicle stated that their "spontaneous declaration of loyalty" proved "most decisively that the system is just and sound."[90] Gladstone wanted news of their status as volunteer special constables broadcast in order to encourage other workers to sign up. He regarded their cooperation as a sign of appreciation for liberal legislation passed on their behalf six years previously. He made no mention of the possibility of extra pay as an inducement.[91] The Times agreed. The coalwhippers knew that "the law embraced their interests", and so they were willing to fight for the constitution.[92]

The pay was not nearly as lavish as the praise, however, and the coalwhippers became disgruntled after April 10. They complained of the "very small pittance shared among the men...in a very unfair manner", which caused "great dissatisfaction among them."[93]

The coalwhippers' chagrin notwithstanding, the "well affected" tried to go beyond praise and pay to honor working class specials. The Times proposed a dinner and public festival in the form of "an ample old English repast". It would "show our poorer brethren" who were "mindful of the wealthier classes in the hour of danger" that the "rich...cherish the remembrance of the service rendered.[94] In June 500 were treated to a dinner at Clapham Common to celebrate their loyalty.[95] A more elaborate gift of thanksgiving was proposed by the Poor Man's Friend Society, a body sponsored by the highest in the nation. Lord John Russell, Sir George Grey, Sir Robert Peel, the Queen and Robert Mayne, the Commissioner of Police, contributed substantially in order to erect a free hospital, baths and washhouses in addition to aiding established institutions helping the poor.[96] In the end, however, the building projects were not carried through.

The contribution of working class special constables to the vision of all classes united against the Chartist danger was not as clear as those celebrating the phenomenon cared to admit. In many cases their employers swore them in instead of magistrates. The threat of dismissal was held over their heads and often their patrol did not extend beyond their place of work.[97] Before April 10 the Home Office received warnings about employers enrolling them "indiscriminately" at large establishments, without character references or householder status.[98] Regardless of all the praise lavished on the working class special constables on April 10, evidence exists to show considerable working class opposition to joining. For example, many workers at the Geological Museum refused to be sworn, and those who consented would serve only in the building. At one large London establishment, all but three turned down the request that they serve.[99] The Marquess of Salisbury was keenly disappointed that workers he knew about refused to become special constables "almost to a man". While most agreed to protect their masters' property, some even refused to do that, declaring themselves Chartists. Therefore Salisbury felt no confidence in working class support on the eve of April 10.[100] Moreover, Prince Albert heard from Lord John Russell that many workers refused to be sworn in on the grounds that the oath contained the Queen's name. Russell assured him, though, that these workers were exceptional to the "general loyalty" shown.[101]

Many other towns and cities had similar experiences as London in dealing with special constables. Manchester had over 10,000 in March alone.[102] Young men employed in the warehouses made up substantial numbers of them, but most patrolled only in their immediate vicinity. Other specials formed a flying squad; some were mounted to patrol and communicate between distant outposts in Lancashire. There was some evidence of men refusing to serve, and of Chartists serving with varying degrees of reluctance.[103] In nearby Liverpool, 3,000 to 4,000 had been sworn by St. Patrick's Day, and Grey claimed that 20,000 more could have been raised.[104] Glasgow could have raised many more as well, and had a large number of factory workers in the specials' ranks.[105] At Stockport, the authorities experienced some difficulties enrolling specials,[106] which was also the case in Leicester.[107] Faced with the reluctance of so many to take up the truncheon, Leicester magistrates swore in what were called "reckless youths" or "swaggering young blades" who "wielded their batons without discrimination" when called into action.[107] In Leeds, a different situation prevailed. Large numbers volunteered readily, convincing the Leeds Mercury that considerable working class support could be counted upon.[108] Attempts to induce workers to serve at some large establishments in Bradford failed. In some instances, workers declared their willingness to defend their employers' property if it were attacked, "but more than this they refused to do."[109]

It is undeniable that many skilled artisans and independent craftsmen in London and elsewhere did identify Chartist with rioter and become special constables out of their own conviction, something that John Saville has pointed out.[110] Even so, many workers saw the Chartists as working class and the special constables as middle class. In other words, many workers saw the confrontations of 1848 as class conflicts. To quote James Bezer, the scene on April 10 showed that "class had risen against class, where there ought to be no classes;...that there was a great gulf fixed between the poor and the rich."[111] Jones, Harney and other class conscious leaders called the specials "the worshipful body of shopkeepers" volunteer organization, and if they could be armed, the Chartists could be armed as well.[112] Kingsley, in an often quoted phrase, described 1848 as a time when "young lads believed that the masses were their natural enemies, and they might have to fight...for the safety of their property and the honour of their sisters."[113]

Chartist leaders stressed the reluctance of workers to serve. Ernest Jones described them as "coerced into an outward semblance of support".[114] Harney pointed out that while The Times gloated over dockworkers serving, others had refused, and expected to lose their jobs as a consequence.[115] A number of anonymous letters appeared in the Northern Star from reluctant specials, pleading that they had been forced to take up the truncheon. For example, a mechanic "who acknowledged the Charter in principle", wrote that he had a family, and if he openly avowed his feelings, "I should lose my situation and they would lose their bread." Therefore, like so many others, he was obliged to "hoist false colours."[116] A former special and a Chartist in Macclesfield condemned the attempt to "overawe the people" with masses of specials. He felt the authorities dare not trust them with anything more than "small pieces of wood" because so many specials would have "not the least objection" to becoming a National Guard.[117]

In Bradford the class conflict in the role of the special constables was fairly clear. Even though "radical reformers" and even some middle class men with Chartist sympathies might be enrolled, they were not regarded as "dangerous" by the authorities. Conservative magistrates had no qualms about swearing them in because they had some property. By contrast, the magistrates felt the poor and ignorant would allow Chartist demagogues to hold sway over them.[118]

Chartists regarded the special constables as a dangerous force, no matter how many individuals in it might be sympathetic to their cause. At the same time that polite society feared Chartists, foreigners, Irish and criminals, Chartists feared overzealous special constables. They called them "bludgeon men", and thought that they would be happy to have "10,000 Chartists thrown into the Thames" on April 10.[119] A Manchester special constable admitted that "there are amongst them not a few Hotspurs who long for the word of command, 'Up, boys and at 'em'." At their assembly points specials were usually plied with alcoholic refreshment, and many of the younger ones were not used to intoxicants.[120] This practice proved to be dangerous for many Chartists before the year was over.

The Times admitted that on April 10 there were "not a few" specials eager to inflict "summary punishment" on those who annoyed them by "pitching into" them.[121] Several Chartists recorded instances of over-zealousness on the part of the special constables. Thomas Frost described Croyden on the tenth, "denuded of police", with specials replacing them "in a state of semi-intoxication", eager to insult "every Chartist or radical whom they met".[122] Also on the tenth, Holyoake saw a "coarse plethoric alderman" in charge of a detachment of specials, who went about from man to man saying: "Strike hard to-day."[123]

The authorities were conscious of the problem of overeagerness on the part of special constables. In fact, the Lord Mayor of London found his "chief embarrassment" on the tenth having "too many special constables to control."[124] At that time and thereafter in 1848, requests that came into the Home Office to arm them with heavier weapons were turned down flatly.[125] The issue had come up before. In 1839, Peel's government reacted against arming them with cutlasses and pistols. Besides the unfortunate victims that might be produced by such a distribution of arms, giving them to specials meant that weapons would be kept in houses and other places where they could not be guarded.[126] When The Times printed letters calling for giving guns to specials, they drew a rejoinder from the Weekly Dispatch, which declared that the "raw lads" would find "pleasure" in "shooting down the objects" of their fears.[127]

One way that Chartists responded to the spectre of the specials' physical presence was with good natured

English jeering. Specials watching a Chartist demonstration march by in Bradford were exposed to a "raking fire of jokes and jibes".[128] One Chartist told how "greengrocers, bacon hucksters, cobbler's clerks and attorneys' journeymen begrimed their upper lips with charcoal and went forth to death, glory and slaughter."[129]

Another approach was to invite specials to Chartist meetings to exchange views. On one occasion Macclesfield was placarded with invitations for them and "others of the middle classes who consider the cause of the working classes identical with their own." None appeared.[130]

Special constables were most effective when they were working as auxiliaries of a well organized police force, which was the prevailing condition in most of the confrontations in 1848. Nearly all of the specials were amateurs with only hasty training, usually consisting of drill in simple military field evolutions.[131] Regardless of the limitations of their capacities, they gave the government an enormous psychological advantage. Although many more special constables than soldiers expressed sympathies with the Chartists, those who did not were apt to bring the hostilities of class conflict to their temporary duties. The force was more middle class than anything else, and the pride that was felt in having numbers of workers wearing the white arm band allowed the boast that the special constables represented "all classes". Some classes, though, were more represented than others, and the adhesion of the working class component was often limited by circumstances. Even so, there were no signs that any group of specials in any place were ready to go over to the Chartist side at any time. Instead, there was every indication that they were more than willing to help put Chartism down. This was another important reason why revolution in England in 1848 was such a hopeless cause.

The Bitter End

Chartist activity subsided by the fall.[132] Cholera replaced Chartism as the dangerous scourge alarming the public mind. This scourge was real. It claimed 72,180 lives in Britain in 1848.[133] At the Home Office, matters became routine again, as reports of Chartist activities became extremely rare. George

262

Grey had time to be concerned over the "malicious" stabbing of a magistrate's horse in Bradford, undoubtedly a 19th century equivalent to tire slashing. Grey offered a reward for information leading to the arrest of the culprit.[134]

Government forces remained vigilant nonetheless, and prosecution of those Chartist leaders still free was urged upon local magistrates.[135] For some reformers, such as the editor of the Bradford Observer, the government had gone too far in its persecutions. He wrote: "A feeling exists...that proceedings against the Chartists have been carried beyond proper limits." Many who had been "loudly censuring the magistrates for allowing the Chartists so much liberty" a few months ago were now "deprecating the perseverence used in hunting these poor wretches out...."[136] He felt that "there is too much trust in soldiers and police...and too little...in the wonderful magic of kindness...."[137]

Arrests continued, some of them of a peculiar nature, as when a Chartist was taken from a coal cellar wearing his mother's clothes, complete with veil and bonnet.[138] Bradford's Watt Tyler or Issac Jefferson was caught at last, a fitting end to the struggle in the north. He went out in style, captured in a comfortable bed at a lonely public house, a pound still in his pocket. He offered no resistance, only liveliness, stating that he was glad that the "old set had come", meaning the old constabulary rather than the new police. The blacksmith admitted that "he was getting tired of the miserable life he had been leading" as a fugitive. How he had been able to wander about for so long without any visible means of support remained a mystery.[139]

Several spies collected their money in the form of an allowance for witness fees in the fall. In addition, several prisoners were very willing to give evidence against their fellows "conditionally".[140] Accomplices could tender Queen's Evidence in the hope of gaining lighter punishments for themselves.[141] The Annual Register remarked sarcastically that "the councils of the Chartists were composed of men whose sole purpose was to betray each other."[142] At the same time that some Chartists betrayed their fellows, others made sacrifices to help. Victim funds did what they could and Feargus O'Connor dipped into his own resources to hire lawyers for them. Wheeler, his trusted aide, busied himself with gathering funds for bail.[143]

Some spies had unpleasant and unforeseen circumstances to face. Robert Emmott, the principal witness against the Bradford Chartists, was attacked by a large crowd of women and boys. He had been staggering along intoxicated, coming home from a pub where he had boasted that he was the means of sending his former Chartist associates to gaol. Emmott was beaten, robbed and flung into a stream. One of the women who participated was eventually charted with assault and highway robbery, but in Emmott's neighborhood 36 cottages became vacant as their tenants fled in fear of government retribution.[144]

Powell, the most infamous spy of all, had to be accompanied by the police all during the period of the Chartist trials. Police also had to guard his house. Although Powell expected a handsome reward, he only got his pay as a witness and a free passage to Australia. Australia turned out not to be to his liking, so he returned to England a few years later, a discontented individual who went about mumbling that he had "saved society" in 1848. Thomas Frost advised that he be left alone: "Leave the wretch to the fate that is sure to overtake him. He will be shunned wherever he goes.... He will be an outcast from the lowest society in London, and he will end his miserable life as miserably as he has lived -- a broken tool that tyrants cast away."[145]

The trials at which these spies performed took place from the summer until December, and commanded what little interest remained for the Chartist movement. 'Where the Borgias used poison the Tudors used the law' is an apt aphorism to explain the judicial murders of the 16th century for the purposes of state. Liberal England in 1848 did not murder its extreme opposition. Opponents were sent to Australia or to gaol, and, as in the 16th century, the legal arsenal was more than ample to carry out the purposes of the state, given the disposition of the jurors to collaborate eagerly in the process.

A total of 266 persons were committed for seditious offenses in 1848. Of these, 35 were sentenced for unlawfully drilling and training, and most of the others for seditious conspiracy to cause an insurrection.[146] Those apprehended in connection with the murder of the policeman at Ashton, those leading the formation of National Guards and those who were caught conspiring in London clubs were all brought before the bar of justice, as well as a number of conspicuous leaders whose speeches were deemed seditious when the government wanted to remove them from the Chartist movement.[147]

The "Gagging Act" proved useful in gaining transportation to Australia for a number of Chartists, including Dowling, Cuffay, Fay, Lacy, Ritchie and Mullins, who were all involved with plotting at the Orange Tree Inn.

The Chartist trials of 1848 are depressing to read.[148] Both sides were incredulous to a substantial degree. The spies brought out all of the rumors of the summer as prosecution evidence, and under cross examination revealed themselves as nefarious characters and agents provocateurs. From the Chartist side came some professions of complete innocence and some contradictory pleas of guilty. All the while, the Northern Star proclaimed that all responsibility for insurrectionary plotting lay with Powell, and wrote off the whole matter as the "Powell Plot".[149]

There were some striking statements that stand out from all of these generally dull, monotonous, and repetitive proceedings. Mullins, for instance, brought forth witnesses to show that he was an excellent clinical clerk at Westminster Hospital, noted for his diligence and morality.[150] Peter Murray McDouall managed to make some stirring statements in his defense. He asked the court to:

> bear this in mind, that the very best men that this kingdom ever knew...your forefathers...through prejudice and reproach, and disgrace, have purchased for you your liberties, were subjected to like trials, and like prejudices...They themselves were trodden down, and humbled to the dust of the earth.

> Perhaps you hate Chartism.... Bear this in mind, that as much as they may be disregarded at the moment, little sympathy as they may find in the bosom of men,... every well-grounded complaint on the part of the poor is a direct appeal to the King of Kings.[151]

The bench managed to make a few incisive remarks of its own in these trials. When McDouall was sentenced to Kirkdale Gaol, he protested that his constitution could not bear it. The judge replied: "You should have considered that before you made yourself amenable to the law." Another judge advised the Chartists who pleaded guilty that "instead of endeavoring to obtain universal suffrage," they should have sought "universal temperance, sobriety and virtue". They should have begun "at the proper end", and sought to become "good and virtuous citizens", and then political power would come to them.[152]

Juries brought in verdicts of guilty with remarkable haste.[153] Sentences varied, from transportation to two years' imprisonment, to lesser terms of imprisonment, to fines and being bound over to keep the peace. Thomas Frost noted that towards the end of the year the sentences tended to become milder.[154]

Of all the Chartist trials of 1848, that of Ernest Jones in July was probably the most important and was certainly the most unique. It deserves consideration in detail. Besides being a national leader, Jones was the only Chartist in the dock educated in law and thereby capable of offering a skilled defense against the government.

Jones was by no means crushed by his arrest and trial. His responses were spirited, didactic and sometimes marked by flashes of humor. Jones said, "I do not feel that I stand as a criminal", instead, "I stand here as an advocate of the British constitution, and the right of public meetings...."[155] The court did not make it easy for him. When Jones tried to range over the whole spectrum of working class grievances, the judge interrupted with: "I am not going to discuss political economy with you. You have your notions upon the subject and are at liberty to retain them."[156] During one of his lengthy statements, Jones noticed that the Attorney General appeared to be asleep, and quipped, "I need not fear offending him" and his "most tender prejudices."[157]

The fact that Jones was a middle class convert to Chartism was held against him. The Attorney General declared, "I blush to state that...the defendant...is a member of my own profession...a barrister,...a profession which...ought to have kept him from offenses like this."[158] While his education might have led him to address meetings in a "more measured language", it also made his language more dangerous, because it gave his instructions "greater weight".[159] All of the other Chartist prisoners were "comparatively illiterate and unimportant", but Jones, with his education and legal knowledge, had "guilt of a far higher character." He could not plead that the wrongs and privations of his life had driven him to acts of desperation in the manner of the poorer, ill-educated prisoners.[160]

Both Jones and the defense counsel, Sergeant Wilkins, responded heatedly to this point. Wilkins said that Jones had cast aside professional "honors and prospects to band with the poor and impoverished and needy", standing up as their "champion". He did so because "his conscience goaded him", and for no other reason.[161] Jones insisted that although someone did not feel the "pangs of hunger" personally, this did not make him devoid of "fine feelings" and "Christian charity" towards the sufferings of others. His own background made him a more able spokesman for the poor, because he could speak "more calmly" and "more dispassionately", and be less likely to sink into the "vortex of passion" and "lead people astray."[162]

Jones was on trial for only one speech at one meeting, held in the open air on the afternoon of June 4, 1848, at Bishop Bonners Fields in London.[163] Two days later he was arrested and arraigned before a Bow Street magistrate. In this case there was no question of whether or not Ernest Jones said what he said. The transcript used in court was almost identical with that reported in the Northern Star. Moreover, at the arraignment Jones heard the transcription from the shorthand reporter, and jauntily remarked: "I can only compliment that gentleman upon the accuracy of his report.... It is a true report of the sentiments I... expressed, and of the sentiments I still entertain, believing them to be the sentiments of justice and truth."[164] The question, then, was entirely over the interpretation of his speech within the close confines of the older laws against seditious speeches and unlawful assembly. The Gagging Act was not applied in his case.

To put it simply, Jones defended himself on the grounds that his speech was designed to motivate Chartists to continue their peaceful agitation. Jones was attacked on the grounds that his words were designed for insurrection. The speech itself is ambiguous enough in key phrases to allow both interpretations.

The Attorney General admitted as much, by saying that
Jones had "not expressed himself in positive language",
although its "meaning" was "clear".[165] Was it?
Hardly. When Jones called upon Chartists to revamp the
organization, to "organize, organize, organize", did
this mean organize for an insurrection, as the Crown
implied, or did it mean, as the defense contended, the
creation of a more effective, peaceful agitation in the
framework inspired by the Wesleyans, which was a "perfectly lawful" form?[166]

     What did Jones mean when he said, "steer clear of
all partial outbreak"? Did this mean, as the Attorney
General maintained, that he was working for a general
outbreak, or did it mean that he foresaw partial outbreaks as the only danger of Chartist militancy?[167]
What did he mean by "Make up your mind,...and whatever
comes, stand to your ground"? What did he mean when
he said, "My duty will be to endeavour to get Leeds and
Sheffield up to the mark to which Bradford and Halifax
are now." Both of these statements, and many more,
were subject to either an innocent or a sinister interpretation. Similarly, when Jones spoke of bringing the
rich man's nose to the grindstone, his defense could
claim that he was being less seditious than many texts
in the Bible.[168]

     On one quotation the defense had to yield ground.
Jones had said that Mitchell and Frost, in exile for
sedition, should be brought back and Grey and Russell
should take their places. In this he went overboard,
or, in the words of the defense attorney, he yielded to
"the zeal and impulse of the moment". Wilkins had to
admit that this statement of Jones was a "very foolish
piece of vapor."[167]

     The prosecution demanded that grave consideration
be given to the circumstances of his speech -- where
and how it was received. A man might say things in
court "with perfect impunity" and not produce any
criminal behavior in others, while the same words would
be "most dangerous" elsewhere.[170] Prosecution witness
told of the violence after the meeting Jones addressed,
which included throwing stones at church windows, ston-
ing the police superintendant and clubbing one policeman with an iron bar. The prosecution sought to hold
Jones' oratory responsible for it, as if he had shouted
'fire' in a crowded room and were responsible for those
trampled in seeking escape. The defense position was
that the meeting was held in broad daylight, at five
o'clock, without any violence or any secrecy, so it

should not be regarded as an "unlawful assembly" striking "terror" in the hearts of citizens. It was wrong to hold Jones responsible for the deeds of others long after the meeting disbanded.[171]

Furthermore, Jones was accused of stirring up the crowd for violence while never putting forth a "sound and practical" system for the social amelioration of the people. He had the right of free speech for good purposes, but he would not take advantage of it.[172] Jones and his attorney vigorously denied this allegation, saying that he had made many such speeches, and all the jury had before it was one speech at one meeting. A "just estimation" could only be made by considering "the whole tenor of that man's life". By citing one speech which was uncharacteristically devoid of "doctrines of social or political amelioration" the attorney general was taking "advantage" of the accused.[173]

Jones' attorney reminded the court of the firey nature of the speeches of Lord Grey and Daniel O'Connell during the great Reform Bill struggle, pointing out that the calumnies of that campaign went far beyond anything Jones had brought forth. Without the great uproar of oratory then, Lord Grey would never have come to power, the Whigs would never have become ascendant, and the very Attorney General in court would not be holding office.[174] Moreover, the defense quoted more than the Whigs of 1832. The works of Bolingbroke, Paley, Hume and Locke were all summoned to the defense of Ernest Jones.

In the eyes of the defense attorney, the trial of Chartism's most prominent and controversial leader was a defense of the right of public speaking and the right of criticizing the government. The jury did not see it that way and took only 17 minutes to find him guilty of making a seditious speech, inciting the formation of insurrectionary bodies, and exciting subjects to general disaffection.[175] He was sentenced to two years of imprisonment, thus bringing his dazzling role in 1848 to an end.

Imprisonment for Jones was brutal. Two Chartists sentenced with him died, Alexander Sharp and John Williams, and Jones barely survived himself in a cold, damp, miserable little cell.[176]

Long before the New Year arrived, editors summed up the course of challenge and response in England in

1848. What had physical force accomplished for France and for England, asked the editor of the Bradford Observer? Martial law prevailed in Paris and in England the historic rights of public meeting and free speech had been tampered with and suspended.[177] Harney, writing in the Northern Star, observed that the "regenerating fever" had come to an end, leaving democracy "more miserably prostrated than ever." Life-long "chains of slavery" had come to some democrats, and others languished "in vilest dungeons". Their families suffered while "popular indifference" to all of these developments held sway. The Chartist organization had become "the merest name -- the shadow of a shade."[178]

So had the Fraternal Democrats. The year which had begun so auspiciously for those voluble internationalists ended rather dismally. September was ordinarily the time of their gala anniversary celebration. In September of 1848, they could not even obtain a suitable public room, and contented themselves with a small private supper for a few members and their friends. They had some new toasts, indicative of what had passed during that exciting year. Salutes to Ernest Jones and Louis Blanc joined the usual toasts to their traditional heroes, Voltaire and Rousseau. No longer did this disappointed, diminished group cry "Vive la Republique!" Now it was "Vive la Republique, democratique et sociale!"[179] Painful lessons had been learned that year.

The Times' conclusion was in a tone that prevailed long after 1848. The year's activities had demonstrated that "the English are not conspirators, with the exception of perhaps one Thistlewood in a century." The nation "abhors it." England could rise only "openly and en masse upon some great provocations, as the nation rose in 1688, but the English would not conspire like the arrested Chartists. The Times did not find them very English anyway: "We doubt if there are half a dozen Englishmen in the whole lot." Some were Irishmen, and Cuffay, "the very chief of the conspiracy", was "half a 'nigger'".[180]

Notes To Chapter VII

[1]Waddington to the Mayor of Birmingham, July 20, 1848, H.O. 41/19; also Waddington to the Town Clerk at Stockport, August 4, 1848; Waddington to the Magistrates at Bradford, August 17, 1848.

[2]Waddington to the Clerk of the Justices, Bolton, July 29, 1848, H.O. 41/19.

[3]Waddington to the Mayor of Birmingham, August 9, 1848 and August 18, 1848, H.O. 41/19.

[4]Waddington to the Clerk to the Justices at Hyde (Chesire) August 15, 1848, H.O. 41/19.

[5]Waddington to the Mayor of Birmingham, July 28, 1848, H.O. 41/19.

[6]Waddington to the Chief Constable at Staffordshire, July 12, 1848, requesting that John Wardle be watched, H.O. 41/19.

[7]Inspector Field to the Metropolitan Police, August 9, 1848, H.O. 45/2410, London.

[8]Waddington to George Pollard, Halifax, August 23, 1848, H.O. 41/19.

[9]Waddington to the Mayor of Liverpool, July 25, 1848, H.O. 41/19. It was difficult to establish a criminal charge against the owners, given the constitutional right to bear arms. But they could be taken from the owners legally, nonetheless. Waddington to the Mayor of Liverpool, July 24, 1848, H.O. 41/19.

[10]William Mayne to H. Waddington, September 11, 1848, Robert Nabbs to Sir George Grey, August 30, 1848, H.O. 45/2410, London. For the objects of the People's Charter Union, the Home Office had a handbill. Handbill of April 17, 1848, H.O. 45/2410, London.

[11]Waddington to the Mayor of Liverpool, August 4, 1848, H.O. 41/19.

[12]Waddington to Sir Thomas Abuthnot, July 3, 1848; Waddington to the Mayor of Bolton, July 31, 1848, H.O. 41/19.

271

[13] Waddington to the Mayor of Liverpool, July 10, 1848, H.O. 41/19.

[14] Annual Register, August, 1848, p. 104.

[15] Leeds Mercury, August 19, 1848, p. 4.

[16] Town Clerk of Lincoln to the Home Office, August 19, 1848, H.O. 45/2410, Part 3, B-Z.

[17] Waddington to the Clerk of the Justices of Bolton, July 29, 1848, H.O. 41/19.

[18] Bradford Magistrates to Sir George Grey, August 15, 1848, H.O. 2410, Part 4, AB-AC.

[19] Waddington to the Magistrates of Hinchley, August 29, 1848, H.O. 41/19.

[20] "Chartist Meetings, Speeches and Trials of July 26-August 25, 1848", Coll. Misc. 208, The British Library of Political and Economic Science.

[21] The Home Office to J. D. G. Tullock, Captain of the Pensioners, the War Office, August 29, 1848. The War Office ordered the enrollment of temporary pensioners discontinued. Confidential Circular, War Office, August 16, 1848, H.O. 45/2410, Part 5, AD-AL.

[22] Weekly Dispatch, June 11, 1848, p. 278; John Mitchell, the Irish patriot, was the most popular hero for Chartist militants. When Ernest Jones became a prisoner he was called the "English Mitchell." Weekly Dispatch, June 11, 1848, p. 280. Historians have given credit to the Irish for the continuation of Chartist strength into the summer. Some have seen the Irish as providing a catalytic effect for physical force Chartists. See O'Higgins, "The Irish Influence in the Chartist Movement"; Prothero "Chartism in London", especially p. 91.

[23] Waddington to the Mayor of Liverpool, July 13, 1848, and other similar letters in July.

[24] Waddington to the Mayor of Bolton, July 28, 1848, H.O. 41/19.

[25] Police Report, K. Mark to the Home Office, June, 1848, H.O. 45/2410, London.

[26]Waddington to the Mayor of Liverpool, September 23, 25 and 26, 1848, H.O. 41/19.

[27]Address of the Bradford National Charter Association, Placard, May, 1848, H.O. 2410, Part 4, AB-AC.

[28]Bradford Magistrates to the Home Office, May 26, 1848, H.O. 2410, Part 4, AB-AC.

[29]George J. Barnsley, The Working Class Movement in the Black Country, 1750 to 1867 (Wolverhampton, 1977), p. 142.

[30]Leeds Mercury, July 22, 1848, p. 9; Bradford Observer, July 20, 1848, p. 8.

[31]Leeds Mercury, July 22, 1848, p. 9.

[32]Bradford Observer, July 6, 1848, p. 5.

[33]Mather, Chartism and Society, pp. 140-7, quoting the deposition of a Chartist seized at Ashton.

[34]Magistrate's report to Sir George Grey, August 15, 1848, H.O. 45/2410; Annual Register, August, 1848, p. 103.

[35]Goodway, "Chartism in London", p. 15.

[36]Royle, Chartism, p. 44.

[37]Metropolitan Police Report, August 13, 1848, H.O. 45/2410, London. The meeting included Mullens, Ritchie and Fay.

[38]Frost, Forty Years' Recollections, p. 162. David Goodway denies that Frost was an accurate source without even substantiating this contention in his London Chartism, 1838-1848, see pp. 94 and 261, M. 395. Also pp. 87-8, 90-6, 228-9.

[39]Frost, Forty Years' Recollections, pp. 146, 162.

[40]Frost, Forty Years' Recollections, p. 165.

[41]Frost, Forty Years' Recollections, p. 150.

[42]Frost, Forty Years' Recollections, p. 163.

[43] Annual Register, August, 1848, p. 104; Weekly Dispatch, August 20, 1848, p. 400; The Times reports the incident involving the broken leg at the South London Chartist Hall, August 17, 1848, p. 5.

[44] Frost, Forty Years' Recollections, p. 164.

[45] Ritchie was seized with 171 cartridges and three "combustible balls". Police Report, August 22, 1848, H.O. 45/2410, London.

[46] Frost, Forty Years' Recollections, p. 165.

[47] Annual Register, August, 1848, p. 104; Weekly Dispatch, August 20, 1848, p. 400.

[48] Weekly Dispatch, August 20 and August 27, 1848; Annual Register, August, 1848, pp. 81 and 103; Leeds Mercury, August 19, 1848.

[49] Leeds Mercury, August 19, 1848, p. 4; The Times, August 17, 1848, p. 5.

[50] R. G. Gammage, History of the Chartist Movement, 1837-1854, 2nd ed. (New York, 1969), p. 338.

[51] Jones wrote that Chartists should "let the shopkeeper feel he need not close his shutters when the Chartists pass", for then "he will not close his heart against the Charter." Chartists themselves should show that they "can punish those who begin a riot." Northern Star, July 1, 1848, p. 3.

[52] Frost, Forty Years' Recollections, p. 162. Frost does not mention Jones by name, but from the description it could be no one else: "A literary Gentleman who had connected himself with the Chartist movement and was a member of the Fraternal Democrats."

[53] Northern Star, August 19, 1848, p. 1.

[54] Northern Star, July 1, 1848, p. 1.

[55] The Times, April 13, 1848, p. 4.

[56] The Times, August 18, 1848, p. 4.

[57] Punch, 1848, p. 154.

[58] Wilson, "The Struggles of an Old Chartist", p. 13.

[59] _Weekly Dispatch_, March 19, 1848, pp. 133 and 137.

[60] _Northern Star_, March 4, 1848, p. 1; also, _Aris's Birmingham Gazette_, March 20, 1848, p. 3, contains a Chartist address extolling how people walked quietly up to the soldiers in Paris and took their weapons.

[61] _Northern Star_, April 1, 1848.

[62] _Northern Star_, April 8, 1848, p. 5.

[63] _Leeds Mercury_, April 8, 1848, Supplement.

[64] _Northern Star_, April 8, 1848, p. 7.

[65] Speech of Taylor, at an Oldham meeting reported in the _Manchester Guardian_, April 15, 1848; Speech of the chairman at a Leeds meeting, _Leeds Mercury_, April 8, 1848, Supplement, p. 9.

[66] Gifford at an Oldham meeting, reported in the _Manchester Guardian_, April 22, 1848, p. 8.

[67] _Weekly Dispatch_, March 26, 1848, speech at Nottingham.

[68] _Manchester Guardian_, June 3, 1848, p. 8.

[69] _Northern Star_, May 6, 1848, p. 7.

[70] _Leeds Mercury_, April 8, 1848, Supplement.

[71] _Morning Chronicle_, April 4, 1848, p. 7.

[72] Gammage, _History of the Chartist Movement_, p. 304.

[73] Division Report, R. S. Humphrey, April 5, 1848. Also John James Allen to the War Office, April 4, 1848, W.O. 30/111.

[74] Superintendent of Police Report, from N. Prince, W.O. 30/111.

[75] John Prest, _Lord John Russell_ (London, 1972), p. 284. Prest quotes the Clarendon Papers, Irish Box 43, John Russell to Clarendon, April 17, 1848.

[76] Harris, _Memoirs of an Ex-Minister_, p. 224.

[77] Hansard, Parliamentary Debates, Third Series, Vol. 98, p. 280.

[78] See in particular, the Weekly Dispatch, March 19, 1848, p. 137.

[79] Haight, The George Eliot Letters, Vol. 1, p. 254.

[80] Marx, "The Class Struggles in France, 1848 to 1850", Engels' introduction, pp. 131-3.

[81] Ibid.

[82] Smith, "Great Britain and the Revolutions of 1848", p. 74; Northern Star, March 14, 1848, p. 5.

[83] Mather, Public Order in the Age of the Chartists, p. 81. Marx remarked that their behavior was "immediately accepted as a model by the entire civic militia" of Germany. Karl Marx, "The Revolutionary Movement in Italy", Karl Marx, Frederick Engels, Collected Works, Vol. 8 (London, 1977), p. 102.

[84] Smith, "Great Britain and the Revolutions of 1848", p. 78 makes this point. Also, Northern Star, April 1, 15, and 22, 1848.

[85] C. E. Treveylan to Lord John Russell, April 4, 1848, Russell Papers, P.R.O. 30/22 7B. David Goodway finds the enrollment of special constables as a "decisive indication that the middle classes were now prepared to ally themselves unreservedly with the ruling class against the threat of proletarian revolt." Goodway, London Chartism, 1838-1848, p. 74.

[86] Weekly Dispatch, April 16, 1848, p. 185.

[87] RA Add MSS C 56, Item 47. Also, Leeds Mercury, April 15, 1848, p. 4.

[88] Colonel Phipps to Prince Albert, April 10, 1848, RA Add MSS C 56 Item 21.

[89] The Times, April 12, 1848, p. 5.

[90] Morning Chronicle, March 27, 1848, p. 4.

[91] Hansard, Parliamentary Debates, Third Series, p. 459.

[92] The Times, April 12, 1848, p. 5; also Colonel Rowan to General Bowles, RA Add MSS J 68/2.

[93] John Day to Sir George Grey, May 23, 1848, H.O. 45/2410, Part 2, London. A total of 1,557 coalwhippers were on duty as specials on April 10, undoubtedly an imposing force. Thames Police Court Report, April 18, 1848, H.O. 45/2410, London, Part 2. For background on the coalwhippers, see M. D. George, "The London Coal Heavers: Attempts to Regulate Waterside Labor in the Eighteenth and Nineteenth Centuries", Economic History, Vol. 1 (May 1927).

[94] The Times, April 12, 1848, p. 5.

[95] Illustrated London News, June 14, 1848.

[96] Poor Man's Friend Society, Private Circular, RA Add MSS C 56, Item 47.

[97] Mather, Public Order in the Age of the Chartists, p. 82. This point was not missed by Goodway, London Chartism, 1838-1848, pp. 131-3. Goodway denies The Times contention that so many workers were enrolled because they opposed Chartist objectives.

[98] R. P. Tyrwhitt, to Sir George Grey, April 6, 1848; Large, "London in the Year of Revolutions, 1848", p. 188.

[99] R. Bingham to Sir George Grey, April 8, 1848, H.O. 45/2410, Part 2, London.

[100] Marquess of Salisbury to Sir George Grey, April 8, 1848, H.O. 45/2410, Part 5 AD-AL.

[101] Lord John Russell to Prince Albert, April 11, 1848, RA Add MSS C 56, Item 28.

[102] Mather, Public Order in the Age of the Chartists, pp. 84-5.

[103] Manchester Guardian, April 5, 1848, p. 6; April 8, 1848; for the railway workers, the Mayor of Manchester to Sir George Grey, March 10, 1848, H.O. 45/2410, Part 1 A. Also Watkin, Extracts from His Journal, p. 252. Nobody over 55 was taken. On April 8, the force rose to 11,000 and some complained when they were left out. Their insignia was a broad white armband and the usual weapons were staves. Smith,

"Great Britain and the Revolutions of 1848", p. 78, mentions the reluctance of some workers.

[104]Mather, Public Order in the Age of the Chartists, pp. 84-5.

[105]Hansard, Parliamentary Debates, Third Series, Vol. 97, p. 460. Edinburgh had a contingent of students among its specials, a bad situation, according to the Northern Star, April 1, 1848, p. 5, because strong feelings existed between the youths and the working classes.

[106]Northern Star, April 8, 1848, quoting West.

[107]Patterson, Radical Leicester, pp. 360-1.

[108]Leeds Mercury, April 15, 1848, p. 10.

[109]Bradford Observer, April 13, 1848.

[110]Saville, "Chartism in the Year of Revolution: 1848", p. 26.

[111]John James Bezer, "Autobiography of One of the Chartist Rebels of 1848", in David Vincent, ed., Testaments of Radicalism: Memoirs of Working Class Politicians, 1790-1885 (London, 1977), p. 155.

[112]Morning Chronicle, April 3, 1848, p. 4.

[113]Mather, Public Order in the Age of the Chartists, p. 1.

[114]Saville, Ernest Jones: Chartist, p. 109.

[115]Northern Star, April 15, 1848, p. 8.

[116]Northern Star, April 29, 1848, p. 2; see also the Northern Star of April 22, 1848.

[117]Macclesfield Courier, April 15, 1848.

[118]Bradford Observer, June 15, 1848.

[119]Northern Star, June 10, 1848, p. 3.

[120]Manchester Guardian, June 14, 1848, p. 7.

[121]The Times, April 11, 1848, editorial.

[122] Frost, Forty Years' Recollections, p. 153.

[123] Holyoake, Bygones Worth Remembering, p. 79.

[124] Large, "London in the Year of Revolutions, 1848", p. 192.

[125] For example, Waddington to Sir Thomas Abuthnot, July 3, 1848, H.O. 41/19.

[126] Mather, Public Order in the Age of the Chartists, pp. 81-2.

[127] Weekly Dispatch, April 16, 1848.

[128] Bradford Observer, June 17, 1848.

[129] Bradford Observer, April 13, 1848. Chartists did not want foreigners to think of the special constables as comparable to a national guard. A Chartist delegation sent to Paris made this point clear: "The National Guards were brave troops" but the English constables "tremble if the weathercock on one of their Churches creaks with a French breeze." Though they might swagger about, truncheons in hand, vowing to put the Chartists down, when the alarm was sounded they would rush back "behind their counters." Northern Star, March 18, 1848, p. 5.

[130] Macclesfield Courier, April 15, 1848.

[131] Manchester Guardian, April 5, 1848, p. 6. Wellington, as a professional military leader, saw much need for improvement in them, particularly in organization. W.O. 30/81.

[132] Large, "London in the Year of Revolutions, 1848", p. 201, wrote that London Chartism "was as quiet as the grave." Saville, "Chartism in the Year of Revolution: 1848", p. 32, wrote that "the Chartist left had been beaten" by then.

[133] Smith, "Great Britain and the Revolutions of 1848", p. 78.

[134] A report by Thomas Leary, September 5, 1848, proclaimed that the Chartists planned to take Rochdale, even at the risk of being shot. H.O. 45/2410, Part 1A. Waddington to the Mayor and Magistrates of Bradford, September 1, 1848, H.O. 41/19 dealt with the problem of

the magistrate's horse. After September, Home Office correspondence had almost nothing at all relating to fresh Chartist activity.

[135] Waddington to the Magistrates of Rochdale, September 11, 1848, H.O. 41/19; Northern Star, September 2, 1848, p. 4.

[136] Bradford Observer, September 21, 1848, editorial.

[137] Bradford Observer, September 14, 1848, editorial. The editor was actually concerned over these questions all through the year. An editorial of June 15, 1848 explained that poverty brought on "pike and dagger Chartism", but not alone. "That supercilious scowl which repels the poor man...drives the iron of contempt into his soul," and the only way to put the Chartists down permanently was to win them over by good treatment. The men employed by good masters were not leading the agitation, the editor maintained.

[138] Weekly Dispatch, September 24, 1848, p. 459.

[139] Bradford Observer, September 14, 1848, p. 5; Leeds Mercury, September 11, 1848, p. 10. Waddington to the Magistrates at Bradford, September 16, 1848, H.O. 41/19.

[140] G. Cornwall to L. E. Rushton, November 13, 1848, H.O. 41/19.

[141] Mather, Public Order in the Age of the Chartists, p. 218.

[142] Annual Register, September, 1848, pp. 121-2.

[143] Stevens, "A Memoir of Thomas Martin Wheeler", p. 46.

[144] Leeds Mercury, September 16, 1848, p. 10.

[145] Frost, Forty Years' Recollections, pp. 166-7, tells of another spy, the policeman Mullins, who was dismissed from the force for misconduct. He became a criminal and, according to Frost, eventually murdered an old woman for a few pounds.

[146] Stevenson, Popular Disturbances in England, p. 266. Forty-six Lancashire Chartists were brought before the Liverpool assizes in December, 1848.

[147] Annual Register, 1848, various items on the Chartist trials from pp. 121-166.

[148] The major Chartist trials of 1848 can be found in J. E. P. Wallis, Reports of the State Trials, New Series, Vol. 6, The Queen against Fussell, pp. 723-782; Williams and Vernon, pp. 775-782; Jones, 783-830. Vol. 7, The Queen against Dowling, 381-466; Cuffey [Sic] and others, 467-484; Cumming, 485-506; Rankin and Hamilton, 505-636; Francis O'Donnell and others, 637-711.

[149] For example, Northern Star, September 30, 1848.

[150] Annual Register, 1848, p. 137.

[151] Philip Murray McDouall, "An Authentic Report of the Trial of Doctor Peter Murray McDouall, at Liverpool in August 28, 1848, compiled from the Shorthand Writer's Notes", (Manchester: Abel Heywood; London: J. Watson), p. 30.

[152] Annual Register, 1848, p. 166; the judge in McDouall's case is quoted in McDouall, "An Authentic Report of the Trial of Doctor Peter Murray McDouall...", p. 41.

[153] Saville writes that they were willing to convict "faithfully" and brought in verdicts with "indecent haste." Saville, "Chartism in the Year of Revolution: 1848", p. 31.

[154] Frost, "History of Chartism", Ch. XII; also, Annual Register, 1848, p. 122.

[155] State Trials, New Series, Vol. 6, p. 826.

[156] State Trials, New Series, Vol. 6, p. 828.

[157] State Trials, New Series, Vol. 6, p. 827.

[158] State Trials, New Series, Vol. 6, p. 785.

[159] State Trials, New Series, Vol. 6, pp. 784-5.

[160] State Trials, New Series, Vol. 6, p. 799.

[161] State Trials, New Series, Vol. 6, p. 802.

[162] State Trials, New Series, Vol. 6, p. 825.

[163] It is reported in the Northern Star, June 10, 1848.

[164] Saville, Ernest Jones: Chartist, p. 102.

[165] State Trials, New Series, Vol. 6, p. 796.

[166] State Trials, New Series, Vol. 6, pp. 803-816.

[167] State Trials, New Series, Vol. 6, p. 809.

[168] State Trials, New Series, Vol. 6, p. 806. Chartists often justified arming and threatening violence on the basis of one or another Biblical quotation. For example, Second Samuel, Ch. 15, was cited to demonstrate that the people of Israel had a "warrant" to rise up and "expel tyrannical rulers". Bradford Observer, April 27, 1848.

[169] State Trials, New Series, Vol. 6, p. 806.

[170] State Trials, New Series, Vol. 6, p. 810.

[171] State Trials, New Series, Vol. 6, p. 803.

[172] State Trials, New Series, Vol. 6, p. 824.

[173] State Trials, New Series, Vol. 6, p. 828.

[174] State Trials, New Series, Vol. 6, p. 803.

[175] State Trials, New Series, Vol. 6, p. 817.

[176] Ernest Jones to the editors of the Examiner, October 10, 1866; Cole, Chartist Portraits, p. 346. Sharp was an engraver and Williams had been a pioneer in the movement for the sanitary improvement of bakeries. Frost, Forty Years' Recollections, p. 150. Harney and others busied themselves with a victim fund. Northern Star, June 10, 1848, p. 1. They were victims of the cholera outbreak.

[177] Bradford Observer, September 14, 1848, editorial.

[178] Northern Star, October 28, 1848, p. 5.

[179] Northern Star, September 30, 1848, p. 8.

[180] The Times, September 29, 1848.

CHAPTER VIII

RECONSIDERATIONS

Leadership Reconsidered

The leadership of the Chartist movement in 1848 has to be reconsidered. Feargus O'Connor remained the foremost national leader until April 10, and deserves rehabilitation. O'Connor has suffered from a very bad press over the years, largely because his Chartist enemies have been favored by nearly all academic historians. Enemies such as Gammage and Lovett wrote books and expressed strong beliefs in the virtues of education, so is it any wonder that these Chartists should be so attractive to academics who share their faith in learning? These Chartist educators passed on their prejudices against O'Connor, and time and again he has been dismissed in modern historiography as weak, vacillating, and incompetent, a windbag, a braggart and a demagogue. In short, he has been written off as a living disaster for British democracy.

Such a negative interpretation seems wide of the truth in 1848. It should always be borne in mind that he was very much a son of Ireland, and perhaps he needs a good Irish biographer to do him justice. A biographer is needed who can understand the boastings, the hyperboles, the teasing jokes, the quick, winking wit that is all summed up by the single descriptive noun: blarney. He had much blarney, and much else besides: compassion for suffering and misery, hopes for human betterment and energy to provide the charismatic leadership that popular, grassroots movements often must have. For the downtrodden going under, such as those in the dying handwork industries, he was their last hope, their opiate. Many in the Dictionary of National Biography have a much lesser claim to fame on humanitarian grounds.

As we have seen, O'Connor had two overriding interests in 1848, the Land Plan and his seat in Parliament. Both did detract from his leadership of a newly aroused, vigorously insistent mass movement swelling behind the National Charter Association.

The Land Plan was a romantic counter to the march of industrialization. It sought to resettle British workers on small farms, which were to become prosperous through intensive spade husbandry. O'Connor's Land Company raised money through massive small subscriptions, purchased estates from the proceeds, broke them into small holdings and arranged for workers to come on to them through a lottery. Profitable operations would mean more and more English estates similarly broken up and more and more British workers self-employed in bucolic bliss. Feargus O'Connor loved the land, and in resettling workers on it he was reacting against the remorseless march of the tall chimneys through England, and all of the dehumanizing factors that modern industry brought. Unfortunately, the Land Plan encountered considerable legal problems, and the small holdings turned out to be less profitable in practice than under the ideal conditions envisaged.[1]

The Land Plan was well underway when news of Continental revolutions reached England. O'Connor's time, energy and enthusiasm was so wrapped up in the scheme that it was difficult to distract him. After the crest of April 10, his energies went back into the Land Plan. Editorial after editorial was taken up with it in June, while repression struck in England and France.[2] Throughout 1848, O'Connor sought to incorporate his reactions to European revolution with lessons about the virtues of the Land Plan. He saw the places free from revolution as those that gave labor a share in the land.[3] Furthermore, he noted that the French revolutionaries were telling their workers that they were entitled to "honor and compensation", but did not say how to get it. But he had his Land Plan, designed to make the rich richer and the poor rich as well.[4] Facing the prospect of a Chartist National Guard, Feargus O'Connor extolled: "What a country this would be, when a million of national guardsmen were placed in their own sentry boxes in their own labor fields."[5]

His initial reaction to the French Revolution of 1848, discussed in chapter one, was cautious, and marked with concern that the all important Land Plan might be jeopardized in some way by it. He saw the Continental revolutions infusing "new blood in the drooping body of Chartism", but was "fearful and apprehensive lest the flood should be too sudden and rapid."[6] All through 1848, he cited Continental examples to discourage any attempts at insurrection in England. His point was that "whenever there is a physical revolution, labor will be the first to suffer." They suffered in France.[7] In Prussia he saw a National

284

Guard of the middle classes established to "keep the working classes down."[8]

He was against republics also.[9] He boasted in the House that he had always been so, and had "published article after article against the republican form of government".[10] Yet he was so appalled at the proposed Gagging Act that he blurted out in the House that if it passed, he should declare himself a republican.[11] Punch was quick to have sport with him on this, declaring that "if he joins Republicanism, the thing is done, as everything else is done that he meddles with."[12]

The myth of O'Connor as nothing but a fool, hypocrite and buffoon simply does not make sense when his other great concern of 1848, his Parliamentary career, is scrutinized. With very little support, and in the teeth of heavy and often nasty opposition, Feargus O'Connor rose again and again to champion the cause of British democracy. A comparison of Hansard with the letters and editorials by him in the Northern Star shows a close correlation. None of the blandishments of the House could wrest him from his causes.

Nor did he mince words. In one debate he told Lord John Russell "that the name of Whig stunk in the nostrils of the country",[13] a statement certainly as vigorous as anything in the Northern Star. He also told the House that Ireland "was stinking with the decomposed carcasses of her starving people...." Shouts of "Oh! Oh!" interrupted him, but he kept on.[14] He had to put up with many such interruptions, sometimes of laughter, shouts, and jibes. Speakers insulted him wittily, and made snide insinuations that he misrepresented the truth. He thought that much of the "odium attached to his own character" came from the fact that he had championed popular movements.[15]

His supporters were far and few between in the House of Commons. A few radicals, such as Hume and W. J. Fox, would rally to his side sporadically, but radicals in the House were not a party. They were idiosyncratic and atomistic, and certainly not a following that O'Connor could rely upon as a power base. But he plowed on, defending the Irish, objecting vociferously to the 'Gagging Act', supporting the petition, and resisting, right down the line, any attack upon popular interests. His role as a Member of Parliament has never been properly acknowledged.

His opposition to the 'Gagging Act' was probably his finest performance in the House. He saw the bill as another step in the pernicious "system of centralization of power" that had gone on since the Reform Bill. To make this point, O'Connor even trotted out the famous saying that the "power of the crown has increased, is increasing, and ought to be diminished."[16] He felt the effects would be disastrous on Chartism, for it would drive the movement underground. Without the "safety valve" of public meetings and free speech, Chartists would turn to secret conspiracies.[17] O'Connor pointed out that he had never closed the doors of any of his associations to the press, and he had "always told the people that they had more liberties and more privileges than any other people in Europe". With the 'Gagging Act' the government was moving to take freedom away to its own peril.[18]

What O'Connor wanted above all else in politics was a popular opposition in the House, with hundreds of members committed, like himself, to espousing the views of British democracy. That was what the Charter was all about, after all, and if opinion in the country was "wild", it was because the people were not represented in the House. Clamping down on free speech would only make it more dangerous.[19] He was proud of his role as the spokesman for democracy, and told his followers that having "one man in the House was worth 'a legion' of men outside of it."[20]

Outside of the House he had to endure sarcasm from Chartists to his left and radicals to his right who were disenchanted with his constitutional opposition. For example, the Weekly Dispatch informed its readers that O'Connor was "growing too respectable to associate with his old companions", some of whom felt they had been "duped" by this increasingly respectable Feargus O'Connor, M.P.[21]

His commitment to Parliamentary opposition and implementing the Land Plan did not keep him from riding the crest of the new wave of enthusiasm in 1848, at least until April 10 and the subsequent ridicule of the petition. Thereafter he pulled back from his conspicuous position of leadership and reaffirmed his interests in the Land Plan and Parliament. Historians have written of his "withdrawl" and his "abdication" in 1848. When the arrest of Ernest Jones came about in June, the N.C.A. did indeed have a vacuum in leadership.[22]

O'Connor spurned the National Assembly in May, calling its legality into question and refusing to sit. His leadership was bitterly attacked during the cantankerous chaos of that body's short lifespan, even though something of a reconciliation was patched up between him and the delegates. In the summer of 1848 he reluctantly turned again to the chimera of a middle class alliance and gave some support to Hume and Bright's Little Charter Movement.[23]

All the while, Lovett and the moral force Chartists and their radical friends kept up a steady disparagement of O'Connor. A handbill for the People's League condemned the "mischievous conduct" of "selfish and unprincipled individuals" who "maintained their notoriety" and acquired an "ascendancy over the multitude" by "lauding their vices...." Such individuals "delayed...reform and...prolonged poverty."[24] While O'Connor was not specifically named, the thrust was obvious.

Meanwhile, from the other side, disappointed and militant Chartists in the north turned their anger on him as well. When one of them complained at a public meeting that they "had too long put their trust in individuals who had basely and scandalously deceived them", there was no mistaking who the target was.[25]

So in 1848 O'Connor was attacked from all directions: right-wing Chartists, many of his former followers in the mainstream, physical force Chartists on his left, the press, the radicals, the Whigs and the Tories in Parliament and polite society in general. Could anybody endure all of this without marked signs of strain? Was it any wonder that he showed signs of physical illness and a willingness to withdraw? During the Chartist crisis of 1839 he had become ill, and in 1848 the symptoms returned: sleeplessness, chest complaints, irritability. The extent to which he used alcohol in that year remains questionable, but by the time of his breakdown a few years later he was gulping glasses of brandy all day.[26] Historians have claimed that the ravages of the spirochete brought him to a deranged state in the early 1850's.[27] It is impossible to say if any symptoms were at play by 1848.

Precarious health did not keep him from compassionate attention to the victims of the judicial process. He helped seek out the best possible defense counsels for Chartists awaiting trial and even bore

some of the considerable cost of their defense. Moreover, when a Parliamentary Committee investigated his
beloved Land Company and found it illegal and dis-
arrayed in its bookkeeping, O'Connor himself was
cleared of any wrongdoing. In fact, several thousand
pounds of his own money had been sunk in the company.[28]
There is also the story of how he informed Lord John
Russell's friends when he heard rumors of an assassination plot on the Prime Minister's life, and gained
Russell's thanks.[29]

     In spite of all of his honesty and dedication,
many contemporaries and nearly all subsequent historians have disparaged O'Connor mercilessly. Perhaps the
touches of egotism have been intolerable, such as his
signing his name "Feargus Rex", or boasting of his
descent from the kings of Ireland, or his pride in the
fact that an 80 year old woman called him "father".[30]
Perhaps Feargus O'Connor has been simply too different
in personality from the craftsmen, Chartist or academic, who have written about him. Perhaps he is a fit
subject for a playwright. If a play were written about
him, it would have to be something of a tragedy enliv-
ened by humor and farce, a true Irish production.

     Just as O'Connor was central to the first stage
of the Chartist challenge in 1848, from February to
April 10, Ernest Jones was the key figure in the second
stage, from April 10 to early June. Before April 10 he
was prominent as well, but second to O'Connor. The
leadership role of Jones in 1848 needs refocusing
rather than rehabilitation. There is no argument about
his significance, and his leadership has been noted at
important points in this study. Many contemporaries
and subsequent historians have acknowledged it. For
example, John Saville pointed out that there was nobody
else "of national stature" to lead the movement after
O'Connor's reputation was shaken in the aftermath of
April 10.[31] The argument about Jones in 1848 is over
his commitment to revolution. Many commentators have
blindly followed Mark Hovell's terse statement that
after April 10 Jones "set to work at once to help in
organizing the movement for a revolutionary attempt."[32]
There is no evidence to support this contention.

     The picture of Ernest Jones, the friend of Marx
and Engels, as charismatic leader of the proletarian
revolutionaries is another myth of 1848. We have seen
his attempt to assure the authorities of the peaceful
intent of the April 10 demonstration at the very time

that his oratory urged Chartists to join him in the
cry, "Down with the ministry; the Charter and no
surrender."[33]   As April 10 approached, Ernest Jones
the O'Connorite insisted that Chartists remain peaceful.   He decried the "alarmists" who feared that Chartists were seeking "strife and bloodshed".   He proclaimed the movement "peaceable and constitutional",
seeking to "mend the constitution" by "constitutional
means".[34]

As an aspiring literary figure, Jones could not
avoid thick romanticism, and romanticism in 1848 meant
colorful if not grandiose exaggeration, florid prose,
plus dire, murky and mysterious innuendo.   Besides,
Jones knew his recent history, which revealed how
reformers had pressured the establishment into accepting the Reform Bill in part through bombast.   Given
these circumstances, should his oratory be anything but
rousing?   Yet it was always sufficiently vague, convo-
luted and qualified to fall short of outright calls for
revolution.   For example, at one meeting leading up to
April 10 he told his audience that "when the electric
fire flashes from high heaven", it should not "be lost
in an unmeaning tumult, but, guided by the limbs of
organization", the impulse should "strike home to its
goal."   Chartists had to be prepared to "have recourse
to extreme measures at last".   Yet in this same speech,
he flatly declared: "I trust and believe not a blow
need be struck in England."[35]

Jones played the old game of bluff and bully, or,
be prepared for revolution so that there will be no
revolution.   This was Chartism's Catch-22 for 1848.
Jones repeatedly denied that he had "exhorted the
people to violence."   He had simply told them that "the
best way to preserve the peace was to be prepared for
war."   He insisted that such exhortations were in the
best style of Lord John Russell himself in the past.[36]

Leaving rhetoric aside, what emphasis did Jones
give to the movement after April 10?   He worked to have
a tighter, more effective organization in the style of
Methodist class meetings.   He foisted this reorganization upon the National Assembly, and it became the only
constructive change instituted by that body.   Reorganization has been construed as reorganization for revolution by several writers, but there is another explanation.

In the Victorian era, the good government was the government that spent little and had a small, balanced budget. Chartist demonstrations were disliked because, from the standpoint of financial expenditure, they were costly and unproductive. Extra police, special constables, the movement of troops and the disruption of trade were exacerbating.[37] Also, time was money to ernest Victorian middle class persons, and policing the Chartists was time consuming. Both Wellington and Peel, in support of the Gagging Act in Parliament, complained of the "severe sacrifices" that the Chartists imposed by their repetitive demonstrations.[38] The Times found it "scarcely possible to exaggerate the exertions and sacrifices" called for to put the Chartists down on April 10.[39]

Jones wanted to keep pushing a wearing, costly and threatening agitation, so that the harried government and weary authorities would concede the Charter. Considerable strength remained in mainstream Chartism after April 10, as we have seen. It is clearly a myth that April 10 broke the power of the movement. While it seems to go too far to say that Chartism was stronger after April 10 than before, the masses still in the mainstream provided a formidable and determined force for Jones' purposes. Determined, unhesitating, clear, controlled and accelerating governmental repression thwarted his aims. No small part of this skillful counterrevolution was his own arrest.

Besides fostering this mode of continuous agitation, Jones supported the Land Plan and opposed middle class collaboration. At times he used his supporters to break up the meetings of right wing Chartists combined with radicals. Such prominence brought him considerable opposition. None was more heated than that of the Weekly Dispatch, which found him talking "treason" to the working classes by urging them to violence. Jones was doing the same things that the "oligarchy" would send an argent provacateur to do. In one instance, the Weekly Dispatch described how his followers broke up a reform meeting, howling and waving their hats, and how Jones "turned his somewhat cadaverous face to those on the platform", as if to say: "You see what...these people think of me!" The Dispatch concluded that Jones was like a "gnat in the eye" or "an earwig in the ear" -- only an "insect", but "we can do nothing until the thing is removed."[40]

The government fulfilled this wish of the Weekly
Dispatch quickly, so that no one can ever know how
effective Jones and his plan of agitation would have
been through the summer. Various Chartists recognized
his arrest as an obvious and deliberate attempt to
decapitate the movement, because the speech for which
he was seized was relatively mild compared to many
other Chartist orations in 1848 and long before.[41]

With Jones gone, the third stage of Chartism in
1848 evolved, from mid-June to mid-August. As we have
seen, this period had three separate and simultaneous
developments: Right wing Chartism continued to seek
collaboration with non-Chartist reformers; the extreme
left, a desperate, determined and isolated minority,
quietly prepared for an insurrection; and in the mainstream a vast number dropped out of the movement
entirely or maintained an interest in the Land Plan
exclusively. Outside of Lovett's continuing traditional low-key leadership on the right, no leaders of
any stature emerged in this third stage. Neither
collaboration nor insurrection got very far, and after
August a period of rapid dissipation took hold.

April 10 and the Historians Reconsidered

When taunted in a seminar with the question, "What
is history?", a brilliant but not entirely sane graduate student answered in exasperation: "History is
whatever the historians say it is!" He never finished
his degree, but his point can be brought to bear on
April 10 and 1848 in England.

Two interpretations of April 10 were put forth by
contemporaries immediately after the event. One was
launched by the establishment, declaring that a
"fiasco" had occurred when the Chartists tried to make
their bid for a French style revolution through
attempting to overawe Parliament during the presentation of their petition. According to this view, what
had saved England was popular support from those who
were loyal and knew that England was different from the
Continent. The ranks of special constables, Sir George
Grey and the Duke of Wellington were the heroes of the
day. The other interpretation, held by most Chartists,
saw a proper moral force demonstration facing an overwhelming counter demonstration of the government's
physical force. Of the two interpretations, the
establishment's view became the standard one for

history until after World War Two. In recent decades, several historians have refurbished the Chartist interpretation and helped to demolish some of the myths of April 10. An examination of the origins and some aspects of the development of both interpretations is in order.

One complication needs recognition at the outset. Not all Chartists shared the Chartist interpretation. Strong anti-O'Connorite feelings flared forth again in the aftermath of April 10 from the right wing as the establishment heaped ridicule on the whole movement. For example, Lovett blamed O'Connor and his "boasting physical force followers" for allowing the Whigs to have a "triumph". April 10 was a "blundering demonstration."[42] Gammage complained of the "boasting", and how O'Connor had encouraged the "empty braggarts" to think up until the last moment that he would take the procession up to the House of Commons. Gammage thought O'Connor was quite right in abandoning the procession, but felt that his tactics caused disunion in the movement, once the "miserable result" was perceived.[43] Since Lovett and Gammage have been highly influential for many writers, their denunciations of O'Connor on April 10 have helped to reinforce the establishment's interpretation as the standard account.

George Jacob Holyoake set forth the Chartist interpretation in Bygones Worth Remembering, in which he denounced the standard interpretation as a "myth". It showed "the wild way" in which history could be written. There had been no revolutionary plans, no disorder was threatened and "not a man was armed." Holyoake wrote that "an extraordinary hallucination" about April 10 "has become historic, and passes as authentic." Holyoake quite correctly insisted that "there was absolutely nothing in the field against the Duke of Wellington." Therefore, no need existed to fill London with troops and put on such a show of force. "There was less ground for alarm," Holyoake wrote, "than when a Lord Mayor's procession passes through the city." Holyoake was furious with the "utterly groundless and incredible representations" of April 10 in Kingsley's Alton Locke and in Thomas Hughes' introduction to that novel. Holyoake was sure that the government knew the truth about the confrontation, because they had informers everywhere. The government had been engaging in "political imposture" in order to gain advantages from posing as "the deliverers of England." That the Duke of Wellington

292

should "compromise his great career by fortifying
London against an imaginary enemy" was lamentable, but
Wellington had "readily lent himself" to the govern-
ment's purposes.[44]

This Chartist interpretation was widespread among
members of the movement in the mainstream, and appeared
in whole or in part in numerous speeches and Northern
Star editorials. Thomas Frost included it in his Forty
Years' Recollections, writing that "nothing could be
further than the truth" when April 10 was described as
"a triumph gained by the supporters of law and order
over the promoters of turbulence and anarchy." He saw
the conference of O'Connor and Mayne at the Horne
Tavern producing a "compromise" leading to some dissatisfaction on both sides. Frost noted the "ill-
temper" of the authorities, "men who were not accus-
tomed to be thwarted", and who were, on that day,
"constrained to make concessions...."[45] George Howell
wrote of this compromise as well, finding "concessions
on both sides."[46]

The Chartist interpretation had its more extreme
explanations also. One of these was that a great
victory had been gained on April 10 because they held
their meeting and showed their resolute moral power.
Writing in 1850, Ernest Jones found the great display
of governmental force "homage paid to our power, and a
tacit admission...that the bulk of the popular feeling
was against the government."[47] Another extreme explanation was that a victory had been won because the
people were heroically resolute in their restraint,
thus depriving the government of its opportunity to
unleash its tremendous forces to butcher the innocent
and the unarmed. According to Reynolds' Political
Instructor in 1850, on the tenth, "the people were
goaded by insult and injury to expose themselves...
unarmed and unprepared" to "murder...by the bayonets,
sabres, and muskets" amassed by the government. But
the "slaughter" was averted, "to the regret of many
thirsting for the people's blood...."[48]

We have seen how the standard interpretation was
created in the euphoric atmosphere immediately after
April 10. It was underlined by countless sources,
enshrined in the cheap, popular histories of the nineteenth century and, of course, featured in textbooks.
There is even an illustrated history showing the Duke
of Wellington on horseback in full field marshall's
uniform inspecting the cannon in Hyde Park as if he

were in Portugal or India once again.[49] As the myth of April 10 entrenched itself, Chartism was written off as an "object of ridicule" from thence onwards.

The Annual Register, a standard source for many historians, was more judicious. It described the Chartists' "real" leaders as being "probably no ways desirous of a national convulsion", but noted that many spokesmen in the movement were "ready for any mischief." The government's measures were described as "forbearing and resolute", while they allowed the constitutional rights of meeting to petition and "proper" presentation of the petition.[50] Less judiciously, the Annual Register probably set the tone for many subsequent descriptions of April 10 by dwelling on the "scorn and ridicule" involved.

The day certainly had its deep and meaningful significance for contemporaries. Chartism was supposed to have been laughed off of the stage, to have come to an end all at once, with the age of Victorian stability immediately ensuing. In Harriet Martineau's words, "From that day it was settled that England was safe from revolution."[51] Karl Marx found it a turning point for all of Europe. He saw the "revolutionary might of the Chartists broken", and, "for the first time", the "revolutionary propaganda...impact of the February victory" was broken as well. The "victory of order" on April 10 gave proof that the "movement which had broken out" in 1848 "was not unconquerable." It was, according to Marx, the first important date "of the European counter-revolution", a "milestone" in which the "outermost" wave of "the revolutionary flood" was stemmed, giving "fresh support to the counter-revolution everywhere", and raising hopes in conservative hearts across Europe.[52]

The myth of April 10 has been so pervasive that even historians of aspects of the British working class movement have uncritically incorporated it in their treatments. For a long time, the standard history of Chartism was Mark Hovell's History of the Chartist Movement. He described April 10 as a "tragic fiasco", the day "the government had finally laid the Chartist spectre" low. According to Hovell, the Chartist challenge had been taken up that day, and afterwards the "ruling classes...feared it no more." Only a "minimum of disturbance and protest" followed the "collapse" of April 10.[53] More recently, David Rowe has written of the "farcical official conclusion of the movement in the Kennington Common meeting"[54] and F. M. Leventhal, in his biography of George Howell, calls the Kennington Common meeting "pathetic".[55]

There have been variations. One recent scholarly article on the subject by an Australian historian, F. B. Smith, contends that the Chartists had a "marvelous opportunity" to "break through on the Six Points" in 1848, but "the madmen at the top spoiled that opportunity."[56] Royden Harrison found April 10 to be "one of the most famous days in the history of the nineteenth century," in which the Chartists "had screwed themselves up for a decisive trial of strength with the ruling classes" and then "shrank back before the prospect of a collision." Instead of a triumphant demonstration of the power of the people, the events of April 10 struck a blow against Chartism "from which it never fully recovered."[57] Yet another variation came forth in 1929. Reg Groves, a communist historian, saw the "ignominious surrender" of April 10 as a disaster stemming from the "centrism" of O'Connor. Centrism, Groves wrote, "appears to advocate mass action, leads the workers almost to the point of struggle, and then falls back into confusion and defeat."[58]

Other historians have reasserted the fundamental Chartist interpretation, beginning in the 1950's, and continuing down to the present day. Raymond Postgate led the way with his rather light and popular account, The Story of a Year: 1848, which deals with Europe as well as Britain. "There was no great victory on April 10", Postgate insisted, "O'Connor's bargain with Mayne was a compromise." Moreover, the Chartist movement did not "disappear,...it came back within the year in some quite serious activities."[59] John Saville's seminal article on Chartism in 1848, "Chartism in the Year of Revolution: 1848", appeared in the Modern Quarterly in the winter of 1952-3. It has inspired all subsequent scholars dealing with the subject through its clear and incisive demolition of the myth of April 10. Nothing that has been written recently on the subject, the present study included, has been without the mark of his influence. Saville vigorously attacked the "commonplace" account of the "fiasco" of 1848 that he found "almost always the same." His main point is that the demonstration of April 10 "was never intended to be anything more than a demonstration." The press and the government blew it up to something else, and "the Chartist leadership were incapable of breaking through the barriers of prejudice and distortion."[60]

The government "had the initiative from the beginning and were able to dictate the order of the day."[61] Another of his contentions has stimulated considerable interest and some controversy. It is that Chartism did not collapse after April 10, but that "it grew steadily in those areas where Chartism had traditionally received support."[62]

Several historians have followed and built upon Saville's modern, scholarly restatement of the Chartist interpretation. John Stevenson, in Popular Disturbances in England, 1700-1870, stresses that the Chartists "conducted their preparations openly" and wanted nothing but a moral demonstration on April 10.[63] David Goodway, in a paper entitled "Chartism in London", put emphasis on the strength of the movement after April.[64] A judicious and detailed recent examination of April 10 by David Large is in a chapter entitled "London in the Year of Revolutions, 1848", part of London in the Age of Reform edited by John Stevenson. Large also points out that the Chartists never intended anything beyond a moral force demonstration, and goes on to say that the government knew better than the press or the public what the outcome was likely to be. He finds the government acted as if it shared "illusions" about the dangers on April 10, in order that they might gain "a substantial political dividend" when it came time to slay the Chartists' "paper tiger". Large mentions that Russell and Grey "kept their heads" because they were so "amply informed", and could see that there was nothing to fear. Russell eventually perceived the credit in store for going along with the demands of the "be up and at 'em" group, according to Large.[65] The hysteria preceeding April 10 has been noted for what it was by Saville, Large and F. C. Mather. Mather makes the important point that the propertied classes did not suffer from an hysteria of "despair and inaction", but one of "assertion".[66]

An important recent scholarly treatment of April 10 can be found in David Goodway, London Chartism, 1838 to 1848. His richly detailed study builds upon the revisionist view of Saville and others, although he does take issue with Large on a few points, such as the size of the Kennington Common meeting. He also explores some of the questions which have been taken up in this study, such as the role of the special constables. In general Goodway finds support for insurrection after April 10 rather widespread, and takes

Chartist conspiracies in the summer seriously. Nevertheless, he emphatically denies many myths surrounding
April 10. He firmly agrees that "the Chartists never
intended April 10 to be anything but a peaceable mass
demonstration."[67]

Finally, the restatement of the Chartist position
has already penetrated to the materials used by under-
graduates, judging by Edward Royle's Chartism, a book
in a series of seminar studies in history. In it he
points out that the attempt to portray April 10 as a
fiasco "is as much ideological as historical."[68]

The full description of April 10 in the foregoing
chapters has attempted to continue on in the rational
directions of the last named historians, dispelling the
myths of April 10 and explaining the emergence of the
two widely different interpretations of the event.
These have been fundamental aims of this study.

1848 In England Reconsidered

April 10 was the most dramatic single event in
1848, but it was only part of the story of the year of
revolutions in England. This study has sought to break
the Chartist movement down into stages over the year:
February to April 10; April 11 to June 12; June 13 to
August 15; August 16 to the end of the year. Each
stage had its own particular emphasis or emphases and
its own variety or varieties of leadership. This
treatment should serve to clarify some of the contro-
versies and questions raised in recent scholarship.

The question of how much revolutionary potential
existed in the movement after April 10 has been a major
concern for several writers. Something of a consensus
exists that the underground movement was not very
strong, either in numbers or potential for success, a
point of view strongly underlined by the findings of
this study. For example, F. C. Mather saw the danger
confronting the government all through the Chartist era
that of "spontaneous tumult" rather than "sedition,...
conspiracy and rebellion."[69] Donald Read and Eric
Glasgow called the plots of the summer "the desperate
last attempts" that had no general support.[70] Read
thought the summer disturbances were "symptoms not of
strength but of weakness."[71] George Rudé, in his
celebrated book, The Crowd in History, did not consider
the disturbances of 1848 as very threatening. They

fell into what he called a "last phase" of the movement which was far less wide-spread and significant than previous manifestations. To him, everything was "in a minor key and on a minor scale", or, "the last flick of the tail of a dying political movement."[72] Rudé comes down close to the earlier pronouncements of Elie Halèvy, who saw Chartism as the "ebb of the big radical upheaval" that began in 1817 and 1819. Halèvy thought 1848 in England was "a mere aftermath" of the French Revolution of February.[73] On the other hand, other historians, most notably John Saville and David Goodway, have laid emphasis upon how revolutionary potential has been underestimated.[74]

One of the more widely celebrated books in political science in recent years has been Ted Gurr's Why Men Rebel. It is an interesting exercise to take some of his conclusions out of context in order to apply them to 1848 in England, when men did not rebel. The process runs some risk of doing an injustice to Gurr's complex work, because out of context some of his conclusions may appear simpler than they really are. Gurr really says little about England in the nineteenth century, except that turmoil was chronic until the middle of the century, and "seldom [my italics] countered with massive force."[75] One of Gurr's hypotheses is that "the likelihood of conspiracy varies inversely with the loyalty of coercive forces to the regime."[76] Applying this to England, conspiracy was not apt to be affective because there was no chance to win over the police, the special constables or units of the army to the Chartist side. Gurr also points out that "if men anticipate severe and certain retribution for pre-scribed actions, they are likely to restrain their anger in the short run."[77] This certainly applied to many but not all Chartists in the confrontations of 1848. Gurr also observes that "discontent leads men to political violence" when the institutional framework is weak enough or opposition organizations strong enough "to give the disaffected a sense of potency."[78] Applying this to England again, it is clear that the insti-tutional framework remained strong while opposition organizations, the National Convention and the National Assembly,[79] were weak from strife and confused in pur-pose. Finally, Gurr declares that the most effective way to handle civil disobedience is with a massive threat of force but a minimal and consistent use of it. He gives as an example the response to the riots after the assassination of Martin Luther King in 1968. He could have drawn examples from a series of events in England 120 years earlier as well.

Britain's ruling elite was effective in handling the Chartist challenge in 1848 in the manner Gurr describes. Massive force was always at hand for their use, but they adeptly applied a minimal but accelerating amount of force. They repressed Chartism with a general consistency and firmness. Several historians have recently cited the skillful responses of the political elite in charge of the administrative machinery to explain why serious clashes were avoided in England in 1848.[80]

In this, England was different, and in much else besides. The argument that England escaped revolution in 1848 because England was fundamentally different from the Continent has endured to the present day. It has been a standard interpretation from the editorials of April 11, 1848, down to the textbooks in current use. Britain allowed greater participation in the political process, guaranteed basic freedoms, provided more effective amelioration of the plight of the poor, operated a less corrupt public administration, had no censorship and could count on the support of the army as well as the satisfied, optimistic middle classes.[81] In other words, while Continental states reached a turning point and failed to turn in 1848, as stated by the famous aphorism of G. M. Trevelyan, subsequently borrowed by A. J. P. Taylor, Britain had reached its turning point in 1832 and turned.

The larger picture of 1848 in England is less controversial than April 10. The standard interpretation remains little changed by modern historiography or by the detailed approach of this study. Many accounts have stressed the fortunate uniqueness of Britain and the key role of middle class loyalty, views first proclaimed by self-congratulatory and relieved Victorians. For example, Priscilla Robertson's Revolutions of 1848 declares: "During the days of 1848, England stood apart, unshaken, apparently unshakable. Her reformers were already in power...."[82] In a recent study of the 1848 revolutions throughout Europe, Peter Stearns focuses on the ways the middle classes abetted Continental revolutions at the same time that they were instrumental in preventing revolution in Britain. He wrote:

> Chartist protest in Britain completely
> failed to make a revolution. In this
> case, segments of the lower classes
> did stir, but they lacked any coopera-
> tion from above, and they were divided
> among themselves, and few of them were
> consciously revolutionary.[83]

These are really restatements of Elie Halèvy's classic
explanation. Halèvy saw "moderate liberalism, combined
with a policy of radical free trade" as the bedrock of
English confidence.[83] While John Saville's treatment
of 1848 differs from the traditional explanation in
several ways, his reasons for the failure of revolution
coincides. He points out that the British government
could count on "wholehearted support" much further down
the social scale than Continental governments could.[84]

Despite all the newer research on Chartism, political violence, crowds and revolution, the standard
interpretation for England's fate remains: middle-
class support for the regime was too powerful and Char-
ist support for an insurrection was too weak. Most
British workers did not draw direct, clear analogies
between themselves and the Continental revolutionaries,
nor did they perceive the same preconditions for revolution in England. They, too, adhered to the view that
England was different in 1848.

NOTES TO CHAPTER VIII

[1] For the Land Company, see A. M. Hadfield, The Chartist Land Company (Newton Abbot, 1970).

[2] See, for example, Northern Star, June 17, 1848, p. 1 or June 24, 1848. Before 1848, O'Connor was described as living in a "state of joyous excitement" over the Land Plan, to the extent that he sought to make the members of the National Executive primarily functionaries of the Land Company. Schoyen, The Chartist Challenge, pp. 148-9.

[3] Northern Star, September 23, 1848, p. 9.

[4] Northern Star, June 17, 1848, p. 1.

[5] Manchester Guardian, March 22, 1848, p. 6.

[6] Northern Star, May 6, 1848, p. 1.

[7] Northern Star, May 6, 1848, p. 1.

[8] According to O'Connor, the King of Prussia "gulled the working classes who gained the revolution" until he gathered enough physical force to defy them. Northern Star, April 29, 1848, p. 1, editorial.

[9] Some xenophobia was mixed with his anti-republican outlook, which made his relationship to Harney, the avid internationalist who was his editor, quite curious. The Northern Star of July 15, 1848, contains some of O'Connor's more pointed xenophobic remarks.

[10] Hansard, Parliamentary Debates, Third Series, Vol. 98, p. 16. He had "never said a word" about abolishing titles or about the "destruction of royalty."

[11] Hansard, Parliamentary Debates, Third Series, Vol. 98, p. 155.

[12] Punch, 1848, p. 173.

[13] Hansard, Parliamentary Debates, Third Series, Vol. 96, p. 1286.

[14] Hansard, _Parliamentary Debates_, Third Series, Vol. 97, p. 1012.

[15] Hansard, _Parliamentary Debates_, Third Series, Vol. 97, p. 1369.

[16] Hansard, _Parliamentary Debates_, Third Series, Vol. 98, p. 41.

[17] Hansard, _Parliamentary Debates_, Third Series, Vol. 98, p. 230.

[18] Hansard, _Parliamentary Debates_, Third Series, Vol. 98, p. 41. O'Connor warned, "Let them pass that law", and within the week "hundreds of secret societies would be organized throughout the kingdom", and sooner or later a violent storm would come from them. (Vol. 98, pp. 230-1.)

[19] Hansard, _Parliamentary Debates_, Third Series, Vol. 98, p. 84.

[20] _Weekly Dispatch_, April 30, 1848, p. 206.

[21] _Weekly Dispatch_, May 7, 1848, p. 222; April 23, 1848, p. 193; Smith, "Great Britain and the Revolutions of 1848", p. 76.

[22] John Saville makes this point in "Some Aspects of Chartism in Decline", p. 18 and "Chartism in the Year of Revolution: 1848", p. 30. Also Large, "London in the Year of Revolutions, 1848", pp. 192-3.

[23] Donald Read and Eric Glasgow, _Feargus O'Connor: Irishman and Chartist_ (London, 1961), p. 137; Frost, _History of the Chartist Movement_, Chapter X; _Northern Star_, April 29, 1848, editorial.

[24] Handbill, "Proposal for Forming a People's League: Addressed to the Radical Reformers of the United Kingdom," Lovett Collection, Vol. 2, p. 288.

[25] _Leeds Mercury_, June 17, 1848, p. 4.

[26] Read and Glasgow, _Feargus O'Connor_, pp. 130-1; 140.

[27] Schoyen, _The Chartist Challenge_, p. 161.

[28] Gammage, _History of the Chartist Movement_, p. 341.

[29] Prest, Lord John Russell, p. 245.

[30] Manchester Guardian, March 22, 1848, p. 6. For a vigorous rehabilitation of O'Connor up to 1842, see Epstein, The Lion of Freedom: Feargus O'Connor and the Chartist Movement, 1832-1842. Epstein explains his use of the politics of intimidation and stresses his constitutionalism.

[31] Saville, "Chartism in the Year of Revolution: 1848", p. 30.

[32] Hovell, The Chartist Movement, p. 343.

[33] Weekly Dispatch, March 13, 1848, p. 141.

[34] Northern Star, March 18, 1848, p. 5.

[35] He also remarked that Chartists stood on "the threshold" of their rights, and "one step, were it only with an iron heel, and they are ours." Northern Star, April 8, 1848, p. 8. At another time he threatened the government with lessons given with "steel pens and red ink." Weekly Dispatch, June 18, 1848, p. 301.

[36] Manchester Guardian, June 10, 1848.

[37] The Leeds Mercury, April 15, 1848, carried the comments of a worker calling upon his fellows to abstain from Chartist movements for fear of disturbing trade. By contrast, the radical John Arthur Roebuck thought the Chartist activities gave the Whigs a wonderful pretext for expense. Leader, Life and Letters of John Arthur Roebuck, p. 203.

[38] Hansard, Parliamentary Debates, Third Series, Vol. 98, pp. 468 and 500.

[39] The Times, April 11, 1848, editorial. In Manchester Absalom Watkin saw some of these sacrifices in May, when "miserably wet" police, specials and troops returned from a threatened Chartist confrontation. Watkin, Extracts from His Journal, 1814-1856, p. 253.

[40] Weekly Dispatch, May 28, 1848, p. 259. For an example of Jones causing discord, the People's League Meeting reported in the Weekly Dispatch of May 23, 1848, p. 254.

[41] The Republican, June, 1882, Vol. 2, No. 3; George Howell, MSS Biography of Ernest Jones, Vol. 2, p. 87. Also Anon., "Ernest Jones, Who is He? What Has He Done?" (A. Heywood, 1868.)

[42] Lovett, Life and Struggles, p. 285.

[43] Gammage, History of the Chartist Movement, p. 331.

[44] Holyoake, Bygones Worth Remembering, pp. 73-83. For another account favorable to the Chartist viewpoint, see Frank Peel, The Risings of the Luddites, Chartists and Plug Drawers, 4th ed. (London, 1968), p. 347. Peel wrote that Feargus O'Connor was "one of the first to realize the grave situation and had the good sense to oppose...mad counsels with all his strength."

[45] Thomas Frost, Forty Years' Recollections, pp. 140, 143. He repeats this in his History of the Chartist Movement, Chapter X.

[46] Howell Collection, MSS Biography of Ernest Jones.

[47] Saville, Ernest Jones: Chartist, pp. 109-11. Saville quotes and open letter in the Northern Star of July 9, 1850.

[48] Reynolds' Political Instructor, March 23, 1850, p. 154.

[49] Edwin Hodder, The Life of a Century, 1800 to 1900 (London, 1901). Also interesting is Mrs. Markham, A Short History of England from the First Invasion by the Romans down to the Present Time (London, 1873).

[50] Annual Register, April 10, 1848, pp. 50-1.

[51] Langer, Political and Social Upheaval, 1832-1852, p. 71.

[52] Marx, "The Revolutionary Movement in Italy", pp. 101-2, Karl Marx found the other important dates of the counterrevolution May 15 and June 25 in Paris; August 6 in Milan and November 1 in Vienna.

[53] Hovell, The Chartist Movement, pp. 292, 343. J. P. T. Bury seconded Hovell's view in what was a significant article, Bury "Great Britain and the Revolution of 1848", p. 186, by calling the event a "débacle" which "effectively spelt the end of Chartism...."

[54] D. J. Rowe, "The Failure of London Chartism", The Historical Journal, Vol. XI, no. 3 (1968), p. 482.

[55] F. M. Leventhal, Respectable Radical: George Howell and Victorian Working Class Politics (London, 1971), p.

[56] Smith, "Great Britain and the Revolutions of 1848", p. 81.

[57] Harrison found the success of the Reform League on May 6, 1867 as an event to avenge the Chartist failure on April 10. Royden Harrison, "The 10th of April of Spencer Walpole: The Problem of Revolution in Relation to Reform, 1865-1867", International Review of Social History, Vol. 7 (1962), pp. 331-400, also "The Hyde Park Rail-Way to Reform", in David Rubenstein, ed., People for People (London and New York, 1969), pp. 98-104.

[58] Reg Groves, "The Class Leadership of Chartism", The Labour Monthly, Vol. 2 (April 1929), pp. 240-4.

[59] Postgate, Story of a Year: 1848, p. 128.

[60] P. 33.

[61] P. 28. Saville found implications for other historical events in April 10. He saw it as the first example of "that extraordinary unanimity which comes over the English press in the face of social revolutions abroad...." (p. 24). Furthermore, this was not the last time that the working class movement "was opposed by a political strategy which combined apparent reasonableness and tact with...ruthlessness." (p. 33).

[62] P. 28. Several of these points were presented again in 1970 in a paper given at a meeting of the Society for the Study of Labor History, reported in "Some Aspects of Chartism in Decline", Society for the Study of Labor History Bulletin, no. 20, (Spring 1970), pp. 16-18.

305

[63] Stevenson, Popular Disturbances in England, 1700-1800, p. 268.

[64] Goodway, "Chartism in London", pp. 13-15.

[65] Large, "London in the Year of Revolutions, 1848", pp. 177-203. For evidence of Russell's reluctance, Large cites his slowness in taking up the plans of Wellington and other "hawks".

[66] Mather, Public Order in the Age of the Chartists, p. 85. Recently Large has restated Mather's assessment, pointing out how "the polite world" demanded firmer action and offered help against the "new bogy" of Chartist revolution, which found a Chartist "under every bed." Large, "London in the Year of Revolutions, 1848", pp. 182-3, 185. John Saville described it as the old fear of Jacobinism reemergent, and suggests that a linking occurred in the minds of the ruling classes between a French Revolution, heretical ideas about property, Chartism, rioting and looting. Saville, "Chartism in the Year of Revolution: 1848", pp. 23-5.

[67] Goodway, London Chartism, 1838-1848, p. 74.

[68] Royle, Chartism, Seminar Studies in History, p. 43.

[69] Mather, Public Order in the Age of the Chartists, p. 26.

[70] Read and Glasgow, Feargus O'Connor: Irishman and Chartist, p. 138.

[71] Read, "Chartism in Manchester", p. 63.

[72] Rude, The Crowd in History, p. 183.

[73] Elie Halèvy, "Chartism", Quarterly Review, Vol. 236 (July 1921), pp. 70-1.

[74] Goodway makes the case that it was the last revolutionary attempt in London, which became the most supported and widespread. Goodway, "Chartism in London", p. 15. Saville's stress on the greater revolutionary potential of the movement after April 10 has been noted previously. Dorothy Thompson suggests that Chartism actually appears to have reduced community violence, and remarks that thousands could gather "in

conditions of great political tension or economic distress" and remain entirely peaceful. Dorothy Thompson, "Chartism as a Historical Subject", Society for the Study of Labour History Bulletin, no. 20 (Spring 1970), p. 12. For the most detailed exposition of Chartist revolutionary potential, see Goodway, London Chartism, 1838-1848, pp. 79-96.

[75]Ted Robert Gurr, Why Men Rebel (Princeton, 1970), p. 246.

[76]Gurr, Why Men Rebel, p. 253.

[77]Gurr, Why Men Rebel, p. 238.

[78]Gurr, Why Men Rebel, p. 155.

[79]The Chartist National Assembly has been cited as the last "anti-Parliament" in British radical history. See T. M. Parssinen, "Association, Convention and Anti-Parliament in British Radical Politics, 1771-1848", English Historical Review, no. 88 (July 1973), pp. 504-533.

[80]Large, "London in the Year of Revolutions, 1848", p. 203; Mather, Public Order in the Age of the Chartists, p. 232. Goodway, London Chartism, 1838-1848, concludes that revolution was avoided in Britain because revolution was avoided in London. London, he maintains, was unique because of the existence of an effective metropolitan police and because of the sheer size and density of the metropolis made organization difficult (pp. 221-5).

[81]Some of the more detailed statements of this point of view are in Postgate, Story of a Year: 1848, p. 48; Halèvy, A History of the English People in the Nineteenth Century, Vol. 4, p. 245.

[82]Priscilla Robertson, Revolutions of 1848: A Social History (Princeton, 1952), p. 405. Also Bury, "Great Britain and the Revolution of 1848", pp. 180-203.

[83]Peter N. Stearns, 1848: The Revolutionary Tide in Europe (New York, 1974), p. 35.

[84]Elie Halèvy, "English Public Opinion and the French Revolutions of the Nineteenth Century", in Alfred Colville and Harold Temperley, eds., Studies

307

in Anglo-French History during the Eighteenth, Nine-teenth and Twentieth Centuries (Cambridge, 1935), pp. 56-7; also A History of the English People in the Nineteenth Century, Vol. 4, p. 245.

[85]Saville, "Chartism in the Year of Revolution: 1848", pp. 23-4.

BIBLIOGRAPHY

Papers

Home Office Papers, Public Record Office
Howell Collection, Bishopsgate Institute
Lovett Collection, Birmingham Central Library
Place Collection, British Library
Royal Archives, Windsor Castle
Russell Papers, Public Record Office
War Office Papers, Public Record Office

Newspapers and Journals

Annual Register
Aris's Birmingham Gazette
Ashton Chronicle
Blackwood's Edinburgh Magazine
Bradford Observer
Fraser's Magazine for Town and Country
Gateshead Observer
Glasgow Examiner
Illustrated London News
Leeds Mercury
Leeds Times
Leicester Journal and Midland Counties General
    Advertiser
Liverpool Journal
Lloyd's Weekly London Newspaper
Macclesfield Courier and Herald
Manchester Guardian
Morning Chronicle
Newcastle Chronicle
Newcastle Journal
The Nonconformist
The Northern Star
Punch
The Reasoner: A Weekly Journal, Utilitarian,
    Republican and Communist
The Republican
Reynold's Political Instructor
Staffordshire Mercury and Potteries' Gazette
Tait's Edinburgh Magazine
The Times
The Voice of the People: A Supplement to all
    Newspapers
Weekly Dispatch

Pamphlets

"Address to the French People from the National Association, London", (London, 1848).

[J. Allport] A Friend to the Working Man, "The Chartists; or, Liberty, Equality and Fraternity", (London, 1848).

Anon. "Ernest Jones, Who is He? What Has He Done?" (A. Heywood, 1868).

Anon. "A Letter From One of the Special Constables in London on the Late Occasion of their being Called Out to Keep the Peace", (London: William Pickering, 1848).

A Conservative Reformer, "On the Disastrous Consequences which might have Resulted had not the Government Adopted Precautionary and Preventative Measures Regarding the Late Expected Monster Meeting of the 10th of April, 1848", (London, 1848).

Thomas Dudgeon, "A Lecture on Radical and Practicable Chartism", (London: Black and Co., May, 1848).

A Fellow Laborer, "What the Chartists Are. A Letter to English Working Men." (London: Thomas Bosworth, 1848).

William Lovett, "Justice Safer than Expediency: An Appeal to the Middle Classes on the Question of Suffrage" (1848).

[Mary Atkinson Maurice] "The Chartist's Friend, by the Author of 'Aids to Development', 'Mothers and Governesses', Etc." (London: B. Wertheim, Aldine Chambers, 1848).

Philip Murray McDouall, "An Authentic Report of the Trial of Doctor Peter Murray McDouall, at Liverpool on August 28, 1848, compiled from the Shorthand Writer's Notes", (Manchester: Abel Heywood; London: J. Watson).

Peter Murray McDouall, "The Charter, What it Means! The Chartists, What They Want! Explained in an Address to the Middle Classes of Great Britain", (London, 1848).

"The People's League to the People of London and Its Vicinity", (London, 1848).

"The People's League for Obtaining Manhood Suffrage", (London, 1848).

The Pimlico Hermit, "An Appeal to the Chartists Proper, in a Series of Letters, Shewing in What Manner the People's Charter May be Rendered Worthy of Being Made a Reality", 2nd ed., Letter I (London: McGowan and Co., 1848).

"Plan of Organization for the National Charter Association of Great Britain and Ireland, Adopted by the

National Assembly, May 1848, to Obtain the Speedy
Enactment of the People's Charter", (Manchester:
Livsey, 1848).
William Stevens, "A Memoir of Thomas Martin Wheeler,
Founder of the Friend in Need Life and Sick Assurance
Society, Domestic, Political and Industrial, with
Extracts From His Letters, Speeches and Writings
(London, 1862).
Benj. Wilson of Salterhebble, "The Struggles of an Old
Chartist, What He Knows and the Part He Has Taken in
Various Movements", (Halifax, 1887).
Peter Wyncoll, Nottingham Chartism (Nottingham, 1966).

Articles

Anon., "Chartism," Fraser's Magazine, Vol. 37 (May
1848).
Anon., "The Chartists of Britain and the Repealers of
Ireland," Tait's Edinburgh Magazine, Vol. 15, no.
173 (1848), pp. 295-300.
Anon., "How to Disarm the Chartists," Blackwood's
Edinburgh Magazine, Vol. 63, no. 392 (June 1848).
Asa Briggs, "Chartists in Tasmania: A Note," Society
for the Study of Labour History Bulletin, no. 3
(Autumn 1961).
J. P. T. Bury, "Great Britain and the Revolutions of
1848," in Francis Fejtö, ed., The Opening of an Era
-- 1848: An Historical Symposium (London, 1948).
Robert Crowe, "The Reminiscences of a Chartist Tailor,"
The Outlook (August 9, 1902).
Ray Faherty, "The Memoir of Thomas Martin Wheeler,
Owenite and Chartist," Society for the Study of
Labour History Bulletin, no. 30 (Spring 1975).
M. D. George, "The London Coal Heavers: Attempts to
Regulate Waterside Labour in the Eighteenth and
Nineteenth Centuries," Economic History, Vol. 1 (May
1927).
David Goodway, "Chartism in London," Society for the
Study of Labour History Bulletin, no. 20 (Spring
1970).
J. H. Grainger, "The View from Britain II: The Moral-
izing Island," in Eugene Kamenka and F. B. Smith,
eds., Intellectuals and Revolution: Socialism and
the Experience of 1848 (London, 1979).
Reg Groves, "The Class Leadership of Chartism," The
Labour Monthly, Vol. 2 (April 1929).
Elie Halèvy, "Chartism," Quarterly Review, Vol. 236
(July 1921).

311

Elie Halèvy, "English Public Opinion and the French Revolutions of the Nineteenth Century," in Alfred Colville and Harold Temperley, eds., Studies in Anglo-French History during the Eighteenth, Nineteenth and Twentieth Centuries (Cambridge 1935).

J. F. C. Harrison, "Chartism in Leeds," Asa Briggs, ed., Chartist Studies (London and New York, 1959).

Royden Harrison, "The Hyde Park Rail-Way to Reform," in David Rubenstein, ed., People for People (London and New York, 1969).

Royden Harrison, "The 10th of April of Spencer Walpole: The Problem of Revolution in Relation to Reform, 1865-1867," International Review of Social History, Vol. 7 (1962), pp. 351-400.

B. G. Iványi, "The Working Classes of Britain and Eastern European Revolutions (1848)," The Slavonic and East European Review, Vol. 26, no. 66 (Nov. 1947).

P. W. Kingsford, "Radical Dandy: Thomas Slingsby Duncombe, 1796-1861," History Today, no. 14 (1964).

Issac Kramnick, "Reflections on Revolution: Definition and Explanation in Recent Scholarship," History and Theory, Vol. 11, no. 1 (1972).

David Large, "London in the Year of Revolutions, 1848," in John Stevenson, ed., London in the Age of Reform (Oxford, 1977), pp. 177-203.

Norman Mackenna, "Socialist Pioneer," The New Statesman and Nation, May 6, 1950.

Karl Marx, "The Class Struggles in France, 1848 to 1850," in Karl Marx and Frederick Engels, Selected Works, Vol. 1 (Moscow, 1962).

_____. "The Revolutionary Movement in Italy," Karl Marx, Frederick Engels, Collected Works, Vol. 8 (London, 1977).

A. L. Morton, "The Interpretation of Chartism," Marxism Today, Vol. 5, no. 6 (June, 1961).

Rachel O'Higgins, "The Irish Influence in the Chartist Movement," Past and Present, no. 20 (November 1961).

Stanley H. Palmer, "Rebellion, Emancipation, Starvation: The Dilemma of Peaceful Protest in Ireland, 1798-1848," in Bede Lackner and Kenneth Philip, eds., Essays in Modern European History (Austin, 1977).

T. M. Parssinen, "Association, Convention and Anti-Parliament in British Radical Politics, 1771-1848," English Historical Review, no. 88 (July 1973).

Iowerth Prothero, "Chartism in London," Past and Present, no. 44 (August 1969).

_____ and D. J. Rowe, "Debates: The London Working Men's Association and the People's Charter," Past and Present, no. 38 (December, 1967).

Donald Read, "Chartism in Manchester," in Asa Briggs, ed., Chartist Studies (London, 1959).

D. J. Rowe, "Some Aspects of Chartism on the Tyneside," International Review of Social History, Vol. 16, Part 1 (1971).

John Salt, "English Radicalism: A Neglected Document," Notes and Queries (September 1966), pp. 332-3.

John Saville, "Chartism in the Year of Revolution: 1848," The Modern Quarterly (Winter, 1952-3).

_____. "The Christian Socialists of 1848," in John Saville, ed., Democracy and the Labour Movement: Essays in Honour of Dona Torr (London, 1954).

_____. "Some Aspects of Chartism in Decline," Society for the Study of Labour History Bulletin, no. 20 (Spring 1970).

F. B. Smith, "Great Britain and the Revolutions of 1848," Labour History (Australia), no. 33 (November 1977).

_____. "The View from Britain I, Tumults Abroad, Stability at Home," in Eugene Kamenka and F. B. Smith, eds., Intellectuals and Revolution: Socialism and the Experience of 1848 (London, 1979).

Dorothy Thompson, "Chartism as a Historical Subject," Society for the Study of Labour History Bulletin, no. 20 (Spring 1970).

Henry Weisser, "Chartist Internationalism, 1845-8," The Historical Journal, Vol. 14, no. 1 (1971).

_____. "The Role of Feargus O'Connor in Chartist Internationalism," The Rocky Mountain Social Science Journal, Vol. 6, no. 1 (April 1969).

_____. "Chartism in 1848: Reflections on a Non-Revolution," Albion, Vol. 13, no. 1 (Spring 1981).

Books

Evelyn Ashley, The Life and Correspondence of Henry John Temple, Viscount Palmerston. London, 1879.

_____, The Life of Henry John Temple, Viscount Palmerston, 1841-1865, Vol. 1, London, 1876.

George J. Barnsley, The Working Class Movement in the Black Country, 1750 to 1867. Wolverhampton, 1977.

Hartley Bateson, A Centenary History of Oldham. Oldham, 1949.

Herbert C. F. Bell, Lord Palmerston. London, New York, Toronto, 1936.

Arthur Christopher Benson and Viscount Esher, The Letters of Queen Victoria: A Selection from Her Majesty's Correspondence between the years 1837 and 1861, Vol. 2, 1844-1853. London, 1907.

The Earl of Bessborough, ed., Lady Charlotte Guest,
    Extracts from Her Journal, 1833-1852. London, 1952.
Frank Gees Black and Rene Métivier Black, The Harney
    Papers. Assen, The Netherlands, 1969.
James Burn, The Autobiography of a Beggar Boy. London,
    1882 and 1978, eds.
David Cairns, ed., The Memoirs of Hector Berlioz.
    London, 1969.
Maria Weston Chapman, ed., Harriet Martineau's Auto-
    biography, Vol. 2. London, 1877.
Alfred Cobban, A History of Modern France, Vol. 2,
    From the First Empire to the Second Republic, 1799-
    1871. London, 1965.
G. D. H. Cole, Chartist Portraits. New York, 1965.
Thomas Cooper, The Life of Thomas Cooper, Written by
    Himself. London, 1882.
M. Creighton, Memoir of Sir George Grey, Bart. New-
    castle upon Tyne, 1884.
T. A. Critchley, A History of Police in England and
    Wales. London, 1978, ed.
C. Stella Davies, A History of Macclesfield. Man-
    chester, 1961.
George Douglas, Eighth Duke of Argyll, Autobiography
    and Memoirs. London, 1906.
James Epstein, The Lion of Freedom: Feargus O'Connor
    and the Chartist Movement, 1832-1842. London, 1982.
Thomas Frost, Forty Years' Recollections: Liberary
    and Political. London, 1880.
    _____, The Secret Societies of the European Revolu-
    tion, 1776-1876, 2 vols. London, 1876.
R. G. Gammage, History of the Chartist Movement, 1837-
    1854, 2nd ed. New York, 1969.
G. P. Gooch, ed., The Later Correspondence of Lord John
    Russell, 1840-1878. London, 1925.
David Goodway, London Chartism, 1838-1848. Cambridge,
    1982.
Charles C. F. Greville, The Greville Memoirs: A
    Journal of the Reigns of King George IV, King William
    IV, and Queen Victoria, Vol. 6. London, 1888.
John Gunn, Violence in Human Society. Newton Abbott,
    1973.
Ted Robert Gurr, Why Men Rebel. Princeton, 1970.
A. M. Hadfield, The Chartist Land Company. Newton
    Abbot, 1970.
Gordon S. Haigt, The George Eliot Letters, Vol. 1.
    London, 1954.
Elie Halèvy, A History of the English People in the
    Nineteenth Century, Vol. 4, Victorian Years, 1841-
    1895. London, 1951.

J. H. Harris, The Earl of Malmesbury, Memoirs of An
  Ex-Minister, An Autobiography. London, 1884.
Philip Henry, Fifth Earl of Stanhope, Notes of Conver-
  sations with the Duke of Wellington, 1831-1851.
  Oxford, 1938 ed.
John Cam Hobhouse, Recollections of A Long Life, by
  Lord Broughton, Vol. 6, 1841-1852. London, 1911.
Steven Hobhouse, Joseph Sturge, His Life and Work.
  London, 1919.
Edwin Hodder, The Life of A Century, 1800 to 1900.
  London, 1901.
_____. The Life and Work of the Seventh Earl of
  Shaftesbury, Vol. 2. London, 1886.
_____. The Life of Samuel Morley. London, 1888.
George Jacob Holyoake, Bygones Worth Remembering, 2
  Vols. London, 1905.
Mark Hovell, The Chartist Movement. Manchester, 1925
  ed.
Lawrence C. Jennings, France and Europe in 1848: A
  Study of French Foreign Affairs in Time of Crisis.
  Oxford, 1973.
David Jones, Chartism and the Chartists. London and
  New York, 1975.
Eugene Kamenka and F. B. Smith, eds., Intellectuals
  and Revolution: Socialism and the Experience of
  1848. London, 1979.
Robert Kee, The Green Flag: A History of Irish
  Nationalism. London, 1972.
Charles Kingsley, Alton Locke, Tailor and Poet: An
  Autobiography, with a memoir by Thomas Hughes.
  London, 1881.
F. E. Kingsley, ed., Charles Kingsley: His Letters and
  Memories of His Life, Vol. 1. London, 1894.
Charles Knight, Passages of a Working Life During Half
  a Century: With a Prelude of Early Reminiscences,
  Vol. 3. London, 1865.
Andrew Lang, Life, Letters and Diaries of Sir Stafford
  Northcote, First Earl of Iddesleigh. Edinburgh and
  London, 1891.
William L. Langer, Political and Social Upheaval, 1832-
  1852. New York, Evanston and London, 1969.
Robert Eadon Leader, ed., Life and Letters of John
  Arthur Roebuck, with Chapters of Autobiography.
  London and New York, 1897.
F. M. Leventhal, Respectable Radical: George Howell
  and Victorian Working Class Politics. London, 1971.
William James Linton, James Watson: A Memoir. Man-
  chester, 1880.
William Lovett, The Life and Struggles of William
  Lovett. London, 1967 ed.

Howard Foster Lowry, The Letters of Matthew Arnold to
Arthur Hugh Clough. London and New York, 1932.
Joseph McCabe, Life and Letters of George Jacob Holy-
oake. London, 1908.
Desmond McCarthy and Agatha Russell, eds., Lady John
Russell: A Memoir. London, 1910.
Justin McCarthy, M. P., Reminiscences, Vol. 2. London,
1899.
Simon Maccoby, English Radicalism, Vol. 3, 1832-1852
(1935).
Norman and Jeanne Mackenzie, Dickens: A Life, Oxford,
1979.
Mrs. Markham, A Short History of England from the
First Invasion by the Romans down to the Present
Time. London, 1873.
Edwin W. Marrs, Jr., The Letters of Thomas Carlyle to
His Brother Alexander, with Related Family Letters.
Cambridge, Mass., 1968.
Theodore Martin, The Life of His Royal Highness The
Prince Consort, 2nd ed. London, 1875.
Karl Marx, Revolution and Counter Revolution, or
Germany in 1848. London, 1971 ed.
F. C. Mather, ed., Chartism and Society: An Anthology
of Documents. London, 1980.
F. C. Mather, Public Order in the Age of the Chartists.
Manchester, 1959.
George C. Miller, Blackburn, the Evolution of a Cotton
Town. Blackburn, 1951.
Robert Newton, Victorian Exeter, 1837-1914. Leicester,
1968.
Alfred Temple Patterson, Radical Leicester: A History
of Leicester, 1780-1850. Leicester, 1954.
Frank Peel, The Risings of the Luddites, Chartists and
Plug Drawers, 4th ed. London, 1968.
Alfred Plummer, Bronterre: A Political Biography of
Bronterre O'Brien, 1804-1864.
Raymond Postgate, Story of a Year: 1848. London,
1955.
John Prest, Lord John Russell. London, 1972.
Donald Read, Cobden and Bright: A Victorian Political
Partnership. London, 1967.
_____, and Eric Glasgow, Feargus O'Connor: Irishman
and Chartist. London, 1961.
Priscilla Robertson, Revolutions of 1848: A Social
History. Princeton, N.J., 1952.
Edward Royle, Chartism, Seminar Studies in History.
London, 1980.
_____. Victorian Infidels: The Origins of the
British Secularist Movement, 1791-1866. Manchester,
1974.

David Rubenstein, ed., People for the People. London
and New York, 1969.
George Rude, The Crowd in History. New York, 1964.
George W. E. Russell, Letters of Matthew Arnold, 1848-
1888, Vol. 1. New York and London, 1895.
Lord John Russell, Recollections and Suggestions, 1813-
1873. London, 1875.
Rollo Russell, ed., Early Correspondence of Lord John
Russell, 1805-1840, Vol. 1. London, 1913.
John Saville, Ernest Jones: Chartist. London, 1952.
A. R. Schoyen, The Chartist Challenge: A Portrait of
George Julian Harney. London, 1958.
Robert Sencourt, Napoleon III: The Modern Emperor.
London, 1933.
F. A. Simpson, The Rise of Louis Napoleon. London,
1909.
Preston William Slosson, The Decline of the Chartist
Movement. New York, 1916.
Alexander Somerville, Conservative Science of Nations,
Being the First Complete Narrative of Somerville's
Dilligent Hope in the Service of Public Safety in
Britain. Montreal and Toronto, 1860.
Peter N. Stearns, 1848: The Revolutionary Tide in
Europe. New York, 1974.
John Stevenson, Popular Disturbances in England, 1700-
1870. London, 1979.
A. J. P. Taylor, Essays in English History. London,
1976.
Malcolm I. Thomis and Peter Holt, Threats of Revolution
in Britain, 1789-1848. London, 1977.
J. J. Tobias, Crime and Industrial Society in the Nine-
teenth Century. London, 1967.
David Vincent, ed., Testaments of Radicalism: Memoirs
of Working Class Politicians, 1790-1885. London,
1977.
Spencer Walpole, The Life of Lord John Russell, Vol. 2.
London, 1889.
J. T. Ward, Chartism. London, 1973.
Absalom Watkin, Extracts From His Journal, 1814-1856.
London, 1920.
Henry Weisser, British Working Class Movements and
Europe, 1815-1848. Manchester, 1975.
Muriel Wellesley, Wellington in Civil Life: Through
the Eyes of Those Who Knew Him. London, 1939.

Miscellaneous Works

John James Bezer, "Autobiography of One of the Chartist Rebels of 1848", in David Vincent, ed., Testaments of Radicalism: Memoirs of Working Class Politicians, 1790-1885 (London, 1977).

"Chartist Meetings, Speeches and Trials of July 26 - August 25, 1848", Coll. Misc. 208, The British Library of Political and Economic Science.

Thomas Frost, "History of the Chartist Movement," Bradford Observer Budget, serial from June 5, 1886 onwards.

Hansard, Parliamentary Debates, Third Series, Vols. 96, 97, 98.

J. F. C. Harrison and Dorothy Thompson, Bibliography of the Chartist Movement, 1837-1976 (London, 1978).

George Howell, MSS "Biography of Ernest Jones", Vol. 2, Howell Collection, Bishopsgate Institute.

George Howell, MSS "History of the Working Men's Association, 1836-1850".

The Statutes of the United Kingdom of Great Britain and Ireland, 11 and 12 Victoria, 1847-8, Vol. 89.

J. E. R. Wallis, ed., Reports of the State Trials New Series, 6, 7.

Index

320

Democratic Committee for the Observation of the French Revolution, 45 (n. 71)
Democratic Party (U.S.), 172
Dickens, Charles, 4, 137
Dissenters, 208
Dohney, Barrister, 29-30
Doyle, Christopher, 26, 110, 117
Dublin, Ireland, 26, 28
Duncombe, Thomas S., 79, 85
Dunkirk, 58

Edinburgh, 33-4, 225, 256
Eliot, George, 137, 255
Ellis, Henry, 73
émeute, 26-7, 30, 33
emigration, 209
Engels, Friedrich, 16, 17, 40 (n. 2), 82, 182, 255, 288
English Channel, 5

Fay, Thomas, 249, 265, 273
Foreign Office, 73
foreigners, in England, see French in England
Fox, W. J., 285
Frankfort Parliament, 176
Fraser's Magazine, 168
Fraternal Democrats, 1, 9-10, 16-21, 23, 28, 46 (n. 80) (n. 87), 110, 165, 167, 210, 273 (n. 58), 270
France, 6, 70, 135, 137-139, 174, 208, 211, 252
and British workers in, 24, 25
June Days in, 182, 187, 190, 210-212, 233 (n. 60)
National Guard in, 6, 18, 21, 255
French in England, 21, 82, 113-114, 118-119,

164, 166, 212, 234 (n. 75)
French Revolution
of 1789, 1, 5, 7, 9, 14, 18, 22-23, 107-8, 168
of 1830 (July Revolution), 1, 11, 17
of 1848, intro, 1, 5-25, 30, 35, 37, 41 (n. 8), 43 (n. 43), 45 (n. 72), 55, 139, 150, 166, 174, 182, 203, 233 (n. 58), 255, 270, 275 (n. 60), 284, 298, 306 (n. 66)
impact after April 10, 210-214
economic implications, 8-9
Frost, Thomas, 87, 108, 115-116, 122, 174-5, 181, 191, 200 (n. 112), 215, 217-219, 237 (n. 113), 247, 250, 261, 264, 266, 268, 273 (n. 38), 274 (n. 52), 293
Fussell, William, 181, 200 (n. 110)

Gagging Act (Crown and Government Security Act), 163-4, 265, 267, 285, 286, 290
Gammage, R. G., 247, 250, 254, 283, 292
Garnier-Pages, Etienne, 18, 21
General Strike of 1926, 257
Germany, 176
Germans in England, 166
Gladstone, William E., 70, 258
Glasgow, Scotland, 171, 254, 259
March riots in, 32, 36-7
Glasgow, Eric, 297
God, invocation of, 129-30, 207
Goodway, David, 200 (n. 112), 215, 235 (n. 88), 247, 273 (n. 38), 276 (n.

322

85), 277 (n. 97), 296–
8, 306 (n. 74), 307 (n.
74) (n. 80)
Gordon, Lord George, 64,
86
Gordon Riots, 64, 86
gradualism, 203–210
Grady, Joe, 245
Graham, James, 38, 74
Greville, Charles C. F.,
69, 73–76, 131–32, 143–
4, 147–8, 187, 208
Grey, Sir George, 34–5,
62–6, 75, 80–1, 112,
121, 128–9, 132, 136–
7, 144, 149, 152 (n.
11), 165, 169, 171,
176, 178, 181, 183–4,
189, 217, 243–4
Groves, Reg, 295
Guest, Lady Charlotte,
57, 129, 187, 208
Guizot, Francois, 12, 167
Gurr, Ted Robert, 298–9

Habeas Corpus, 59
Halévy, Elie, 133, 298,
300
Hansard, 285
Harney, George Julian,
intro., 3, 16–20, 37,
42 (n. 13), 44 (n. 54),
56, 81–2, 88, 110, 117,
119–120, 147, 150, 166–
7, 173, 182, 191, 204,
210–211, 223, 233 (n.
58) (n. 65), 252, 260,
270, 280, 301 (n. 9)
Harrison, Royden, 295,
304 (n. 57)
Hetherington, Henry, 3,
137, 204–5, 229 (n.
15), 244
Heywood, Abel, 204
Holyoake, George Jacob,
37, 87–8, 138, 205,
229 (n. 13), 244, 261,
292–3
Home Office, 21, 31, 34,
56, 66–7, 75, 83, 106,

127, 141–2, 169, 171,
177–9, 182, 184–5, 188,
201 (n. 124), 212, 216,
243–245, 258, 261–263,
279 (n. 134)
Horne Tavern, 114–115, 146,
293
House of Lords, 69, 165
House of Commons, 85, 128,
141, 144, 165
household suffrage, 203,
204, 212
Hovell, Mark, 288, 294–5
Howell, George, 293
Hume, Joseph, 63, 141, 149,
166, 203–4, 206, 208,
285, 287
Hunt, Henry, 3

internationalism, Chartist,
1, 3, 16, 82, 165, 167,
211, 301 (n. 9) See also
Fraternal Democrats
industrial revolution, 4
Ireland, 2, 13, 20–1, 25–
31, 67, 119, 155 (n. 57),
163, 165, 179, 213, 283,
288
Dublin, 26, 28
Irish Chartists, 26, 30
Confederates, intro., 3,
26, 28, 35, 53 (n.
192), 56, 107–8, 116–
117, 119, 131–2, 163,
165–6, 179, 188, 212,
216, 245, 285
conspiracies and con-
spirators, intro., 27,
30–1, 35, 53 (n. 192),
57, 165, 188, 212, 215,
240 (n. 165), 245, 247,
270, 272 (n. 22)
fraternization with
English Chartists, 26–
31, 35, 50 (n. 141),
171
in London, 49 (n. 136)
oratory, 27, 29–30, 86
revolution in, 26–7

323

and the Roman Catholic
  Church, 29-30
United Irishmen, 28-9
workers, 24-5, 28
Young Ireland, 26, 49
  (n. 132), 166
Isle of Wight, 74

Jacobinism, 58
Jefferson, Issac (alias
  Watt Tyler), 177, 245-
  6, 263
Jewish disabilities, 20
John Street Institution,
  229 (n. 15)
Jones, David, 215, 223
Jones, Ernest, intro., 3,
  11, 13, 16, 18-20, 28,
  56, 59, 62, 81-4, 110,
  119, 138-9, 142, 147,
  150, 173, 175, 176,
  187-8, 211, 223-4, 226-
  8, 250, 253-4, 260,
  266-270, 271 (n. 22),
  274 (n. 51) (n. 52),
  286, 288-291, 293, 303
  (n. 35)
July, agitation and
  repression in, 214-220
July Revolution, in
  France, 1, 11, 17
June, agitation and
  repression in, 214-220
June Days (in France),
  182, 187, 190, 210-212,
  233 (n. 60)
juveniles, 36

Kee, Robert, 26-7
Keen, Charles, 9, 16
Kennington Common
  in 1842, 38
  in March, 38, 39
  on April 10, 55, 87-8,
    108-9, 114-115, 117
King, Martin Luther, 298
Kingsley, Charles, 57,
  206-7, 260, 292
Kydd, Samuel, 164, 175,
  191, 219, 227

Labour Party, 172
Lacey, William, 249
Lafayette, Marquis de, 10
Lamartine, Alfonse de, 15,
  21, 166
Land Plan, 2, 4, 7, 15-16,
  118, 138, 141, 158 (n.
  105), 173, 175, 177, 206,
  214, 248, 284, 286, 288,
  301 (n. 2)
Large, David, 116, 133,
  296, 306 (n. 66)
law, 34, 67, 75-6, 163-5,
  183, 191, 199 (n. 90),
  201 (n. 115), 178, 243,
  264, 267-9, 290
  Alien Act, 164-5, 167
  Bill of Rights, 64, 75
  Blackstone, Sir William,
    221
  Charles II, statute of,
    64, 74-5
  Gagging Act (Crown and
    Government Security
    Act), 163-4, 265, 267,
    285-6, 290
  Habeas Corpus, 59
  Riot Act, 246
Leach, James, 175, 227
Ledru-Rollin, Alexandre, 18
Leeds, 105, 171
Leicester, 105, 179, 259
Le Marchant, Sir Dennis, 81
Leopold, King of Belgium,
  35, 61, 127
Leventhal, F. M., 295
Lightowler, Daniel, 167
Lincoln, 244
Linton, William James, 31,
  171, 195 (n. 36), 205,
  244
Little Charter, 203-4, 212,
  287
Liverpool, 170-1, 245, 259
Locke, John, 269
London
  Chartism in, 3, 4, 11
  in 1848, 3, 66, 105-6,
    170-1, 173, 187, 192,

223, 244, 247, 306
(n. 74), 307 (n. 80)
government preparations
in, for April 10, 65-
78
March disturbances in,
31-2, 34, 36, 38
June meetings, 188-190,
192
Seven Dials, 249, 254
(See also August, dis-
turbances and repres-
sion)
London Corresponding
Society, 22
Lot, Parson, 207
Louis Napoleon, 70, 95
(n. 85)
Louis Philippe, 6, 11-12,
20, 133, 135, 167
Lovett, William, 3, 14,
137-8, 177, 205-6, 209,
211, 229 (n. 15), 283,
287, 291-2

Macaulay, Thomas B., 73
Macclesfield, 262
Mackay, John H., 253
Magna Carta, 222
Malmesbury, Earl of, 57,
73, 113, 128, 144, 149-
150, 166, 254
Manchester, 3, 11, 21,
24, 28, 33, 69, 80,
142, 179, 212, 244, 259
Mansfield, Lord (Judge),
64
March disturbances, 31-9,
60
Marines, 72
Marseillaise, 14, 17
Martineau, Harriet, 133-
4, 206, 294
Marx, Karl, 16, 17, 19,
40 (n. 2), 82, 182,
255, 276 (n. 83), 288,
294, 305 (n. 52)
Marxism, 19, 211
Mather, F. C., 58, 60,
215, 218, 296-7

Maurice, F. D., 206-7
May, 1848, disturbances
and repression, 170-181
Mayne, Police Commissioner,
106, 114-116, 121, 144,
146, 293, 295
Mazzini, Giuseppe, 205
McDouall, Peter Murray,
10, 34, 37, 74, 139, 173,
175, 189, 200 (n. 112),
217, 227, 247
McGrath, Philip, 16, 18,
20, 110, 114, 227
Methodism, 175, 289
Metropolitan Delegate
Council, 4, 8
Metternich, Prince Clemens
von, 58, 133
Middle class(es), 68, 135-
6, 190, 205, 209, 211-
212, 220, 232 (n. 53),
256-257, 260, 262, 299
alliance with Chartists,
4, 150, 204, 226, 229
(n. 12), 287
Military, see army
Militia, 72
Mill, John Stuart, 23
Mint, 72
Mitchell, John, 26, 180,
185, 218, 226, 268, 272
(n. 22)
mobilization, of the gov-
ernment in 1848, 10, 57,
61, 65-78, 81, 147-9
Morley, Samuel, 231 (n. 37)
Mullins, George, 247, 249,
273 (n. 37), 265

Napoleon I, 7, 136
Napoleon III, Prince Louis
Napoleon, 70, 95 (n. 85)
National Assembly, 167,
169, 171-176, 197 (n.
59), 210, 225-226, 254,
287, 289, 298, 307 (n.
79)
National Association, 14,
15

75-76, 79, 83-85, 88,
108-9, 111, 114-115,
117-118, 120-121,
144, 146, 176, 181,
186, 191-192, 196 (n.
58), 202 (n. 126),
216, 218, 244-250,
252-253, 262-263,
290, 298, 307 (n. 80)
in provinces, 178-180
political economy, 60,
209
Poor Law, 60, 171, 179,
221
Poor Man's Friend
Society, 257
Post Office, 72
Postgate, Raymond, 49 (n.
132), 133, 247, 295
Powell, Thomas, 219, 237
(n. 113), 247, 264-5
Press, intro., 18, 22-3,
25, 35-6, 39, 58, 105,
129-132, 134-5, 168,
219, 226, 250-1, 286
Prussia, 284-5, 301 (n.
8)
Punch, 27, 32, 140, 168,
224, 243, 251

Railroads, 67
Read, Donald, 297
Reform Bill of 1832, 1,
11, 17, 60, 136, 203,
211, 223, 269, 286,
289, 299
republic and republican-
ism, 177, 205, 211,
223, 285
revolution, 46 (n. 46)
(n. 88), 131, 135, 138-
9, 228, 233 (n. 65),
247
Chartists and, 133, 135,
138, 200 (n. 112),
179, 213-220, 227 247,
248-252, 284, 288-9,
294, 296-300
continental, in 1848,
intro., 41 (n. 5),

55-6, 58, 145, 252
in France, see France
Fraternal Democrats and,
17, 18
in Ireland in 1848, 26-7
rhetoric of, 37, 220-228,
246, 289
Irish rhetoric of, 27,
29-30, 86
Reynolds, G. W. M., 9, 21,
31-2, 43 (n. 43), 44 (n.
58), 79-80, 117, 119, 293
rhetoric, Chartist physical
force, 220-228, 246, 289
Richmond, Duke of, 254
Rider, William, 88, 102 (n.
185)
riots, in March, 31-9, 60
Riot Act, 246
Ritchie, Joseph, 248, 265,
273 (n. 37), 274 (n. 45)
Robespierre, Maximillien,
5, 136
Robertson, Priscilla, 299
Rochdale, 279 (n. 134)
Roebuck, John Arthur, 145,
303 (n. 37)
Roman Catholic Church, 29,
30
romanticism, 13-14, 26, 79,
86-7, 117-118, 289
Rose, John, 235 (n. 88),
247
Rousseau, Jean Jacques, 20,
270
Rowan, Lieutenant Colonel
Charles, 75-77, 98 (n.
129), 131, 209
Rowe, D. J., 215, 294-5
Royal Archives, 116
Royle, Edward, 247, 297
Rugby school, 69
Rudé, George, 31, 297-8
Russell, Lord John, 12-13,
20, 26, 57-62, 65-6, 77,
81, 98 (n. 129), 99 (n.
137), 112, 121, 127-8,
131-2, 135-6, 140-1, 163,
169, 171, 181, 186, 216,

violence, in general, 49
(n. 135)
Voice of the People, 206
Voltaire, Francois M. A.
de, 20, 270

Walpole, Spencer, 209
war
against France, 24
World War One, 68
War Office, 254, 272 (n.
21)
Waterloo, 130
Watkin, Absolam, 303 (n.
39)
Watson, James, 3, 137,
205, 229 (n. 15), 244
Webber, George, 221, 249-
250
Weekly Dispatch, 21-22,
35-37, 56, 82, 116,
140, 143, 146, 150,
187-8, 212, 219, 226,
227, 234 (n. 67), 252,
255, 257, 261, 286,
290-1
Wellington, Duke of, 59-
60, 62, 72, 75-8, 98
(n. 129) (n. 134), 111-
112, 128, 140, 148,
163, 201 (n. 115), 279
(n. 131), 290-294, 306
(n. 65)
West, John, 222
Wheeler, Thomas Martin,
80, 102 (n. 187), 108,
110, 123 (n. 13), 263,
264
Whig interpretation of
history, 136
White, George, 186, 221,
249-250
Wilkes, John, 2
Wilkinson, W. P., 80
Williams, John, 269, 282
(n. 176)
Wilson, Benjamin, 251-2
World War One, 68

xenophobia, 15, 24-5, 113-
114, 165-168, 212, 301
(n. 9)

Yeomanry, 72, 96 (n. 100)
York, Duke of, 72
Yorkshire, 33
Young Ireland, 26, 49 (n.
132), 166